SHAPING THE WAVES

SHAPING
THE
WAVES

A History of Entrepreneurship
at Harvard Business School

Jeffrey L. Cruikshank

HARVARD BUSINESS SCHOOL PRESS
BOSTON, MASSACHUSETTS

Printed in the United States of America
09 08 07 06 05   5 4 3 2 1

Library of Congress Cataloging-in-Publication

Cruikshank, Jeffrey L.
  Shaping the waves : a history of entrepreneurship at Harvard Business School /
Jeffrey L. Cruikshank.
      p. cm.
    ISBN 1-59139-813-4 (hardcover : alk. paper)
    1. Entrepreneurship—Study and teaching (Graduate)—United States. 2. Indus-
trial management—Study and teaching (Graduate)—United States. 3. Harvard
Business School—Curricula. I. Title.
  HB615.C78 2005
  650'.071'17444—DC22

                                                                    2004027869

The paper used in this publication meets the minimum requirements of the
American National Standard for Information Sciences—Permanence of Paper
for Printed Library Materials, ANSI Z39.48-1992.

This book is dedicated to the countless graduates of

Harvard Business School who have pursued

their entrepreneurial dreams,

and also to the many generations of

HBS faculty who have helped them in those pursuits.

Arthur Rock (M.B.A. '51) and

Professor Howard H. Stevenson (M.B.A. '65, D.B.A. '69)

embody these proud traditions, and—through their tenacity,

skill, and courage—have helped shape and lead

entrepreneurship, both at HBS and in the world.

Contents

Acknowledgments

THIS BOOK EVOLVED over the course of more than seven years. Many people along the way made it happen.

The two constants were Bill Sahlman and Howard Stevenson, HBS faculty members who believed that the story of HBS in the field of entrepreneurship—teaching and doing—was fascinating and deserved to be told. Mike Roberts joined my informal advisory board somewhere in midproject and helped carry the project through to completion. Thanks to all three of you. All along the line, someone always had faith, even when the rest of us were flagging. Somebody was always throwing a good idea into the mix.

Kristin Lund deserves special credit as well. She joined my company as a staff writer shortly after we took on this project, and she wrote initial drafts of several of the chapters. Although the book continued to evolve—including the elimination (due to space constraints) of about a million colorful sidebars that she and I put much time into—after Kristin went into business on her own, I can still see her strong influence in the manuscript.

Almost everyone quoted in the book sat down for at least one interview and, in many cases, follow-up interviews. Thanks to you all. Thanks especially to the senior members of the venture capital communities in Boston, New York, and Silicon Valley, who helped re-create a very exciting juncture in American business history. Similarly, thanks to the senior and retired HBS faculty members who shared their recollections. I'm glad to have had the chance to hear firsthand from Mace about how poker players in Hawaii led, indirectly, to the first entrepreneurship course at HBS.

Closer to the present day, I'm particularly indebted to the folks at Staples, Zoots, Orbital, and Cinemex, who talked, provided materials, squired us around the premises, and talked again. Thanks to Bob Reiss—with whom I had previously collaborated on a fun book, *Low Risk, High Reward*—for giving more insight into the (low overhead!) entrepreneurial mind. Special thanks to the Not Your Average Study Group, in which I'll include Kim Moore. Dave Perry, Stig Leschly, and Paul Conforti talked candidly about things that sometimes weren't easy to talk about. And because this book took so long to finish, Dave had to do it not once, but twice.

Laura Linard's staff at Baker Library Historical Collections made some key resources available to me, including Pat Liles's papers. Thanks again for making books like this possible—a compliment that of course extends to my friends at the HBS Press.

Jeffrey L. Cruikshank
Milton, Massachusetts
September 2004

Foreword

IN 1947, Professor Myles Mace introduced a new course in Harvard Business School's elective curriculum. Entitled "Management of New Enterprises," its aim was to teach returning servicemen how to run their own businesses. By 1997, this initial course had evolved into a deep and wide-ranging set of activities at the School. More than twenty entrepreneurship courses were offered in the M.B.A. program, and student enrollment in them accounted for a remarkable one-quarter of all second-year course work. A full-fledged Entrepreneurial Management unit had been formed, which by that time comprised nearly two dozen faculty members. Additionally, research, cases, and courses developed at the School had influenced scholars and practitioners in the United States and around the world.

We believed this fifty-year milestone merited chronicling and celebrating. We saw an interesting story: about the School and its faculty, and the role they—and our students and alumni—played in developing a new and more expansive definition of entrepreneurship.

What we began in 1997 has grown beyond our original conception of the project. We discovered a far richer story than we initially imagined; moreover, entrepreneurship and entrepreneurial management went through a set of remarkable changes in the late 1990s and early 2000s. We wanted to include these important years and the insights we gained during them. In 2003, when Arthur Rock (M.B.A. '51) made a very generous gift to the School and endowed the Arthur Rock Center for Entrepreneurship, we felt the first chapter in our history—longer than the fifty years we originally had envisioned—finally had an appropriate conclusion.

Howard Stevenson, Bill Sahlman, and Mike Roberts led this project, and I am grateful for their efforts and all the work they and their colleagues have done to advance the understanding of entrepreneurship. We were fortunate to enlist Jeff Cruikshank in our undertaking; I appreciate his patience and perceptiveness in eliciting the tale that appears here. Frank Batten (M.B.A. '52) helped support this project with a very generous gift; we are grateful for this and the wonderful entrepreneurial example he sets for us all. Finally, thanks to the many alumni and friends of the School whose gifts allow the Division of Research to fund innovative research and course development.

This is a story about our students, our alumni, and our faculty, and the ideas that have arisen from their collaboration and interaction over the years. It's a story that goes to the heart of what makes this institution unique.

Dean Kim Clark
Harvard Business School

Prologue

THIS IS A BOOK about networks, relationships, bonds, legacies, and debts. It is a book about attitudes: toward people, and toward business.

Finally, it is a book about people bound together by the common link of entrepreneurship—whether they admit it or not. (Why wouldn't they admit it? Because being an "entrepreneur" has not always been seen as a glamorous condition.)

The stories in this book are about people who have discovered and shaped waves of change. These individuals are not easily categorized, and they don't share a lot of common characteristics. They are not necessarily firstborns, or misfits, or motherless, or the apple of their mothers' eyes. But almost without exception, they love the *game* of entrepreneurship.

These stories are also about an institution—the Harvard Business School—that for more than half a century has been exploring ways to give structure to (and exploit opportunity within) the unruly field of entrepreneurship. These stories are about restless academics who can't quite stay out of business—or alternatively, about entrepreneurs who can't quite stay out of the academy.

And finally, the stories in this book are about how the Business School, its graduates, and larger economic opportunities intersect. What creates a wave of opportunity? Do the skills learned from shaping previous waves pertain to the next one? Are there cautionary tales that we should carry over from the last wave? Or will that simply slow us down and close our eyes to the *real* opportunity?

The stories in this book have unfolded over many decades and multiple business generations. They are unusual, but not unique. Stories like them unfold regularly on the pages of the *Wall Street Journal*, in venture capitalists' boardrooms, and in the basements, warehouses, garages, and home offices where entrepreneurs chase opportunity, all around the world.

We open this book with a dramatic example of entrepreneurial success: Staples, the "Office Superstore." Tom Stemberg's amazing creation (as of 2004 1,600 stores, nearly $14 billion in annual sales, 60,000 jobs) was all about spotting a wave and then shaping and exploiting it skillfully for the next two decades.

In retrospect, shaping waves looks easy.

But that wasn't the way it *was*, of course.

1

From Shelf Space to Cyberspace

TAKE YOURSELF BACK to the early 1980s. Jimmy Connors is still grunting and fist-pumping his way to Grand Slam championships. LPs and turntables rank as the music-delivery system of choice. Aerobics and mountain biking appear to be catching on. Camcorders and video games are hot. In California garages, teenagers are piecing together the very first personal computers.

It is the dawn of the Reagan era. The Fed, applying tough fiscal discipline, has broken the back of double-digit inflation. The Reaganauts' supply-side economic program has provoked and survived a nasty recession, and is now inspiring a resurgent stock market. Junk bonds are lubricating a wave of mergers. And although Wall Street once again is starting to feel its oats, the domestic manufacturing sector is still reeling. A sharp *de facto* revaluation of the dollar has killed U.S. exports. Once-proud Chrysler has been reduced to seeking a federal bailout to avoid bankruptcy. Up in Milwaukee, Harley-Davidson—the last U.S. motor-cycle manufacturer—seeks tariff protection against foreign competitors.

At the Harvard Business School in the winter of 1982–1983, students in the middle of their second year study this economic landscape carefully. Many make plans to join consulting firms and investment banking houses after graduation. These industries traditionally pay high salaries to recently minted Harvard M.B.A.'s, and high salaries help retire mountainous student-loan debts. Another plus: Consulting firms and investment banks appear to be immune to the competitive problems that are buffeting other sectors of the economy.

Todd Krasnow is not among the would-be consultants and I-bankers. A second-year M.B.A. student, he isn't sure exactly where he wants to wind up after graduation. But he *does* want to get into the extremely popular second-year Retailing elective taught by Walt Salmon. The retailing sector is far from hot, but the soft-spoken, red-haired Salmon —a senior and highly regarded member of the faculty—is an authority in his field, and his course is consistently overenrolled. Krasnow approaches Salmon and begs for a dispensation: Can't he *possibly* get into the Retailing course?

Salmon can't do much more than encourage this eager student to attend the first few class meetings. That way, if someone drops out of the course, Krasnow can step into the slot.

Krasnow agrees. For several days, he goes to the large amphitheater classroom in Aldrich Hall, perches on one of the steps leading down to the pit—all of the seats are full—and takes notes, hoping for the best. Finally, Salmon has to tell him that no spaces are going to open up. Krasnow has to stop sitting in the aisles. He has to abandon the course.

Now, fast-forward some two decades, to the early years of the twenty-first century. "Looking back," Krasnow says, "I find it ironic. Maybe two people graduating from HBS that year went into retailing, and I was one of them. But I just *couldn't get into that class.* It would have been my first-choice course."

History tends to record outcomes rather than dead ends and might-have-beens. In the early months of 1983, a student tries to pursue a passion, a professor takes note of youthful determination—and nothing much happens. *End of story.*

A few short years later, however, Todd Krasnow and Walt Salmon found their paths crossing again: this time as part of the team that helped Thomas Stemberg (M.B.A. '73) launch an astoundingly successful company—a rocket-ship start-up that blasted its way past even the most optimistic forecasts.[1]

THE STAPLES STORY TIES TOGETHER several cities and a sequence of different (but related) industries. It involves several generations of businesspeople who compete with and help each other—people who are nothing if not individualistic, and yet possess complementary strengths. As the interaction of these people works unlikely magic, opportunities are cracked open and fresh corners of the economy exposed, clearing the way for other innovators and enterprises to follow. And all along the way, millions of dollars in new wealth and tens of thousands of jobs are being created.

Very often, this story threads its way back to the Harvard Business School. The School's long-standing nickname—the West Point of Capitalism—underscores its close relationship with the largest companies in the United States (and more recently, the world). But that somewhat dated nickname implies a static posture, a one-way communication, like a farm team's relationship to a major-league ball club. A better metaphor would conjure up a much more active image. Picture a flask—the place where volatile elements come together, combine, respond, and react. What if we put this old idea into that new distribution channel? Or, what if we put this *new* idea into that *old* channel?

The School's well-manicured campus on the banks of the Charles River helps skew the picture in this direction, too, conveying a strong sense of place, purpose, and permanence. Yes, first bonds are formed in this tranquil setting: among students and between students and teachers. But these bonds are subsequently tested and reinforced in a thousand roiling centers of business activity around the world. Call them "network nodes," and call the Soldiers Field campus a specialized node in that system.

It is a system of remarkable scope and power. It is *not* the "old boy network" of walnut-paneled dining rooms, late-afternoon sherry, and commercial safe havens. (If that world ever existed, it is long gone.) Instead, it is an organic, evolving, self-renewing, and stimulating web of relationships, within which people rewrite the rules of the game, change some corner of the commercial world, and sometimes get very wealthy in the process. It is less like a Rolodex and more like a neural network—constantly rewiring itself. Three classmates meet up, years after graduation, and decide to found a company. One M.B.A. finds a critical pot of venture capital for another, who uses that stake to launch an enterprise that transforms an industry, makes history, and sets in motion a string of other ventures. (That story, among others, is told in this chapter.) An introduction is made over the phone; this leads to a small and informal joint venture; in due time, a tentative collaboration leads to a full-fledged enterprise.

It is a network of both breadth and depth, says Todd Krasnow:

> *You end up with very good contacts, with some degree of history back-*
> *ing them up. And the people you are connected to are in all sorts of dif-*
> *ferent fields. If you're looking for help with raising money, or with*
> *figuring out the right way to structure something, or how to think about*
> *insurance, chances are somebody from your class will be off doing some-*
> *thing significant in one of those fields. And it helps.*

Meanwhile, back at Harvard—the specialized node—ideas are being generated and batted around. One professor spends months or years field-testing a set of ideas in a company set up by a former student. (Sometimes, professors come to believe so much in these companies that they are among their first investors.) Another HBS faculty member, drawing on her experiences as a director of several start-ups, writes a case that pushes the thinking of an executive education group—often the context where new ideas get worked out—and eventually a battle-hardened version of that case makes its way into the M.B.A. classroom. Working papers bounce back and forth among offices, and between Harvard and the "real world." A new idea pops up; a new link is forged.

The School also engages in a form of network management. At reunions, in specialized course offerings, at meetings of the School's governing boards, and in dozens of other contexts, people come to-gether and build connections. Often this happens in Boston, but it may also happen in the context of the School's Silicon Valley research center, at its overseas research centers, during a regional alumni con-ference, at an HBS club meeting, or even by satellite hookups. The pot gets stirred. New ingredients get thrown in.

The best way to flesh out these complex mechanisms is with a case in point: Staples, the Office Superstore. But it turns out that we can't start this story by walking into that first stark, concrete-floored Staples store in Brighton, Massachusetts, in 1986. (*Todd—we have no customers!* *Do something!*)

Instead, we have to trace this venture one step further back in time. We have to begin with yet another HBS graduate: a man who firmly believed that ambitious young M.B.A.'s interested in retailing should get some firsthand retail experience before setting foot on the corporate ladder.

ROOTS: THE JEWEL COMPANIES

Twenty years before Tom Stemberg stepped onto the Soldiers Field campus, Donald S. Perkins left it, freshly inked M.B.A. in hand.

Perkins, a native of St. Louis, had gone to Yale on a scholarship. He completed his undergraduate degree in 1949, after a two-year stint in the Merchant Marine. He briefly considered a career in law, but decided instead to aim toward business—in large part because the Harvard Business School was willing to extend financial aid. In 1951, he graduated from HBS and began a tour of duty in the U.S. Air Force. Three years later, ready to return to civilian life, Don Perkins was pleased to discover that a variety of companies were knocking at his door, eager to hire someone with his combination of education and experience.

After some debate, he chose to sign up with the Chicago-based Jewel Companies, a major Midwestern supermarket chain. For one thing, he appreciated the fact that Frank Lunding, Jewel's chairman, recruited him in person. And although Perkins didn't think of himself as an "entrepreneur," he nevertheless had formed some novel ideas about management and training, and several top Jewel executives seemed to share his convictions. For example, he was drawn to Jewel in part because he was able to request a particular kind of experience for his first year of employment.

"I wanted to be a trainee," Perkins explains. "I wanted to learn about the business before I sat down behind a desk in a more typical job." Granting this wish, Jewel president George Clements started him off in 1953 at the bottom, selling groceries door-to-door for the company's Routes Division.

Jewel also satisfied several other of the criteria that Don Perkins had in mind. It dealt in consumer goods (his primary area of interest), it was financially strong, and it was well managed. Despite his M.B.A. credential, Perkins felt he knew almost nothing about the real practice of management. He hoped to find someone at Jewel to learn from, someone who would act as his mentor. Initially, the person who filled this role was another M.B.A.—Jewel's first, in fact. Don Booz (M.B.A. '47) was the company's personnel manager and had known Perkins at HBS. Although their paths rarely crossed at Jewel, the two men lived close to each other and began to drive to and from work together. Their conversations during their shared commute provided Perkins with his first meaningful mentoring relationship.

"I don't know that anyone has ever succeeded in any business without having some unselfish sponsorship or mentorship," Perkins said in a 1978 *Harvard Business Review* interview. "Everyone who succeeds has had a mentor or mentors. We've all been helped."

During his first year at Jewel, Don Perkins learned the ropes at a variety of sites, familiarizing himself with every aspect of food retailing. He recalls vividly when his mother came to visit him about six months into the informal internship program. It was close to Easter and Perkins, decked out in a long, starched white apron, was stacking candy at the end of the aisle in one of the Jewel Food Stores. He recalls the scene:

> *Picture the world's largest candy display. In walked my wife with my mother in tow. When they spotted me, my mother—who could always smile, at anything—actually stopped smiling. Her face just froze. Two steps later, she managed to get the smile back.*

Perkins spent a total of six years in the Routes Division. All that time, he says, he had no inkling that Frank Lunding was thinking of him as a potential successor to Clements. Not until 1959, after being promoted to assistant head of operations in the Food Stores, did Perkins suspect that a remarkable opportunity might be opening up for him. At that point, the company's chairman and president began making it clear that they wanted to hear his suggestions for improving the business.

"Clements wanted to bring more talented young people into the company," Perkins says, "and I suggested they develop a recruiting program that would offer the same kind of training they offered me. Actually, a lot of people at Jewel didn't like this idea. I had to convince them." Jewel's management, finally persuaded, began to recruit M.B.A.'s in 1960 using a Perkins-inspired invention called the Corporate Sponsorship Program. It was a resounding success, according to Perkins. "Basically," he explains, "they couldn't help but love the people who came in because of the program."

Many years later, Perkins recalls, he and his senior colleagues personally took advantage of the Corporate Sponsorship Program to recruit M.B.A.'s as often as possible. "The point of the program," he would tell them, "is to give you a chance to learn as much about our company as you possibly can in one year. You start out by getting your hands dirty." Every trainee—and almost every other new employee at Jewel—was assigned a mentor from the ranks of Jewel executives.

In 1961, Perkins was named vice president of the Routes Division. As he saw it, this was a mixed blessing at best. He had been with Jewel for eight years and had spent the last two years influencing corporate policy. Now he was being given a divisional position—and a tough one at that. "We were starting to franchise the Routes," Clements explained in a 1978 interview, "and if [Don] could help make that work, he'd have a success in store operating, merchandising, and management." Briefly, Perkins tried to talk Lunding and Clements out of this banishment to divisional purgatory. But his superiors held firm. They felt that Perkins needed a "real tough baby" (as Clements put it) to showcase his talents.

Evidently, the showcase was effective and the talents were ample. Four years later, in 1965, Perkins was named the president of Jewel. Only thirty-seven, he had been at Jewel for just twelve years. (Five years later, he would become the company's CEO.) It was a remarkable ascent in an industry famous for sluggish career advancement. "I like to use myself as an inspirational example," he says. "I replaced the man who was the president when I was first starting out. I tell people, 'If I could do this, think what *you* could do!'"

THE SECOND GENERATION: TESTING ITS WINGS

The Corporate Sponsorship Program thrived during Perkins's years at the helm of the Jewel Companies. Countless young M.B.A.'s were drawn by the lure of this unusual training experience, including one named Thomas Stemberg.

Stemberg received his M.B.A. from Harvard in June 1973. A year later, he was settling himself in Boston. He had been accepted into the Corporate Sponsorship Program at the Jewel Companies, where he began in Jewel's Star Markets division by tackling a sequence of entry-level jobs: stocking shelves, taking orders at the deli counter, and, of course, bagging groceries *(heavy items first!)*.

An HBS classmate, Fred Lane, lived in Watertown, Massachusetts, across the street from the Star Market where Stemberg was working. On his way home from work, Lane would often stop in to pick up some groceries. "I would always say hello to Tom," he recalls. "There I'd be in my cheap Brooks Brothers suit, and he'd be doing fruit. I had enormous respect for him. He was working in a real-world job, while I was doing this nebulous thing called public accounting."

Stemberg also kept up with other HBS friends and members of the faculty. "He and I would meet for breakfast or lunch once in a while," recalls Walt Salmon, who taught retailing to Stemberg at HBS and also guided him through a field study there. "I liked him. He struck me as extraordinarily energetic—perhaps even *neurotically* energetic. Very committed, too, and with a remarkably strong interest in retailing."

Salmon, from what he knew of Stemberg, thought the retailing industry might be a good fit for his former student. "You need a lot of energy for retailing," he explains, "because you're constantly being asked to make tactical decisions, and make them quickly. And sometimes you have to *remake* them, five minutes later."

From Stemberg's point of view, retailing demanded more than energy. It demanded a particular "yielding" quality—the willingness to put the customer first, always:

> *I took marketing with Ben Shapiro during my first year at HBS. He helped me to see the one most crucial thing: that it all starts with the consumer. Even today in business, as I look around at what's going on, whether it's marketing plans, business plans, business ideas, or whatever, 99 percent of it is an idea looking for a market. And Ben taught me way back then that the great ideas are* markets *looking for a* solution.

The Corporate Sponsorship Program at Star gave Stemberg an understanding, from the ground up, of how a food retailing business actually worked. His marketing training and his own determination to *put the customer first* complemented this understanding and would serve him well, more than once, in the course of his business career.

One notable illustration came in the late 1970s. That was when Star began to fall behind in a ferocious competition with other local supermarkets. Stemberg, then at work in Star's marketing department, started to cast about for ways to reverse this ominous trend. His front-line experiences with Star's customers helped him decide to introduce in Boston the pioneering concept that would rescue his division: generic-brand foods.

In the supermarket industry of the 1970s, generic brands were almost a complete novelty. In fact, only the Jewel Food Stores, out in the Midwest, had experimented with them. Tom Stemberg suspected that the generic products, less costly to supply and priced lower than the corresponding branded foods, would appeal to a large segment of Star's shoppers. He was right. Star's sales shot up. Stop & Shop and Purity Supreme remained Boston's leading supermarket chains, but Stemberg's innovation helped put Star back in the running.

Star's generic line of foods succeeded partly because Stemberg's timing was perfect. With inflation pushing grocery prices ever higher, Boston's consumers were eager for the price break that generics offered. Again, for Stemberg, the experience "confirmed the power of identifying and satisfying a customer's need, a lesson that had been drummed into me at Harvard." Star executives—and of course, Jewel executives farther up the line—loved these results. Tom Stemberg, buoyed by his highly visible success, began eyeing the top job at Star.

Meanwhile, Stemberg's innovation had hardly gone unnoticed among the local supermarkets. The grocery trade is characterized by low margins and cutthroat competition. Leo Kahn, CEO of Star's archrival Purity Supreme, concluded—not for the first time—that this young upstart, Stemberg, was a worthy competitor, and therefore worth imitating. Soon, generics could be found in the stores of all the major Boston supermarket chains.

In 1981, Tom Stemberg began participating in Jewel's recruiting process. He interviewed young hopefuls at business schools across the country. The Harvard Business School, his own alma mater, was an obligatory stop on this circuit. On his first pass through Harvard, he interviewed a woman named Myra Hart who was receiving her M.B.A. degree in that spring of 1981. Impressed, he submitted a highly favorable recommendation. When Jewel offered Hart a job, both Stemberg and VP of operations Jack Avedisian offered to be her official mentor in the Corporate Sponsorship Program.

Hart was an unusual M.B.A. student, and—at least on paper—an unlikely candidate for a job at Jewel. Already fifteen years out of college, the mother of three children, she had run her father-in-law's real estate company in her hometown of Chicago for several years. Next, she moved to Michigan with her husband and children, where she was a college administrator and instructor. She eventually applied to business schools. Harvard accepted her, and Hart enrolled eagerly.

Once again, the family relocated. But this time, Hart—formerly the teacher, now the student—was looking for a credential that would let her put down roots in Boston. She also hoped to find a certain kind of work environment. "I was looking for a job where I could thrive and be valued for what I was," she says, "not some place where they were looking for a malleable young person they could train to be whatever they wanted."

When the Jewel Companies recruited her aggressively, she felt much encouraged. "They seemed to value the fact that I was both a woman and older," she recalls, smiling. "Perhaps they saw me as the consummate consumer." Retailing may have been somewhere in her blood—as a child, she had enjoyed visiting her grandfather's retail store in downstate Illinois—but before graduate school, Hart had no direct retail experience. Jewel clearly saw something in Hart other than a dyed-in-the-wool retailer.

Accepting Jewel's offer was a relatively easy decision for Hart. But the other offer—of mentoring from Tom Stemberg—was a tougher call. Eventually, Hart asked to be assigned to the VP of operations in the Jewel organization. "I felt our training was too similar," she recalls. "I wanted someone in the organization who had a very different background." Hart then left for a summer of rest and relaxation in Switzerland: her last long vacation before beginning her new career at Star. For this ambitious professional woman who had already remade her life several times, it seemed as if things had come together almost perfectly.

She returned to find chaos in the division. A new president had been selected for Star, but it wasn't Tom Stemberg and it wasn't Hart's mentor, both of whom had been touted (and had thought of themselves) as candidates for the top job. Hart's mentor left the company somewhat abruptly to start his own food-retailing venture. Bruce Kruger, the new president of Star, stepped in to fill his departed colleague's role as mentor to Hart. "And as it turned out," Hart says, "I couldn't have gotten a better one." The brushfire was extinguished, the divisional alarm bells were silenced, and Hart rolled up her sleeves and went to work.

Hart may have been reassured, but Tom Stemberg was not. In fact, he now saw his career at Star heading in one of several possible directions, none of them attractive. For the next six months—which would be his last at Star—he investigated potential options at other companies.

In the meantime, he tended to his corporate responsibilities. He also kept a watchful eye on Myra Hart, whom he had recruited into the organization. True, mentoring Hart was the divisional president's formal responsibility. But Stemberg had always appreciated the attention paid to him by Don Perkins, earlier in his own career, and now he was determined to do the same for Hart. Contact between the two Star colleagues was only intermittent, but it was a constant for both of them amid much organizational change. Like Stemberg before her, Hart was immersed in the Corporate Sponsorship training program at Star, "learning everything from running a warehouse to cutting meat and cleaning fish." Stemberg often called and invited her to lunch when he was touring the stores, and sometimes he encouraged her to attend his merchandise meetings.

The relationship—part mentor/mentee, part collegial, part friendship—was put on hold in 1982. Star Markets had clawed its way up to a position of rough parity with market leaders Stop & Shop and Purity Supreme. Tom Stemberg decided it was time for him to leave the Jewel Companies behind for good.

ANOTHER M.B.A. AT JEWEL

This was, coincidentally, the same year that Todd Krasnow petitioned Walt Salmon to let him enter the oversubscribed Retailing course at

HBS. Although that campaign had failed, as he neared his graduation from HBS, Krasnow was convinced that retailing would definitely be part of his plan.

Krasnow had arrived at retailing by a roundabout route. Before entering business school, Krasnow had worked at General Foods as a food chemist. This was mostly an accident. He took a food chemistry course his senior year of college because he needed the two credits to graduate. Although an A student in his other courses, he proved to be a subpar food chemist. "I slept through the midterm, missed the final exam, begged the teacher and got a D−, and I was able to graduate," he recalls.

Off Krasnow went to General Foods, mainly because it appeared to be a setting where he would be allowed to be creative. Very quickly, he was put to work inventing new foods. His "crowning achievement," he recalls wryly, was a fast food product line: frozen foods that, when removed from the oven, would hit the palate like fried foods. "The goal was to have it taste like McDonald's or Kentucky Fried Chicken," he says, deadpan. The team of which he was a member invented a special oven tray that elevated the food and was pierced with airholes; with air circulating around it, the food cooked more uniformly and acquired the right consistency. Krasnow and his colleagues eventually won a patent for the process.

The creative side of food inventing was appealing, but Krasnow had larger ambitions. A quick survey of the corporate hierarchy at General Foods revealed an interesting pattern: Most of the company's decision makers, such as the product managers and brand managers, were business school graduates. Krasnow decided that he should follow suit.

Harvard Business School accepted Krasnow after he had spent two years at General Foods. By the end of his first year there, he knew that his emerging career interests were unusual. "I wanted to get involved with something other than consulting or investment banking," he says. "I wanted instead to learn something about running a business."

Krasnow investigated, among other things, the Corporate Sponsorship training program Don Perkins had established at the Jewel Companies. Looking through alumni records, he discovered that people like Tom Stemberg and others who were once part of Perkins's program had gone on to hold senior positions, either at Jewel or elsewhere. A summer stint at Jewel seemed a requirement to enter the sponsorship program later. Convinced that he had cracked the code for success at a company like Jewel, Krasnow interviewed for, and was ultimately accepted into, the summer program.

Coincidentally, he came very close to encountering Tom Stemberg during the interview process. Stemberg's name was on the original interview schedule, but someone had slashed an X through it. Krasnow later learned that Stemberg had left the company just one day earlier. "I missed him by this much," he recalls, holding up a thumb and forefinger in a nearly closed circle.

By the time of his departure from Star, Tom Stemberg had achieved near-legendary status at Jewel. Many people at both the parent company and the divisional level thought him utterly brilliant; others found him intimidating. That summer, Todd Krasnow met his future wife, who by another coincidence had worked for Stemberg. "And all that summer," says Krasnow, "while I was romancing my future wife, I heard nothing but these marvelous Tom Stemberg stories."

After graduating from HBS, Krasnow returned to the Jewel family to take a permanent job at Star. His first position, of course, was bagging groceries—at the Brighton Star Market near HBS. "Then I was a produce manager," he recalls, "then I worked in the meat department, and then the deli. All the different jobs. I was even on the night crew."

One memorable moment came early in his tenure in Brighton; it was almost a reenactment of Don Perkins's encounter with his mother, some three decades earlier. Krasnow was at the end of a checkout line, busily bagging groceries for customers. At one point, he looked up from his work to find himself eyeball-to-eyeball with one of his HBS professors. "First she lights up with genuine excitement," Krasnow recalls. "She blurts out, 'Todd!'—and then, a split second later, her whole face drops. Obviously, in that split second, she decides that something *truly horrible* has happened to me." This was a professor, Krasnow says wryly, who had always emphasized the importance of learning a business from the bottom up.

Krasnow went on to manage one of Star's worst-performing stores, in the Massachusetts city of Attleboro, on the Rhode Island border. Within six months, Krasnow had turned the store around, and it had begun making a profit. His turnaround strategy was simple: work hard and get the job done. Although he was the store manager, he would jump to open an extra register whenever the checkout lines got too long. "Common sense," he recalls, "but apparently, it had been years since customers at that store had seen a manager ring a register."

He was practical, compassionate, and lucky: three good traits for almost any manager. One day he came across a woman in a checkout line who was making a huge purchase—several carts full—and had come up $20 short. She was anxious and embarrassed. A "scene" seemed to be unfolding. All eyes swung to the young and relatively inexperienced store manager. Krasnow took out his wallet and loaned her $20. She departed gratefully, promising to return.

Shortly thereafter, the woman came back to repay the $20, and let slip that she was a candidate for the state senate in that district. (The huge food-and-beverage purchase had been for a fundraiser.) Store volume shot up in the wake of the incident. Many of the new shoppers made it clear that they had come to the store mainly to get a look at this odd young manager who had helped their candidate for the senate.

Krasnow managed the Attleboro store as if he owned it. "I really didn't see any difference," he explains. "To me, that was *my* store, and I had to make it work." This meant putting the customer first. At Thanksgiving, his warehouse failed to ship the turkeys that he had promised to his customers. Gritting his teeth, Krasnow went out and bought turkeys from all his competitors, just to ensure that his store could honor its commitments.

In 1984, at the end of his first year at Star, Krasnow moved into a marketing job that had been held by Tom Stemberg ten years earlier. His new boss was Myra Hart, who by then had been made head of marketing. The circle was closing. Within eighteen months, they would both be gone.

ZEROING IN

Leaving certainly was not at the front of Myra Hart's mind. "I had a great job at Star," she says. "It was really a lot of fun. I was just getting

my feet wet with the agency, filming commercials and putting together a new staff. Everything was going my way. Why would I leave?"

In fact, the wheels of change were already in motion. First, American Stores' hostile takeover of Star changed the calculation. Next, a
headhunter had called her. This was not unusual, in and of itself; Hart
was accustomed to getting calls from headhunters. This time, though,
there were rumors in the air about a new business that Tom Stemberg
was supposedly starting. Based on the headhunter's description, Hart
deduced that Stemberg was behind the contact. As it turned out, she
was right.

By this time, of course, Tom Stemberg had a high profile in his industry. He had been tagged with lots of adjectives: *outspoken, remarkable, determined,* and *brash* among them. (Competitors often used saltier
words.) When he left the Jewel Companies—irritated because someone else had been chosen to head up Star Markets—he wanted an opportunity to "blow the doors off" and underscore the fact that Star
had let a star get away.

That next job turned out to be the presidency of the Edwards-
Finast Division of First National Supermarkets. Plagued by losses, the
division appeared to be a perfect candidate for a generic-brands rescue. Stemberg delivered. "The stores' rock-bottom prices," he recalls,
"were the result of the rock-bottom costs associated with buying in
volume and operating a no-frills store."

Once again, Stemberg turned a supermarket chain around. But
once again, and within a very short time, he found himself heading for
the door. First National Supermarkets went up for sale in 1984, and
Stemberg—who thought the business should be grown, not sold—
was fired in January of 1985.

He was just thirty-six years old. He had one year's severance pay in
his pocket. He had a young family to support. Not surprisingly, he
paused to consider with care exactly what he would do next.

Fortunately for Stemberg, at this same juncture, a like-minded man
was casting about for new opportunities in retail. Leo Kahn, who had
once eyed Tom Stemberg's generic-brands successes from across a
competitive fence, had sold his Purity Supreme supermarket chain in
1984. By now, Kahn and Stemberg regarded each other with mutual
respect. They also shared a love of basketball. Stemberg, the president

of Friends of Harvard Basketball, had often invited Kahn to games. As soon as he heard that Stemberg had been fired, Kahn contacted him, and they began casting about for a plan that would suit them both.

Various avenues lay open before them. Both men had extensive expertise in the supermarket industry, of course, but both were well aware that the Boston supermarket trade was fragmented, deadly competitive, and had scant room for newcomers. Quietly, systematically, they kept probing their possibilities.

Stemberg, who was recently inducted into the Marketing Hall of Fame, in 1985 suffered serious doubts about his future. "Let's face it," he says, "I was an unemployed executive. I may have had a lot of good ideas and whatever else, and I had some talent and experience, but I was unemployed."

Leo Kahn helped Stemberg dig himself out and regain his self-confidence. Assistance arrived from other sources as well. "When I think back to who I should thank," Stemberg says, "Harvard Business School looms large." For example, Walt Salmon—Stemberg's former professor and now friend and confidant—played a critical role along the way. In 1985, Stemberg met a number of times with Salmon to pick his brains. One day in late spring, faced with an opportunity to buy a division of Star Markets that had come on the block, Stemberg and Kahn took Salmon to lunch. The two would-be entrepreneurs wanted his opinion: Should they pounce on the opportunity to own a piece of Star? Salmon looked Stemberg in the eye and asked, "Do you really think you can out-execute Star and Stop & Shop?"

Stemberg didn't have to think long for his answer. "No," he admitted.

"Wouldn't it be wiser to simply *use* what you've learned from the supermarkets? You should take their modern distribution techniques and apply them to a business that's underserved and overpriced."

Stemberg nodded his agreement. Recently, partly in response to Kahn's prodding, he had been leaning in a similar direction. ("Leo had been whispering 'specialty retail' in my ear," recalls Stemberg.) And Stemberg himself knew in his gut that this was the right track. The very same idea had been hovering at the edge of his mind ever since his visit to a Makro warehouse-style store in Langhorne, Pennsylvania, several months earlier. But Stemberg was already thinking *office products*. Even while he and Kahn were working up some sketchy business plans in other directions, Stemberg had been thinking about Makro and office products. Could those two ideas be brought together somehow?

Salmon continued to provide helpful advice. He gave Stemberg the name of a recent HBS grad who had spent a year as Salmon's teaching assistant. Marci Dew (M.B.A. '75) was then living in the Boston area and running a consulting firm with her husband, also an HBS grad. The goal was to identify a growth industry, preferably one that would happily support a new enterprise. With Dew's help, Stemberg and Salmon began to zero in on the specialty retail categories that had shown high growth rates over the previous decade and also held out the promise of continued expansion. One of these, still somewhere toward the front of Stemberg's brain, was office products.

The clincher came as much from the real world as from research and consultants. Specifically, it came from Tom Stemberg's own experience just before the Fourth of July weekend, when he found himself driving all over Connecticut in search of a ribbon that would fit his printer. One store was closed; another (BJ's Wholesale Club) had only a limited selection of office supplies, which didn't include the right kind of printer ribbon. Suddenly the crucial concept was there, right in front of him. "A vision blindsided me," says Stemberg.

Soon, Dew's research confirmed his suspicions. Among the specialty retail categories, pet foods and supplies were hot, but *office products* topped the charts.

FORMING A TEAM

The Jewel tradition had created a second generation of HBS innovators. The Perkins-inspired training program turned M.B.A.'s from places like Harvard, Stanford, and Chicago into hands-on retailing executives—managers who learned the realities of supermarket storerooms and deli counters before they teased out the nuances of the boardroom. In a very real way, Don Perkins gave Tom Stemberg this critical leg up. For his part, Stemberg cleared the path that both Myra Hart and Todd Krasnow would follow.

But Hart wanted to think it over. As noted, she was reasonably happy at Jewel when she received that particular headhunter's call in 1985. The likelihood that Tom Stemberg and his mysterious new company were behind the call intrigued her and piqued her interest, but this unnamed opportunity didn't seem to have the potential to change her life. She agreed to meet with the headhunter almost on a lark: *What's Tom really up to?*

Then she read the mysterious company's business plan. She was floored: "I looked at it and thought, 'This is incredible! This can't possibly lose!'" After confirming that the plan was indeed Stemberg's work, she called him up and offered her compliments.

"But I'm a marketing person," she told him. "I don't read business plans for a living. Do you mind if I have a pro look at it?"

With Stemberg's permission, Hart brought his proposal in confidence to another HBS friend in the venture capital community— Linda Linsalata (M.B.A. '82)—who handed it back a few days later. "Frankly," Hart recalls Linsalata saying, "we don't usually invest in retailing, but we'd definitely be interested in *this*."

Hart concluded that Stemberg's plan was even better than she had thought. Her curiosity was turning into fascination. Meanwhile, though, her own life had grown more complicated. Now a single parent, she had primary responsibility for three children, two of whom were in college. She was reluctant to risk their future. In an effort to resolve her dilemma, she asked Tom Stemberg to meet with her.

"I really want to do this," she told him, "but I have a mortgage and kids in school, and not much of a cushion. What if it all falls through?"

"Tell me the truth," Stemberg replied in his blunt way. "How long will it take you to find another job if this venture folds? Two months? Ten months?"

Hart considered her success at the Jewel Companies. She thought about all those calls from headhunters. "Three months," she said finally. "Six, if I want to be sure the job is perfect."

"Six months," replied Stemberg, "and that's all. So that's what you'd be risking, and nothing more. That seems like a risk you can afford to take."

Looking back to that pivotal day, Myra Hart (now a professor at HBS) concludes:

Once you can put things in that kind of perspective, then you realize
you're not really sacrificing anything. That was an important insight for
me, and it still is. I try to share it with my students. When you think
about risk, you think you're putting your whole life at risk, but you're
not. You're risking a few months while you look around for what's next.

Hart agreed to join Tom Stemberg's enterprise in September 1985, although she kept quiet about the impending move as she continued with her job at Star Market. Todd Krasnow was then her assistant head of marketing. That fall, she told him she was leaving. "But I can't tell you what I'm doing," she added. The reason was simple: She hadn't yet told Star of her plans and knew that even when she did, she would be discouraged from recruiting (or *appearing* to recruit) at Star.

Hart and Krasnow had a comfortable, professional relationship. Although Hart was never Krasnow's official mentor at Jewel, she was in many ways his indirect sponsor and trusted sounding board. When she told him she would soon be changing jobs, he grew curious. By the end of 1985, she was gone, and in February 1986, Todd Krasnow read an article about Tom Stemberg and the business he was launching: an office-supplies superstore. Krasnow put two and two together, and called Hart. His message was simple: He wanted in.

"During that first phone call," Hart recalls, "I had to tell Todd that although I appreciated his interest and valued him highly, we didn't need him."

Within a few short weeks, however, she found herself calling him back. The start-up management team needed someone new to handle marketing. Stemberg's original choice (an individual with proven expertise in creative advertising work, but with no comfort or familiarity with direct mailings and promotions) had thrown in the towel.

Todd Krasnow needed no persuasion to join the team. Stemberg's business plan looked superb, the prospects were thrilling, and—since Krasnow and his wife had no children yet—the risk was low.

"I went into Star planning to be CEO," says Krasnow, who was twenty-eight at the time, "and that would have been a fine career. But then this terrific opportunity presented itself. When I talked to Tom and saw the business plan, I just loved it. And it was exciting to be going from a fairly predictable, low-margin business, where you really had to grind it out, to something involving a lot of high-powered people who were going to shake up retailing. Hey, I'm glad Tom hired a marketing guy who didn't fit in with the retail mentality. Otherwise, I might never have had the opportunity."

Myra Hart adds a slightly different perspective. "We didn't consider the departure of our first marketing manager a disaster," she says, "because we knew we had a brilliant alternative. Todd was head and shoulders above the competition. He joined the company about two weeks after we called him, and I have always considered him one of the founders."

The new company's management team was in place. More than half of them—Tom Stemberg, Myra Hart, and Todd Krasnow—held M.B.A.'s from Harvard and had been trained in the Corporate Sponsorship Program at the Jewel Companies. The legacy of Don Perkins would soon be put to the test.

THE STAPLES GENERATION

If you compress the timeframe enough and lose enough of the details, Staples, the Office Superstore, was indeed a rocket-ship start-up. The first store opened in Brighton, Massachusetts, in May 1986, and the second opened that November. In its second full fiscal year, the company reported close to $40 million in sales, nearly a 500 percent increase over the previous year. Its initial public offering (by which time 25 stores were up and running) raised $36 million in April 1989. Between 1989 and 1995, a new store was opened once every eight days, on average. At the end of 1991, there were 123 Staples stores. By 1996, Staples had 500 stores, and was the sixth company in the history of the United States to achieve annual sales of $3 billion within ten years of its founding.[2]

But the key players remember exactly what it took to get the rocket ship off the ground. By the time his headhunter contacted Myra Hart, Stemberg and Leo Kahn (with the help of Walt Salmon and Ben Shapiro, also at HBS) had researched the office superstore idea exhaustively. They also had attempted to secure initial financing for the venture.

Despite their solid reputations in retailing, however, Stemberg and Kahn had trouble convincing investors that this would work.

One investment professional who *did* believe in the Staples concept was Bob Higgins (M.B.A. '70). Higgins accompanied Stemberg on some of his field-research trips, and was persuaded that the Staples concept could succeed. Briefly, Higgins's firm—Charles River Partners—considered becoming the first major investor in Staples, but backed out. "Higgins was great in those early days," Stemberg recalls, "even though his partners wouldn't do the deal. He educated me in what I needed to do, including putting together a complete management team."

The strange thing about the investment community's reluctance to bet on Staples was that the evidence arguing for the viability of the venture seemed to be *overwhelming*. While trying to figure out just how much a company actually spent on office supplies, Stemberg had discovered that most small business owners grossly underestimated their costs. People had no idea that pens and stick-on notes were draining the coffers. One friend of Stemberg's, after checking his off-the-cuff estimate—$10,000 a year—against his invoices, was aghast to discover that his company actually spent close to *$50,000* a year on office supplies.

Stemberg persuaded other business owners to double-check their figures, with much the same results. On average, office supplies were costing small businesses $1,000 per employee per year, and this figure reflected only consumables. Add in equipment and furniture, and the sum climbed far higher. It was a case, Stemberg recalls, of listening to and learning from the customer:

> *I didn't start out saying we should build a stationery superstore. We started with the* customer. *I went to the customer's office and saw what was there. I would look around and see writing pads, and marker boards, and telephones, but I'd also notice the bottle of water. Hey, we should probably carry bottles of water, because the customer buys that. And the customer makes copies; we probably ought to put a copy center in there. And the customer doesn't just buy supplies, he buys machines and desks and file cabinets.*

Stemberg wanted to offer one-stop convenience and affordability to small-business managers who were buried under layers of markups. By now, he knew that the giant office-supply companies routinely cut great deals for their favored corporate customers—the IBMs and Coca-Colas of the world—and just as routinely imposed huge markups on smaller enterprises. He wanted to give the "little guys" the same deals that the big guys enjoyed.

But even the rude awakening ("Binder clips are costing us *how much??*") was not enough to persuade people that they *needed* an office-supplies superstore. Nobody seemed eager to abandon the delivery services and other perks that came along with using a rep to buy supplies. Convenience? Nothing was more convenient than having everything delivered by the rep. Low prices? Saving a few pennies here and there will hardly make a difference. Besides, who'll give me the occasional ticket to the ballgame?

Nevertheless, Stemberg was certain he could win them over, given the chance. He wasn't going to save them just a few pennies; he was going to save them big bucks. Small and moderate-sized businesses would understand once they could *see* his trump card: the lower prices—the much lower prices—he could offer by buying in bulk and selling in volume. Seeing would be believing.

He envisioned aisles peppered with printed cost comparisons showing how his superstore was offering you—the customer, *the little guy*—50 percent discounts off list prices. *Fifty* percent, he pointed out to the venture capitalists to whom he made these pitches. They would listen hard, nod, and take the occasional note. Then they would lean forward in their chairs and ask the tough questions. For example: Who, exactly, will be *managing* this strange new enterprise?

Stemberg and Kahn were caught in a position well known to many entrepreneurs: between potential investors asking about management and potential managers asking about money. They solved the problem in the classic manner: by working both ends as best they could. But money was increasingly a problem.

Once again, Tom Stemberg found Harvard Business School useful, in a roundabout way. He had met months earlier with John McArthur, then dean of HBS, because he was considering buying the Edwards-

Finast division (which had so recently been his responsibility) of First National Supermarkets. "I need to raise fifty million bucks of equity in two weeks," he told him. "Who do you think I should see?" McArthur—a former finance professor with a reputation for extraordinary corporate turnaround skills—sent Stemberg to Sherman Hall, where Stemberg repeated his story to Chuck Sethness (M.B.A. '66).

Sethness was a former investment banker and U.S. Treasury official, and—coincidentally—a high school classmate of Myra Hart's. He was then an associate dean at HBS, but had retained his close ties to the financial community. After hearing Stemberg out, he introduced him to Charlie Downer (M.B.A. '66) and Bob Reilly of the investment banking firm Downer & Co.

The firm was not prepared to fund the proposed start-up itself, but Bob Reilly volunteered to help Stemberg hammer the business plan into shape. He knew exactly what elements were needed to help pitch the idea to his industry peers. In August of 1985, with the plan now in presentable form, Reilly agreed to assist in the search for the necessary venture capital.

As it turns out, other Harvard Business School connections also helped Stemberg and Leo Kahn in their money chase. Two HBS graduates—Felda Hardymon (M.B.A. '79), then a partner at Bessemer Venture Partners, and Mitt Romney (M.B.A. '74), founder of Bain Capital and many years later the governor of Massachusetts—were among the first venture capitalists to take Stemberg seriously. Bain conducted a thorough investigation into Stemberg's plan, talking to many companies to assess their office-supply spending habits.

Once again, the initial findings were disappointing: Companies told Bain that they spent only around $200 per employee. Stemberg, who knew from his previous research that these figures were impossibly low, convinced Bain to go back and look at the actual invoices. This time, the results painted a very different picture. Companies were spending an average of *four times* what they had estimated, and Romney was now definitely intrigued.[3]

Stemberg found another interested partner in Fred Adler, an attorney from New York. Adler had been dabbling in venture capital, but was less experienced in this realm than either Bessemer or Bain. He was also more ready to jump into the fray, and was the first investor to commit to the fledgling venture.

The summer drew to a close, and Stemberg and Reilly—who together had come up with the name Staples, the Office Superstore—wrestled with their venture capitalists over the valuation of the company. Also involved in this wrestling were Stemberg's four first lieutenants: Myra Hart, Paul Korian (from Osco, another Jewel company), Bob Leombruno (who had saved Mammoth Mart), and the soon-to-depart marketing manager, who had been working with a Connecticut advertising agency.

Todd Krasnow arrived on the scene just weeks before the first store opened its doors on May 1, 1986. Last to the party, he was under perhaps the most intense pressure of all during those very first days that Staples was in business. As the head of marketing, it was his job to get people in the doors. For the first store's grand opening, the Staples employees and officers had invited virtually everyone they knew. "That first day was a great success," Stemberg recalls, "but on the second day, we had only sixteen customers. On the third day, it was about the same number."

In other words, it looked like a disaster in the making. Krasnow—concluding that desperate measures were called for—decided he would *pay* people to come in and give Staples a try. First, he contacted the office managers of some two dozen local small businesses and got them to agree to come in and shop Staples. Then he sent each of them a $20 bill as an additional inducement—a lot of cash out the door for a store with no customers. After waiting a week or so, he recalls, he called them up to get their reactions to Staples:

> None *of them had come in! I couldn't believe it. They took the money, but they didn't come in. I was beside myself. My whole career was flashing before my eyes. I was thinking,* Oh God, I'm failing, and I've only been here for three weeks.

Throwing subtlety to the wind, he began hounding the twenty-five managers relentlessly: *Come in and try us!* Of the nine who finally set foot in the store, all of them loved it.

So the trick was to get people in the door. Krasnow began creating incentives at a frenzied pace. (Krasnow credits Rowland T. Moriarty—a 1980 graduate of the School's D.B.A. program, then an associate professor of marketing at HBS, and a founding member of the Staples board—with helping immensely in this dark phase as well as later key junctures.) Krasnow offered coupons and deals, organized direct mailings, and collected data on the customers. The free Staples "savings card" helped consumers save money by cutting prices even further, but also helped Krasnow compile marketing statistics based on information from the card applications. ("At the time," notes Stemberg, "such database marketing was almost unheard of in retailing.") The customer list grew longer and more detailed.

Yet Stemberg and his team were still deep in the woods. During the second round of financing, the question of valuation proved to be a potential roadblock. It seemed that the venture capital firms were closing ranks, stonewalling Stemberg, and refusing to value Staples as highly as he'd hoped. He returned to HBS and sought out Professor William Sahlman, the School's authority on venture capital, for advice. "How do you break this?" he asked.

Sahlman suggested that Stemberg seize control of his own destiny. *Go directly to the institutions: the pension funds and insurance companies,* he told Stemberg. *They may be limited partners of the venture capital firms, but often they resent handing off 20 percent of the profits instead of keeping it themselves. Add new sources of capital to the mix.*

Following this advice, Stemberg found his options vastly expanded. He also decided to make a direct appeal to high-net-worth individuals. ("When someone said he wanted 10 percent of the company, we'd say, 'Fine, that'll be $3 million.' And he'd say 'Fine'—and like magic, the company had a value.") Several of Stemberg's friends from HBS, including Scott Meadow (M.B.A. '80) and Michael Cronin (M.B.A. '77), decided they wanted in.

Meanwhile, persistence in the venture realm also paid off, in part because another HBS friend was helping Stemberg push open those sticky doors. Fred Lane —the classmate who years earlier used to visit Stemberg as he was bagging groceries at the Watertown Star Market—

had risen to the post of managing director for investment banking at the New York–based firm of Donaldson, Lufkin & Jenrette. Stemberg had approached DLJ during Staples's two rounds of financing, but to no avail. Despite Lane's staunch support, others at DLJ found Stemberg a little too aggressive in his approach, and they disagreed with his valuation of the company. Though Lane and his wife, Wendy, wound up putting about $75,000 of their own money into Stemberg's vision, he couldn't interest his DLJ colleagues in the venture, and eventually had to send Stemberg elsewhere.

When Stemberg came around a third time, Lane once again pushed DLJ's Sprout Fund to take a look. Lane first signed on Janet Hickey—an experienced venture analyst—and her approval helped win over the rest of the DLJ crew. This time, Sprout served as lead investor, and the deal became a very successful venture for the DLJ venture offshoot.

DOERS, DREAMERS, AND TEACHERS

Meanwhile, down at street level, the new enterprise struggled forward as many new enterprises do, encountering dead ends and wrong turns and countless small setbacks. "The greatest story about our first office," says Stemberg, in his characteristic rushed and staccato delivery, "was when the toilets broke down completely, probably sometime in 1989. Everyone was going up the street to our neighboring McDonald's to use their bathrooms. Finally, McDonald's put a sign up on their door saying 'No Staples people, please.' We had to send in the special troops."

Joe Vassalluzzo, who later became Staples's vice chairman, was the de facto commander of the special troops. "He began by guaranteeing them we would buy a certain number of lunches if we could use the facilities," says Stemberg.

Also in 1989, Stemberg hired a 1979 graduate of the Harvard Business School named Ron Sargent. Sargent was perhaps the only person in the Staples organization who was more deeply steeped in supermarkets than Stemberg himself. He had started working for the Cincinnati-based Kroger chain at age sixteen, worked there every summer for many years, and had gone back to Kroger after business school. So he was on a solid, safe career track with a century-old, $25 billion company when the call came in from Stemberg:

> *They were looking for somebody to open stores in the Midwest. They wanted somebody from the Midwest who was connected with people and knew retail. So they called a headhunter, and that person knew I was with Kroger, and that's why I got the call.*
>
> *At that point, there were probably fifteen or twenty stores in the chain, but it was still pretty entrepreneurial, and still felt like a start-up. I felt that people were running around like chickens with their heads cut off, especially compared to Kroger, where the trains tended to run on time. But I saw the concept, and I thought it could work. I told my wife, "Either I'm going to be very happy I joined this little start-up or I'm going to be unemployed within the year."*

The company gained momentum slowly, but even this modest success bred competitors. Within two years of its founding, Staples was faced with twenty new entrants into the office-supply trade. Office supplies somehow had become the darling of the venture capital community. In 1989, Tom Stemberg was asked how it felt to be the father of the office-supplies superstore industry. "I wish I had worn a condom," he replied brusquely.

That was the bad news. The good news was that he and his hardy band had vastly underestimated their market. From one perspective, it didn't matter how many new competitors entered the fray. The market simply refused to become saturated. Stemberg was amazed: "The core appetite for our products and expertise just continued to grow." The numbers were, and are, astounding. During its first twelve years of operation, Staples sold more than 5.5 *billion* paper clips.

THE ZOOTS GENERATION

Ask almost any professor at Harvard Business School about dry cleaning and you are likely to get handed three or four cases on the subject, all pointing the insightful student to the same basic conclusion: *Dry cleaning is a losing proposition.*

"They say it's a terrible business, and you don't want to be in it," says Todd Krasnow. "God, I *love* 'em for that!"

Sometimes the best opportunity hides in the pile that has been thoroughly picked over. Zoots, "the Cleaner Cleaner," is the most recent manifestation of the creative bonds between entrepreneurs Tom Stemberg and Todd Krasnow. Having already turned an uninspired industry—office products—into a field of opportunity, they set their sights on dry cleaning.

Krasnow—who had left Staples early in 1998, wanting to get back to a more entrepreneurial setting—had to create a dry cleaning company that offered something *different*, and thereby could prove the Harvard professors wrong. In some ways, the industry was similar to that of office supplies twenty years ago: fragmented, dominated by small local chains or single-location enterprises, and rarely able to offer cut-rate prices. Getting your dry cleaning done was a lot like buying office supplies used to be—"a chore, a necessary evil," as Krasnow puts it. Nobody expected or demanded improvements, so a huge industry had the luxury (or bad luck) to remain static.

Tom Stemberg, for his part, had been taking notes on dry cleaners for years. "I experienced a lot of problems as a customer," he recalls. "You'd get your shirts back with two buttons missing, and the stores were never open when you wanted." His file on the industry, dating back to before the founding of Staples, had grown large enough to convince him that a new kind of dry cleaning company might succeed.

Eventually, the subject came up in a conversation with Todd Krasnow. As Krasnow recalls:

> Over the years, we had talked on and off about doing something after Staples. When I finally decided that I wanted to get back to a more entrepreneurial environment, I approached Tom, and we decided his dry cleaning concept was the best of the bunch.

Could the techniques that worked for Staples also help transform the dry cleaning industry? The answer was yes—and no. Krasnow and Stemberg wanted to offer the same kind of benefits customers enjoyed at Staples: improved service, lower prices, and greater convenience. "But dry cleaning is different from Staples," says Krasnow. "Staples was low price with the right selection. In dry cleaning, we can offer all those services, but if we don't do a good job cleaning, you're not going to use us."

He and Stemberg turned the problem over in their minds. "What do customers deserve to have?" they asked themselves. "Forget about the problems in delivering it. What would make it a good experience for customers?"

Convenience, they decided, had to be the linchpin. For example, a drive-through window would help enormously, especially in bad weather. So would a twenty-four-hour kiosk, with lockers where customers could pick up or drop off cleaning any time of day or night.

A robust Web site would be a big help. In addition to showing the location of the nearest store, it could provide access for customers wanting to check the status of an order, print out cost-cutting coupons, or request valet pickup and delivery. It could allow customers to describe their own profile and change their preferences online.

The company Stemberg and Krasnow developed—Zoots—was founded on these kinds of innovations. During late 1998 and early 1999, the first stores opened in the small Massachusetts cities of Danvers and Attleboro. The second wave came in the Boston suburbs of Newton, Wellesley, and West Roxbury, where the first drive-through windows and twenty-four-hour kiosks were clustered.

A bright white decor dominated. Button replacement was free. Customers who registered with the company received a Zoots customer ID and a Zoots password; the numbers were part of a system that enabled people to get faster service (using personalized garment bags and/or the Web site) and access to the all-hours lockers in the kiosks.

According to Krasnow (who ran Zoots's day-to-day operations for five years and today serves as its chairman, while Tom Stemberg serves as chairman of the company's executive committee), obtaining customer data for marketing purposes in the dry cleaning industry was a snap, compared to office supplies. "When people give you their clothes," he explains, "they *want* you to know who they are. We don't have to fight to get their names and other information—they give it to us."

The plan was to broaden the customer base and turn this handful of stores into a nationwide chain. "Even more than Staples," says

Krasnow, "we faced the challenge of building very, very quickly— getting to scale, and doing it extremely well from the get-go." Like Staples a generation earlier, Zoots had to build a loyal following, *fast*. As if to underscore the point, well-financed competitors in North Carolina and California jumped into the business shortly after Zoots, clearly intending to pursue the same strategy as Krasnow's company.

But getting customers to change dry cleaners, and at the same time building loyalty to Zoots, was easier said than done. Most people simply patronize the dry cleaner closest to home or the one they pass on the way to work. In many cases, they've been friendly with the counter staff for years. Habits like this don't change unless someone puts a far better value proposition on the table.

"We make a pledge to all of our customers," announced the first iteration of Zoots' Web site. "Cleaning done right—or it's free." Patrons who were unsatisfied could decline to pay. "If you are satisfied, then you do pay us, and presumably you'll become a customer. Has any other dry cleaner ever made you an offer like this? So there is nothing to lose and lots to gain."

As of this writing, Zoots is still a picture in the painting. Jim McManus (M.B.A. '90) has taken over as chief executive officer of the company. As Stemberg explains:

> *We suggested to Todd that he should hire a big-time COO at Zoots, because at this scale, it's an operations-focused business, and Todd ain't an operator. So Todd went us one better. He said, "I don't want to hire a COO. I want to be a venture capitalist. So let's go hire ourselves a CEO."*
>
> *So we found McManus, who's doing a phenomenal job. He sees the same things we see: that if we operate this thing right, we could do really, really well. And it's already the biggest dry cleaner in the country, so that's a good sign, right?*

The chain's fifty-plus stores are both spiffy and efficient, thanks to high levels of automation, and its cleaning process has been lauded as environmentally sensitive. So far, customers in more than two hundred communities in ten states can take advantage of Zoots's free pickup and delivery service. Early in 2003, Krasnow announced proudly that his company had won sixteen "2002 Readers Choice Awards" in states stretching from New Hampshire to Virginia. A year later, it won another sixteen, in part by introducing an automated system to allow customers to get their garments back at all hours. And, in a symbolic closing of several loops, Zoots in 2003 entered into negotiations with a supermarket chain—Stop & Shop—to begin putting Zoots stores in selected locations.

THE MOTHER SHIP ADDS A CHANNEL

There's another parallel Staples story that needs to be told, involving yet another generation of young businesspeople, and also calling upon some of the same technologies that helped fuel Zoots's growth.

The story begins sometime in late 1996 or early 1997. The IS head at longtime rival Office Depot had put together a relatively low-cost Web site, and Office Depot was starting to do a brisk business through the site. Stemberg became aware of the success of this site in part through due diligence related to a proposed merger between Staples and Office Depot.

Although the Federal Trade Commission eventually blocked the merger, Stemberg kept thinking and worrying about the Internet. Would this new channel prove to be the way to serve large customers most effectively? Or maybe *small* customers? And looking sideways at what Amazon was threatening to do to Barnes & Noble: Would the Web threaten traditional bricks-and-mortar enterprises? Stemberg's concerns were fueled by the counsel of his chief strategist, Jeff Levitan, who was pushing strongly for a Web presence, and also by his friend Bob Higgins. Higgins was now with Highland Capital Partners, which had already made a number of successful Internet investments—including MapQuest, e-Toys, Ask Jeeves, and others—and was on the lookout for more such opportunities.

Those concerns were further underscored, Stemberg recalls, by a presentation made by HBS professor Warren McFarlan:

> *Warren McFarlan, of all people, gave a speech showing us how Amazon's market cap was way up here, and Barnes & Noble's was way down there. Same with e-Toys versus Toys "R" Us: up here, down there.*

*I mean, this isn't some wild-eyed e-commerce guy; this is McFarlan,
telling us this is the future.*

*At our next board meeting, [HBS professor] Bill Sahlman gave an-
other presentation. He said, basically, that even if it turned out to be a
bubble, we could go ahead incrementally, take advantage of it, and have
no disadvantage from a cost-of-capital point of view. Meanwhile, he
said, we sure didn't want this thing spinning out of our control. It was
too integral to our business.*

*So I finally said, "You know, we've got to get into this thing. Yes, I
think there's a bubble aspect to it, but we need to move on this."*

To head up the new Staples Internet venture—dubbed Staples.com—
Stemberg tapped Jeanne Lewis. Lewis, a graduate of Wellesley College
and HBS (M.B.A. '92), had spent the summer of 1991 at Staples, working crazy hours (for what she once calculated to have been something
like $8 per hour) as a marketing intern for a local legend named Todd
Krasnow. After getting out of business school, Lewis turned down a job
offer from Staples—looking for a slightly less crazy work environment,
as she recalls—and went to work for Fidelity Investments instead. She
didn't last long at Fidelity. "Great place," she says in retrospect, "but a really bad fit for me."

In 1993, she rejoined Staples as a marketing manager and quickly
climbed the still relatively compressed Staples corporate ladder. After
spending a successful year as director of operations for Staples's New
England stores, she headed up merchandising for 150 East Coast
stores. In 1996, she became one of five merchandising vice presidents,
where again she distinguished herself—and began working closely
with marketing head Todd Krasnow. And on February 1, 1998, after a
year of apprenticeship, she succeeded Krasnow as the head of marketing, thereby stepping into the shoes of a Staples legend.

She didn't get much time to celebrate her arrival at the top of the
Staples marketing organization. She initiated a series of changes in
the existing department, many aimed at pushing responsibility farther down into the ranks. At the same time, however, Stemberg was
pushing ever harder on his organization to develop a credible e-busi-
ness presence. As head of marketing, Lewis was the obvious choice to

succeed strategist Jeff Levitan as head of the e-commerce project. As Stemberg explains:

Jeanne Lewis is one of the most talented executives/entrepreneurs I've ever had work for me. She's extremely entrepreneurial. She's really strong-minded. I mean, I used to kid her that I'd appreciate her at least informing me what her decisions were, maybe half the time. Very, very good. She was just perfect for this.

Staples.com launched in November 1998, with Lewis at the helm. A month later, it became an "independent" business with its own growth targets and staff. From the start, though, Staples.com lived in a complex relationship with its parent. It was billed as more or less a freestanding entity, and yet it was completely dependent on the same purchasing, warehousing, and fulfillment functions that the parent company's seven-year-old catalog division already drew upon. The model that Stemberg had in mind was the relationship between the New York Times Company and its Web offspring: a mother ship with a feisty satellite, which looked and acted differently from its parent, but at the same time depended entirely on that parent for content.

On September 15, 1999, the Staples board announced plans to issue a tracking stock for Staples.com. Again, the New York Times Company precedent—which also involved a tracking stock—served as a useful model, although there were numerous other examples in recent corporate history. The goal was threefold: to give the dot-com access to relatively inexpensive capital, to create competitive incentives to recruit and retain employees, and to create a transparent system of accounting for this substantially different sort of business. The tracking stock was a relatively easy device to create, and also relatively easy to undo, if the parent chose to fold the offshoot back into the core of the company. And if Staples went the other way—in the direction of spinning out the dot-com in an IPO—then the satellite had the advantage of a clear valuation.

Two months later, after winning the approval of the company's shareholders, Staples issued a 5 percent equity stake in the dot-com to five venture capital and private-equity firms, including Bob Higgins's Highland Capital. For a business that was then doing something like

$20 million annually, the $200 million valuation that resulted seemed high, but not outlandishly so, in the midst of Internet fever.

FREE COFFEE AND CULTURES

In January 2000, Lewis hired a design team to rebuild her dot-com's physical space in the Staples headquarters building. By this time, the Staples.com staff had grown from a few dozen to more than four hundred, and space had become an issue. Stemberg had originally encouraged Lewis to find space physically separated from the mother ship, but she persuaded him that businesses that were so closely tied logistically should not be physically separate. At the same time, she desperately wanted, in her own corner of the second floor, to overcome the "*Fortune* 500" feel of corporate headquarters—"the four flags out front, the trophy case, the security guard"—and create the feel of an entrepreneurial endeavor.

Helping Lewis feel her way down this complicated path was Staples board member Meg Whitman—president and CEO of eBay Inc., the online trading site, and along with Ron Sargent, a member of the HBS class of 1979. Stemberg, Levitan, and Lewis all made treks out to San Jose to get a feel for this new kind of business, as practiced by eBay. As Stemberg says of Whitman:

> She was huge. She just had great ideas about how to look at these things. How to negotiate with all the other sites. How you build a sense of community. Stickiness: How you create stickiness was a big thing. And sending out e-mail reminders about your toner cartridge running out, and creating your personalized shopping list—all things that Meg inspired Jeanne to do.

Whitman showed Lewis her cubicle at eBay's San Jose headquarters—a space no bigger or smaller than that of her administrative assistant—and explained how a relatively open and democratic floor plan helped communications flow across a fast-moving company. Lewis adopted the bright-colors/eight-by-ten-cubicles approach and also found money in her budget for a game area (including a pool table and the requisite foosball game) and free coffee, soda, and cookies.

These little perks created some frictions within the larger organization. People in the "old" Staples began grumbling, wondering aloud why *they* couldn't have free coffee as well. "So much so," Lewis says with a somewhat pained smile, "that at one point, Tom said to the leaders of the other areas, 'Great. You want free coffee and donuts? Go sit in cubicles, and save us some space. You can have all the donuts you want.'"

By now, she recalls, the dot-com was going like a house afire, which both generated better numbers and exacerbated the cultural issues:

> *The business side of it was relatively easy. I always compared it to try-*
> *ing to open a surprise package when you're running at a hundred miles*
> *per hour. Hard to run that fast, hard to look at the prizes along the way.*
> *But the business stuff was fairly easy, compared to some of the cultural*
> *stuff within the organization.*
>
> *And the problem really was that it was* a different way of doing
> business. *We created a subculture that was foreign to a lot of the folks*
> *at Staples. There were a lot of twenty-somethings walking around the*
> *building in really nice eyewear—really interesting glasses!—and*
> *dressed a little differently. So once we could see our way clear to prof-*
> *itability, I spent a lot of my time building bridges between this foreign*
> *entity—Staples.com—and the base business.*

Almost from the outset, the big question was whether Staples.com would simply cannibalize existing customers and accounts. Publicly, Staples argued that their model—clicks and mortar—was the best of all possible worlds, but privately, many inside the organization worried. Would Staples.com simply "steal" all the catalog division's customers? Would it empty the retail stores of warm bodies? *If so, so be it,* Stemberg told the troops, well behind the scenes. *Better that we canni-balize ourselves than have somebody else do it to us.*

To minimize interunit rivalries, Staples established a system of blended stock options, whereby Staples employees were offered the opportunity (and loaned the money) to buy Staples.com stock, and vice versa. This tactic helped knit the organization together and underscore the mutual dependencies and synergies among its component parts.

Meanwhile, interesting things started happening in the retail stores that reinforced this thrust. The bricks-and-mortar stores could physically stock only 7,000-plus SKUs. The standard Staples catalog offered some 15,000 items, plus another 40,000 or so through specialized catalogs. But Staples.com offered more than *100,000* products. Gradually, Staples's retail employees relearned the lessons they had learned when the catalog division got started in the early 1990s, under Ron Sargent's direction: Done right, multiple selling channels means both increased penetration and reduced customer attrition.

If we don't have it, the retail salesclerks started telling customers, *we can find it on our Web site.* Meanwhile, the Web also gave Staples's corporate merchants the opportunity to test new products in a relatively low-risk way. Rather than bringing untested items into 1,500 stores, they learned to put the item up on the Web site, track the new product's progress, and then make the decision as to whether or not to roll out the product across the retail chain.

CANNIBALS AND KIOSKS

Then came the implosion of the Internet bubble, with major reverberations for both Staples and Staples.com. Just before the bubble burst in the first quarter of 2000, some analysts were suggesting that a Staples.com IPO would fetch as much as $7 *billion*—a valuation that some suggested might position the satellite to buy the mother ship. ("We would have held on to 80 or 90 percent of the dot-com," scoffs Stemberg, "so that wasn't going to happen.") But as people ran away from Internet stocks, the frame around Staples.com changed. Instead of applauding the dot-com for losing money, analysts complained that the satellite was dragging down earnings. It was no longer likely that $7 billion was out there on the table, waiting to be scooped up.

Briefly, Stemberg and his colleagues tried to stay on their charted course, announcing plans to invest an additional $150 million in its online venture (up from $75 million only a few months earlier). Partially in response, Staples stock sagged almost 30 percent between March 1 and mid-April. Meanwhile, analysts began hammering on the parent to include the dot-com's business expenses in the parent company's overall results. When the SEC made the same request in August—as a result of changing its own practices regarding the reporting of losses from Internet units—Staples complied, and Stemberg began talking publicly about folding the dot-com back into Staples, Inc.

At the same time, though, Stemberg continued to thump the Internet tub with the zeal of a recent convert. In a mid-August interview with CNBC, he acknowledged that some cannibalization had gone on between the Internet and the retail stores. But as customers moved to the Web, he emphasized, they spent twice as much on a per-employee basis ($150 in the stores, $300 online).

Cross-selling between channels, Stemberg was convinced, more than made up for any cannibalization. And Stemberg himself had helped shove this integration process along. Somewhere in the early months of 2000—looking sideways at his Zoots experience—he suggested putting kiosks in the retail stores that would tie directly into Staples.com. If a customer wasn't finding what he or she needed on the floor, an alert salesclerk could steer the customer to a kiosk and find the item online. The result? Another happy customer, who very often had the items delivered to the office the next day. The kiosks—dubbed "business solutions centers"—were introduced in August 2000, and quickly proved their worth. "And today," says Stemberg, "we're running something like $300 million a year through those kiosks. Huge."

But in the larger context, especially with the SEC demanding consolidated financials, it made little sense to maintain the separate tracking stock. In April 2001, the Staples board voted to convert Staples.com stock into Staples stock—and to rescind their personal stakes in Staples.com. The directors also voted to sell back their own shares in the dot-com at the original purchase price, thereby forgoing any personal gain on the transaction. And that was the end of the quasi-independent Staples.com.

Bob Higgins—who today works part-time as a venture capitalist and part-time as a senior lecturer at HBS, teaching entrepreneurship—recalls that Highland Capital and the other venture partners made a respectable return on their investment, on the order of three times what they had put in:

I think the return to the investors was pretty fair. It wasn't the ten- or twenty-fold return that we were expecting when we invested, but we also weren't expecting to have to cash out in less than a year and a half. And I'm sure many of us would have preferred to stay in, given the kinds of phenomenal numbers and meteoric growth that Staples.com was generating.

Over the next two years, in fact, the dot-com continued to grow at a dizzying pace. In 2003, Staples.com did something in excess of $2 billion—"two *big* ones," Stemberg underscores, happily—and as of 2004 makes roughly a 10 percent return. It is the fourth-largest Internet business in the world. Close to 80,000 people a month use Staples.com to find the nearest Staples retail score, underscoring the symbiotic relationship among the various Staples channels.

DREAMERS AND DOERS

Staples now has annual sales approaching $13 billion. It employs more than 50,000 people, who operate some 1,500 stores in the U.S., Canada, the United Kingdom, France, Italy, Spain, Belgium, Germany, the Netherlands, and Portugal as well as thriving businesses in the catalog and contract arenas. In its Staples.com venture, as we've seen, the company successfully navigated the tricky waters of the Internet, and came out more than whole.

Despite this success, founder Tom Stemberg stays on his toes and looks over his shoulder. "I always had doubts," he says, a little gloomily, "and I keep having doubts. I guess they never go away." Entrepreneurs, he adds, need to have thick skin and an abiding vision. "You have to live reality, but dream the dream." Beginning in February 2002, Stemberg began dreaming his dreams one step back from the front lines, when he was succeeded as CEO by longtime operations chief Ron Sargent.

Jeanne Lewis also is watching proudly from the sidelines. Toward the end of 2001, she came to a strange realization: that she was in the office-products business:

Up to that point, the office supplies were kind of the "oh, by the way" of our lives. The excitement came from new channels, new customer segments, new geographies, new product lines. All the crazy stuff we

*did never felt like work to me. But as I contemplated going back into
the core business in late 2001, it just felt less like a high-growth company, and more like an office-supplies retailer.*

She resigned in November, was cajoled into taking a promotion
and staying on the job, and then resigned for good early in 2002.
Today, along with an HBS classmate, she is looking for her next opportunity—preferably a smaller, high-growth company like the Staples she joined in 1993.

Tom Stemberg hears of this plan with great interest. "Whatever her
next deal is," he says, "I'm investing."

Myra Hart—now a professor in entrepreneurial management at
HBS—also grew apart from Staples. Having started out as the company's
vice president of operations, Hart had watched the company blossom
with the pride of a founder—and also the occasional pang of regret. The
company's success soon caused her job to change; within a year of its
founding, she became the executive vice president of growth and development, and gradually her responsibilities became more administrative.

"I'm very operational," she explains, "and I prefer hands-on work.
But soon I had two secretaries and a staff doing everything for me. It
really stopped being as much fun." The company's initial public offering gave her financial independence, and she decided to explore her
"unfinished work" back at Harvard Business School.

During her second year at HBS, Hart had completed a field study
under Chris Christensen, the legendary case-method teacher. He encouraged her to enroll in the doctoral program. She decided against it
then, but after Staples went public, she contacted Christensen, then
applied to HBS and was accepted. After receiving her doctorate, she
stayed on to teach.

"In retrospect," she says, "I think I was an entrepreneur back when
I was running my father-in-law's real estate business. It just wasn't a
word that was on the tip of my tongue then; that wasn't the way I
framed it in my thoughts." Although she considered herself to be running a business, and although she took steps to shake that business up,
the word *entrepreneur* simply never came to mind.

Her experience with Staples changed all that. "There I definitely
thought of myself as an entrepreneur. And yet I'll be the first one to tell

you that it wasn't my idea. I don't think you have to be the inventor or the creator to be the entrepreneur. You have to be the *doer*."

Over at Zoots, Todd Krasnow agrees wholeheartedly. No matter what the final verdict on his dry cleaning venture, Krasnow plans to keep acting on great ideas, in the company of great people. "My hope is to work with people whose attitudes are like Tom's was twenty years ago, and Myra's and mine were ten or fifteen years ago," he explains. "I want people who will roll their sleeves up, and dive in, and *make something happen.*

"It's just a mind-set," he concludes, "but you can't do without it."

Stemberg, Sargent, Lewis, Hart, Krasnow, and the other protagonists in the Staples story embody the classic attributes of entrepreneurial success: deep industry knowledge, operating skills, vision, determination, and *luck*. But the specifics of their careers also underscore the importance of the extraordinary network that exists among HBS alumni—an active connection that bridges generations, different fields of interest, and wide geographic distances.

That network has been many decades in the building. It has played a critical role not only in the lives of entrepreneurs, but in the very definition of entrepreneurship, as that word has been understood at the Harvard Business School.

And one of the first HBS researchers to worry about that definition, and to benefit from that network, was a young lawyer turned statistician turned professor named Myles Mace.

CHAPTER 2

The Light Goes On

IN THE WANING YEARS of World War II, Myles Mace—a member of the Harvard Business School class of 1938 and a lieutenant colonel in the U.S. Army Air Forces' Statistical Control School—was serving a tour of duty in the South Pacific. Although the end of hostilities was not yet in sight, it was clear to many that the tide of warfare was turning slowly in favor of the United States and its allies. Slowly, the Axis powers would be ground down, and someday, for those who survived the brutal conflict, life would return to normal.

Mace was stationed at Hickham Field on Waikiki. A deceptively idyllic setting, Hickham Field several years earlier had been a main target in the Japanese attack on Pearl Harbor. At Pearl, the burned-out hulk of the U.S.S. *Arizona* still lay half-submerged at an unnatural angle in the harbor, silent testimony to the terrors of war.

But for Mace, as for many others in uniform, those terrors were mostly remote. Contacts with the enemy were rare punctuation marks amid long periods of routine, even tedium. Mace, a midlevel officer in what was informally known in military circles as the Stat School, was then spending his days trying to help the still mushrooming Army Air Forces (AAF) get control of itself.

This was a major challenge. Earlier in the war, the AAF had realized that it was unable to answer an absolutely critical question: *How many planes do we have—right here, right now—that can fly, fight, and bomb?* The AAF had turned to the Harvard Business School for help, and the School assembled a cohort of bright and ambitious young men to develop a new approach to organizing the flow of statistical information across a fast-growing organization. One was Robert McNamara—then a young assistant professor of accounting—who later helped create the postwar field of control at the Ford Motor Company, rose to the presidency of Ford, and became an international figure as Secretary of Defense in the Kennedy and Johnson administrations and president of the World Bank.

Another was Myles Mace. From his Waikiki base, Mace traveled all over the Pacific, launching and nurturing AAF Stat Control in places as far-flung as Manila, Guam, Saipan, and Tinean. "All those little air bases throughout the Pacific that were then bombing the hell out of the Japanese," Mace recalls. "I covered them all."

Although not a gregarious man, Mace was friendly and accessible. He enjoyed fraternizing with enlisted men and officers alike. He was a good listener and discreet, and was therefore someone in whom fellow officers and subordinates felt free to confide. Such informal contacts also helped him be more effective at his job, which involved training officers to set up effective ways to collect and disseminate information, and therefore required trust and cooperation across all the ranks of the AAF.

On one otherwise unmemorable morning, a captain under Mace's command strolled into Mace's office. He looked quite full of himself. Engaging Mace in conversation, he soon made an amazing announcement. He had won $25,000 in a high-stakes poker game the night before.

At that time, $25,000 was a staggering amount of money. Mace, the son of a locomotive engineer, had been raised in modest circumstances in the small town of Montevideo, Minnesota; he had never seen anything like $25,000 in cash in one place. After digesting this astonishing news, Mace made a strong suggestion to the captain. "You go down and get a money order," he said, "and send that money to your wife right now! If you don't, you're going to go back and blow it at that gambling table."

The captain agreed. "Sir, I'll take your advice," he said, and left the office.

The next day, the same captain showed up in Mace's office. This time, he looked forlorn. "Colonel Mace, I'm sorry, sir," he said. "I should have taken your advice. I went back to the table, and I blew it all."

The episode stuck with Mace—not only for its lessons about the powerful lure of the poker table, but also as part of a larger picture that Mace was then piecing together in his mind. Eventually, this war would be over, and the young soldiers and sailors who were fortunate enough to survive it would be returning home. As Mace knew from personal experience, these future veterans were looking forward to returning to civilian life—with a vengeance.

"Many of them had come to hate the constraint that being in uniform represented," Mace remembered a half-century later. Many were determined to escape the regimentation, facelessness, and routine that characterized their military service. As he recalls:

> *They were fed up with being a serial number in a large organization. They were saying, "When I get out of this damn uniform, I can tell you that I'm never, ever going to work for a large corporation and just be another number! I want to be part of a small organization. Maybe I'll start my own business."*

Some were merely daydreaming, of course. But others were very serious about acting on their entrepreneurial impulses. The war had tested and hardened them, shown them far broader horizons than they could have known under any other circumstances, and made them mature before their time. And many, it seemed, would be coming home with cash stakes in their pockets. Following his encounter with the poker-playing captain, Mace had done some informal investigating, and had been astonished to discover how much cash was sloshing around in the giant American military machine, largely in the pockets of young GIs.

Many of these young men were ambitious, versed in the ways of the world, and strong-willed. Many felt that they had to make up for lost time. And most, Mace suspected, hadn't the slightest idea about how to start and grow a new business. But the young lieutenant colonel began to think that, thanks to his unusual background, he might just be in a position to help them.

A decade earlier, in the depths of the Great Depression, Mace had worked his way through law school at the University of Minnesota and the St. Paul College of Law, and was admitted to the Minnesota bar. But the hard times were afflicting law school graduates and sharecroppers alike. Mace was lucky to secure a job as a bill collector for a fuel oil company. "It was knocking on doors from eight in the morning until five at night, five and a half days a week," Mace recalls. "And in Minnesota, in the winter, there were days when it was thirty below."

Mace wanted more out of life. He dreamed of working as a high-powered lawyer in New York City, but he knew that his credentials were far too modest to let him realize these ambitions. After talking things over with his fiancée, Bunny, he decided to enroll at the Harvard Business School. Perhaps the combination of a Midwestern law degree and a business degree from Harvard would give Mace the edge he needed to push his way into the upper reaches of New York's legal profession.

Mace did well at the Business School. He particularly enjoyed his second-year elective course with Professor Nathan B. Isaacs, the School's authority on legal issues in business, whom Mace recalls as "one of the finest professors I've ever had." Isaacs evidently took a liking to the young lawyer from Minnesota. An Orthodox Jew, Isaacs often asked Mace to come over to his house on Friday evenings to light the stove and perform other tasks that Isaacs was prohibited from performing after sunset on the Sabbath.

Following his graduation from Harvard in 1938, Mace and Bunny— married in the summer between the young lawyer's first and second years at HBS—drove to New York, where Mace had interviews with a half-dozen of the best law firms in the city. He received job offers from all of them, including one that promised an astounding starting salary: $18,000 per year. "That," Mace recalls with a smile, "was a *hell* of a lot of money." But as the Maces toured the city, they had an unexpected realization: They really didn't want to live in the kind of environment that New York promised them. "It was an awful big city," Mace explains, "for two kids from Minnesota."

Giving up on his dreams of a high-powered legal career, Mace landed a far less lucrative position as a young HBS faculty member and research assistant to Professor Isaacs. Now back on the HBS campus in a different role, the Maces set up house on the second floor of Sherman Hall. The household budget was tight; Mace was making a tenth of what he would have made in New York City. Professor Isaacs, however, watched out for the young couple. Noticing one cold winter day that his research assistant had only a lined raincoat to wear, for example, Isaacs the next day brought in one of his cashmere overcoats as a gift to Mace.

Soon the war intervened, but the School's family-like atmosphere continued to provide benefits to Mace and his new family. Mace and his young faculty colleague, Robert McNamara, were commissioned as lieutenant colonels in the infant Army Air Forces statistical control network. Shortly before their departure for England—where they would distinguish themselves by helping to make the U.S.'s Eighth Air Force a more effective fighting unit—Mace and McNamara stopped by the office of HBS dean Donald K. David. "Basically," Mace admits, "I wanted to show the dean my fancy uniform."

But David had far more practical matters on his mind. "Does either of you have any life insurance," he asked them, "in the event that something should happen to you?"

The question struck Mace and McNamara as being just this side of absurd. "On $1,800 a year," Mace recalls responding, "we should be buying life insurance?"

"Well, *that's* crazy," David replied. Mace later learned that the dean had immediately called an insurance broker and taken out policies on the two young officers, naming their respective wives as beneficiaries.

THIS ENVIRONMENT bred an intense kind of loyalty. It was no surprise, then, that Mace—contemplating his postwar options from his vantage point in the South Pacific—wanted to return to the Harvard Business School after the war. He hoped to teach, to complete a dissertation—a prerequisite for staying on the faculty, even in that less academically rigorous era—and to research business topics of interest to him. And increasingly, given his experiences with the young soldiers, sailors, and airmen at Waikiki and elsewhere, he was interested in new and small businesses.

But new and small businesses were decidedly *not* the traditional province of the Harvard Business School. For the first three decades of its existence, the School had mainly catered to the nation's largest businesses. This was more a practical necessity than a philosophical bent. Large corporations controlled the resources that were needed to help the School survive its underendowed infancy. At the same time, they created the jobs that were supposed to be filled by the School's graduates.

The installation of Donald David as the School's dean in 1942 only cemented the close relationship between HBS and big business. David was himself a successful businessman, extremely well connected in business and financial circles. He drew heavily on these informal ties to advance the School's interests and worked hard to bring the heads of America's most powerful corporations into more significant relationships with HBS. A glance at the roster of the School's Visiting Committee in the immediate postwar years—which included people like the chairman of the board of AT&T, the president of Procter & Gamble, and the chairman of the board of Chase National Bank— makes the point. The Harvard Business School was an institution that, for very practical reasons, defined "success" in very specific ways.

At the same time, the School was not monolithic. Since its founding, there had always been a handful of faculty members interested in small businesses. During the School's first two decades, for example, its Bureau of Business Research had attempted to establish operating norms for small companies in a variety of retail trades—jewelry, grocery, shoes, and so on. Specialized industry-oriented courses, subsidized by the industries on which they focused (printing, lumbering, etc.), often looked at companies in the early stages of their existence. And of course, many of the teaching "cases" for which the School was becoming celebrated focused on smaller companies embarking on growth. Finally, most of the huge, publicly traded companies that formed the nucleus of the School's corporate support traced their roots to small, privately held companies.

But these pursuits tended to be the exceptions to the larger institutional rule. So when Mace returned to the Business School at the end of the war, he asked for a meeting with Dean David. At that meeting, in the spring of 1946, he sketched out his vision of a wave of returning GIs eager to invest in a future of their own making. These men, Mace asserted, had drive, maturity, and—in some cases—start-up capital. But, as he explained to the dean, "They don't have the slightest idea of what's involved in putting whatever capital you have or can raise into a new enterprise. Not a smidgen of an idea."

David asked Mace how his ideas might be applied to the School. Mace had a ready answer: "I'd like to start a course on the problems of starting and running small businesses."

"Fine," Dean David said. "Go ahead."

As it turned out, that off-the-cuff endorsement launched more than a half-century of creative instruction in small-business formation and development, the raising and deployment of capital, and a host of other issues that in recent years have come to be grouped under the term *entrepreneurship*. Of course, neither Mace nor David was predicting a durable success would grow out of that meeting early in 1946. But Dean David had ample reason to support Mace's new venture and to take any steps he could to help it succeed.

First, David's own background made him sympathetic to Mace's plea. Although he had spent twenty years in industry, eventually becoming president of American Maize Products Company before assuming the deanship at Harvard, David came from small-business roots. His father ran a department store in the modest city of Moscow, Idaho. And David, like other thoughtful businesspeople and academics in the immediate postwar period, had been thinking a great deal about the prospects of the American economy. The return of American servicemen at the end of the First World War—who were almost literally dumped on an unprepared economy that was then contracting due to postwar demobilization—had helped spark the severe recession of 1920–1922. Conversely, nearly two decades later, it was the Second World War that finally pulled America out of the Great Depression of the 1930s. Would the end of the war usher in a return to depression? If so, what could Harvard do to help head that off?

A related factor that inclined David to support Mace's proposal was the recently implemented Elements of Administration program,

the revamped M.B.A. curriculum approved by the faculty early in
1945. Among other things, the Elements of Administration program
was intended to produce what David called "risk takers" for the postwar economy.

The Elements of Administration, however, focused on the first year
of the School's two-year program. This was in part because the war
was not expected to end quickly, and the demobilization that would
follow the war was expected to last several years. Harvard's president
James Conant was among the select few who knew about the progress
being made toward the development of the atomic bomb; he nevertheless predicted in November 1944 that demobilization would begin
in the fall of 1946 and continue for three or four years. The Harvard
Business School's second-year program, it seemed, could wait.

All of these predictions were washed away in the flood tide of returning GIs that hit the Harvard Business School when, in the fall of
1945, the School announced that it would resume civilian instruction
in February 1946. Within a few months, nearly 6,000 men had expressed an interest in attending the School. This was an astonishing figure for an institution that had graduated only 7,757 in its entire history
of nearly four decades. Many of the ambitious young soldiers and
sailors of World War II, the kinds of young men who had so impressed
Myles Mace in Hawaii, wanted business skills, and decided that Harvard was the place to get them.

The School took aggressive steps to respond to the unprecedented
demand. A plan to run year-round was confirmed, with three separate
entering dates: February, June, and October. The size of these entering
classes was increased from 550 to 900. Second-year students—those
returning to complete studies that had been interrupted by the war—
would be admitted in June and October. But the second-year program
was still largely up in the air. A beleaguered faculty, as noted, had tacitly
agreed to deal with the second year when circumstances permitted.

Now, looking forward from the spring of 1946, Dean David could
see that there was no time to waste. Individual faculty members had
pulled together thirty elective courses that could constitute the second-
year program for that year's forty-four second-year students. (Not all
of these courses would be offered, of course; enrollments would de-

termine what would actually get taught.) The following year, though, the School would need to offer at least forty second-year courses, to accommodate more than *six hundred* second-year students.

So when Myles Mace presented his plan for a novel second-year course in starting new businesses, the dean didn't hesitate. "Fine," he said. "Go ahead."

ANNOUNCED IN THE COURSE LISTING for February 1947, Mace's course was titled Management of New Enterprises. According to the catalog, the purpose of the course was to "center attention on the opportunities, risks, and management problems involved in establishing and operating new enterprises. The course is intended primarily for students who contemplate going into business for themselves." The students would be expected to grapple with "management issues faced by individual entrepreneurs" and the "implications and individual responsibilities of the small management group in a new business."

This was the first time an HBS course would focus entirely on the problems faced by fledgling companies. It was also the first time the word *entrepreneur* appeared in an HBS course description. These were the modest beginnings of a faculty effort that would take nearly a half-century to come into its own.

Mace intended to teach Management of New Enterprises using the almost universally accepted mode of instruction at the School: the case method. He himself was a product of the case method, and he subscribed wholeheartedly to it as an effective and interactive way of conducting professional education. (The Stat School experience, which involved training legions of relatively elite AAF officers, had reinforced this conviction.) But there were two major catches.

First, Mace would have to build the course from scratch, in a hurry. "The most urgent thing," Mace recalls, "was to get some teaching materials together. There wasn't a word in the files on any of these problems. There wasn't a single case that had any relationship."

And at the same time, Mace had to learn his subject. "The fact was, I didn't know anything about starting a small business," Mace admits cheerfully. "So I had to learn fast." Again, the Stat School experience gave Mace a necessary measure of confidence. In that context, Mace and his colleagues had more or less invented a subject, drawing on several content areas, and then gone out into the field and developed the materials needed to teach it. At times, the Stat School faculty members were only a week or two ahead of their students. Living on the pedagogical edge was not new to Mace.

With the help of research assistant Don Booz—M.B.A. '47, son of one of the founders of the consulting firm of Booz Allen Hamilton, and much later a mentor to Don Perkins at the Jewel Companies— Mace began assembling the cases and supporting materials that he would need to teach his unprecedented course. One of the first people he called upon was Louis Kovacs, a fellow member of the class of 1938. Mace and Kovacs had met as "can-mates" (members of a group of eight students sharing common bathroom facilities) in Chase Hall and had become fast friends.

By this point, Kovacs was working at a company founded ten years earlier by his father and grandfather. Vitamins Inc., on Chicago's South Side, was a small business focused on developing innovative ways to supplement the nutritional value of foods and pharmaceuticals. Vitamins were starting to be understood by both science and industry, and Vitamins, Inc., was in the vanguard. For its largest customer, the cereal giant Kellogg, the company had devised a method of spraying vitamins onto cereals.

The younger Kovacs was both an executive of the company and a member of its board. When Mace came to see Kovacs, he was looking for guidance in shaping his new course, and hoping that Vitamins, Inc., might serve as the basis for a case or two. Kovacs went him one better: He not only offered to help Mace think through his course materials, he also offered the young faculty member a seat on the company's board.

"I figured," Kovacs recalls, "that Myles would be exposed to a wide variety of issues above and beyond what would normally be board-of-director type problems." The company was in a state of transition on many fronts, inventing both new products and new processes. It was changing and growing; at the same time, it was still small enough that a board member would be immersed in its day-to-day challenges.

The argument was compelling, and Mace agreed to serve as an out-side director of the company. He soon found himself sitting in on meet-ings with key suppliers and customers, and observing as the company began taking the difficult steps necessary to develop a presence in coun-tries outside the United States. "Louie Kovacs and I learned together lots of things about running a small business," Mace says. "He was most helpful in teaching me exactly what's involved. And for my part, I did my best to avoid making any egregious mistakes in my role as director."

Kovacs gives Mace more credit, suggesting that the young Harvard Business School professor made real contributions to the business. At the very least, Mace's calming presence—and his status as an out-sider—helped ease some of the tensions that often arise in businesses involving several generations of the same family. "I don't think he found those problems very pleasant," Kovacs comments, "but I'm sure they were educational."

They were—so much so, in fact, that Mace soon replicated the small-company immersion experience that Kovacs had invented for him. In short order, he was also serving on the boards of (and becom-ingly intimately acquainted with) a maker of architectural models and a manufacturer of industrial plastics. Stories from each of these settings—often disguised, sometimes not—made their way into the growing collection of teaching materials being put together by Mace and his research assistant, Don Booz.

Many years later, Mace recalled two of the principles that he wanted his course to convey. First, *make sure that your company's financ-ing is adequately secured.* Second, *make sure that your company's market is clearly identified.* "Know what the hell your market is!" as Mace puts it. "There are so many bad business ideas out there without a sound, sen-sible idea behind them." Not conceptual breakthroughs, to be sure—but solid fundamentals for would-be entrepreneurs to take to heart.

MANAGEMENT of New Enterprises was formally launched in Febru-ary 1947. Many of the 188 enrollees were precisely the people for whom Mace had invented the course: returning veterans. They were outstanding students, hard-working and creative, and they repaid Mace's personal investment in the course in the most gratifying way possible. "They knew what the hell they were doing at the Harvard Business School," Mace says, his admiration obvious a half-century after the fact. "They were deadly serious. They were determined."

Mace required all students to complete a term report, which, according to the course catalog, might consist of "the presentation of a complete plan for starting a small business." It was the best way Mace could think of to get his students out in the field, talking to small-business owners, much as he had done with Kovacs. In Mace's opinion, many small businesses failed because their owners were both ignorant and isolated. He was determined to keep his students out of these traps: "I wanted to get them out to actually see what's involved in starting your own company. I wanted to get them talking to guys who were successful. And they did it."

For these and other reasons, Management of New Enterprises was an intensely *practical* course. It offered real and useful insights into how good small businesses actually worked. As a result, course ratings were high, and enrollments hovered around two hundred students the first three times Mace taught it. Clearly, Mace had tapped into a significant tributary of student opinion. A survey published in an August 1947 edition of the *Harbus* revealed that 59 percent of fourth-term Business School students hoped to make their careers in companies of small or medium size. Although enrollments dipped in the fourth run of the course, an October 1948 *Harbus* article reported that "Management of New Enterprises was in marked demand by 147 scions and relentless hunters of golden opportunities."

At the same time, entrepreneurship in the context of small businesses was slowly gaining respectability. No longer was small business perceived as a haven for amateurs and also-rans. When Charles Edward Wilson, then the president of General Electric, spoke at the Business School in November 1949, his topic was "Bigness in Business"—but much of his address concerned new and smaller enterprises. The small-business sector played a vital role in the economy, according to Wilson; since 1900, it had grown at a faster rate than large business, so that it now constituted 35 percent of enterprises overall.

Few records exist, but it appears that few of Mace's graduating students launched businesses upon leaving the School. On the other hand, many eventually did start companies, usually after spending a number of years in large corporations. (This became the pattern for many of the ensuing classes.) In the early 1990s, Mace attended an alumni gathering at which he was very warmly received. "It seemed to me," Mace says, with evident satisfaction, "that the people who took my course were represented in very large numbers. And it was gratifying to me that they had been very successful, and made a lot of money, and gave me credit for that."

Those students had taken risks, but their professor had taken risks before them. He had ventured into a field that, for all practical purposes, didn't exist. He had agreed to sit on the boards of several small companies, a step that was highly unusual at the Harvard Business School of the 1940s and early 1950s. ("Nobody around here that I know of has ever sat on the board of directors of a small corporation," Mace's faculty colleague and mentor Melvin T. "Doc" Copeland told him, and Copeland—who had been at the School since 1909—was in a position to know.) While he was frantically assembling the materials needed to teach Management of New Enterprises, Mace was also mapping out an unorthodox dissertation, which focused on analyzing the appropriate role of the boards of directors of small corporations. The dissertation was published in 1948 as a book, *The Board of Directors of Small Corporations*, and despite the many risks he had taken, Mace's position as an innovator in a field largely of his own design seemed secure.[1]

But Mace was already planning the next phase of his life, and it would turn out to have a very different focus. "I didn't see much future in being a great expert on small businesses," Mace says today. "Maybe that was wrongheaded. But right or wrong, I decided it would be better to focus for a while on large organizations." In 1950, Mace began teaching in the School's Advanced Management Program (AMP), which served senior executives in large companies. Anyone plotting Mace's trajectory at that time would have concluded that he had settled into one of the more typical career patterns at the Harvard Business School.

But in 1955, Mace's career took one more surprise turn. When the call came from an old friend to come to California and help a struggling company get off the ground, Mace found the offer irresistible. The friend was Charles B. "Tex" Thornton, former head of the Army's Statistical Control Division, and the company was a fledgling electronics firm, the Litton Company, with some $3 million a year in sales. Over the next three years, with assistance from Myles Mace—who knew something about growing small companies—Litton's annual sales increased to more than $80 million. For the first time, Mace was a direct player in the entrepreneurial game, and he loved it. "We were growing like crazy," he recalls, "and taking a lot of risks. We worked like hell, and it was a lot of fun."

Mace returned to Harvard in 1958, mostly because he missed the intellectual excitement of the place. "The professors there are a tremendously stimulating group," Mace explains. "They're bright, they're resourceful, they have broad-ranging interests. And it's an environment where you basically have the freedom to fulfill your own potential."

Mace did not return to the course he had created. Management of New Enterprises was taught by a succession of instructors throughout the 1950s and the early 1960s. Although some of these instructors went on to distinguished careers outside the School—most notably Thornton F. Bradshaw, who taught the course between 1950 and 1952 and later headed electronics giant RCA—the entrepreneurship course started by Myles Mace mostly languished for a decade and a half. Student demand never dipped low enough to permit the School to exit the related fields of small business and entrepreneurship, but none of Mace's successors commanded the same respect or elicited the enthusiasm that he had. It was not until the arrival of another engaging young instructor in 1963 that entrepreneurship again enjoyed a strong champion at the Harvard Business School.

Unless, of course, one looks to the example of Georges Doriot, the formidable and idiosyncratic teacher who taught a unique, freestanding course, shaped generations of Harvard Business School students, and—almost out of his back pocket—helped invent a new industry.

CHAPTER 3

The First Venture

THE WAR AGAINST the Axis powers, which in the South Pacific gave a young Myles Mace ideas for a course he might teach about new businesses, also presented interesting challenges to another member of the HBS faculty. His name was Georges F. Doriot.

By 1941, when he received a commission in the U.S. Army, Doriot already added a unique flavor to the faculty. Born in France at the very end of the nineteenth century—in September of 1899—he was the son of an engineer who had helped invent the first motor car for Peugeot. The senior Doriot, hoping that his son would follow in his footsteps, urged Georges to enter a top-notch engineering program once he finished his studies at the University of Paris in 1920. When the young would-be engineer arrived in Cambridge, Massachusetts, in 1921, he planned to study industrial management at the Massachusetts Institute of Technology.

At this point, fate intervened. Harvard's president, A. Lawrence Lowell, was introduced to the young Frenchman, and liked what he saw. The imperious Lowell—himself the scion of one of New England's most accomplished industrial families—strongly urged Doriot to give up on the idea of MIT and instead enroll at the Harvard Business School. (Lowell, who had helped launch the Business School little more than a decade earlier, remained an energetic salesman for the institution.) Doriot—headstrong but impressionable, willing to take a risk, and flattered by all this personal attention from one of America's most famous educators—allowed himself to be wooed and won by President Lowell.

"At least," says Canadian entrepreneur Ralph Barford (M.B.A. '52), who many years later worked for Doriot, "that's the story he always *told.*"

Doriot spent a single year at HBS as a special student before leaving for a job in New York City with the banking firm Kuhn, Loeb. (Special students were sometimes admitted in those years to fill the occasional empty seat, and departures after one year were not uncommon.) But the School would not let Doriot get away so easily. In 1926, Dean Wallace Donham persuaded him to return to HBS as one of several assistant deans. Before long, however, Doriot's administrative responsibilities took a back seat to teaching: first in a course called Manufacturing Industries, and then (in 1928) as the head of a section of the required second-year Business Policy course. In 1929, he was named a professor of industrial management. Doriot had found his life's work.

Although he became an American citizen, Doriot remained an intense Francophile all of his life. Somehow, during his many years in the United States, his strong French accent became even more pronounced. He carried himself formally, almost stiffly, which tended to make his short and slender frame more imposing. From his earliest days at Harvard, he was a solitary, quietly theatrical person, given to the well-chosen expression, the purposeful arch of the eyebrow, and the seemingly casual *bon mot.* "When Georges Doriot left France," a senior colleague said many decades later, "the Comedie Française lost one of its greatest talents."

A personal milestone for Doriot came in 1937, when he first taught a second-year elective called, simply, Manufacturing. In the course catalog, Doriot wrote that his goal for the elective was to "train the students in the thorough analysis of and in the administrative control of a manufacturing company. . . . The intent will be to show markedly the basic differences between analyzing, advising, and actual executive work. Efforts will be made to help students develop a realistic grasp of executive problems and fitness for the discharge of managerial duties."

Like Doriot himself, the Manufacturing course was not exactly what it seemed. As students soon discovered, Doriot used the setting of the manufacturing company as a pretext for talking about what really interested him: "executive work" and "executive problems" at the highest levels of management.

The Harvard Business School already offered a range of courses in what it called "production"—in fact, there was a formal faculty group devoted to the teaching of that subject. But Doriot had nothing whatsoever to do with these colleagues. (Indeed, in an academic setting that was notably collegial, Doriot had nothing to do with *most* of his faculty colleagues.) He played no part in shaping the offerings of the Production group, and the Production faculty were not invited to contribute to his Manufacturing course.

Doriot's real "competition" was to be found elsewhere. His Manufacturing course was, in fact, a rival to the required second-year Business Policy course. That course, as Doriot knew well from having taught it himself, attempted to integrate the various functionally oriented lessons of the first-year curriculum. Doriot decided that he could do better.

The young Frenchman distinguished himself in another way, which became increasingly noticeable over the years. Dean Wallace Donham had introduced the case method to HBS in the early 1920s as a means of bringing the complex and fast-changing reality of business into the classroom. During almost his entire twenty-four-year tenure in the deanship, Donham pushed his faculty to abandon their lectures and embrace case-method teaching. Most eventually either complied or left the School. Doriot did not. Ignoring Donham's unsubtle pressures, Doriot continued to lecture—by all accounts, powerfully and brilliantly.

OFF TO WAR

When World War II broke out, Georges Doriot (who had served as an artillery officer in the French army during World War I) now looked for a way to serve his adopted country. Having become a naturalized U.S. citizen in 1940, he was eligible to serve in the U.S. armed forces. When word reached Washington that Doriot was in search of a suitable posting, a former student—Major General Edmund B. Gregory, then the Army's quartermaster general—arranged for Doriot to be commissioned as a lieutenant colonel and chief of military planning for the Quartermaster Corps.

Once again, Doriot put himself in the right place at the right time. Logistics is the deepest backwater of the military during peacetime, but an absolutely vital function during wartime. Doriot, drawing on his training in industrial management, took full advantage of his position. A tribute to Doriot in the Quartermaster's Hall of Fame lists the following accomplishments, among others:

> *Under his direction, many of the country's best academic researchers, scientists, technologists, and industrial planners were brought together to support the war effort. The Military Planning Division's unprecedented accomplishments under General Doriot included the development of all new uniforms and equipment for use in every kind of climate and geographic region around the world; a whole family of new field rations (for example, B-, C-, D-, and K-Rations, 5-in-1s, 10-in-1s, Assault and Accessory Packs) along with stoves, food containers, openers, and cook tents for various climates.* [1]

According to some accounts, Doriot also played a crucial role in the later stages of the European war. In late 1944, as U.S. troops pushed across France and into Germany, General Dwight D. Eisenhower sent a cable to Doriot recommending that he begin to slow the wheels of industrial production. If the worst of the fighting was behind them, Eisenhower allegedly reasoned, it was probably time to start backing off the throttle on the great American war machine.

Doriot, as the story goes, did not agree with Ike's assessment. Ignoring the suggestion from the top, the diminutive quartermaster kept the heat on his suppliers to maintain a full pipeline. If true, it was a fortunate bit of insubordination. When an unexpected German offensive led to the Battle of the Bulge—and some of the fiercest fighting of the war, under miserable winter conditions—the supplies kept coming. "Thanks in large part to Doriot," says longtime HBS colleague and friend Vernon Alden, "we had the supplies we needed to regroup and go on and win the war."

Doriot's logistical successes earned him the rank of brigadier general in 1945; for the rest of his life, he was "General Doriot" (and less respectfully, "Le Grand Général"). But as implied above, Doriot's work was not limited to the all-important lines of supply. For much of the war, he also served as the deputy director of research and development for the War Department. It was a unique posting—in a very real sense, a window into the future. Every day, proposals ranging from the harebrained to the visionary landed on his desk. The most outlandish of these schemes were rejected out of hand. But Doriot and his staff carefully combed through the rest, searching for innovative ideas that might advance the Allied cause—whether by accomplishing an old task in a new way or by doing something important that had never been done before.

In particular, Doriot looked for ways to save time, money, and materials. He knew, for example, that the army had to curb its appetite for strategic materials such as copper and chrome or risk running out of those precious resources altogether. Focusing on these real or looming material crises, Doriot's division came up with a string of improvised solutions. They asked questions that forced thinking in new ways: *Why did uniform buttons have to be made out of tin?* When plastic was substituted for tin, the result was a perfectly adequate button—and a savings of ninety tons of tin for each production run. Doriot's division lobbied successfully for the use of wood, rather than steel, in military bed frames, and organized a system for making shoe soles out of reclaimed rubber. Doriot also spurred his division to develop tents and uniforms with new thermal properties and improved abrasion resistance to better withstand extreme forms of weather. At his urging, the army began to experiment with (and eventually use) freeze-dried foods, powdered coffee, and armored vests.

Perhaps Georges Doriot's fascination with visionary concepts and technical innovations dated back to his childhood, when his father participated in the birth of the French automobile industry. But certainly this fascination intensified through his work for the Pentagon.

For years he had taught about the importance of planning and foresight in the manufacturing setting. Now, in wartime, he went through a unique, intense immersion in high-stakes product development, where human lives hung in the balance. He experienced first-hand the astonishing innovative capacities of American engineers, inventors, and tinkerers, and he also learned how difficult it was to get even great ideas off the laboratory bench and into the military "marketplace."

Somehow, in some context, he intended to carry forward and apply these lessons.

BACK TO MANUFACTURING

As described in chapter 2, the early postwar years were dynamic and turbulent ones at the Harvard Business School. Veterans, subsidized by the GI Bill and determined to make up for lost time, enrolled at the School in record numbers. For several years, HBS admitted three entering classes per year, a policy that required year-round teaching.

When it came time for the School to field a schedule of second-year courses, some professors (including Myles Mace) scrambled to invent new offerings. But Georges Doriot simply picked up where he had left off. Beginning in 1946, Manufacturing once again appeared in the School's course catalog. And once again, it offered a formative experience to many of those who took it. In fact, for the rest of the century, eminent graduates of the School—including such self-described "Doriot men" as Philip Caldwell, John Diebold, William McGowan, James D. Robinson III, and many others—would volunteer that they owed a large part of their success to Georges Doriot's Manufacturing course.

The course remained an anomaly. Its length (two full semesters) and pedagogical approach (lectures and field work, no cases) made it a special animal. The course content became more idiosyncratic in the postwar years, reflecting Doriot's broader perspective. In the 1953 course description, Doriot provided a concise summary of what his course comprised: "This is not solely a production course—it enters many areas of business interest."

In fact, the course entered many areas of human interest. "He taught a philosophy of life," explains Ralph Barford. "It had a huge impact. He taught us to work hard and lead an honest life. Even now, almost fifty years later, I sometimes catch myself thinking, 'Whoops, that isn't exactly what *he* would have done.'"

Doriot achieved this impact almost in spite of himself. He remained a cool and somewhat remote figure who made no effort to establish personal bonds with his students. He was difficult to find outside the classroom. In the classroom, he could be tough, even tyrannical. "I would rather have you respect me in five years than like me now," he said on more than one occasion. He told his students what to read (three newspapers a day: the *Wall Street Journal*, the *New York Times*, and the best available local newspaper). He told them how to dress, where to work, and even what kind of woman to marry.

"Georges Doriot was one of the only men I ever met who had spent enough time thinking about life to come up with a widespread, consistent philosophy—and it worked," says David Powers (M.B.A. '54), a Doriot acolyte who spent several decades working for large companies (Westinghouse, Texas Instruments) before founding Hybrid Enclosures, Inc. "In class, he gave advice on almost every subject you could think of, and he made everything fit together."

"It was like finishing school for business students," adds Arthur Goldstein (M.B.A. '60), president of Ionics, Inc. "Doriot made us aware of all the different variables in the equation." Goldstein and other former Manufacturing students recall being mesmerized by Doriot, in part due to his exotic Gallic appearance and accent, which necessitated careful listening. Doriot referred to the "ca-*pee*-talist system," and strongly encouraged his students to become "ca-*pee*-talists." Once a student was so bold as to imitate this pronunciation in class—telling Doriot that he hoped to become a ca*pee*talist after graduation—and was expelled from Manufacturing on the spot.

Somehow, Doriot pulled together many of the strands of human existence and wove them into captivating and essential truths. He would stand in the "pit" at the front of the amphitheater classrooms in Aldrich Hall, making occasional forays up and down the tiered aisles, lecturing more or less continuously. Questions were discouraged and were extremely rare. Doriot peppered his commentary with aphorisms: *I'd rather have a Grade B idea and a Grade A person than a Grade A idea and a Grade B person. If you want to know what's going on in a company, ask the guards, janitors, and secretaries. If you want to know how good a company is, go out in back and look at the scrap pile. Be wary of investment bankers; they've got a totally different view of the world. Don't put lawyers on your board.* Most students took copious notes during his lectures, for fear of missing even one profound nugget. The silence in Doriot's classroom, recalls Vern Alden, "bordered on the evangelical. You could hear a pin drop when he was talking. Everyone was writing, writing, writing."

Doriot complemented his own perspectives with contributions from distinguished guest speakers. One class in the early 1960s, for example, heard from scientist Leslie Groves (on the development of the atomic bomb), a brilliant twenty-four-year-old chemist named John Deutsch (later MIT's provost), and J. Irwin Miller, chairman of the Cummins Engine Company, who addressed the class on the subject of corporate social responsibility. These were individuals who rarely accepted invitations to speak at business schools, but willingly responded when the call came from Georges Doriot.

To some extent, Doriot implicitly encouraged a "cult of personality" around himself and his course. (Most of his students would have been astonished to learn how nervous the seemingly imperturbable Doriot was before each class session, and that he forced himself to eat corn flakes and milk before every lecture to settle his anxious stomach.) Doriot's personal mystique surely added to the impact of the course and promoted learning. But Doriot also tried to stress a contradictory point: that received wisdom (even including the wisdom received from him) had to be tested. Yes, he emphasized, it was important to take notes in class and to refer to those notes in subsequent months and years. But one reason to do so was to compare Doriot's precepts with one's own perceptions and experiences, and then decide which of life's lessons to believe.

"Indeed," recalls James A. Henderson (M.B.A. '63), a Doriot research assistant who later became CEO of Cummins Engine, "the General stood up there and said, 'Look: I want you to keep a Manufacturing notebook. In it will be your notes on my lectures, but I hope there will be other observations of your own. And I want you to *read* that notebook from time to time, and decide if there's wisdom there that applies to your situation.'"

In addition to the lure of General Doriot and distinguished guest speakers, many students took the course simply to test themselves. "With some students," says Henderson, "it was almost like the Citadel, or the Marines. It was understood that Doriot's course was a huge amount of work. If you could take Doriot's course, you were one tough hombre."

This mystique was reinforced by presentations made in the spring by students who were then finishing their second term with Doriot. (Doriot himself never attended these sessions.) Their audience was first-year students who were deciding whether or not to take the course. In the spring of 1960, one such presentation was made by a bright young second-year student named Henry B. Schacht, who many years later served as CEO of both Cummins and Lucent Technologies. In the audience that day was Jim Henderson. "Henry's message was that it was clearly a choice," remembers Henderson with a smile. "And the choice was something like, 'Hey—you wanna go be a brown-shoe Navy man, or do you wanna join the Marines?' The clear message was that in Doriot's course, you were going to work your *tail* off."

But it wasn't the volume of work that sold the course; it was the kinds of opportunities that the course provided. Unlike most other courses at the School at that time, Manufacturing gave students the chance both to work in teams and to conduct field studies in the "real world." Students organized themselves into groups ranging from nine to twelve students. They then picked two companies to study. (There were no limits on these choices, although companies in the Boston area were favored because they were easier to handle logistically.) The groups' assignment was to prepare two reports on these companies. The first report was an industry study, and it was expected to include a ten-year projection of the prospects of that industry. The second focused on solving a particular problem faced by one or both of the subject companies.

In this process, they got almost no help from Doriot and only limited help from his teaching assistants, who gave guidance to the teams as they got organized, and (in the vast majority of cases) graded the papers the students ultimately produced. But this lack of direction also pertained to those assistants. When confronted with a request for direction from a beleaguered or confused assistant, Doriot was very likely to say, "*You* figure that out." On the other hand, Doriot rarely overruled his young assistants. "Once," says Ralph Barford, "I gave one of his favorite students a High Pass instead of a Distinction. Doriot looked over the list, nodded, and handed it back without saying a thing."

So both teaching assistants and their students were more or less left to fend for themselves, according to rules of their own devising. "In our case," recalls Jim Henderson, remembering his student days, "we put a team on each company, a team on the reports, and we'd meet as a large group to keep the whole thing together. In other words, we compartmentalized, as I think most groups did; but we all signed the reports. The teamwork aspect of it was very important—and that was something that was rarely emphasized, in those days." The bonds that were formed in these Manufacturing groups proved amazingly durable over the years, with some groups holding informal reunions to celebrate and reinforce those ties.

Team members wrote letters, conducted surveys and interviews, and otherwise investigated their subject companies and their industries. Perhaps reflecting Doriot's own interests, many teams focused on cutting-edge industries: atomic energy, fuel cells, integrated circuits, and so on. Others studied fields—such as factory automation and pleasure boating—that seemed to have great growth potential.

For some students, this exercise initiated a lifelong passion. John Diebold (M.B.A. '51) was one of these. He and his team wrote in 1951 about something they called factory "automation" (an old word that Diebold appropriated for use in his team's report). Diebold later emerged as one of the world's leading authorities on that subject.

"Doriot bailed me out," admits Diebold, whose impatience with traditional approaches to education dated back to his undergraduate days at Swarthmore College. "With Doriot, you could do what you wanted, so as long as he approved."

Having signed up for Doriot's Manufacturing course because of a genuine interest in manufacturing, Diebold was surprised and motivated by the General's offbeat lectures. He was particularly inspired by the team report, a central component of the course. "What he wanted," Diebold says, "was to get you out into the real world, where you could study it. He wanted you to have ideas."

Diebold realized this was his chance to follow through with the ideas about "automatic factories" that he had developed as a midshipman in the Merchant Marine during World War II. His ship's antiaircraft fire control mechanisms employed crude self-correcting devices. "That interested me," he recalls. "I kept thinking, if we can build tools and if we have automatic antiaircraft fire control, why can't we have an automatic factory?"

Doriot suggested that Diebold create (on paper) a factory that would build a specific product. "But I don't know anything about products," Diebold protested. Reaching up to a shelf behind his desk, Doriot brought down an automotive piston, possibly a relic from his father's days in the French automotive industry. "Here," he said, holding out the piston. "Design a factory to make this."

Diebold and his team of classmates did exactly that in their report, "Making the Automatic Factory a Reality." In the text, the students explored (through the context of a piston factory) how new and growing technologies could help (and hinder) the mechanization of industrial functions. They went so far as to propose that a central computer could be used to control all of the automatic machines.

The second-year student decided he wanted to write a book on the subject that had captured his interest, and had gained a name: *automation*. "People say I coined this word," he recalls, "but it wasn't the word so much as the *use* of the word. Ford Motor Company called it 'automation' when they initiated automatic loading and unloading of the machines in the punch press division—but this was mechanical movement, with no feedback, like the eighteenth-century automatons. What I meant when I used the word was *automaticization*. The problem was, I was a bad typist and a terrible speller, and I found I was typing 'automation' over and over. Then people started using it the way I had used it. I don't claim to have invented the word, just the use of it."

After graduation, Diebold accepted a job offer from Griffenhagen & Associates, a venerable New York–based management consulting firm. The choice irritated General Doriot. "Doriot had contempt for consultants as he had contempt for professors," says Diebold. "When I told him I'd landed a job with the oldest firm in the industry, he said, '*What* industry?'"

Diebold's book, *Automation*, was published in 1952. (It was dedicated to Georges Doriot.) Besides shedding light on the computer revolution, which was just passing out of its infancy, the book addressed the problems of integrating computers into nearly all aspects of a business. It was an enormously influential work, then and for years thereafter. *Automation* was reissued as a "management classic" on its thirtieth anniversary, and celebrated again on its fortieth.[2]

Diebold's case was unusual, but not unique. Other students, too, found that their manufacturing research not only influenced their own subsequent careers, but also reached a broader audience. A report on creative collective bargaining by Jim Henderson's team, for example, was published by Prentice-Hall and was used as a textbook for several years in the mid-1960s.[3]

Doriot encouraged his students to aim for publication—a high hurdle that a surprisingly large number of his students cleared. Regarding a report on the pleasure-boating industry, a *New York Times* article in May 1960 said that the report was "certain to become a syllabus, even a sort of Bible, for years to come." As a result of this kind of admiring publicity, Doriot's office was flooded with letters requesting copies of various reports. This was ironic, in light of the fact that Doriot himself never even read many of the reports his students generated. "From his perspective, that wasn't the point," Jim Henderson says. He explains:

> *Rather, his goal was to assemble a bunch of talented and aggressive M.B.A.'s, set a high standard, give them autonomy, get them access, and set them off and running. It wasn't the specifics of a particular industry he was looking for. It was a* process *he was trying to teach them. And they learned that process by doing it.*

In retrospect, Doriot's Manufacturing course was a prescription and a recipe for entrepreneurship. Despite its Gallic roots, *entrepreneurship* was not a word that Doriot used much. But by changing the way students looked at opportunity—and the way they looked at themselves—Doriot helped encourage the entrepreneurial instinct. "In Doriot's course," Dave Powers explains, "the viewpoint was always that of the individual. One couldn't help but feel, by the end of the course, like someone who has had his own company."

For many students, it was a short and quick step to founding that company. Ralph Barford's first enterprise, which he set up when he finished his term as Doriot's research assistant, produced plastic phone book covers with advertisements on them. Others bided their time, waiting for the right opportunity to come along. Dave Powers founded his company (which made hermetic enclosures for microelectric circuits) several decades after leaving the Harvard Business School.

And although "entrepreneurship" did not get top billing in the Manufacturing course, new products and new companies were at its heart, especially after World War II. The course description (which changed little from year to year) noted that "special attention will be given to the study of products, new ideas, new developments, and . . . the problems involved in starting new companies." At least one of Doriot's lectures every year emphasized how satisfying it was to start a new company from scratch and to watch that company grow and prosper under one's careful guidance. "Clearly," says Ralph Barford, "his philosophy gave us a bias toward entrepreneurship."

Long after his retirement from the School and more than a decade after his death, Doriot's influence is still felt on the campus. As an academic who wrote only one book, published early in his career, Doriot was never embraced by his more theoretically inclined colleagues. But those colleagues who prided themselves on their teaching took note of Doriot's obvious success. When Professor Harry Hansen launched his Creative Marketing Strategies course in the late 1950s, that highly successful course included a team- and field-based learning experience that closely resembled the core of the Manufacturing course. And time has caught up with the approach that Doriot, Hansen, and others pioneered. Today, graduate business education is far more experientially oriented and emphasizes team building to a far greater extent than in the past.

But Doriot's real impact is to be found in the world of business. More than seven thousand students took his Manufacturing course, many of whom listened carefully to Doriot's entrepreneurial message and discovered ways to apply that message to their own careers, whether in the context of a large corporation or in the launching of small and new companies. *Look ahead*, he advised. *Be prepared, persevere, be patient, be flexible, be strategic. Reinvest; don't milk. Don't imagine that change can be had without cost. Take a commonly used item and find new uses for it, or put a new product into established channels of distribution. Above all, stay hungry; avoid complacency.* "Somebody, somewhere, is designing a product that will make your product obsolete," he told generations of talented and ambitious young men. "The man who understands the future is the man who will move up."

BACK TO A BIGGER STAGE

For many people, the experiences of World War II were powerful but self-contained: The lessons of wartime did not translate easily to a peacetime economy. This was not true in Georges Doriot's case. His ability to anticipate trends and evaluate novel products and processes served him well both in war and peace.

Despite his distinguished stint in the Quartermaster Corps, Doriot never stepped all the way out of the civilian economy. In 1941, Massachusetts governor Leverett Saltonstall asked him to serve on the Committee on Post-war Readjustment. By accepting, Doriot placed himself at the center of an ambitious effort to revive and redirect the struggling regional economy of New England.

After the war, as before, the region appeared to be headed for deep trouble. Relatively few of the federal dollars allocated for the construction of buildings, roads, and other infrastructure associated with the war mobilization had gone into the Northeast states. Even more troubling, most of the large, federally subsidized manufacturing plants (some $4.6 billion in plants and equipment between June 1940 and August 1941 alone) were steered toward the nation's heartland—into cities like Detroit and St. Louis—far away from the presumed threat of enemy bombers.

Early postwar trends only accentuated the problems that had beset New England for several decades. The formerly dominant textile and shoe industries continued their wholesale relocation to southern states—in part to escape New England's unionized workforce, but also to reap the benefits of modern facilities where both land and electricity were relatively inexpensive. (Crowded New England, far from reliable supplies of fossil fuels, had the highest energy costs in the nation.) As people and institutions began to lose faith in the future of the region, personal and institutional investment dwindled. And as demobilization led to large-scale layoffs in defense-related industries, New England seemed doomed to replay the downward spiral into depression that had followed World War I. This time, however, it appeared that other regions of the country would flourish while New England stagnated.

Hoping to head off this potential disaster, government leaders, members of the regional business community, and leading academics (including prominent professors from both Harvard and MIT) agreed to put their heads together. The Readjustment Committee—headed up by Melvin T. "Doc" Copeland from the Harvard Business School—accepted the task of assessing the situation.

The results of their initial investigations were discouraging. Boston and other New England cities had once been centers of business innovation, technological advances, and entrepreneurship. They were the cradle of Yankee ingenuity, which nurtured the first industries on the North American continent. Now, though, they were economic backwaters. The local families and businesses that had once distinguished themselves through the boldness of their vision—throwing off the mercantile system imposed by the British king, opening up the China trade, building whole cities in north-central Massachusetts to support the manufacture of textiles, boring tunnels through the Berkshires to promote trade with Albany and points west, damming local rivers and transmitting inexpensive hydropower over unprecedented distances—were now risk-averse. The financial institutions that managed Yankee fortunes were equally apprehensive. Blessed with affluence and cursed by a crippling conservatism, New England had turned into a region of defensive trust-funders and coupon-clippers.

Some members of the Readjustment Committee, including its Harvard Business School delegation, thought that New England's salvation lay in bringing its "locked-up" capital back into circulation. Increased levels of investment could provide a much-needed boost to the regional economy by encouraging new companies and industries to take root and grow. Ralph Flanders—a committee member, the president of the Federal Reserve Bank in Boston, and later a U.S. senator from Vermont—was convinced that new business ventures were the key to a strong economy. "American business, American employment, and the prosperity of the citizens of the country as a whole cannot be indefinitely assured," he wrote, "unless there is a continuous birth of healthy infants in our business structure." [4] Doc Copeland and General Doriot agreed wholeheartedly.

But Flanders's prescription was easier written than filled. Before the First World War, private investment in a new venture was appealing in part because neither the enterprise's earnings nor the growth in value of that investment over time were subject to heavy taxation. The tax burden at both the state and federal levels had increased dramatically since that time, and both income and capital gains taxes were effective disincentives for individual investors. This was already the subject of a heated national debate. In a November 1944 speech in St. Louis, for example, industrialist Henry J. Kaiser called for the creation of a new government entity to provide what he called "risk capital" to existing and new businesses in the postwar era. A month later, New York Stock Exchange president Emil Schram declared publicly that although the nation desperately needed "venture capital" to move forward, the tax system discouraged this kind of investment.

Perhaps because of his highly visible perch atop the regional Federal Reserve Bank, Flanders shied away from embracing a large-scale governmental intervention. He was convinced that large financial institutions could and should provide the necessary funds. This opinion was seconded by Merrill Griswold, another powerful voice on the local financial scene. Griswold was the chairman of the Massachusetts Investors Trust, by most accounts the world's first mutual fund, created in the 1920s and widely imitated in subsequent decades. Griswold, although certainly a conservative thinker, was personally offended by the fact that 45 percent of the considerable wealth of New England then resided—safe, snug, and unproductive—in the cautious hands of banks and insurance companies.

The third ingredient in this mix was the local academic community. Both Harvard and MIT had made significant contributions to the biggest technological breakthroughs of World War II, including the computer and the atomic bomb. The Harvard Business School—recognized before the war as the nation's most successful school of management—had engaged in novel wartime experiments, including teaching statistics to air force officers and logistics to naval officers. As a result of these and other successes, these academic institutions did not lack for confidence. Some, moreover, were frustrated by their inability to capitalize on their institutional investments in high technology, the benefits of which often accrued to private industry.

What was needed was a new entity—one that would extract money from unproductive accounts and redirect it into productive arenas. Early in 1946, Flanders and Griswold joined forces with other committee members, including Georges Doriot, Karl Compton (president of the Massachusetts Institute of Technology), Frederick S. Blackall Jr. (president of the New England Council), Ira Mosher (chairman of the board of the National Association of Manufacturers), and Bradley Dewey (of Dewey and Almy Chemical Co.). These men agreed to form a new kind of investment company—similar to the private, family-owned venture operations run by the Rockefeller and Bessemer families, but *publicly* held. The new company, formally launched in June of 1946, was called American Research and Development (ARD). Its goal was to bring scholars and savants face-to-face with their peers in the world of practical applications—a combination that was expected to be heady, creative, and profitable.

For their first president, ARD's founders hoped to snare Georges Doriot. "He was the natural choice," explains Ralph Barford. "ARD was hoping to find and finance technologically advanced projects, and Doriot was dealing with these every day in the Army." Doriot said he was willing, but felt he had to finish his hitch at the Pentagon first.

Ralph Flanders, determined to get the new enterprise off the ground as soon as possible, agreed to serve as ARD's president for the second half of 1946, after which Doriot would take over.

These two men, so different in their backgrounds, shared some fundamental beliefs. Most important among these was the conviction that the creative investment of capital could help New England (and the rest of the country) out of the economic doldrums and into exciting economic territory. "There is no lack of new and hopeful ideas for new enterprises," Flanders wrote. "Our country is boiling with new ideas." Capitalizing on those ideas, moreover, was not a luxury, but an obligation. "After all," Doriot explained, "if we want a strong nation, we must not drift along indefinitely on the courage and thoughtfulness of the preceding generation." Yes, it might be possible to "live on the risks our forefathers took," Flanders acknowledged. "But we capitalists must take risks of our own to keep building up our country."

American Research and Development, the first venture capital company that hoped to be publicly held, was itself taking a considerable risk. For one thing, this was to be a very visible experiment. According to the August 9, 1946, *New York Times*, ARD was being established "for the express purpose of garnering venture capital for the 'fullest exploitation' of recent advances and discoveries. The latter, the new company believes, will lead to an era of new devices, processes, and products, and they, in turn, will bring forth new enterprises as well as recast old ones."[5] *Finance* magazine gushingly called ARD "one of the potentially most important projects this country has seen," while also noting that "most such companies would appear as 'wild dreams' of theorists, or at best a flight of fancy."[6] Pundits debated the company's chances of success. As ARD prepared to offer shares to the public, both the business world and the larger public watched closely.

Like most good entrepreneurial ventures, ARD did everything it could to tip the odds in its favor. First, and by far most important, the company's managers and directors represented a staggering reservoir of talent and connections. Doriot was not well known outside his specialized circles, but the same could not be said of MIT professors Karl Compton, Edwin Gilliland, and Jerome Hunsacker. "If this company does not pan out," commented the *Boston Herald* that August, "it will not be because it does not have plenty of the right kind of brains behind it."[7] And although the local institutions that spawned it were not direct investors, they and their leaders felt some direct responsibility for the success of the fledgling company. Behind the scenes, influential people were pulling for ARD.

Initially, ARD offered 200,000 shares (of an authorized 3 million) of $1 par value common stock, to be sold at $25 each. Thanks to an SEC-granted waiver of regulations governing the sale of stock to investment trusts, institutional investors could purchase minimum lots of 1,000 shares, and individuals could purchase minimum lots of 200 shares.

Through this first public offering, ARD hoped to raise a minimum of $5 million. But there was an interesting wrinkle. According to ARD's charter, also blessed by the SEC, at least $1.5 million of the $5 million *had* to come from institutional investors. Through this maneuver, ARD's founders hoped to kill two birds with one stone: Thirty percent of the start-up capital that ARD would provide to new companies would come from the very banks, insurance companies, investment trusts, and other institutions that had impounded the capital in the first place. New England's most conservative financial institutions, in other words, would bankroll the region's most adventurous new companies.

By the end of October 1946, enough shares were subscribed and paid for to permit ARD to begin operations. Fiduciary organizations, broadly defined, had purchased more than the required 60,000 shares. (Registered investment companies had put in $1.2 million, life insurance companies had come up with $300,000, and educational institutions had contributed another $225,000.)[8] Although one could argue that insurance companies—which dominated much of the regional economy—were underrepresented, ARD had cleared its first hurdle.

Georges Doriot arrived at ARD in December 1946. Thus began Doriot's career as a half-time HBS professor and half-time business executive—a circumstance that for the next quarter-century generated irritation and envy among some of his academic colleagues. Ralph Flanders, nominated by Vermont's Republican Party to run for the U.S. Senate, happily handed over the reins to Doriot, according to the previously agreed-upon schedule. Flanders moved north to mount what turned out to be a successful Senate campaign.

Doriot had one important resource already at hand: Vice President Joseph Powell Jr., a member of the HBS class of 1926. Powell was from a prominent Rhode Island family, and (in the words of a colleague) a *salesman*—"an incredible, outward-going, gregarious, happy salesman." He was as energetic as Doriot and every bit as committed to the high-minded mission of ARD. This shared sense of mission counteracted the personal friction that sometimes arose between these two strong-willed individuals.

With a strong management team in place, ARD now began the hard work of delivering upon its vision. This involved not only identifying start-ups with potential, but also evaluating each company's needs and prospects and putting together an intelligent financing plan for each. Prior publicity both helped and hampered this early phase of the operation. When ARD opened its doors in downtown Boston, literally hundreds of projects were waiting on the doorstep, ready for consideration. According to an October 1947 *Investor's Reader* article, Joe Powell said the company received "every nutty idea that had been on everybody's back burner."[9]

Many of the schemes—which included several techniques for perpetual motion, a sleuth's rearview mirror fitted to a pair of eyeglasses, and a massive treadmill for airplanes (for cutting down on the space and time needed for takeoffs and landings)—could be written off quickly. Others, especially those with significant technological components, were far tougher to evaluate. But ARD's financial resources were finite, and the company could not afford to make too many mistakes. In fact, the firm's leaders desperately wanted a strong debut. Of the 296 initial proposals, the company finally picked three that it deemed worthy of funding.

"We started in a garage," Doriot once said metaphorically of ARD. "We cleaned the place up. We took the grease off and removed the old cars."

Actually, ARD was housed in pleasant offices at 79 Milk Street in Boston's financial district, although the top-floor offices, which weren't air-conditioned, tended to get uncomfortable on hot summer days. But when it came to putting down its initial bets, ARD bet twice on garages, of sorts. The first of these was in nearby Cambridge, where three men were building particle accelerators for atomic research. This small operation would eventually achieve renown as the High Voltage Engineering Corporation. The second garage, located in Cleveland, Ohio, housed a new creation from Circo Products Company: a gun-like hand tool capable of vaporizing a chemical solvent and injecting it into automobile transmissions, thereby dissolving and flushing out accumulated grease.

The third enterprise that received ARD funding was an adventurous Boston-based company called Tracerlab, Incorporated. The men behind Tracerlab had figured out productive ways to use the radioactive isotopes in the atomic pile at Oak Ridge, Tennessee. Tracerlab's founder, William E. Barbour Jr., credited Georges Doriot and ARD with saving the company. "I started out with a hatful of ideas and a lot of long-range plans," he said, "but in a couple of years, I got bogged down in the details. Doriot stepped in just in time to pull me out of that rut."[10]

From Doriot's point of view, this was an urgently important part of ARD's work. More than most private or institutional investors, ARD was determined to contribute in significant ways to the successful *operation* of its portfolio companies. It wasn't enough simply to lure unproductive capital back into the economy; now the companies into which that capital was being invested had to be made to succeed. This was where the Harvard Business School connection in general—and the Doriot connection in particular—was called upon heavily.

But success for ARD's companies was no simpler than for any other companies, high-powered help notwithstanding. When the Circo degreasing project was derailed by a nationwide shortage of chlorine in 1947, Doriot hired a member of the HBS class of 1940, Fenton M. Davison, to conduct an exhaustive (and ultimately successful) search for a replacement product line. "Better," Doriot said, "to tell my directors that one of us has died from overwork than to lose a company. We can't take a capital loss the way some of our friends can."

Of course, as time went by and more investments were made, some of ARD's investments did bellyflops. Island Packers, a tuna canning company, was an early casualty. So was Apple Concentrates, which tried to do for apples what Minute Maid had already done for oranges. As a result, ARD's progress was anything but a straight march upward. By 1949, the company's shares could be purchased for $22, or almost $4 below the stated asset value of 1948. Critics of ARD's early track record earned a curt response from Doriot. "In recent months," he wrote in the company's 1949 annual report, "American Research has been erroneously compared to well-known, long-established investment companies. The Corporation does not invest in the ordinary sense. It creates. It risks. Results take more time ... but the potential for ultimate profits is much greater."

In fact, there were cases at ARD in which profit making took a back seat to parenting. Doriot regularly demonstrated his paternal and protective feelings toward both ARD and its fledgling offspring. As he put it many years later, "If a child is sick with a 102-degree fever, do you sell him? I do not have any company doing well today that did not at some time have a crisis."

Sometimes Doriot brought together his former students and ARD's portfolio companies, presumably for the benefit of both. Arthur Goldstein, for example, graduated from Harvard with an M.B.A. in 1960. He went to work for an ARD company: a small research-and-development enterprise called Ionics Incorporated. "My plan was to accept a job in New York," he explains, "but General Doriot, who was chairman of the board at Ionics, called me up one night and spent four hours on the phone with me, convincing me to give Ionics a shot." Goldstein finally agreed.

The company focused on researching techniques for purifying water. After twelve years of work, it still had no products to market. But Doriot and ARD had seen the potential of the field. "I think in some ways, we were their favorite company," Goldstein says. "Ionics and American Research had a very close working relationship. Sometimes we would help them evaluate new projects they were thinking of funding." Under the guidance of ARD, Ionics developed the separation technology that it needed to analyze, treat, and purify water, and readied itself to offer products to potential customers.

Goldstein became president of Ionics in 1971. By then, it had sales of about $8 million. He moved quickly to broaden its base. Rather than simply manufacturing and selling equipment for treating water, the firm began treating water in-house and selling that as well. With Goldstein at its helm, Ionics grew to more than $400 million in annual sales.

"Anybody who is creating change in a system, in an organization, a company, a product line, is an entrepreneur," says Goldstein (who won Rensselaer's Entrepreneur of the Year Award in 1997). "We took unusual risks that leapfrogged us ahead of where people expected the industry to be." And it was General Doriot, Goldstein says, who taught him to think this way. "Doriot was unusual in that he put aside the current buzz. He was always willing to take the long-range view of things."

FIGHTING TO CREATE SOMETHING

In the spring of 1950, when American Research was only a few years old, Doriot was asked to share his experiences at a Life Insurance Association of America gathering. It was an interesting choice of venue, given Doriot's disdain for those conservative institutions that had tied up so much of New England's desperately needed capital. His speech that day reveals a great deal about both himself and the venture capital firm he had done so much to bring into being.

He explained to the assembled insurance executives that the life of a venture capitalist was not a peaceful one. ("Finance something that doesn't move," he advised, "and that doesn't call you at two o'clock in the morning.") Of the more than eighteen hundred projects studied by ARD by that point, only eighteen had been judged worthy investments. "We have a single-minded viewpoint that we want to succeed, no matter how much effort it costs," Doriot explained. "But it has been extremely difficult."

Perhaps assessing the interests and inclinations of his audience, and perhaps speaking for dramatic effect, Doriot strongly advised his audience to avoid the business of starting new companies. "It is an impossible task!" he declared. In any small company, he explained, the human element was a huge factor—and one that was greatly magnified by the fact that a seemingly small, seemingly isolated human problem could easily become a threat to the entire enterprise. "It is one crisis after another!"

Was this a midlife recanting from a man who was already established as a source of inspiration for entrepreneurs? Hardly. Even while discouraging his listeners from entering the nascent field of venture capital, Doriot also spoke of the immense rewards that he himself was enjoying every day, as he worked with young entrepreneurs. "You would feel twenty years younger," he told the insurance executives, "if you came to Boston and visited some of those new small companies. You would see the spirit, the attitude—the driving power of outstanding young Americans who are fighting to *create* something."

Georges Doriot and his colleagues at ARD did not yet know that they, themselves, were helping to create a new industry: venture capital. Nor did they know that their biggest triumphs and greatest satisfactions as venture capitalists were still to come.

CHAPTER 4

Bringing in the Entrepreneurs

THE 1960S WERE A DECADE of rare prosperity and tumultuous change. Much of that change originated in Washington, initiated by the "new generation of leadership" that the country's youthful president celebrated in his inaugural address. Although the Eisenhower years held portents of things to come—early salvos in the desegregation battles, the emergence of an infant counterculture, and isolated voices raised against Washington's virulent anticommunist crusade—the ascension of John F. Kennedy to the presidency marked the true changing of the guard.

Some of these changes were symbolic. Kennedy dined with poets and cellists. He disdained hats, and almost overnight, the grey-fedoraed legions of the Eisenhower era looked dowdy and old fashioned. His wife sparked fashion trends and undertook the restoration of a White House that had fallen into a genteel shabbiness. Their young family, prominently displayed in the national media, reinforced a calculated imagery of vitality and change.

But far more than image making was going on. The new administration was fully committed to an activist federal agenda, the likes of which had not been seen since Franklin Roosevelt's day. The energetic young president took on adversaries ranging from the Soviet

Union to the domestic steel industry. The Justice Department—notably business-friendly during the Eisenhower years, but now headed by the president's combative brother—began scrutinizing proposed corporate mergers far more aggressively. Times had changed, and not necessarily in a direction that big business liked.

Meanwhile, the administration's "New Frontier" economic policy included such novelties as the Area Redevelopment Administration (ARA), which funneled federal money into economically depressed areas of the country where bank loans for industrial development were traditionally difficult to obtain. Another novelty was the Kennedy administration's focus on small businesses, which finally were being recognized by the government as a key driver of the U.S. economy. The money funneled through the ARA program, for example, was aimed specifically at small and undercapitalized firms, which were expected to help jump-start their local economies. The Small Business Administration (SBA)—created in 1953, but not put on a permanent footing with substantial capital until the passage of the Small Business Investment Act in 1958—also enjoyed strong support from the New Frontier's strategists.

To some extent, Kennedy's economists were only riding a wave that had already started to crest. The Small Business Investment Act had minimal impact in its first full year of operation: only 62 Small Business Investment Companies (SBICs) were established in all of 1959. But in 1960, 115 new SBICs were authorized—almost double the previous year's total. And by early 1961, applications for new SBICs were arriving at SBA headquarters at the rate of between 40 and 50 *per month*.[1]

On this issue, at least, Wall Street and the Kennedy administration found themselves seeing eye-to-eye. The booming stock market had been fueled in part by new issues—and Wall Street hungered for a steady stream of such new issues. And from the federal government's perspective, helping small business was both good economics and good politics.

Few academic institutions involved themselves in—or even noticed—these shifting economic and political tides. One that did was the Harvard Business School, which would struggle for the better part of two decades to figure out ways to meet the unique needs of small and growing businesses.

CHANGE AT THE LOCAL LEVEL

Later in the 1960s, the fires of social and political change would engulf Harvard University. Harvard Square would emerge as a national center of student rebellion and activism, and the university would regain its reputation for left-leaning politics—an image it had been struggling to shed since the 1930s.

But in September 1961, during the first year of the Kennedy administration, life in Cambridge was still relatively calm. The university had broken ground on an ambitious, $4 million multiuse building in the heart of Harvard Square—a stark and imposing monolith soon to be named Holyoke Center—but the Square for the most part was still a sleepy, low-rise academic neighborhood. Bookstores, coffee shops, and inexpensive bars and eateries abounded. Parking spaces could be had for $5 a month. The Harvard Coop barbershop featured $2 haircuts.

And in that same September, just across the river at the Harvard Business School, a low-profile faculty group called the M.B.A. Study Committee turned in a report titled *Planning for Change*. This turned out to be a document that, in its own way, fomented local revolutions and counterrevolutions.

The report was the product of a small group of hardworking Business School professors, collectively known as the Anthony Committee after its chairman, Robert Anthony. They had taken seriously their charge to review and make recommendations for the revision of the School's M.B.A. curriculum. It had been more than fifteen years since that curriculum had been examined formally, and changes in the outside world since the end of World War II underscored the need for such a review.

Taken at face value, *Planning for Change* proposed only modest adjustments in that curriculum and didn't seem to contain sparks that would lead to a conflagration. (Among other things, the report called for a new term system and restructured courses for the first-year

M.B.A. program.) But in part because of some process mistakes—the report was printed, bound, and distributed before most faculty members had any inkling of its contents—and in part because both the Ford and Carnegie Foundations recently had issued their own highly visible reports castigating business education as unscientific and inept, faculty nerves at the School were raw.

The report landed; a heated debate erupted. The proponents of dramatic change criticized the report's proposals as too unadventurous. Faculty barons, who felt their baronies were threatened by the (slightly) more quantitative approach of the proposed new curriculum, fought back.

In the academic world, this was serious business, and there were casualties. Dean Stanley F. Teele retired unexpectedly, his health broken in part by the acrimony and ill will surrounding the debate. His successor, George P. Baker, devoted much of his first year in the deanship establishing a consensus and restoring calm to the institution.

Almost lost in this acrimonious debate was some interesting speculation near the end of *Planning for Change*—speculation that opened the door to some substantial long-term changes in the way the School did business. This section of the report was devoted to the question of whether HBS should develop a postdegree program for its M.B.A.'s.

"The need for continuing education does exist," the Anthony Committee noted. Few Harvard M.B.A.'s had expressed interest, however, possibly because "the right format has not yet been developed." The Harvard Business School Alumni Association was then looking over some proposals it had received, but the Anthony Committee recommended against initiating such a program. It questioned whether M.B.A.'s required postgraduate courses that were different from courses aimed at businessmen in general. "Unless M.B.A.'s do have special needs that can be identified," the report concluded, "there is no need for a special program, for graduates will find no shortage of other educational opportunities designed for the practicing businessman."

Indeed, some of those opportunities were already available at Soldiers Field. The School was heavily involved in what it called executive education programs, which were by any measure "educational opportunities designed for the practicing businessman." Its Advanced

Management Program, first offered in 1943, had been in operation for nearly twenty years. A second executive program was then in development. It debuted in 1962 as the Middle Management Program, and was later renamed the Program for Management Development.

But these two programs served very specific constituencies. The AMP was aimed at CEOs in training—senior executives in large corporations who needed an overarching perspective. The MMP (later PMD) was intended for younger managers with a functional specialization who were deemed capable by their companies of assuming broader management responsibilities. Again, the prime consumers of this program were large corporations, which paid the tuitions of those who attended.

These patterns had grown out of recent history. Defense-related industries had sent many of the first AMP participants during World War II. Westinghouse and other large corporations helped call the MMP/PMD into being. Economic trends, as well as tradition, reinforced the strong ties between HBS and the *Fortune* 500. "Companies suddenly started to grow," explains HBS Professor Howard Stevenson. "The multinationals were expanding very rapidly. They were going from small to large, and from national to international. All of a sudden, they needed legions of managers who could speak the same language, both literally and figuratively."

The Harvard Business School was well positioned to take advantage of these trends, and it derived many benefits from specializing in executive education aimed at large corporations. A reasonably stable revenue source was only one of these benefits. In addition, these client companies hired graduating M.B.A. students, supported the School's research financially, and in many cases welcomed HBS casewriters into the very heart of their operations. It was a virtuous circle.

But this focus on large companies left substantial market segments uncovered by the School. By the early 1960s, local business organizations, HBS alumni, and even some faculty had begun to suggest that the School should think seriously about adding new kinds of executive education programs. The School had proven very adept when it had set out to capture the "high ground" of executive education. Were there other segments out there to be captured?

CASTING A WIDER NET

One such opportunity seemed to lie in the field of entrepreneurship. At the same time that large companies were getting larger, the number of smaller companies was increasing dramatically, and the population of small-firm owners and managers was approaching 7 million. The booming stock market sparked a renewed interest in fledgling ventures. The SBIC stampede mentioned earlier had a dramatic multiplier effect: In 1963 alone, SBICs received applications for financing from almost thirty thousand small companies.[2]

Some of this interest came from the Harvard Business School's own graduates. Despite the School's reputation as handmaiden to the *Fortune* 500—a reputation that resulted from the growing success of the School's graduates within those companies—more than a sixth of Harvard's M.B.A.'s in this period joined start-ups or smaller enterprises immediately after their graduation. Available evidence, moreover, suggests that at least *half* of all the School's graduates were engaged in small business. True, many of them had begun their postgraduate careers in large corporations, but at some point many had made the shift to a smaller business, often with their own names on the door. A 1957 survey, for example, revealed that "the typical 1942 man" was working in a firm with fewer than a hundred employees by the time of his fifteenth HBS reunion.

For smaller enterprises and the people who managed them, Harvard's AMP and PMD programs were not particularly useful resources. For one thing, they were time-intensive and—in terms of schedule— inflexible. Participants were required to spend up to three consecutive months on campus. Tuition was steep. The typical *Fortune* 500 company paid full freight (tuition, salary of the participant, and salary of his temporary stand-in back at the office), and—judging from the frequency of repeat business—called it a smart investment. A smaller company, by and large, simply couldn't afford this luxury.

Perhaps an even greater disincentive for managers from small companies was the curriculum of the executive programs. The School was almost universally case-oriented, and the cases discussed in AMP and

PMD classes were primarily focused on the problems and opportunities of large corporations. The owners, managers, and employees of small or recently launched companies didn't derive a lot of benefit from putting themselves in the shoes of General Electric's chairman, or Ford's head of R&D, or Nestle's vice president of international sales.

Not that the entrepreneurial population was entirely overlooked or ignored. Entrepreneurs occasionally made their way into the M.B.A. classrooms or showed up to speak to student groups. And for years, a large number of "outside" seminars and short courses had been offered on campus to meet the demand for training in a wide variety of specialized topics; a few of these programs now began to address the problems of smaller companies and start-ups. But these were not "Harvard Business School" programs. Even those offered at HBS and staffed primarily by HBS faculty were not formally sponsored, or even sanctioned, by the School.

The result in many cases was confusion and a blurring of the lines. "They weren't School courses," recalls Howard Stevenson, "but they were run on the School's campus by the School's faculty, so it was extremely hard to *tell* they weren't School courses. My uncle, for example, came to a specialized program on campus. Right up until he died, he thought of himself as a Harvard Business School graduate." It didn't much matter to these outside-program participants that they didn't attend commencement or receive a Harvard diploma. What mattered was that they had attended the *Harvard Business School*.

For the most part, these programs were entrepreneurial faculty ventures. Some, such as the Presidents Seminar (attended by members of the Young Presidents Organization and first held in 1952), ran every year and by the 1960s were well established. Others were entirely new, reflecting the evolving interests of faculty members and changing market demand. Faculty members received compensation for their efforts, but they also made valuable research contacts in industries of interest to them, and got exposure (at least in some cases) to knowledgeable professionals on the cutting edge of their fields. Again, it was a virtuous circle, of benefit to both parties.

Marty Marshall, then a young professor in the School's Marketing area, organized and conducted three such outside programs in the late 1950s and early 1960s. Like most of these programs, they reflected both the professor's interests and a demonstrated market demand. Marshall designed one program for the International Marketing Institute, another for the National Association of Broadcasters, and a third for the American Advertising Federation. The programs were successful, both in terms of content and enrollment—so much so that Marshall soon received an unusual request.

"I was filling up the goddamn School with people," Marshall recalls with a grin. "So Dean Baker called me into his office one day and suggested that I think about making some of these courses official."

Baker's novel proposal to "officialize" the best of these outside programs made good sense. By bringing these programs under its wing, the School would discourage people from thinking of the campus as merely an ivy-covered conference center. Faculty members running the courses would use their talents and energies for the direct advantage of the School, rather than for outside institutions. Last but not least, the School would make more money, at a time when budgets were stretched thin.

"We started with the International Marketing Institute," recalls Marshall. "People said it wouldn't work, but I made it into a three-week marketing program for the School." The other two marketing programs soon followed suit. Admissions standards were raised, the curriculum was better coordinated internally, and course quality was improved. Participants of these much-revised programs—which in a very real sense represented the voice of their respective marketplaces—could rightfully claim to have been part of an official Harvard Business School program.

ENTREPRENEURS INTO THE FOLD

Despite George Baker's push for a gradual "nationalization" of key School accounts—that is, bringing the strongest of the outside programs into the institutional fold—strong countercurrents persisted. This was especially true in the small-business arena, which continued to be a difficult sector for the School's traditional research and teaching mechanisms to serve.

In the fall of 1961, when *Planning for Change* was released, two organizations were sponsoring ongoing programs (on campus, but still "outside") that focused specifically on the issues of small business. One of these organizations—the Smaller Business Association of New England, or SBANE—held two-day seminars at HBS in both the summer and the winter. This series started in February 1958, when SBANE's pilot conference brought together representatives from large and small companies to discuss their shared goals and also their perceived grounds of conflict. (School administrators no doubt took note that while trying to drum up interest in this first seminar, SBANE's president had emphasized the fact that participants would be learning "*under the same conditions* as do top business executives from national as well as worldwide companies through the Advanced Management Program.") In subsequent years, semiannual SBANE conferences and seminars continued to focus on the issues of smaller enterprises.

Left unattended, this activity might have remained well outside the HBS mainstream. There, it most likely would have expired from institutional neglect. Fortunately, however, the SBANE series attracted the attention and support of a strong ally: HBS professor Frank Tucker.

Tucker was an experienced businessman, hired by the School in 1957 in part due to his strong background in accounting and finance. Before coming to HBS, Tucker had spent twenty-two years working for General Radio Company—Genrad—in Cambridge. One person who worked closely with Tucker after his arrival at Harvard was Charlie Leighton (M.B.A. '60), one of Tucker's teaching assistants. Leighton recalls an explanation he once heard for why Tucker left Genrad and went to teach at HBS:

> He was a Texan, and a very warm, human person. I remember one day he told me a story. He had driven home to his house in Concord from his office at Genrad. He was all excited at dinner, telling his wife that he had found a new way to drive home—one that would allow him to cut three minutes off his commute! He was so excited about this new route. So his wife looked at him and said, "Frank, you've been there

twenty years. And this is the most exciting thing you have to tell me about your work? Maybe it's time for a change." He said that just hit him, and he looked at his wife, and said, "Yes!"

Tucker's early years at the School were spent teaching finance, but he quickly gravitated toward the emerging field of entrepreneurship. In particular, he decided to keep a close eye on the School's involvement with new and small enterprises. Tucker began attending the SBANE annual meetings, and in short order was facilitating all of their HBS-based conferences.

Tucker soon expanded his portfolio to include the Seminar for Small Business Owners and Managers, sponsored by the National Small Business Men's Association and also held at the School. Attending this conference, first held in July 1959, were men from small companies that produced a vast array of goods: lumber, concrete, oil, elastic fabrics, lithograph varnish, furnaces, and many others. As with the SBANE conferences, Tucker did whatever was needed to help the event succeed. In some cases, he played only the coordinator's role; in other cases, he took to the podium as a featured speaker.

Within a few short years, these activities proved to be a fortuitous investment, both for Tucker and for the School. When Professor Arnold Hosmer retired in 1963, Tucker took over not only Hosmer's idiosyncratic Small Manufacturing Enterprises course, but also Management of New Enterprises (the course started by Myles Mace after World War II, and taught by a succession of instructors in the interim). These were the School's only two courses in entrepreneurship at that time, and the contacts and experiences that Tucker had gained through his "moonlight" work now came to bear directly on the School's second-year curriculum.

Meanwhile, Tucker continued to devote whatever hours he could spare to SBANE and other smaller-business groups. It was this close work with SBANE and other small-business organizations, and also the experience of teaching entrepreneurial electives in the second-year program, that led Tucker to a new and related cause in the mid-1960s. At that time, a small group of Tucker's HBS colleagues was quietly urging the School to consider creating a continuing education program for entrepreneurs. Loosely organized under the informal leadership of Professor Arch Richard "Dick" Dooley, the group that Tucker joined included Professors Michael Donham, Patrick Liles, and John Whitney as its other members. Their goal was to secure the administrative approvals necessary for an interesting experiment: School-sponsored executive courses that would concentrate specifically on the concerns of start-ups and small businesses.

Dick Dooley, chair of the School's Production area—traditionally linked to large manufacturers—might have seemed an unlikely candidate to lead this quiet charge. But he was no stranger to hard work, academic experiments, and institutional politics. He also understood life as it was lived at street level. His father, an appliance salesman who had peddled washing machines to small-town shops across Oklahoma's dust bowl during the Great Depression, died when Dooley was nine; his mother then became a schoolteacher so that she could support her family. In 1965, Dooley—who received his M.B.A. from Harvard in 1950, joined the faculty four years later, and earned his doctorate in 1960—became a full professor, having made his way up through the ranks of the Production area. A pioneer in some of the School's more successful overseas executive ventures and collaborations with other schools of management, Dooley also helped teach in a wide variety of focused seminars held on the campus throughout the late 1950s and early 1960s.

In short, Dooley was someone who could spot and exploit opportunity in an academic setting. He turned this talent to an analysis of the market coverage of the AMP and PMD programs—the School's flagship executive programs. "Someone with a $17 million business making preserved jams and jellies," he observed pointedly, "doesn't get that much out of studying giant corporations." He, Tucker, and their coconspirators were determined to develop an executive education program that would meet the needs of companies like Dooley's apocryphal jams-and-jellies maker: small, niche-oriented, successful, and managed primarily by the people who owned them.

Gradually, they roughed out a vision of the course. Central to this vision was the concept of *sequential sessions*: a program offered in installments, such as one session each year for three successive years.

Under this kind of scheme, participants would be expected to be away from their businesses for no more than, say, three weeks at a time—an interruption in leadership that most businesses could survive. The iterative rhythm of this scheme also had pedagogical appeal: Participants could come to the School, study intensively for three weeks, and go back to their businesses. There, they could try to apply what they had learned and begin preparing for next year's session at Harvard. Dooley and his colleagues grew increasingly excited about the concept, and—although the wheels of administration ground slowly—Dean Baker and his administrative team offered encouragement to the slightly undercover program designers. Dooley, Tucker, and others with experience in teaching entrepreneurs began combing through their files for teaching materials that might be adapted to use in such an unusual executive program.

During this time, Frank Tucker continued his work with "outside" on-campus seminars for entrepreneurs. He lobbied intensively to win official School sanction for those that were (at least in his mind and the minds of his outside-world collaborators) well established and likely to be repeated. In December 1970, for example, he formally requested "special program" status for a summer seminar that had been held on campus for six years running. This three-day seminar was sponsored by the National Association of Smaller Business Investment Companies (NASBIC) and staffed by HBS faculty. The 1970 NASBIC seminar focused on the hows and whys of providing venture capital to entrepreneurs. But official sanction was not something that the faculty awarded lightly. When the seminar was held again in the summer of 1971, it was still an outside program.

Others might have stopped pushing this particular boulder uphill, but Tucker persisted. His writings from the period suggest that he was increasingly convinced the School could make a meaningful contribution to the field of new and small ventures, and that he was increasingly excited about the prospect. He expected more, not less, from the School. In a letter sent in the fall of 1971 to Lew Shattuck (then executive vice president of SBANE), for example, Tucker expressed his conviction that HBS would soon provide "additional curriculum offerings, programs of research (both project research and case development), and additional short programs for businessmen (small business)."

Soon enough, Tucker's prediction panned out. In early 1972, the experimental executive education program that he, Dooley, and others had been championing was finally given the green light by Dean Lawrence E. Fouraker, who had succeeded George Baker two years earlier. Having cleared the hurdle of administrative approval, the trio of course developers now faced a more substantive challenge: creating a program that would *work*. Meetings proliferated, and—between meetings—memos flew among Tucker, Dooley, and the increasingly active Patrick Liles. They batted around ideas about the overall concept of the course, including its novel sequential structuring, and teased out details about how the program would function on a day-to-day basis.

The first session of the Smaller Company Management Program (SCMP) was convened that summer, from August 13 to September 1, 1972. Dick Dooley served as chair of the program. Sixty business executives (fifty-nine men and one woman, who seven months earlier had become the twenty-nine-year-old vice president of her family's steel-barge leasing company) had agreed to pay $1,500 per session for the privilege of going back to school. "You should refrain from conducting any business for your companies while you are here," they read in a welcoming letter. "And you should leave your families behind." Waiting for them in their rooms were bundles of cases covering topics such as policy, finance, and marketing.

Among these pioneering participants were owners of retail shops and restaurants, managers of firms that manufactured parts and components for OEMs, and presidents of construction companies and communication firms. And although they represented a wide range of industries, most of these executives shared two key characteristics: They were *generalists*, and they were *decision makers*. More than half of them were company presidents or chairmen. "Every time the phone rings," course head Dick Dooley remarked, "these people have to be prepared to make decisions in any area of the business."

Dooley took steps to make sure that his executives would be isolated from the demands of their everyday lives—and at the same time, would be fully immersed in this odd new peer-group experience for which they had signed up. As in the AMP and PMD, the SCMPers were divided into "can groups" of six or eight people, whose individual rooms were linked by a common living area, study space, and bath-room. Members of each group were carefully chosen according to how they might complement, and also strike sparks against, each other.

Dooley and his colleagues wanted to cultivate an environment that would be characterized by both intellectual intensity and cama-raderie, and by both trust and challenge. It was a difficult but critical balance to strike. These were unusual students—self-made individuals who didn't give up three weeks of their time lightly, and who had high expectations of the Harvard Business School. They were pre-pared to be dazzled; at the same time, they would be intolerant of "beginner's mistakes."

Increasingly, the burden of creating success fell on the shoulders of Dick Dooley. Frank Tucker retired from the faculty in the summer of 1972. With his departure, Pat Liles took over as course head for the venerable second-year entrepreneurship elective (which Liles had re-named Starting New Ventures) and had less time to give to SCMP.

Soon it was clear that HBS had tapped into an underserved mar-ket. More than eighty qualified candidates had applied for SCMP's first sixty spaces—far from a land rush, but very encouraging to those faculty members who had worried that they might be looking out over rows of empty seats. Rather than disappoint the twenty "extra" applicants, Dooley and the SCMP faculty immediately began making plans to offer another three-unit cycle starting in January 1973.

Seats in the January and August 1973 sessions remained in strong demand, despite the uncertainties created by the energy crisis, Water-gate, and a falling stock market. Participants returning for their sec-ond (and eventually their third) sessions were increasingly vocal about the benefits of SCMP to themselves and to their businesses. The "co-hort bonding" among the SCMP classes soon rivaled that of the School's M.B.A. sections—a phenomenon not often seen in the ex-ecutive programs.

But the course content was far from perfect. Well before the end of that first 1972 session, Dooley knew that additional entrepreneurship cases were needed, and they had to be created from scratch. This was true in part because the School's case "library" continued to be thin on small-company materials. But it was also due to the unusual nature of the course participants. Most of these entrepreneurs had learned by doing. Some had little or no formal education, and very few had been taught (or had taught themselves) the full range of business basics. SCMP first had to fill in the gaps. Accordingly, early sessions focused on issues such as policy formulation, strategic planning, and the management of finances and personnel.

Later sessions taught SCMPers how to encourage growth, increase productivity, and negotiate a merger, acquisition, or sale. As information flowed back and forth between the early participants and the faculty, the program gained a sharper focus. Between June of 1974 and June of 1975, for example, faculty members wrote fifty new cases for SCMP, and the courses began to reflect a greater understanding of smaller-company issues: special tax concerns, growth strategies, family involvement, team versus one-person management, product innovation, niche positioning, and the like.

Marty Marshall, the academic entrepreneur mentioned earlier, joined the SCMP faculty in 1975. Marshall first came to HBS as a naval officer assigned to Soldiers Field during World War II. After the war, he returned to complete an M.B.A. in 1947. He stayed on as a casewriter, tried his hand at teaching, and decided to get his doctorate, which he finished in 1953. Marketing became his specialty, and Marshall found himself increasingly curious about these people he was now teaching. Who was signing up to be an SCMP student? Into what categories did the program's participants fall? He conducted a survey, and was intrigued by the patterns that emerged from the resulting data.

"About a third of them came from family-owned businesses," recalls Marshall. "These were the mavericks, the ones who wanted to do something different and had to butt heads with the people who didn't want change." The rest of the owner-managers were either high-tech entrepreneurs or problem solvers who had happened upon the kind of solutions that spawned companies.

Not every participant had founded a business. Some were what Marshall eventually came to think of as "hired guns"—professional managers who had responsible positions, but no ownership stake in the enterprise that employed them. It was clear to Marshall that no love was lost between hired guns and owners. "The hired guns were jealous of the owners," he recalls, "and coming to Harvard didn't necessarily help. They'd attend our program, and then go back and make trouble for their companies, saying they wanted equity. By and large, though, relatively few of them wanted the *risks* that came with ownership. Most of those guys really didn't want the responsibility. They wanted a security blanket."

In Marshall's opinion, the people who benefited most from SCMP were those who had started companies, or at least had nurtured them into the kinds of entities that now needed "systemic management" in order to function effectively. And so, as the 1980s loomed, Marty Marshall made preparations to focus the program with even greater precision.

"SCMP now had to do two things," he recalls. "First and most important, we had to become a program for owner-managers only." In 1981, Marshall took over from Dooley as the program's chair. One of the first things he did was tighten who could participate. Henceforth, SCMP would be open only to CEOs with at least ten years of managerial experience, who owned all or most of the equity in their companies, and whose companies had sales of between $3 million and $75 million annually. This change reflected the changing composition of the participants; nearly all of those signing up for the program were owner-managers. "The message was, 'If you don't own the company and manage it, don't come,'" Marshall says flatly. "No more hired guns."

The second priority was to change the program's name. This was in part a symbolic gesture, but it was one that was important to Marshall. He had learned that some SCMP graduates felt embarrassed by the name. "Smaller" was purely the result of a faculty group thinking in isolation about a new program only in its Harvard context; the name had little relationship to outside-world realities. "Say I'm a graduate," Marshall explains, "and I'm in a small town, and I run the biggest company in that town. Well, I don't necessarily want people to hear I went to the *Smaller* Company Management Program!" A new name, Marshall concluded, would also reflect and reinforce the changing nature of the participant group.

Marshall wrestled with the challenge of a new name on and off for about a year. Eventually, he found himself toying with a list of ten alternatives, but neither the faculty nor the program participants seemed fond of any of his choices. His faculty colleagues, in particular, proved to be a unexpectedly reactionary influence. "Everyone who had been teaching there year after year loved being called a 'scampie,'" he says. "And nobody was going out of their way to help me change that."

The decision was ultimately spontaneous, and—for the consensus-driven Business School—surprisingly high-handed. When the program administrator arrived in Marshall's office to announce that SCMP would need new program brochures for 1985–1986, Marshall seized the opportunity. "I had to make sure they took new photos," he says, "because the clothes of the people in the photos were so out-dated. And since we were going to be making changes on that order of magnitude, I just went ahead and wrote in a new name: the "Owner/President Management Program" (OPM).

Although he didn't particularly want to draw attention to his one-man coup, Marshall understood the value of publicity. To make key constituencies aware of the change and minimize confusion, Marshall took out an ad in the *Wall Street Journal* celebrating the new name. (He subsequently distributed more than six thousand reprints of the ad.) He also sent new certificates to all SCMP graduates, congratulating them on their new status as graduates of OPM.

There was no counterrevolution. In fact, Marshall recalls with some amusement, certain members of the faculty did not notice the change until months after the fact.

Under Marshall's leadership, the course workload—already celebrated as heavy—only increased. A typical day for an OPM participant included at least three seventy-minute class discussions, and each case might require up to several hours of individual and group preparation. The workweek, moreover, was a full six days. Not all participants appreciated this intensity—but most wound up valuing the deep exchanges and strong friendships that grew out of it.

Marshall also tailored the program to take better advantage of its episodic nature. "Between the first and second sessions," he explains, "they had to take a look at the outside environment affecting their business. They had to ask, 'What's going on that's important?'—and then render a report of their findings. A second task was optional: They could present a business plan. Well, all kinds of people who went through OPM will tell you that as a result of these assignments—as well as the casework, being with the faculty, and being with other people, of course—they ended up doing something totally different with their businesses."

Happily, the diversity of industries represented did nothing to deter the exchange of useful information and the forging of personal bonds. Some OPMers, Marshall admits, came from industries he didn't even know existed. Nevertheless, they found ample common ground to learn from each other. He suggests that this was because many of them shared a few key characteristics: "Most of them are loners, in one way or another. They're running their companies, and until they come to OPM, they don't have anybody to share things with. Here, they do, and that process of sharing opens their eyes to things that they simply haven't thought about."

DRUGS AND FISH

Two cases help make the point: one involving a chain of drugstores, and the other involving a chain of fish stores.

"I'd been working in drugstores since I was eight years old, so I knew how to run a drugstore," recalls Jeffrey Ross, a member of the fifth run of the Owner/President Management Program. "But I didn't know how to negotiate a bank loan, I didn't know how to read a balance sheet, and I had no idea what strategic planning was."

Finding himself suddenly responsible for his family's chain of drugstores—Ross was thirty when his father died unexpectedly—he soon discovered that he needed help. Not that the company was in trouble. "On the contrary," says Ross, "we were *growing*. Every year, the volume of sales was increasing: 22 percent, then 33 percent, and then 25 percent. The result was that I couldn't do business with the small banks anymore. So here I was, going into Boston to visit with the big banks, and I didn't know anything about doing projections or budgeting, or even how to *talk* to these guys."

Marty Marshall asked me what business I was in, and I told him I was in the restaurant business. This was during my first session. So Marty told me to do an "environmental analysis" of the business, and hand it in during the next session a year later. When I did, he didn't even look at it; he just held it up in front of the class and said, "All right, Berkowitz, what business are you in now?" I told him, "The fish business." And it was true. Fish was the core of our enterprise, and I had realized that I could open other restaurants, but they should always be seafood restaurants.

Subsequently, Roger concludes, the family "stuck to fish."

A PROGRAM MATURES

In 1997—a typical recent year for OPM—114 people participated in the program. More than half of them were company presidents, and 11 percent of the presidents also were CEOs.

About half of the companies represented had sales ranging from $10 million to $50 million; another third had sales ranging from $1 million to $10 million. About 35 percent of the companies represented had between 100 and 500 employees, about a quarter had between 50 and 100 employees, and a slightly smaller number had fewer than 50 employees. No single industry dominated the program, although about 10 percent of the participants came from the "food & lodging/other service" industry.

Marshall, who retired as head of OPM in 1993, sees the program as a permanent fixture at—and contributor to—the School. He looks back on his years with the program as some of the most satisfying of his academic career. He has no doubt that OPM has had a strong and beneficial impact on many of the entrepreneurs who have attended, and on the companies they lead. "Over time," Marshall says, "I've had many people come to me and say, 'You know, OPM caused me to really change what I did—and make millions because of it.'

"I always say, 'Fine. So how about giving me 5 percent?' "So far," he concludes, smiling, "no takers."

CHAPTER **5**

A Tale of Three Cities

VENTURE CAPITAL, in the broadest sense of the term, was at least centuries old when Georges Doriot and his fellow New Englanders founded American Research and Development in the anxious years immediately following World War II.

For example, Ferdinand and Isabella were venturers, of a sort, when they bankrolled a young entrepreneur named Christopher Columbus. The nineteenth-century English capitalists who funded the canals and railroads that helped tame the North American continent were venturers, too, sinking their money into highly speculative enterprises in hopes of spectacular gains. And when American industrialists built large fortunes in the late nineteenth and early twentieth centuries, they too deployed amassed riches to generate even more wealth.

But venture capital, strictly defined, is really an invention of mid-twentieth-century America. And although it has been practiced in dozens of cities and towns across the nation, the essentials of its story can be told by focusing on three hotbeds of activity: New York City, the Boston-to-Route 128 region, and the fabled peninsula that stretches south from San Francisco to Palo Alto. Each region has had its special strengths and weaknesses.

Within the venture capital community, moreover, many of the most creative and lucrative deals were put together by a small handful of people—many of them M.B.A.'s from Harvard or engineers from MIT, Stanford, and other leading technology centers. The ways that these individuals competed and cooperated played a critical role in the development of the nation's astoundingly productive economy in the second half of the twentieth century.

NEW YORK ROOTS

The story begins in NewYork.The nation's financial capital has always funded businesses: new, middle-aged, and old. By the 1920s, backing new businesses was a $4 billion-per-year industry, and much of it was centered in a few square blocks on the southern tip of Manhattan.

The Depression throttled this industry, cutting investment by roughly 50 percent throughout the 1930s. But the damage was more evident on the investment banking side of venturing. Throughout the troubled decade of the 1930s, America's wealthiest families continued to make judicious investments in selected industries. Some did so to protect and grow their fortunes. Others did so out of a sense of urgency and obligation: If they didn't do their part to save capitalism, who would?

Bessemer Securities Corporation, for example, was founded by the steel-rich Phipps and Guest families in 1924. It engaged in start-ups, second- and third-stage financings, and leveraged buyouts throughout the 1920s and 1930s. H.E. Talbott & Co.—organized to invest on behalf of a wealthy Chrysler director—was active and successful in the 1920s. The Nashville-based Equitable Securities Corporation gained some public notice by buying stock in fledgling companies, developing them, and then taking them public. Even the government did some "venturing" of a sort: The Reconstruction Finance Corporation, established in 1932 to combat the Depression, began making loans to start-ups in 1938.

Perhaps the most successful individual venturer before World War II was Laurance S. Rockefeller, grandson of the oil baron, whose fascination with technology and aviation led him to move some of his personal wealth out of Standard Oil shares and into new ventures. Working on his own, Rockefeller would spot an opportunity—for example, World War I flying ace Eddie Rickenbacker's new Eastern Airlines, or the aircraft-manufacturing start-up proposed by James McDonnell—and he would offer his brothers and sister the chance to invest in the proposed deal.

Another prewar venturer was John Hay "Jock" Whitney, heir to a New York newspaper fortune. Like Laurance Rockefeller, Whitney made some speculative solo investments in the 1930s. His wartime experiences, including his internment as a prisoner of war, reinforced his determination to do good—helping capitalism triumph over evils like Nazism—and also to do well. But the postwar Whitney efforts were designed to be *professional*, competent to do the necessary due diligence that would be required to make sound investments. J.H. Whitney & Co. opened its doors in February 1946, backed by $10 million of Whitney's own money and staffed by six professionals. "J.H. Whitney was formed with some perceptible measure of altruism," Whitney later commented, "as well as the hopeful purposes of making money."

Industry legend also has it that the Whitney firm invented the term *venture capital*. Jock Whitney was supposedly tired of seeing his firm referred to by the *New York Times* as an investment banking firm—which in fact it was not. A brainstorming session over lunch led to a new company description: a *private venture capital investment company*. The name stuck, and its abbreviated form was eventually adopted by an entire industry.

Sometime in its first year of operation, J.H. Whitney & Co. played host to a diminutive but impressive man with a pronounced French accent. The firm's guest was General Georges F. Doriot, who spent several days with the Whitney organization asking questions and taking notes. The already legendary Harvard Business School professor was then making plans to launch his own venture capital company, American Research and Development. Although ARD would be very different from the Whitney organization—among other things, it would be publicly held, and was intended to raise money from more than one source—Doriot did his homework carefully. Both as an academic and as a businessman, he wanted to learn as much as possible about this "venture capital" business before plunging into it himself.

BOSTON JUMPS FORWARD

Despite Doriot's careful preparations, ARD proved to be something less than a spectacular success in its first several years of operation. Perennially strapped for cash, the company started charging management fees to its portfolio companies in 1948. (These took the form of either straight fees for services or directors' fees, all of which went directly to ARD.) Still, in 1949, ARD fell $44,000 short of covering its operating expenses. A public offering of ARD shares in 1949 attracted little interest: No investment banking firm was willing to underwrite the offering. A year and a half later, 57 percent of these new shares remained unsold.

The company had hoped to realize gains by 1949. But in that year, only six of the eleven companies in which ARD had invested were in the black. Several of ARD's initial investments were in deep trouble. None was as yet a star performer.

But in the face of growing criticism of his company's performance, General Doriot remained unflappable. More than half of the companies in which ARD had invested were brand new, and were pioneers in their respective fields. Building great companies, Doriot acerbically reminded his critics, was not a short-term proposition.

By 1952, ARD had invested $4 million in sixteen major ventures, which were then registering gross sales of $60 million. Progress was slow, and even worse, the *perception* of progress lagged behind reality. In 1953, the company's net asset value was still only $9.50 per share, representing an average annual increase of only about 2 percent a year since ARD's founding.[1] In an effort to enhance the public's perception of his company and push up its share price, General Doriot (in February 1953) staged an exhibition of the products of ARD's portfolio companies, called Products with a Future. Some four thousand visitors viewed inventions ranging from a self-cooling pillow to a rapid-tanning process for shoe leather. This turned into an annual event, centered around the ARD shareholders' meeting, with portfolio company CEOs talking up their products—and by extension, ARD—with both shareholders and media representatives.

Inevitably, the highlight of these annual events came to be Doriot's address to the shareholders. One year, he apologized profusely for not having performed sufficient *due deeligence* in the case of one investment in which ARD had lost money. The audience's curiosity mounted: Which portfolio company was about to be humbled? Which leaders had not been sufficiently vetted in advance? "We weel have to be more careful in the future," Doriot concluded, with an actor's timing, "about investing in . . . *Treasury beels*." The crowd roared.

But theatrics couldn't stand in for performance. The following year, ARD's board of directors decided that ARD's investors had waited long enough for signs of progress, and it was time for a cash dividend. (In addition, certain institutional investors couldn't hold stock in companies that didn't pay dividends.) Doriot reluctantly agreed to declare a dividend—which, given ARD's cash shortage, would require the sale of some of the company's stock holdings. The stocks were sold, and a modest dividend of twenty-five cents per share was paid out. In this same period, ARD quietly bailed out of its unsuccessful investments in (low tech) apple- and shrimp-processing companies. "From now on," Doriot told shareholders at the company's 1955 annual-meeting gala, "you are free to eat anybody's *shreemp* you want to."

Criticism mounted. As an article in the February 28, 1955, issue of *Barron's* put it:

> *Despite the advantage of top financial and scientific help from Harvard, MIT and State Street, [ARD] has proved disappointing profit-wise. In its nine years of existence it has operated in the red more often than in the black; its capital losses have outweighed its capital gains; and it has paid exactly one dividend, of 25 cents per share. Most of the time its common stock has sold below the original offering price of $25 per share. Some of its early stockholders have lost patience—and, if they sold out, quite a little money, too.*

But one of ARD's original investments now showed signs of real progress. High Voltage Engineering, an MIT spin-off in which ARD had invested $200,000 in 1946—started to click. ARD began distributing shares of High Voltage to its investors in 1956, and this annual distribution brought the cash value of ARD's dividends up to $2.40 per share by 1958.

ARD's circumstances still lent themselves to conflicting interpretations. Without the contribution from High Voltage, ARD's dividend would have been an unimpressive three cents a share, and this led to grumbling. But one astute observer—Belmont Towbin, partner in the Wall Street firm of C.F. Unterberg, Towbin & Co.—took a very different view. As he told *Barron's*:

> *There are only 300,000 shares of ARD out. If the stock of one of the affiliates really took off, it could have quite an impact on the parent concern. Look how popular electronics shares are: Anybody with a soldering iron and a piece of wire can sell stock these days. Some of them are bound to be lemons. With a selection like ARD's, you minimize the risk.* [2]

Maybe some of ARD's investors would have stuck with the struggling company indefinitely, waiting for General Doriot's long-term vision to pay off. As it turned out, they didn't have to. In the spring of 1957, William H. Congleton—a youngish ARD staffer and a 1948 graduate of the Harvard Business School, with the nonrevealing title of "technical director"—was invited by Horace Ford, then treasurer of MIT, to visit MIT's Lincoln Labs. ARD, according to Congleton, was short on technical know-how at this stage in its development, and often leaned heavily on its MIT contacts. While visiting Lincoln Labs, Congleton mentioned his interest in computer business opportunities in the private sector to computer pioneer and MIT researcher Jay Forrester. Forrester was then focused primarily on academic pursuits, but he steered Congleton toward two young engineers in Building X who had been muttering about "starting something": Ken Olsen and Harlan Anderson.

Olsen was the more dynamic of the pair. He had a master's degree in electrical engineering from MIT and had attended the U.S. Navy's Radar School and served in the Navy during World War II. With Forrester, he had led the development team at Lincoln Labs that had created "Whirlwind," celebrated as the world's fastest computer and a central building block in the U.S. Air Force's Semi-Automatic Ground Environment (SAGE) defense network. Olsen had served as liaison between MIT and IBM (which was the prime contractor on SAGE), and was an expert in the use of transistors in computer applications. When transistors replaced vacuum tubes in a piece of equipment, that equipment went from being "analog" to "digital." Olsen and his team had developed various kinds of digital equipment—laboratory testers and so on—for use in their government work.

Congleton was intrigued, and recommended to Olsen and Anderson that they write up a business plan to take these products to market. His involvement didn't stop there: When the two subsequently submitted a four-page outline, Congleton offered some suggestions about how to give the plan some added depth. He also recommended that the engineers downplay the "computer" aspects of their proposal, concentrating instead on the possibility of creating digital building blocks. These individual pieces could be sold to labs, which in turn would evolve them into full-size computers.

Congleton knew there were good reasons to downplay computers. Though an exciting concept, the minicomputer still seemed too speculative a bet to many at ARD, and at least one member of the ARD board was convinced that the waterfront was already fully covered by Univac, Sperry, and IBM. Olsen and Anderson agreed to these suggestions, including changing the name of their proposed company from Digital Computer Corporation to Digital Equipment Corporation.

ARD's board liked the revised plan, and in the summer of 1957 ARD invested $70,000 in DEC, a sum sufficient to purchase 78 percent of the new company's common stock. Olsen leased nine thousand square feet in a decrepit woolen mill in Maynard, Massachusetts—the rent was twenty-five cents per square foot—and began cranking out digitally based testing modules. Budgets were tight. "The nice thing about seventy thousand dollars," Olsen later told a group assembled to celebrate his firm's twenty-fifth anniversary, "[is that] there are so few of them you can watch every one." Remarkably, in its first year of operations, DEC made a small profit on $94,000 in sales.

"I am sorry to see this," Doriot told Olsen, scowling theatrically at

Olsen's first year's financial statements. "No one has ever succeeded this soon and survived."

Public descriptions of what was actually being *made* out in Maynard were vague. (Competitors, and maybe even one or two of ARD's board members, were being screened from the whole story.) "Engineers and scientists will use these DEC units to develop and test circuits and components employed in all types of computers," an ARD newsletter told shareholders in October 1957, "up to the largest and most advanced now existing or contemplated."

But Olsen had no intention of stopping there. This was an era when computers were room-sized affairs, run by technicians and given commands through punch cards. There was no "user interface." Users of a centralized computer resource turned over their inquiries to the white-coated technicians and hoped for the best. Olsen wanted to build a smaller, more flexible machine, which would be programmable *by the user.* He called his vision the "programmable data processor," or PDP. It would use semiconductors, rather than vacuum tubes. It would include a keyboard to allow direct input from the user, and (by means of a cathode ray tube) give the user a "window" into what was actually going on. The first generation of PDPs—the PDP 1—was ready to ship by the end of 1960.

ARD board members got a sneak preview of the PDP 1 and its capabilities and were impressed with what Olsen, Anderson, and their colleagues had been able to accomplish on their shoestring budget. One longtime staffer remembers, though, that when the team returned to Boston, they were "a little nervous about having to break the news to General Doriot." Computers were still that dangerous field in which only IBM could make money.

The rest, of course, is computer history. DEC was an astounding success. Ensuing generations of the PDP got smarter, faster, and cheaper—and sold in amazing quantities. Almost single-handedly, Olsen and DEC had invented the "minicomputer" market, and they—and their original sponsors at ARD—were richly rewarded for that creativity. DEC went public in 1966 at an asking price of $25 per share, and overnight, ARD's $70,000 investment was valued at $37 million.

Subsequent increases in DEC's share price floated ARD's tiny boat ever higher. When DEC's share price topped $80 in the summer of 1967, ARD's investment was worth something like $140 million. (Three years later, the figure was more than $260 million.) By the end of 1967, about two-thirds of ARD's total portfolio value was represented by the DEC holdings. A dollar invested in ARD in 1946 was now worth $30.[3]

To his credit, General Doriot sang the same tune in good times and bad. In his 1968 message to shareholders, he sounded a cautionary note:

It is many years between the inception of a small company and a level of profitable stability. There are many disillusions in the early years, and many accidents with which to cope.

Perception, courage, and hard work may not be enough to solve problems. It is hard to determine when a hope is no longer a hope . . .

No forecasts can be made, and shareholders should be reminded that venture capital is a dangerous, but constructive, business.

Dangerous, but constructive: the phrase captured much of what was unique about ARD's approach to venture capital.

BREEDING COMPETITORS

Even as the DEC investment was finally validating the ARD patient-capital philosophy, three other challenges were coming to the fore. Each would breed new competitors to American Research and Development, and contribute to its ultimate demise.

The first challenge, unfortunately, was General Doriot himself. Self-consciously European, he was a complicated, brusque, and exacting taskmaster. The kinds of highly talented young people ARD recruited—smart financial types from HBS, technically savvy engineers from MIT—eventually bridled at the tightness of the reins at ARD. This was Doriot's show, pure and simple. In the early 1960s, Doriot approached a rising young venture capitalist on the West Coast and asked if he might be interested in joining ARD. The implication was clear: When Doriot finally stepped down, this young man would be in line to take over as head of ARD.

"General Doriot," the young man responded coolly, "the only thing that might be worse than moving to Boston would be working for you."

A second problem faced by ARD was the extraordinary commitment it demanded from its staffers. Jefferson Asher was a Doriot student at HBS who, after graduating from the School in March of 1948, turned down the opportunity to serve as Doriot's teaching assistant because of family demands. A year later, however, he happily accepted Doriot's invitation to join the ARD staff. The staff then consisted of four young men—two HBS grads and two MIT grads—who combined their skills to screen the never-ending stream of requests for funding that poured into ARD's offices.

In some cases, moreover, the staffers were expected to go fix the portfolio companies that got into trouble. From Doriot's perspective, no personal sacrifice was too great when an ARD company was in peril. But this intense commitment, as Asher recalls, sometimes caused problems of its own:

> *I got assigned something that I had not been initially responsible for— a company called Coulter Corporation, which was the largest shrimp company on the Gulf Coast. It basically consisted of twenty-five boats, a large freezer, and a proprietary automatic deveining process. And even though everything looked like it was going great, we kept losing money.*
>
> *So I followed it for about a year, and I said, "Hey, there's something wrong. Somebody is screwing up the works down there." So the General says, "So go on down and fix it." Well, I couldn't bring my wife and two little girls down there, because it was just a miserable environment. So I left them in Boston, and went down and lived in Texas for a year.*
>
> *I solved the problem. I closed down four of the five receiving stations, made everybody come into one so that there wouldn't be massive stealing at the dock. By cutting down the stealing, all of a sudden we started making money. But I was really annoyed that Joe [Powell] and the General had left me down there, and left my wife and two little girls in Boston, and I let them know that. So the General calls me back, and he says, "What's the matter with you, Jeff? Don't you want to be the shrimp king of the world?" And I said, "No, damn it, I don't want to*

be the shrimp king of the world." And he more or less said, "Well, this
is your job, you know? You've got to do this." So I said, "The hell with
you," and I quit.

Others at ARD made similar sacrifices without complaint. ("Hey,"
recalls one, "we were all fresh out of the service, and here was a *general*
telling us what to do. He could have sent me anywhere, and I would
have loved it.") But happy or not, ARD's young staffers were sometimes called upon to turn entire companies around. In those contexts,
they discovered that they were helping to create a great deal of wealth,
in which they were not sharing.

And this raised a third and related problem. Legally, ARD was a
Small Business Investment Company, and the Securities and Exchange
Commission had ruled that employees of regulated investment companies couldn't be granted options on their own stock. For Doriot—
who was at heart an academic and an economic missionary—this
meant little. (Recognizing the threat to his company, Doriot ultimately did make several efforts to get the SEC to change its relevant
rules, to no avail.) But for the ambitious young men around him, who
were helping make other people rich, the arrangement was hard to
take. One young ARD staffer took on a struggling ARD portfolio
company—in which ARD had an investment of a few million dollars—and parlayed that liability into a multimillion-dollar "win" for
ARD. His reward? Goodwill, and a $2,000 bonus.

Another point of contention was stock options in portfolio companies. Those who were lucky enough to get directors' stock options in
a company like DEC got rich; those who weren't, didn't. It was a hit-
or-miss situation, which didn't sit well with ARD's staffers. DEC, for
example, gave shares in the company to everyone on its board, including ARD staffers Bill Congleton, Dorothy Rowe, Wayne Brobeck, and
Harry Hoaglin. When DEC shares went through the roof, these members of the ARD staff were well rewarded financially, while others who
had also been deeply involved in the company weren't.

Not surprisingly, many at ARD were unhappy with this system.
Several ARD staffers, including Congleton, had lobbied Doriot several
times to set up a cache of portfolio stock options that Doriot could

then distribute among the staff as bonuses or rewards. For one reason or another, however, Doriot never adopted this concept of incentive compensation, and resentments continued to smolder.

One of the first out of the ARD fold was Joseph Powell Jr., a member of the HBS class of 1926 and Doriot's right-hand man since the founding of ARD, who left the company in 1951 to take an operating job with a Cleveland-based company. (Another HBS graduate, William Elfers, M.B.A. '43, who also had been with ARD since its founding, took over as vice president.) In 1960, Powell returned to Boston to help found Boston Capital Corporation, which went public as one of the first Boston SBICs in September 1960. More than 1.5 million shares were sold, which netted the company more than $20.3 million—"the largest single offering ever made of venture capital shares," as the company's 1964 annual report boasted.

BCC was created very much in the mold of ARD. Like ARD, it drew heavily on the resources of both MIT and Harvard. Its patron was the celebrated Harvard-educated financier John P. Chase, while its operating head, Powell, was Doriot's alter ego. Charles Draper, head of MIT's Department of Aeronautics and Astronautics, agreed to take a seat on the BCC board. Early indicators suggested that BCC might well tap into the same vein that ARD was exploiting so successfully. BCC's $220,000 investment in Berkey Photo, Inc.—supplier of photofinishing services for all types of color and black-and-white film—quintupled in value within five years.

Boston—the second city into the venture capital game—was competing admirably. Boston could still learn from New York, but now it could teach a few lessons of its own.

A NEW YORK INTERLUDE

Two hundred miles down the coast, meanwhile, the original venture community was evolving in its own distinctive direction.

Unlike Doriot and his Boston-based colleagues, New York's venture capitalists were not particularly concerned about their home territory being left behind by a fast-moving postwar economy. New York was the center of the financial universe and the home of corporate America. This seemed unlikely to change any time soon.

And unlike Boston, New York had no particular tradition of innovative engineering. There was no MIT to turn to, no Lincoln Labs, no local community of talented and ambitious Ken Olsens. Instead, New York had a centuries-old tradition of *financial* engineering. This legacy tended to focus the New York venture capitalists on the money flows involved in a particular deal, rather than the technologies. Venture capital was the first and riskiest activity on the broad spectrum of corporate finance—but after all, it was only *one* of those activities. And indisputably, New York led the world in every other activity on the investment-banking spectrum.

On the venture capital end of that spectrum, moreover, most of the key players knew each other socially as well as professionally. The Rockefellers, Whitneys, Phippses, and Guests summered together, were educated together, and gathered at events ranging from balls to board meetings.

Perhaps as a result, the New York venture capital group was intensely interested in *pedigree*. Who were the individuals behind the deal, and how well connected were they? Were they the "sort of people" with whom one would want to associate? One former New York–based banker, now a West Coast venture capitalist, recalls how a New York venture firm once turned down an opportunity to invest in what appeared to be an attractive proposition. The reason, he was told, was that the proposed head of the company had been discharged from the Army for being a bed-wetter: *not the sort of person we'd want to associate with.*

But the New York venturers—still led by the Rockefellers and the two Whitney concerns (Jock Whitney had gained a friendly competitor in 1947 when his sister, Joan, put $5 million into her own firm of Payson & Trask)—were still refining their approach to bankrolling new speculative ventures. From the 1950s forward, they increasingly took what might be called a "milestone" approach, providing injections of funds to deserving portfolio companies when those companies reached a new stage of development. The first round of investment might support, for example, product development; the second round, product testing; and so forth.

In each round of funding, the New Yorkers looked for partners to share the risks. Most often, they looked to each other. But it was also common to look northward to Boston, and in particular, to ARD.

ROCK MAKES HIS MARK

One day sometime in the mid-1950s, Arthur Rock's secretary knocked on his office door and asked if he would agree to an unscheduled meeting with an insurance salesman.

Rock, a member of the HBS class of 1951, was then working at the New York headquarters of Hayden, Stone & Co., a venerable investment banking firm and brokerage house with major offices in New York and Boston. Rock worked in the Corporate Department, which underwrote corporate issues of all shapes and sizes. Although most of Hayden, Stone's business came from well-established companies, the firm also dabbled in new ventures. According to a 1958 company publication:

> *With the help of Assistants David MacNeil and Arthur Rock, Hayden, Stone & Co.'s Corporate Department is busily investigating the hundreds of hopeful small businesses that need financing, and the firm has already established a reputation for its knowledge of the newer fields of industry, particularly in electronics, nucleonics, and instrumentation.*

The corporate brochure emphasized, however, that although new business was "exciting in its potentials," old business was still the "lifeblood of the Corporate Department." MacNeil and Rock were more or less a colorful sideshow. But Rock didn't care; he liked the kinds of people that his work put him in touch with—scientists, engineers, and inventors—and he enjoyed putting good deals together. In 1955, for example, Rock assembled a funding package for General Transistor, the first independent manufacturer of semiconductors. Its target market was hearing-aid components. "I liked [General Transistor CEO] Herman Fialkov," Rock recalls, "and he had already demonstrated that transistors had a practical use. It seemed to me that this opened up a whole new field."

Not for the first time, Rock had the feeling that he was looking into the future. Transistors had been invented in 1947 by three scientists at Bell Labs, and were only now finding their way into the marketplace. "I always had the ability to see where things were going, more or less," Rock says. "Not necessarily understanding them, but being able to figure out that some things were garbage, and other things had a future." Transistors, Rock was convinced, had a future.

But at this particular moment, Rock was surprised and a little annoyed at being interrupted by his secretary. Having recently suffered through a rash of sales calls from insurance agents, Rock had summarily banned them from his office.

"I *asked* him if he was in the insurance business," the secretary explained apologetically, "and he said, 'Yes, I'm with the John Hancock.' But he said he thought you might recognize his name—Georges Doriot—and that you might agree to see him. I think he's French."

The normally reserved Rock chuckled and agreed to the unscheduled meeting. He had never been a student of Doriot's, but was well aware of the general's prominent role in the Boston venture community (and his less-important role as a member of the John Hancock board of directors). On this day, as it turned out, Doriot was pitching not life insurance, but the opportunity to buy a small piece of a Chicago-based tape-transport company called Magnacord. Hayden, Stone eventually went into the deal—and wound up regretting it when Magnacord went belly-up.

But failure was routine in venture capital, and Rock continued to look for interesting opportunities, especially among the creative engineers and scientists with whom he enjoyed spending time. One day in 1957, a Hayden, Stone colleague forwarded to Rock a letter from someone named Eugene Kleiner. Kleiner was then working for William Shockley, one of the three Bell Labs scientists who had invented the transistor and had since set up a laboratory on the West Coast. For all his brilliance, Shockley was an extremely difficult individual to work with, and seven of his top scientists, including Kleiner, had agreed to try to seek employment together elsewhere. They had a vague notion of setting up a research department for an existing company, and hoped to get equity positions. They wrote to Hayden, Stone—where Eugene Kleiner's father had a brokerage account—and asked if the New York firm had any ideas.

Rock arranged a meeting in San Francisco, was impressed with the restless scientists, and proposed a different approach. "My idea," Rock recalls, "was that they would become a subsidiary or division of some other company, so that they could get management help and reap some of the rewards if they were successful." The group—now joined by an eighth colleague, Robert Noyce—agreed to be "shopped" in this way. They also agreed to an 80/20 split: Each of the eight would get 10 percent, and Hayden, Stone would get the remaining 20 percent. Each of the eight agreed to put in $500.

Initial results were discouraging, as Rock recalls:

> *We canvassed all of the big companies, and there were dozens of them that said they wanted to get into scientific-type things, new frontiers. The war was over, and there were new technologies, and they all wanted to do it—or so they said. But none of them did. They all said, "We can't do it. We like the idea. But we can't fit this into our organization." And we got turned down by something like thirty-five companies before we met Sherman Fairchild.*

Fairchild was a unique character who played a key role in the development of the U.S. economy in the postwar period. He was the son of George Fairchild, who had persuaded Thomas Watson Sr. to leave National Cash Register and take over the Tabulating, Computing, and Recording Company—later renamed International Business Machines. The Fairchilds were well rewarded for their contributions to IBM. By the 1950s, Sherman Fairchild was the company's single biggest shareholder. He was also an inventor in his own right and had set up Fairchild Camera and Instrument, as well as Fairchild Engine and Aircraft, to exploit his own discoveries in aerial photography. He bought Rock's pitch, and Fairchild Semiconductor—a separate company financed by Fairchild's company—was born. The parent company put in $1.5 million and reserved the right to buy all the outstanding stock for $3 million.

Two years later, in 1959, Fairchild Camera and Instrument exercised its stock-purchase options and bought out Hayden, Stone and the "Fairchild Eight," as they had come to be known. All parties to the deal came away from the table happy. Fairchild now owned its most profitable subsidiary outright; Hayden, Stone received a handsome payout; and each of the Fairchild Eight received $250,000 worth of

Fairchild Camera and Instrument stock. On the announcement of the consolidation, the stock promptly doubled, giving each of them $500,000.

And more important, in the long run: A new bridge was built between the New York venture community and the high-flying engineering community then centered in the eastern foothills of the Santa Cruz mountains, in the backyard of Stanford University.

PENINSULA ROOTS

Jefferson Asher, the former ARD staffer and reluctant Gulf Coast shrimp king, was finishing up an unusual job on the West Coast in the summer of 1961 when he received a call from Joe Powell, his former ARD colleague. Asher had been working with Kirk Douglas for several years, trying to straighten out the actor's tangled personal finances. Douglas had made millions of dollars over the previous several years, and yet somehow had a negative net worth and owed the U.S. government millions of dollars. As it turned out, he had been bilked systematically for years by unscrupulous advisors. "I probably learned more doing that job," Asher recalls, "than I learned at the Harvard Business School or at any of my other jobs. I was *amazed*—all the phony deals and the crazy things that go on in that business."

Powell asked if Asher would be willing to head a West Coast office of the Boston Capital Corporation, launched with much fanfare the previous year. Asher, fed up with the slippery ethics of Hollywood, jumped at the chance. In the fall of 1961, he opened BCC's branch office on Wilshire Boulevard in Los Angeles.

Asher thereby joined a surprisingly small community of West Coast venture capitalists, at least as the business was then being defined in New York and Boston. In the mid-1950s, a company called Spring Street Capital—consciously conceived of as a West Coast counterpart to General Doriot's ARD—was underwritten, but it never got off the ground. (It was eventually taken over by an operating company.) The SBIC Act of 1958 encouraged banks to get into the venture capital business, and most West Coast banks—including

Bank of America—sooner or later took the plunge. A company called Electronics Capital Corp. was launched in 1959 in San Diego as a publicly held SBIC; it is remembered today as a relatively flamboyant outfit that was skilled at raising money. In the same year, General William H. Draper Jr., a former investment banker and a leading figure in the postwar reconstruction of Germany and Japan, used Rockefeller and Lazard Frères money to launch a West Coast venture firm called Draper, Gaither, and Anderson, which did business for approximately a decade. Continental Capital Corporation, led by Frank Chambers (M.B.A. '39), began its long history of backing early-stage technologically oriented companies.

But at the beginning of the 1960s, much of the real action took place within informal networks based in San Francisco. Entrepreneurial individuals as well as deal makers in corporate settings—for example, the legendary Reid Dennis of the Fireman's Fund—would get together over lunch and listen to a pitch from an engineer with an idea. Anyone who liked the pitch had the opportunity to kick in money. This was "passing the hat" raised to a new level. An articulate engineer with a seemingly solid idea might go home with $100,000 in pledges of backing for his new venture.

Many of these engineers were developing their ideas in an emerging hotbed of technical creativity: the campus of Stanford University and the surrounding neighborhoods of Palo Alto. There, a farsighted MIT graduate and member of the Stanford Engineering Department, Fred Terman, had almost single-handedly created a crucible of high-tech entrepreneurship. Terman persuaded Stanford in 1951 to set up the Stanford Industrial Park on a corner of the University's expansive campus. (There was plenty of land to work with: After Moscow University, Stanford's is the largest campus in the world.) Hewlett-Packard, which had been created by two of Terman's former students, was an early distinguished tenant, moving into the complex in 1954. In subsequent years, a torrent of ideas and products came out of the industrial park and its surroundings.

So the West Coast had a wealth of good ideas. But it still lacked the kind of capital that was available on the East Coast, and it lacked an organized way of hooking up money with ideas.

MOVING WEST

Arthur Rock had greatly enjoyed his most recent look into the future, as he had helped transform a group of eight disaffected scientists into Fairchild Semiconductor. Rock decided to once again go with his instincts—which by 1961 were telling him to relocate to the West Coast.

The proposed move, he recalls, went against the prevailing wisdom among his New York colleagues:

> *People thought I was nuts. But I saw enormous opportunities. There was very little capital around in the West to finance any of these companies. There were no organized groups like the family foundations in the East, which historically was where a lot of the money had come from. I knew where that money was. I met Tommy Davis, and we just decided we'd do it.*

"It" was hanging out a shingle in San Francisco as the brand-new venture capital firm of Davis & Rock. Rock's new partner, Tommy Davis, had been vice president and resident idea man for the Kern County Land Company, where he had responsibility for investing the land trust's royalties and other income profitably. He had made one successful investment in a new venture—the Watkins-Johnson Company, a high-tech manufacturer spawned down at Stanford—and was eager to make more like it. He discovered to his dismay, though, that Kern's management was not as aggressive as he was. When the opportunity to team up with Rock arose, Davis bolted.

The first thing that Davis and Rock did was to work out a new approach to venture capital—one that sidestepped the compensation issues that were already plaguing ARD. They agreed that Davis & Rock should be organized as a *partnership*, rather than as an SBIC or a publicly held company. Rock suggested, and Davis agreed, that the capital gains on the firm's investments should be split 80/20 between its limited partners (i.e., its passive investors) and its general partners (Rock and Davis).

On this basis—which became the model for almost all venture capital firms organized subsequently—Rock called on his East Coast contacts and quickly raised $5 million. ("A princely sum then," he says wryly. "Somewhat more princely than now.") Then Davis & Rock set about investing that money.

This was an assignment they never completed. By the time the partnership was dissolved in 1968, Davis & Rock still had some $1.6 million of that original $5 million to draw upon. In the meantime, they had generated some $90 million in capital gains for their investors.

The "failure" to invest the full $5 million reflected, in large part, the intensely personal way Rock and Davis did business. They not only scrutinized their proposed deals thoroughly in advance, but continued to serve their portfolio companies as hands-on advisors throughout the duration of the investment. They got to know their CEOs, their CEOs' spouses, and their CEOs' families. They served on their companies' boards. The word quickly spread: An investment by Davis & Rock was very likely to be the beginning of an intense relationship.

As much as anything else, this reflected the times. As Rock recalls:

Remember: There wasn't any competition. It's not like the late 1990s, where you had to go out and knock on doors to find things. People came to us when they heard what we were doing. We had plenty of time to investigate. Nothing was done on Internet time. So we were able to assess whatever needed to be assessed. And, of course, luck plays a big part in these things.

The partnership demonstrated that it had good timing, was lucky, and was very, very good at what it did. Over its seven-year history, Davis & Rock racked up a 54 percent compound growth rate. Their biggest successes came through investments in Teledyne—on whose board Rock served for thirty-three years—and Scientific Data Systems (SDS). It was the success of the SDS investment, in fact, that led to the amicable dissolution of the Davis & Rock partnership. In 1968, Rock was serving as the chairman of SDS's board. The SEC made it clear that investors in Davis & Rock couldn't sell SDS stock as long as Rock chaired the SDS board. Rather than give up the SDS relationship—which Rock enjoyed enormously—Rock and Davis gave up Davis & Rock.

MORE IMMIGRANTS

One other set of "immigrants" turned West Coast venturers in this time period deserves special mention.

William H. Draper III (M.B.A. '54) was the son of the celebrated General Draper, a cofounder of the pioneering West Coast venture firm of Draper, Gaither & Anderson. After graduating from the Harvard Business School, Draper took a job with Inland Steel, where he met another HBS graduate named Franklin Pitcher Johnson (M.B.A. '52). "Pitch" Johnson focused on mill operations, while Draper eventually migrated into sales. As Draper recalls, it was an unglamorous but highly educational posting:

> We both lived in East Chicago, Indiana—a real mill town. If you washed the car on Saturday, you could plan on washing it again on Sunday. Coke dust, an oil refinery nearby, and a cement factory—all that stuff ended up on your car. I stayed with Inland for five years, and by '59, when I joined DG&A, I had learned a great deal about what industrial America was all about.

Draper moved west to join the firm then being founded in San Francisco by his father. The launching of DG&A received considerable public notice—including a write-up in *BusinessWeek*—due in large part to the prominence of its founders. Draper spent five years at DG&A learning the venture capital business. Then, in 1962, he struck out on his own. Teaming up with his former Inland Steel colleague, Pitch Johnson, he launched Draper & Johnson Investment Company, a Palo Alto–based SBIC.

After a few years of struggling to establish Draper & Johnson and also make ends meet—the two partners paid themselves a paltry $10,000 a year—Draper and Johnson decided in 1965 to team up with another SBIC called the Sutter Hill Land Company, which specialized in shopping-center ownership and financing. The new company, Sutter Hill Capital Corporation, took its president Bill Draper from one predecessor company and its vice president Paul M. Wythes from the other. "We merged mainly to share the Xerox machine and the receptionists," Draper recalls. "We were all getting along on peanuts."

With a clear focus on the operating side of young businesses—all of Sutter Hill's early partners had served in operating roles in established companies—Palo Alto–based Sutter Hill quickly established a sharp profile in the West Coast venture game. One early success was the Santa Clara–based Measurex Corporation, a start-up that made digital control systems for the pulp and paper industry. Because Measurex needed $1.25 million for its 1968 launch, and because Sutter Hill had to observe a $250,000 limit on its investments, Draper and his colleagues were compelled to scout for some additional partners. New York–based Bessemer, among others, signed up.

Measurex shares went for a dollar apiece in 1968. Two years later, they were valued at $40 apiece, and Sutter Hill won a National Venture Capital Award (an annual honor bestowed by the Harvard Business School) for its creative backing of Measurex. Measurex filed in December 1971 for its first public offering, and its stock soon began trading on the New York Stock Exchange. In 1997, the company was sold to Honeywell for $600 million.

Sutter Hill's search for money led to one unexpected fork in the road. Draper recalls the circumstances:

> *Georges Doriot was a friend of mine. We were looking for new money. We were thinking about what to do, so I went up to Boston to talk to him about it. He said, "Why don't you become the West Coast operations of ARD?" Well, I entertained that for a while, but the more we talked, the more clear it was that every decision was going to be made in Boston. I'd be presenting deals to a board in Boston, and I'd be on the board, but it wasn't going to be independent at all.*

Eventually, early in 1970, the search for backing led Sutter Hill into the arms of Genstar Ltd., a large NYSE Canadian industrial company. Genstar's $10 million investment secured 80 percent of Sutter Hill's profits as the firm's sole limited partner; the remaining 20 percent would go to general partners Bill Draper and Paul Wythes. Over the next three decades, Sutter Hill would assemble an astounding track record. Investing in more than two hundred companies with a market capitalization of more than $50 billion, Sutter Hill would generate average annual returns in excess of 35 percent.

The 1969 dissolution of Davis & Rock and the 1970 reconfiguration of Sutter Hill marked the end of one era and the beginning of a new one. In the increasingly self-confident and economically exuberant region that stretched from San Francisco to Palo Alto, the stories of Draper & Johnson, Sutter Hill, and especially Davis & Rock were told and retold. Inspired, legions of competitors prepared to enter the once-sleepy field of Western venture capital.

BOSTON: NEW BEGINNINGS

By 1965, ARD's vice president Bill Elfers was increasingly unhappy with his career options. After almost two decades at ARD and fourteen years as General Doriot's number-two man, he had learned all that he was likely to learn within the confines of Doriot's operation. Although Elfers seemed to be in line to succeed Doriot, there was no hint that Doriot intended to retire any time soon. Like most of the other talented people whom Doriot had hired over the years, Elfers wanted to make his own mark in venture capital. And finally, he—like most of his colleagues at ARD—wanted to do better for himself financially than he was ever likely to do at ARD.

With all of these incentives lining up in the same direction, Elfers began looking for backing for a company he had already started to call Greylock—named, offhandedly, for the Wellesley Hills street on which he lived. Here, his personal contacts, as well as the many contacts he had made over the years at ARD, served him well. Members of the prominent families who had been impressed with Elfers's contributions to some of ARD's portfolio companies now agreed to back him in his new venture.

"This was Greylock's 'first first,'" Elfers notes. "With the possible exception of Davis & Rock, Greylock was the first partnership that represented multiple families." One family asked if it could be Greylock's sole investor; reluctantly, Elfers said no. He was looking forward to a future in which Greylock would outstrip the capacity of a single family to bankroll it. In addition, he wanted to be able to draw upon the talents (as well as the bank accounts) of a variety of investors.

One target Elfers had in mind was Sherman Fairchild, who had gotten to know Elfers as a fellow director of the Pasadena-based G.M. Giannini Corporation. (Fairchild was on the board protecting his own investment; Elfers was representing ARD's interests.) Coincidentally, this was about a year after Fairchild's company had bought out the Fairchild Eight and brought Fairchild Semiconductor—the company invented by Arthur Rock—fully into the corporate fold. Fairchild was then sixty-nine years old and clearly didn't need the money; he backed Elfers because he respected his younger counterpart, and—in Elfers's estimation—because he simply enjoyed the sport of backing new ventures.

Elfers needed to find partners as well as investors. His first recruit was Daniel S. Gregory (M.B.A. '57), a rising young star in the Boston investment community. Elfers described to Gregory his novel vision: a venture capital organization that would (as an organizational memo to investors described it) invest in companies that had "qualified and dedicated managements, enlightened ownership, substantial capital resources, and patient investment programs." Greylock would be private—thereby avoiding some of the compensation problems encountered by ARD and other public SBICs—and would go beyond the single-family base of the Whitney and Rockefeller organizations. Gregory, who was ready to carve out his own niche in venture capital, signed on eagerly. The Greylock Management Corporation was formally launched in October 1965.

Bill Elfers had no particular intention of populating Greylock exclusively with Harvard Business School graduates. But as Greylock grew, it seemed to grow most often by signing on bright new M.B.A.'s from HBS. In 1966, with General Doriot's cooperation, Elfers signed on five-year ARD veteran (and former Doriot teaching assistant) Charles P. Waite (M.B.A. '59). Three years later, Elfers and his partners recruited Henry F. McCance (M.B.A. '66), who was then finishing up a stint as a civilian strategic planner for the Defense Department. Ultimately, eleven of Greylock's first fourteen partner-track hires were graduates of the School.

In its first decade of operations, Greylock did fifty deals. It established itself as one of the leading venture firms in Boston—and by extension, the nation. By 1973, of those fifty companies, seventeen had gone public and four had been sold to larger companies. Going where ARD had been reluctant to tread, Greylock decided to bet on the infant cable television field. Its investment in Continental Cablevision—a 1963 start-up headed by Amos B. "Bud" Hostetter Jr. (M.B.A. '61) and H. Irving Grousbeck (M.B.A. '60)—proved to be its most successful of all, and also helped cement Greylock's reputation as a long-term investor. (Henry McCance served on Continental's board for a quarter-century.) Greylock also carved out a position as a savvy investor in the medical field, based in part on its successful backing in 1967 of Damon Corporation, which—after its Greylock-inspired merger with another Greylock investment, International Equipment Company—returned on a five-for-one basis.

Greylock often worked in partnership with other venture firms, in Boston and elsewhere. One of these was ARD, with which the Greylock management team was careful to maintain good relations. (In addition to mutual respect, there was simply too great an overlap of interests to allow any other approach.) Another was Boston Capital. It was BCC's Joe Powell, for example, who brought Continental Cablevision to Greylock's attention.

Still another friendly competitor was T.A. Associates, Inc., founded in 1967 by Peter A. Brooke (M.B.A. '54). After getting out of the Army, Brooke had gone to work for the First National Bank of Boston, where he started a then-offbeat venture called the High Technology Lending Group. As he recalls:

> *The bank wasn't lending money to companies in the New England area because the companies here were dying. The textile industry was moving south, the shoe industry was moving west, and so on. So the local banks had shifted to investing in nationally significant companies.*
>
> *And I said, "You know, we're never going to build a local franchise by doing that." I wrote a paper arguing that the bank should concentrate its assets on the one thing that we had in this region that could make us economically self-sufficient: high technology. At that time, MIT and Harvard were getting tons of contracts, and there were lots of spin-offs, and the bank was disregarding that sector completely. So I went out and started developing relationships and providing loan capital to these small, emerging high-tech companies.*

Brooke next spent two years with Bessemer Securities, learning the venture capital game as it was played in New York. In 1963, he set up his own investment company—Tucker, Anthony & Co., Inc.—under the auspices of the Boston-based investment banking firm of Tucker, Anthony & R.L. Day. Brooke's firm made a few investments, but mostly generated fees by placing venture capital securities with Besse-mer, the Rockefellers, and other New York investors. The company was extremely profitable—so much so that the IRS ordered Brooke to distribute its profits in dividends. After declaring a liquidating divi-dend large enough to pay the partners' taxes, Brooke used the remain-ing capital to set up a new venture fund, Advent 1, with a new entity, T.A. Associates, as the general partner of that limited partnership.

Under the direction of Brooke and partner C. Kevin Landry, T.A. Associates eventually became the manager of one of the largest group of venture capital partnerships in the country. Through a network of subsidiary and affiliate companies and with Brooke's active encour-agement, T.A. Associates and its successor in the international arena, Advent International Corporation, became the first U.S. firm to "ex-port" the venture capital concept. And finally, T.A./Advent served as a training ground for an extraordinary number of young venture capi-talists who left to start their own firms. One of these was Claflin Cap-ital Management, Inc., formed in 1978 by Tom Claflin (M.B.A. '74). Another was Burr, Egan, Deleage & Co., started in 1978 by William P. Egan, Craig L. Burr (M.B.A. '70), and Jean Deleage. Yet another was Summit Venture Partners, formed by E. Roe Stamps (M.B.A. '74) and Steven Woodsum in 1983. Finally, David Croll (M.B.A. '73) started Media Communications Partners in 1987. These second-generation managers, all graduates of T.A. Associates, have created a third genera-tion of industry leaders. In the aggregate, T.A./Advent and its second- and third-generation spin-offs have raised billions of dollars and have financed countless start-up companies.

ARD: THE END

While Greylock and T.A. Associates were taking root and prospering, their spiritual parent—American Research and Development—was slipping into decline.

The company didn't lack for successes in the late 1960s and early 1970s. (Its investment of slightly less than $1 million in Boston-based Teradyne, Inc., for example, returned almost $15 million when that company went public in 1970.) But a quarter-century of domination by one individual—even one as talented as Georges Doriot—and an uncompetitive corporate structure had taken their toll. ARD was no longer the only game in town. Talent flowed outward toward a dozen competing firms. At the end of 1971, according to ARD's annual report, "shares were selling at a discount of 23 percent from net asset value, the largest discount seen in years."

Early in 1972, unexpectedly, the curtain came down. ARD and Rhode Island–based Textron, Inc., announced plans to merge. Under the terms of the agreement, ARD shareholders would receive three-quarters of a share of DEC stock and a third of a share of Textron stock for each of their ARD shares. On the face of it, the deal seemed to make sense. Doriot and Textron's president, G. William Miller, had served on each other's boards for years. Textron agreed to Doriot's precondition that ARD could maintain confidential information about its client companies, some of which competed with Textron subsidiaries. Doriot, then seventy-two years old, also announced his retirement from the active management of the business.

In Boston, few people rejoiced. The reaction of longtime shareholders ranged from skepticism to deep anxiety. Portfolio companies, too, were upset. The CEO of one client company commented that the merger was like watching his father make a mistake and not being able to do anything about it. This same CEO noted pointedly that of all ARD's portfolio companies, only DEC had been consulted in advance about the merger. The ARD family was dissolving.

The merger also sparked a new wave of out-migration of talent from ARD. In January 1973, twelve-year ARD veteran John Shane left the company to set up the Palmer Organization. As Shane recalls, it was not a close call:

> *I did not favor the Textron merger. We at ARD had spent a lot of time with early-stage companies. Entrepreneurs came in with an idea, and we'd bring them along to the point they might start a company. I didn't feel that an entrepreneur who wanted to have his own show would go to a conglomerate for help. That would be like a chicken going to a fox.*
>
> *I also had several discussions with Textron about compensation. I pointed out to them that if they had a venture firm that was part of a*

*bigger organization, they'd have to accept the fact that the compensa-
tion of the group in the venture department was likely to be out of
synch with the rest of the organization. And I suggested some things
that they might do to make that attractive to a venture capitalist. They
said they couldn't do that. So both the environment and the compensation were going to be unattractive.*

*So I made a deal with the General. I said, "I'll stay to the last day
that ARD is independent; then I'm leaving." And that's what I did.*

Shane was joined at Palmer several months later by his former
ARD colleague, Bill Congleton, who had played a key role in launching DEC. Palmer raised upwards of $13 million from thirty-six limited
partners, including individuals, families, nonprofit institutions, and corporations. Though equal partners, Shane and Congleton continued to
play to their individual strengths by more or less sticking to their long-
standing ARD roles: Shane working mainly with existing portfolio
companies and Congleton sniffing out new investment opportunities.
Within three years, Palmer had invested $4.6 million in fourteen com-
panies, and was on the lookout for new and bigger opportunities.

In retrospect, Palmer was perhaps a little too cautious; much of the
firm's capital was not used in the first years of operation. Although
Palmer had a friendly relationship with both Greylock and T.A. Associates, Palmer never quite made it into the inner circle of the Boston
investment scene. This may have been partly due to Congleton's lack of
interest in building and maintaining the necessary political fences. Nevertheless, though Palmer didn't enjoy the spectacular success of a DEC-
type investment, the firm did have several big wins. The first of these
was Cintas, a uniform company that returned on a 100-to-1 basis.

Subtle competitive shadings soon emerged between the Boston
venture firms that had spun off from ARD. Greylock, under Elfers's
careful hand, was less interested in start-ups; Palmer was somewhat
more interested. T.A. Associates eventually began favoring later-stage
investments over start-ups, and later profited significantly from its participation in restructurings and leveraged buyouts.

But the overriding spirit of the day, in the intimate Boston venture
capital world, was cooperation and collegiality. All of the major players

knew all of the other major players. (Many had either a Harvard Business School or an ARD connection, or both.) They respected each other, and also respected each other's turf. When a deal started to come together, it was understood to be a Greylock deal, a T.A. Associates deal, or a Palmer deal, but the other firms often were invited in. These intimate ties connected not only the Boston venture capital firms, but also connected those firms with their counterparts in New York City.

OLD MEETS NEW IN NEW YORK

One of those counterpart firms was a new incarnation of one of the oldest venture traditions. For the first quarter-century or so after the end of World War II, Laurance Rockefeller had continued his informal (but successful) venturing efforts. In 1960, he and his three colleagues—including the legendary venturer Charles B. Smith—hired a well-traveled young Harvard M.B.A., Peter Crisp (class of 1960), to help make their operation run more smoothly. But it wasn't until 1969 that the Rockefellers decided to professionalize the family venture operation. As Crisp explains:

> *We felt we needed to act more quickly. We could no longer run around collecting checks from twelve family members. So we formed Venrock, with seven investments that were contributed by family members. Our total capital in 1969 was $7.5 million, of which $1.5 million was a call for additional capital.*

Venrock Associates continued Laurance Rockefeller's tradition of investments in aviation, instrumentation, and other pioneering fields. The limited partnership soon made good on its intention of getting into new technological arenas. Several of its first investments, including one in a new company called Intel, went into West Coast start-ups with a heavy technology component.

As a rule, the Rockefellers shunned publicity. Unlike other venture companies, most of which didn't mind having their successes celebrated publicly, Venrock rarely appeared in the pages of financial publications. For the most part, the patterns of the Rockefeller venture investments can only be inferred. When longtime Rockefeller associate and Venrock general partner Charles B. Smith died in February 1974, for example, pundits took note of the boards on which he had been serving at the time of his death: AVX Corp., Iomec, Playback Associates, Inc., Plasmachem Inc., Thermo Electron, and Ventron. He had previously served as a director of Electronic Specialty Company, Elron Electronics Industries Ltd., and Fansteel, Inc.

Another window on Venrock's investments opened in September of 1974, when Nelson Rockefeller's holdings were made public in connection with the Senate confirmation hearings on his nomination for the vice presidency. As *Venture Capital* magazine reported:

> *The clever reader could pick out many of the venture projects that the family has financed over the years . . . Autex, Cambridge Memories, Coherent Radiation, EOCOM, Data Science Ventures, Evans & Sutherland Computer, Intel, Iomec, Kaspar Instruments, New England Nuclear, Plasmachem, Scidata, Thermo Electron, UMF Systems . . . Worthington Biochemical Labs, and some others.*

As a rule, when Venrock distributed $10 to investing family members, the family put $2 back into Venrock to fund the next round of investments. (The exception came when small stakes were sold for cash.) When a security became marketable, it would be distributed to the family, who would use these low-basis stocks to meet their philanthropic commitments. But Venrock's very success in its first quarter-century of operations led to a major policy change in the mid-1990s. At that point, the Rockefellers' financial advisors suggested that family members had too high a percentage of their net worth in venture capital. Venrock's senior managers—including Peter Crisp and Ted McCourtney (M.B.A. '66), Anthony Sun (M.B.A. '79), and Ray Rothrock (M.B.A. '88)—then invited six leading educational institutions to join as limited partners in Venrock II. All accepted, thus expanding Venrock's base beyond its founding family.

Venrock's track record paints an compelling picture of the power of venture capital over the past thirty years. In that period, according to Peter Crisp, the partnership invested in 272 companies. Of these, 159 were clear winners, with gains of $1.9 billion. Another 71 were losers, generating losses of $93 million; the jury is still out on the re-maining 72. As of the end of 1999, these companies had aggregate rev-enues of $330 billion, and employed 1.3 million people. Of the 103 investments distributed by Venrock by the end of 1999, the value at the date of distribution was $1.5 billion. If held, that value at the end of 1999 would be $9.2 billion.

SPROUT TAKES ROOT

Also launched in New York in 1969 was the Sprout Capital Group, a venture partnership formed by the entrepreneurial investment banking firm of Donaldson, Lufkin & Jenrette, Inc.[4] One day in the late 1960s, DLJ executive vice president Richard M. Hexter was sitting in his New York office, dreaming of a venture capital fund that would not only allow DLJ to generate a superior investment return, but would also grow fu-ture investment banking clients for the firm. Hexter's office was filled with plants of all shapes and sizes, and he gradually began associating his vision with his office environment—hence the name "Sprout."

Although Hexter didn't carry his bright idea forward personally, the chairman and chief executive of DLJ Capital Group—John K. Cas-tle (M.B.A. '65)—did. Sprout Capital Group (later known as Sprout I, to distinguish itself from subsequent Sprout funds) was launched in late 1969 with $11.5 million in backing. It was the first venture fund di-rectly sponsored and controlled by an investment bank.

The concept of Sprout I evolved over the summer of 1969. Melvyn Kline, an early recruit, was responsible for the initial draft of the Sprout I projects, while Castle created the structure. Having had success with the partnership concept with many prior one-off deals, Castle applied this methodology to a portfolio of investments. The model was tax-free at the partnership level and primarily targeted in-stitutional investors and pension funds.

By September, Castle's team had begun to take shape. Stephen W. Fillo (M.B.A. '63) was among the initial recruits, L. Robert Johnson (M.B.A. '65)—who was drafted into the project from another division of DLJ—became involved in a number of the fund's investments, and Kenneth Yarnell (M.B.A. '69) also came on board.

Sprout I's initial $11.5 million was fully invested by mid-1972, and by the fall of that year, DLJ reported that Sprout had been generating a pretax compound growth rate of 23.6 percent. Meanwhile, Sprout II—formed in December 1971 with $18.2 million in capital—was also well launched. Its limited partners included the retirement plans of General Mills and Atlantic Richfield, several family trusts, and a number of foundations.

Although Sprout was a small operation—consisting of five full-time project managers as well as Castle and his two other general partners—it prided itself on digging deeply into proposed investments. A project manager presented a proposed investment to the general partners' committee. If the proposal was approved, the project manager then would continue to work closely with the portfolio company's management team.

The formula seemed to work: Only one of Sprout's first twenty-five investments went under. By 1972, three of Sprout's portfolio companies had gone public, and Sprout had an unrealized gain of $3.4 million on a total investment of $1.7 million. Sprout's 1970 investment in Media Networks grew at a 50 percent annual rate between 1970 and 1973, and its investment in Advanced Micro Devices returned on a ten-to-one basis.

By the time Sprout I went into liquidation in 1976, at the end of its seven-year lifespan, it had slightly underperformed expectations, returning profits of between 11 and 12 percent per year compounded, before fees. Viewed in the context of the times, however, this number is more impressive; when Sprout I was founded the Dow Jones was hovering around 1,000, but over the next several years it was down as much as 45 percent.

Sprout II, meanwhile, which came to life in a far more congenial economic climate, was outperforming its older brother substantially, generating returns of around 36 percent annually compounded (before management fees). Sprout II had several home runs, including Shugard Associates, a floppy disc company in which Sprout II invested half a million dollars in 1974. Within a year, Shugard was sold to Xerox Corporation for $40 million, of which Sprout's share was $20 million. Sprout's combined record was appealing enough to enable the same management team to raise an additional $20 million for Sprout III—including $14 million from investors in Sprouts I and II.

The Sprout story is retold here at length because it underscores a recurrent theme in the larger saga of New York venture capital. The Sprout funds were invested primarily in ongoing businesses that were undergoing some sort of shake-up, and only secondarily in start-ups. Because New York's financial traditions were so strong, and because such large pots of money were so close at hand, later-stage financing tended to predominate over early-stage investments, and financial engineering tended to predominate over other kinds of engineering.

In and of itself, this was neither good nor bad. But it was in marked contrast to what was then happening on the nation's other coast.

FUNDING THE VALLEY

One day in the summer of 1968, several months after the Davis & Rock partnership had dissolved amicably, Arthur Rock got a call in his San Francisco office from his old friend and camping buddy Bob Noyce.

In the decade since Rock had helped Noyce and his seven fellow refugees from William Shockley's lab set up Fairchild Semiconductor, all but two of the Fairchild Eight had left their company. Only Noyce and Gordon Moore remained with the organization, and both had done well. Noyce was now group vice president with the Fairchild parent organization, and Moore was head of Fairchild Semiconductor's R&D division. But both missed the pace and drama of the start-up environment, and once again were eager to break new ground. As an added incentive, an aggressive new company, National Semiconductor, was stealing away Fairchild's skilled technicians and its markets, and Fairchild seemed unable to stem the tide. Sherman Fairchild passed away, and the management of Fairchild Camera and Instrument did not want to award options to the employees in the semiconductor business, which Noyce and Moore felt essential to growing their business.

So now—as Noyce told Arthur Rock—it was time to move on. He and Moore wanted to go into business together again. They thought they had figured out a way to use semiconductors to make memory modules for computers. If they could drive the cost of semiconductor-based memory down dramatically, they could displace magnetic core memory devices. Coming in at the low end of the market—at, say, 64-bit or 256-bit memory—was especially tempting, since magnetic cores made no economic sense at that small scale.

So, Noyce asked: Was Rock willing to try to raise money for the new venture? Rock's answer came immediately: *yes.* Rock was in no sense a technician, and had no special insight into whether or not the semiconductor-memory idea was a good one. But he had enormous confidence in the abilities of Noyce and Moore, and that was enough. ("I never assess technology," Rock explains. "I always assess people.") He and Noyce agreed to get together and work out a business plan for the new company—a document that wound up being all of a page and a half. Rock explains:

> *This was before lawyers got into the act. The lawyers of today would never bless the kind of business plan that Bob and I came up with. Plans grow thicker every year, as the lawyers find more ways to put things in to prevent lawsuits. But with so much more institutional capital going into investing, maybe that has to be done.*

With this succinct document in hand, Rock called fifteen potential backers, and got fifteen acceptances. Now—like Bill Elfers back in Boston—Rock had the luxury of trying to put together a "portfolio" of investors who could bring complementary skills to the new venture. (Rock actually cut back some "allocations" to broaden the base of initial investors.) Venrock's Peter Crisp, another longtime friend of Rock's, later remarked that this may have been the only venture capital deal in history that was done by invitation only. Rock and Crisp went in for $300,000 each, both Noyce and Moore put in $250,000, and Rock raised another $1.9 million.

The infant company now had leaders, a product, and backers. But it still needed a name. Noyce and Moore initially favored NM Electronics, but were talked out of it on the basis that it sounded old-fashioned. Moore then suggested Integrated Electronics, which Noyce proposed to shorten to Intel. The new venture was launched on July 16, 1968.

Over the next three decades, Intel revolutionized the chip-based memory field. It also invented and developed the microprocessor: the "brains" that not only drive every PC in the world, but also direct the activities of countless other kinds of "smart" equipment, ranging from toasters to Toyotas. In less than fifteen years, Moore's $250,000 stake in Intel was worth more than $100 million. Once again, Arthur Rock had helped a team of brilliant technologists change the world— and had helped a lot of people get rich in the process. Rock reflected, "I knew a little about the memory business through my association with Electronic Memories, run by one of my HBS classmates. When he heard about the deal, he told me that I was nuts—there was no way semicon-ductors would replace cores. It turns out that if it weren't for semicon-ductors, it would take the entire world's population to string enough core memory for today's computers."

THE NEXT GENERATION

The Intel triumph, combined with the prior success of Davis & Rock and Sutter Hill Capital, opened the floodgates of West Coast venture capitalism in the early 1970s. Some individuals set themselves up in the Arthur Rock mode—more or less solo operators who liked to put together their own deals and pour themselves into the companies they were helping to grow. "I really never thought about growing my own company," Rock recalls. "I was a company builder only in the sense that I wanted to help those companies that I invested in to grow."

One of these solo artists was Pitch Johnson, Bill Draper's former partner in Draper & Johnson and Sutter Hill. Johnson's Palo Alto–based company—Asset Management Company, launched in 1972—was structured like Arthur Rock & Company up the road in San Francisco, except that Johnson managed his own money exclusively. Johnson also immersed himself in the affairs of the Stanford Business School, teach-ing that school's venture capital classes for a dozen years.

But other would-be venture capitalists were decidedly more inter-ested in institution building. Among these was Tom Perkins (M.B.A. '57), Hewlett-Packard's former director of corporate development and general manager of the Computer Division, and more recently a cofounder of University Laboratories, a private concern that was sold to Spectra-Physics. Perkins was a hot property in the venture field and was wooed by both Arthur Rock's junior partner and ARD back in Boston. ("He was an exceptional person," recalls John Shane.) Instead, Perkins hooked up with Gene Kleiner—an original member of the Fairchild Eight, and more recently a private investor—in 1972, and the two of them decided to set up shop together, combining their respective computer and semiconductor expertise. This particular season was a rough one for venture capital and for the financial markets in general; Kleiner, Perkins set out to raise $10 million, but gave up after assembling commitments for only $8.4 million.

They never had as much trouble raising money again. After enduring a series of less-than-stellar investments—and the demoralizing market crash of 1974—they scored their first coup in 1975, when they fronted $50,000 for another former Hewlett-Packard employee and Kleiner, Perkins limited partner, James Treybig, to study the market for so-called "fault-tolerant" computers. They liked what Treybig came up with and agreed to back his proposed venture: Tandem Computers. Perkins signed on as chairman of the board and was soon devoting up to half of his time trying to help Treybig make a go of it.

It was a huge win. Kleiner, Perkins later pointed to this happy-ending story as evidence that it had more or less invented the "incubation" of a start-up by a venture capital firm.

Only a year later, Kleiner, Perkins solidified its reputation as one of the hottest venture firms by backing the first genetic engineering company: Genentech. It was founded by a former Kleiner, Perkins partner, Robert Swanson, who resigned to chase his dream of commercializing recent advances in biology and genetic engineering. Kleiner, Perkins put up $100,000 for 25 percent of the company. By the third round of financing, a scant year and a half later, the company was valued at $11 million. And by the time Genentech went public in 1980, it was valued at $300 million—a 750 percent increase within four years.

In 1977, Kleiner and Perkins were joined by Frank J. Caufield (M.B.A. '68) and Brook Byers—Pitch Johnson's former understudy at Asset Management Company—and the name of the firm was formally changed to Kleiner Perkins Caufield & Byers (KPCB). The following year, the firm raised $15 million in its KPCB1 venture fund.

At the time, this was a staggering amount of money. But it was only the beginning of a transformation of the scale, pace, and very nature of venture capital—a transformation largely led by KPCB. The $15 million fund lasted two years. KPCB2, floated in 1980, raised $55 million—and this fund, too, lasted only two years. Then came KPCB3: a blockbuster at $150 million.

What lay behind this sea change? Beginning in January 1978, the Labor Department's ERISA Advisory Council started calling for changes in the "Prudence Rule" regulations (also known as the Prudent Man Rule) governing investments in small and new companies by pension plans. Prior to this time, the federal government had actively discouraged such investments on the grounds that they were too risky. Now, the Labor Department reversed course. The risks of such investments seemed to be outweighed by the potential gains. At the same time, government officials concluded, loosening the reins on pension funds might head off a nationwide shortfall of investment capital that was anticipated for the 1980s.

"The prudence of an investment decision," wrote the Labor Department in July 1979, in a ruling notable for the turgidity of its prose, "should not be judged without regard to the role that the proposed investment course of action plays within the overall plan portfolio." In other words, venture investments by pension plans were acceptable as long as they made sense in the context of a larger investment strategy. Within the year, pension funds became the single biggest supplier of new venture capital.

And suddenly, venture capital was a whole new business. It was light years removed from a young staffer at ARD trying to turn around a struggling shrimping business, or an Arthur Rock working with a Bob Noyce to write up a business plan for a company, or even a Tom Perkins working to help a Jim Treybig define a successful strategy. The new model of a venture firm was a highly professionalized, industry-oriented operation—one deploying huge amounts of capital; betting on technologies, rather than people; and in some cases even helping to develop those technologies.

One advantage to this approach was that it helped solve the chronic problem of succession: How does a venture capital firm survive the departure of a founder? Through scale and system, KPCB (for example) created a way for Tom Perkins and Gene Kleiner to retire in the late 1980s, making room at the top for the firm's rising stars, such as John Doerr (M.B.A. '76), who joined KPCB in 1980. Doerr's successes with Compaq, Netscape, At Home, Amazon.com, and Healtheon subsequently established him as one of the most successful venture capitalists in history.

Scale, therefore, has great benefits, and the KPCB pattern has been repeated at many other venture firms. New Enterprise Associates, for example, founded on both coasts in 1978 by Arthur Rock's former junior partner C. Richard Kramlich (M.B.A. '60), Frank Bonsal, and Chuck Newhall (M.B.A. '71), floated an initial fund of $8 million. Its eighth fund totaled $550 million.

But funds on this scale also pose challenges of their own. For one thing, they create a certain level of performance anxiety. A $500 million fund is expected to return $2 billion, more or less—no small assignment. And the emphasis today is necessarily on the *team*, rather than the individual. For these reasons and others, it is harder to find the kinds of intimate, long-term relationships that used to exist between venture capital firms and their portfolio companies. *Time* is all-important: the speed to deal completion necessarily accelerates year by year. The young venture capitalist may get enough hands-on time to watch the new building go up and see the parking lots fill up for the first time. But he or she is unlikely to attend meetings in the boardroom over a decade or more, watching a young CEO (and a young company) grow into the job. There simply isn't time.

CONSORTING WITH ANGELS

So is old-fashioned venture capital dead? Not exactly. Today we have "angels": wealthy individuals who invest their own money in new ventures and then—in many cases—invest themselves in the heart and soul of that enterprise. In a sense, the industry has come full circle. Like the Whitneys and Rockefellers of a half-century ago, wealthy and experienced individuals continue to help young people realize their entrepreneurial dreams. Angels work out of New York, Boston, and San Francisco—and also out of the dozens of other centers of venture capital that have sprung up in recent years, very often in proximity to pockets of high-tech entrepreneurship.

Today, for example, Arthur Rock is an angel of sorts, although he is quick to say that he is now far more likely to participate in other people's deals than to hunt up his own. Standing at his writing table in a downtown San Francisco office that affords a spectacular view of the Golden Gate Bridge, Rock skims the scores of unsolicited business plans that come over the transom (including the e-mail transom) every week. Still a Harvard Business School loyalist, he confesses to looking a little more carefully at ideas being promoted by fellow HBS alumni. ("When someone calls up and says, 'I'm an HBS graduate,' I'm liable to listen to that person a little longer than I would to someone else.") He also takes care to return calls from other angels whose opinions he respects—for example, Mike Markkula, the former Intel employee whose excited phone call a quarter-century ago eventually led Rock to invest in a tiny company called Apple Computer.

"If Mike calls," Rock says, with the slightest of smiles creasing his normally stern visage, "I'm very likely to return the call."

CHAPTER 6

Voting with Their Feet

IN THE SPRING OF 1962—a few years before Frank Tucker, Dick Dooley, and their younger colleagues embarked on the long process that ultimately led to the Owner/President Management Program— the Harvard Business School was engaged in a difficult process of self-evaluation. This was partly a result of the hotly debated recommendations of the 1961 *Planning for Change* report, described in chapter 4. As soon as tempers had cooled sufficiently, members of the various faculty factions (course heads, area chairs, and so on) sat down together to plot an institutional strategy. In local terms, the stakes were high. Pieces of courses, and maybe even whole courses, might be on the block.

Among the committees organized was one that was asked to examine the School's position regarding the very field Tucker and others were beginning to find so promising. The Ad Hoc Committee to Review the School's Work in Small and/or New Businesses was convened in part because of the impending retirement of Professor Windsor Hosmer. Hosmer's Small Manufacturing Enterprises course, introduced in 1958, was still in the early stages of its evolution, and now its chief designer was leaving his laboratory.

Only thirty-two students had enrolled in the first session of the course, but that was because Hosmer wanted to run the class as a seminar, and therefore hoped to limit enrollment to thirty. This cap was removed after a year, reimposed in the third year, and thereafter dropped. By the spring of 1962, sixty-three students were signing up for the course.

This was not a particularly impressive number. In the same period, for example, the Management of New Enterprises course (launched originally by Myles Mace, and taught in this period first by Paul Donham and later by Herbert F. Stewart) was averaging more than a hundred students per run, and sometimes attracted more than two hundred students.

On the other hand, something like a tenth of the second-year class was signing up to learn about entrepreneurship from Windsor Hosmer. The Harvard Business School faculty had long been sensitive to student interest, as reflected in course enrollment patterns. When students "voted with their feet," they helped shape the M.B.A. curriculum in critical ways.

Given Hosmer's impending retirement, his course surely would be dropped if the faculty did not take active steps to save it. Should the faculty take those steps?

PASSION WITHOUT STRUCTURE

To answer that question, the committee had to figure out (among other things) whether Hosmer was separable from his course. The School's history was full of examples of popular second-year courses that embodied the life's work of a unique individual, but which were unable to survive the departure of their inventors.

Who was Windsor Hosmer? His public notices were spare. "During the past few years," the alumni-oriented *Harvard Business School Bulletin* reported in a spring 1963 issue, "Professor Hosmer has been closely associated with the School's activities in the small business area. A number of recent Business School alums who, through preference, took jobs with small companies are former Hosmer students."

Hosmer came to the small-business field relatively late in life. Born in Riga, New York, in 1894, he graduated from Harvard College in 1918 and served in the ambulance corps with the French army in World War I. He received an M.B.A. from Harvard in 1921, taught Business Policy at HBS for two years, and then went back to his home state to teach economics at Hobart College in Geneva, New York. In 1931, he returned to Boston to accept a position on the HBS faculty.

Economics, particularly applied economics, was Windsor Hosmer's forte for many years. He was promoted to associate professor of accounting in 1932 and to full professor in 1937. In 1934, he achieved some measure of notoriety when he testified at a public hearing that the Massachusetts judicial system lacked adequate financial controls, and that public money was possibly being misspent. Hosmer had labored hard in advance of this hearing to track and make sense out of the judicial system's cash outflows. After three solid months of work, however, he still felt his estimate of the court system's real costs might be off by as much as $500,000 in either direction—an astounding margin of error for the relatively small Massachusetts judicial system of the 1930s. The courts, Hosmer argued forcefully, badly needed a modern system of accounting.

Hosmer published several accounting textbooks, and in 1939, his *Problems in Accounting* casebook was hailed as a "wealth of material" that was "carefully collected and marshalled." (The book received a mention in the "Notes and Comment" section of *The New Yorker*.) Throughout his career, Hosmer continued to apply his accounting expertise to solve problems encountered—or created—by large governmental bodies. In the 1950s, for example, he served as an advisor on accounting practices for the Atomic Energy Commission, which was then experiencing wrenching growth pains.

Through all of this, however, the questions closest to Hosmer's heart were those that pertained to small business. It was a field that Hosmer himself tilled as well as studied. In and around his academic responsibilities, Hosmer had established and helped manage two small New Hampshire–based companies. In an August 1955 letter to A. G. Bardes, a Milwaukee-based manufacturer, Hosmer explained that the arena of small manufacturing enterprises "is one which has interested me for 30 years, and in which I have had substantial experience as chairman of the board of the Richard D. Brew Co. and president of the Hosmer Machine and Lumber Co."

The challenge that Hosmer faced was to integrate his personal interest in small business with the curricular realities of the Harvard Business School. This meant first getting permission to put together a new second-year course—a permission that he secured in 1956. Hosmer then immodestly announced that he planned to offer to the School's M.B.A. candidates "the first major in [the administration of small business enterprises] ever given in a major university."

This was hyperbole; the School in fact offered no "majors." (Graduating students earned the Master of Business Administration degree, which was by design a generalist's training.) But Hosmer was by then working hard to develop the entrepreneurship course he would call Small Manufacturing Enterprises, and he saw the need for some hype. In a March 1956 letter to former and future colleague Myles Mace—Mace at the time was serving as vice president of Litton's Beverly Hills–based Electronic Equipment Division—Hosmer explained that he expected the course research to take two years, and that he planned to emphasize "the strategy of size"—in other words, the purported advantages of being small. He was fascinated by "what can be done with a well-conceived operation in an industry where the strategy of size is favorable and where a good management of five or six men can do a real job."

As he prepared for his course, Hosmer wrote to countless small companies, asking for the details of their enterprises. Cement companies, tool manufacturers, paper companies, potato growers, chemists, makers of plastic envelopes—all intrigued him, and the responses from many seemed to validate his notions about the "strategy of size." Hosmer evidently took pleasure in teasing out underlying patterns in a field that most of his colleagues scorned as either boring or unsystematic.

To the vice president of one small company (Alcon Labs, Inc.), for example, Hosmer wrote, "The very early period in industrial enterprises from the original conception and planning through the actual origin when one family or a group undertake to live on what the customers will pay and through the subsequent establishment and growth is extremely interesting. We haven't devoted enough attention to this subject here at the School and we haven't devoted enough to small as opposed to large enterprises." In another letter, Hosmer—citing 1951 statistics—pointed out that twice as many people in the country were employed by small manufacturing firms (ninety-nine employees or fewer) than were employed by General Motors, Ford, Chrysler, Studebaker-Packard, American Motors, AT&T, U.S. Steel, and Standard Oil Company combined.

Hosmer's research for his new course culminated in two products. The first was an article for the *Harvard Business Review* (November–December 1957), titled "Small Manufacturing Enterprises." The second was the course itself, launched in February 1958.

Although Windsor Hosmer embraced entrepreneurship with the enthusiasm of a youthful convert, he was already in his sixties, and close to retirement. He explicitly referred to his pursuit of this new-found passion as the final phase of his academic career. Arnold C. Cooper (D.B.A. '62), who wrote cases for Hosmer from 1959 to 1960, recalls his faculty sponsor:

> *His hair was snow white. He was very much at the end of his career. Always had stories to tell, but he'd had two heart attacks, and that slowed him down some. He would take the elevator instead of the stairs, and sometimes his voice would quaver. But he could still be very tough, and very determined.*

Hosmer put his determination to work on behalf of students who expressed an interest in finding jobs with small and entrepreneurial companies. He launched an individual campaign to bring HBS students and graduates together with appropriate smaller enterprises. He wrote letters to friends and colleagues, plugging his students' talents: "We have at this School a substantial number of men who do not want their careers in large corporations, and who have the pioneering instinct, the courage, and the stamina to seek careers in small manufacturing. This group includes some of our ablest men." He called on contacts in both industry and academia. In a June 1958 letter to a friend at the Carnegie Institute of Technology, for example, he implored his Carnegie Tech counterpart to spread the word among small to medium-sized manufacturing companies: Harvard M.B.A.'s want to work for *you*.

Hosmer's enthusiasm for matching his students up with smaller enterprises stemmed not only from his belief in the vital role played by such operations—and the high quality of management displayed by many of them—but also from the feedback he got from his former students. "I hated office politics," as one of them (a freelancing manufacturers' agent) wrote in a letter to Hosmer, "and was never very good at it. I'm delighted to be free from it. I have never done anything that I enjoyed more or found more absorbing, interesting, and satisfying." Another graduate and small-company employee emphasized the welcome unpredictability of small business: "I never know when I get here in the morning what I will be doing at ten o'clock, except that I will be doing what has to be done. I love it, and would not trade it for a job in a big company for anything."

Hosmer seems to have felt the same way about his own job. As his course took shape along satisfactory lines, he began collaborating on a textbook with casewriter Arnold Cooper and recently arrived colleague Frank Tucker. The result, *Small Business Management*, was published in 1966, and eventually was adopted by instructors at more than thirty universities in the United States and abroad. And while course enrollments were far from overwhelming, they were respectable. Hosmer had reason to believe that his message about the importance and relevance of small business was getting heard.

In retrospect, though, the *content* of that message seems somewhat unclear. Hosmer obviously felt that small businesses were important in and of themselves, and that they also could serve effectively as a metaphor for larger enterprises. "While the course is limited to small manufacturing firms," he noted, "all administrative functions within these firms are dealt with. The course is, in a sense, one in Business Policy concentrated within this segment of the economy."

The "small business as metaphor" notion was sound enough, up to a point. In fact, some of the School's most successful cases over the years have used the problems of a small business as a jumping-off point for a discussion of larger issues. But another foundation of Hosmer's course—the "strategy of size" concept—was less solid. Hosmer wrote in his first course description that the course would "examine the hypothesis that we may have in manufacturing in the next 20 years a reversal of the trend toward bigness of the last 90 years."

This hypothesis ultimately proved untenable; it was quietly dropped from the revised course description that was published only two years later. "He was a very nice guy," Myles Mace observed many years later, "but he didn't know what the hell he was talking about in *that* statement."

Hosmer's story is included here at length because, in a very real sense, he embodied much of what was both good and bad about the early decades of entrepreneurial studies. Hosmer had passion and commitment in abundance—but he lacked the kind of organizing hypothesis around which he could structure a successful field of study. Among his fellow faculty members, he won no converts, and trained no successor. When advancing age finally forced him to leave his course in 1963, no one stepped forward to carry on.

THE COMMITTEE'S VERDICT: YES

The Ad Hoc Committee to Review the School's Work in Small and/ or New Businesses, set up as part of the larger curriculum review of 1962, was well aware of Windsor Hosmer's recent struggles to help put small business on the School's agenda.

But was finding a faculty successor to take over Hosmer's course worth the effort? Should this course (and for that matter, Mace's course, with its substantially higher enrollments) be continued? Did the issues of entrepreneurship constitute a field distinctive enough to warrant specialized courses? More generally, were entrepreneurial ventures and careers in small business rewarding and satisfying enough to justify steering Harvard M.B.A.'s in that direction?

After a year of investigation, the committee announced that its answer to all of these questions was yes.

The committee concluded, in a report delivered during the spring of 1963, that Hosmer's course (and for that matter, Mace's) deserved an extended life. One reason was the enrollments cited earlier: Student demand for courses in entrepreneurship was consistently high. The students were, in the HBS tradition, "voting with their feet." Assuming minimal overlap between the Hosmer and Mace courses, about a quarter of second-year students each year (some 150 out of approximately 600 students) were signing up to acquire the generalist's skills that were required of the entrepreneur.

The committee noted, too, that in 1963, many M.B.A. candidates at Harvard had chosen to market themselves to smaller companies, rather than simply allowing themselves to be slotted into the jobs being offered on campus by larger companies. These students were making a special effort to reach out to enterprises—mostly small—that could not afford to visit and recruit on campus.

Another key factor in the committee's reasoning was that alumni-sponsored surveys had shown that graduates working in start-ups and small businesses were often more satisfied than their counterparts at large companies (and, for the most part, they were earning at least as much). The class of 1949, for example, was then en route to being celebrated by journalists as the "Class the Dollars Fell On." Translated from journalese, this meant, roughly, "the class that boasted an amazingly large number of CEOs of huge companies." But in response to one survey, about 60 percent of this seemingly Establishment-oriented class of 1949 said that being a success meant "being my own boss." More than a third of them urged students to "work for yourself, not for somebody else." Only 16 percent recommended working for a large company.

For these and other reasons, the committee concluded that the Hosmer and Mace courses should not be dropped. It also recommended that active research and course development in the field of new and small businesses should be supported and encouraged.

Frank Tucker (in an article in the October 1963 *Bulletin*) wrote that HBS students should rejoice over these clear and forceful recommendations. He was firmly convinced, he wrote, that many students came to HBS with a strong interest in small business—only to have that interest "brain-washed out of them." Too many of them, Tucker wrote, had overlooked or missed out on "opportunities for satisfying and profitable careers in small business." But with the School now committed to keeping two entrepreneurship courses firmly in place, and with research opportunities for faculty opening up in the field, it seemed more likely than ever that HBS students would be able to explore whatever avenue interested them, including entrepreneurship.

STUDENTS AND SMALL BUSINESS

The *Bulletin* was distributed to HBS alumni, and they were the primary audience for Tucker's rhetorical call for celebration. As a result, few HBS students would have come across Tucker's call to arms. But on their own, even without encouragement from faculty members, HBS students were already taking active steps to ensure that entrepreneurship would not be ignored at the Harvard Business School.

In the fall of 1958, for example, 150 second-year students—25 percent of the class, a percentage more or less identical to that taking second-year entrepreneurship courses—had chipped in $15 apiece to start a unique enterprise: the Student Small Business Placement Program (SSBPP). This was primarily student-financed and student-run, and as such, it was unique. In a laudatory January 1959 article, the *Boston Globe* reported that "no other business school student body has initiated such a program."

The SSBPP was designed to complement the ongoing activities of the School's placement office. Not surprisingly, this office concentrated its efforts on large enterprises, which had a proven track record when it came to hiring graduating M.B.A.'s. Large companies were the placement office's strongest allies: Their representatives showed up when they were supposed to, hosted off-campus receptions, made attractive offers to HBS students, and helped keep the placement office's key statistics (percentage of graduating students employed, starting salaries, etc.) impressively high. In many cases, these companies had relatively recent HBS grads among their ranks, and these young men, obviously well versed in the needs and expectations of Harvard Business School students, were particularly effective recruiters.

Smaller companies, by contrast, usually couldn't afford to visit the campus or host receptions. Many lacked even the most rudimentary materials to get their case in front of HBS students, and few had HBS alumni available to make pitches on their behalf. And many owners of small businesses either assumed that a recruitment effort on the HBS campus would fail to yield results, or—perhaps worse—that it might yield a Harvard M.B.A. who would be far too full of himself to fit comfortably into a small-business context.

All of this meant that HBS students had to *actively* demonstrate their interest in working for entrepreneurial businesses. Opening a network of "area chairmen" across the country, the SSBPP undertook "regional employment campaigns." SSBPP members distributed resumes to enterprises of interest and sent program brochures and personal letters to HBS alumni, small-business managers, banks, professional placement firms, manufacturers' associations, and SBICs—to any person or organization, in fact, that might help the SSBPP make productive connections. Twice a year, in December and March, SSBPP representatives flew to major cities across the country and endeavored in person to match program participants with companies. The program also sponsored on-campus discussions and workshops. In March of 1963, for example, the SSBPP called a meeting to introduce itself to new students, who then observed while second-year students brainstormed about how to prepare for interviews with small firms.

This particular late-winter meeting ended with a question-and-answer period that was presided over by Professor Windsor Hosmer. Hosmer, then on the verge of retirement, had served as an informal advisor to SSBPP since its formation. In this realm, too, Hosmer's impending retirement raised important questions. Although the SSBPP had more than proven its abilities as an effective advocacy group, having a well-connected faculty member in its corner was a great asset. Who on the faculty would step forward to help the School's entrepreneurially minded students help themselves?

STEPPING FORWARD

Several candidates were already on the scene, although not specifically in the context of the SSBPP. One of these was Professor Marty Marshall, who—although then fully occupied teaching two sections of Marketing—was impressed by the continuing student interest in small and growing businesses. "In the late 1950s," he recalls, "we had all these students who wanted to learn more about entrepreneurship. I decided that I wanted to help."

Marshall was unhappy that, although these entrepreneurially oriented M.B.A. candidates were active and creative in their outreach efforts, they received only limited faculty guidance. Windsor Hosmer and Frank Tucker were doing what they could, but demand was far exceeding supply. And although Marshall had no entrepreneurship course or other official peg to hang his interest on, he figured that he could make a contribution on an informal basis. One day, while meeting with a delegation of the students who were lobbying most persistently for new ways to study smaller business, Marshall made an unusual offer. "Let's meet every Wednesday," he suggested. "We'll have lunch in Kresge, and we'll talk about what interests you."

Thus began what Marshall calls his "ad hoc seminar." By design, the "class" would never show up in a formal course announcement. Instead, it was a freewheeling forum—a context for discussing the implications of working in small companies, and working for oneself. In the parlance of a later day, this was a "small business support group." There were no prerequisites, other than an interest in entrepreneurial businesses.

Attendance at Marshall's forum tended to reflect the rhythms of the larger School calendar. "We usually started every year with thirty or more students coming to the first few meetings," Marshall says. "And then, particularly after January, the group would shrink down to a core group of four or five people." This reflected not only midyear burnout, but also the shifting interests of students. Inevitably, some students decided that, at least in the early years of their business careers, they were better off betting on large companies.

January was also the beginning of the on-campus recruiting season. This was the season, Marshall recalls with amusement, when he "went on alert." Large corporations were setting up shop on campus and making seductive offers of employment. Marshall suggested an informal decision rule for those Wednesday seminar attendees who were serious about carving out a future in small business: *no on-campus interviews*. "Believe me," he warned them, "you'll get sucked in by those corporations." Over time, Marshall recalls, adherence to this guideline emerged as the best way to distinguish committed entrepreneurs-in-the-making from those who were merely dabbling.

And to those who established themselves as hard-core, Marshall offered substantive assistance. "As things got rolling," he explains, "I'd ask the students to bring in proposals as to what they would do when they left the Business School." This was, in effect, an informal system for drawing up business plans, guided mainly by Marshall but also by student members of the group. Bad ideas got weeded out; good ideas got improved.

Marshall also drew on his outside-world contacts to match graduating students with appropriate opportunities. One student, for example, had demonstrated leadership potential and a commitment to entrepreneurship, but failed to come up with a compelling business concept. Marshall suggested to this student that he contact bankers for leads on companies in trouble that were in search of "heroes." Through a Chicago bank, the student found just such a company in a town in Nebraska. "Within a year," Marshall recalls, "he had purchased half the company and established himself in a splendid small-town life and career."

A somewhat more roundabout example is provided by Lloyd Cotsen, a member of the M.B.A. class of 1957. "I had him in my first-year Marketing class," remembers Marshall, "and then he vanished."

Where had he gone? Halfway through his business training, it turned out, Cotsen had detoured to Yale, where he earned a master's degree in archaeology. Then he came back to Harvard. "Now I've got to make some money," he told Marshall.

Cotsen joined the group of entrepreneurial students who lunched with Marshall every Wednesday. Together, the group spent many hours mulling over the opportunities and challenges of risk taking in business.

After receiving his M.B.A. Cotsen went to work for Natone, his father-in-law's company in Los Angeles. Natone was a small cosmetics company. Founded in 1930, it began by providing specialty items to beauty salons serving members of the film industry, and then aimed its products at a more general consumer market in the 1940s. One of Natone's most unique products was a bar of clear, mild glycerine soap. Emanuel Stolaroff, the company's founder, had discovered this soap in the mid-1950s while on a business trip to Europe. In 1957, he decided to place this fledgling division of Natone in the hands of son-in-law Lloyd Cotsen.

At that time, the Neutrogena soap bar accounted for $80,000 of the company's $500,000 in sales. Over the next few years, Lloyd Cotsen built Neutrogena into a brand name that could stand on its own. Among other steps, Cotsen retained Marty Marshall to come to California and consult with the company on the process of developing the new brand. In subsequent months and years, Marshall continued to provide advice on advertising and pricing. "Lloyd would send me cases of Neutrogena, and I'd give it out to the secretaries at the Business School and ask them what they thought," says Marshall. "My connection to the company was informal—I was a background advisor—but it was great fun."

Before long, Neutrogena soap demanded greater attention. Cotsen founded the Neutrogena Corporation in 1961 and took it public in 1973. Effective marketing, based on a super-clean image and the first labels to boast "dermatologist recommended" products, reached out to consumers across the country. By the time Cotsen sold his company to Johnson & Johnson in 1994, he had achieved sales of more than $300 million.

This kind of Cinderella outcome was the exception, rather than the rule. "I would say that very few of those students went out and became huge success stories," Marshall says. "But most of them ended up in small companies, many went into business for themselves, and most of them did pretty well." More to the point, Marshall concludes, these M.B.A.'s "did what they were dying to do."

REVERSE RECRUITING

In the fall of 1963, one hundred second-year M.B.A. candidates signed up for the Student Small Business Placement Program, or SSBPP, believing (as reported in a *Bulletin* student-viewpoint article) that smaller businesses would provide them with interesting challenges, responsibilities, opportunities, and a high degree of personal satisfaction.

True, the SSBPP was by then losing its friend and advisor, Windsor Hosmer, who had retired from the classroom that fall. But the SSBPP had reason to look forward with confidence: More than 15 percent of the graduating class was committed to careers in entrepreneurship.

An article in *Business Week* about the SSBPP brought in twenty job offers from small companies in the late spring of 1966. By then, the SSBPP (now in its eighth year, and boasting a membership of 130) had twenty-one area chairmen working ten distinct geographical areas.

Celebrity inspired a new tactic. In the fall of 1966, the SSBPP placed an unusual ad in the *Wall Street Journal*: "Several Harvard M.B.A.'s, with varied backgrounds and training, desire eventual control and ownership of small to medium sized enterprises. Prefer challenging, demanding opportunities."

At least fifty responses came in. The students were encouraged to invest in franchises such as a specialty junkyard and a popcorn vending machine business. A new invention—the "collapsible one-room house," intended as competition for the pup tent—was offered for a mere $20,000. Management opportunities were offered by companies dealing in medical appliances, computer components, burlap bags, and steel.

Through the 1960s and 1970s, the student-run placement program continued to conduct "reverse recruiting." The effort was now almost twenty years old, and had been widely imitated. (By the spring of 1967, business school students at Chicago, Columbia, Stanford, and Wharton had all started similar placement programs.) While the name of the program changed over the years—from SSBPP to other equally cumbersome monikers (such as "HBS Students Seeking Careers in Small Business")—its goals remained the same. Many of its tactics, having proved successful, were repeated and elaborated upon. In the fall of 1978, for example, more than 250 M.B.A. students with an interest in working in small business "passed the hat" and chipped in $20 apiece. The resulting $5,000 was spent on a *Wall Street Journal* ad (appearing in December) that encouraged the owners and managers of smaller enterprises to consider Harvard Business School students for both summer and full-time jobs. Within weeks, more than 270 companies responded.

DEMANDING MORE

Beginning in 1963, Frank Tucker took over Small Manufacturing Enterprises from the retiring Windsor Hosmer. In the winter term of that year, Tucker also took on the responsibility of teaching Management of New Enterprises, the course originated by Myles Mace and taught by a succession of instructors in the intervening decade and a half.

Tucker taught both courses for the next six years. In that span of time, enrollments in Small Manufacturing Enterprises more than tripled (to an average of almost 170 students per course). More students took Management of New Enterprises than ever before, and the numbers went up relentlessly every year (from 223 in 1963–1964 to 318 in 1968–1969). In his last year of teaching, Tucker taught a total of

479 students. Even allowing for overlap, Tucker in many years was teaching entrepreneurship to between one-third and two-thirds of the second-year class.

Like Hosmer before him, Tucker also logged countless extra hours helping students think through the challenges of entrepreneurship, and advocated for these entrepreneurial students in the ears of key School administrators. As the faculty advisor to the students' New Enterprise Club, for example, he urged the School to devote "more attention to student and alumni placement in small business." He pointed out that as of 1965, the nation's supply of small enterprises was showing a net increase of 50,000 a year, and asked pointedly if the School's priorities reflected that reality.

Also like Hosmer, Tucker worked his own networks on behalf of his students. Ever attentive to matchmaking possibilities, Tucker maintained companion files of entrepreneurs (looking for financing) and investors (looking for opportunities), hoping to make a match now and then.

For all of these reasons, Tucker's retirement in 1969 was a blow. But student enrollment patterns strongly suggest that student interest in entrepreneurship was increasing year by year, and that this enthusiasm was more or less independent of whichever professor was standing in the pit of an amphitheater classroom in Aldrich. Tucker himself never received particularly high student ratings—one colleague later commented that Tucker remained a "green-eyeshade, financial type" throughout his teaching career—but the students kept coming. In the spring of 1969, Tucker's last year, the *Bulletin* described Management of New Enterprises as "one of the most popular second-year electives."

A 1970 Student Association survey showed that more than 70 percent of first-year students, and an even greater number of second-year students, planned to seek careers in small businesses. That winter, the School's two courses on entrepreneurship were so popular that "students must register early for them or be turned away." A group of M.B.A. candidates who launched a search for international small-business opportunities were able to raise thousands of dollars to finance their efforts. The trend only intensified in the middle and later 1970s. According to the March–April 1975 *Bulletin*, the campus was populated with "substantial numbers of M.B.A. students who are now actively seeking jobs with small enterprises." Surveys from this same period were suggesting that a majority of Harvard Business School alumni who were twenty to twenty-five years out of school were working in small business.

Dean Lawrence Fouraker took note of this phenomenon in a "From the Dean" letter published in the March-April 1978 *Bulletin*. Although (as Fouraker explained) about 10 percent of the CEOs in the country's largest industrial and financial corporations were Harvard M.B.A.'s, it was also true that for every *one* of those CEOs there were *fifty* Harvard M.B.A.'s heading up smaller organizations such as banks, insurance companies, small manufacturing firms, newspapers, and retail enterprises. "We should take a new look, and a continuing look, at the curriculum," wrote Fouraker, "to make sure that the problems of small business and starting new ventures will not be neglected."

The fact remained, however, that it had been two decades since a new course in entrepreneurship had been added to the curriculum. And now, based on the state of the faculty, the entire field of entrepreneurship appeared to be in danger of abandonment at HBS—despite overwhelming student interest. The manufacturing-oriented entrepreneurship course originated by Hosmer had passed from Tucker's hands to Dick Dooley's, but only briefly; in 1970, the course was renamed Management of Small Enterprises: Operating Problems and Strategies, and soon hit hard times. ("When a course changes its name a lot," as one senior faculty member once commented, "that course is in trouble.") An odd assortment of older and younger faculty members was called upon to teach the course, which began to resemble an unwanted child.

Myles Mace's course, now called Management of Small Enterprises: Starting New Ventures, fared somewhat better, at least at first. This was primarily because it captured the imagination of a young assistant professor named Patrick Liles.

Almost by stealth, Liles—a Louisiana-born graduate of Harvard College who received his M.B.A. from the Business School in 1964 and his D.B.A. in 1970—sparked a quiet revolution in the School's entrepreneurship offerings. According to his friend and colleague Howard Stevenson, "Pat took a course that had become reasonably dull and turned it into one that focused on *deal making*. Mace's course, over time, had become like a mini–Business Policy course: Here is a small business. How do you manage problems in the in-box? But look at Pat's book: *New Business Ventures and the Entrepreneur*. It's about deals. It's about making offers, about pricing, about how you bid, things like that. This intrigued the students."[1]

Liles shifted the focus of the course away from the problems of operation. As Stevenson notes, he encouraged his students to concentrate on *how to make deals*, and how to understand the perspectives of the various players involved. This shift was accomplished in part through sleight of hand. "The suggestion that a newly coined assistant professor, as Pat was in 1970, might start a *new* course would have been unacceptable," Stevenson explains. "On the other hand, it was perfectly OK for him to say he was just differentiating his version of this course from other versions that might be out there. So he put a colon in the name, added a second name, and pretty soon the course became known by its second name: Starting New Ventures."

Why would a talented young assistant professor, working in one of the most popular fields at the School, move so cautiously? The answer lies in academic traditions. Core business school subjects—marketing, accounting, finance, and even fairly recent arrivals like organizational behavior—had well-established career paths for young academics to follow. There were conferences to attend, journals to get published in, mentors to call upon for help and guidance, and colleagues around the country to collaborate with. None of this was true for the field of entrepreneurship, which most business schools didn't even offer as a formal subject. Entrepreneurship, to most academics, was too general, too broad, and too hard to systematize and study. As one HBS professor once put it, entrepreneurship was an intellectual onion: After peeling away layer after layer, you'd get to the center, and there'd be nothing there but you—crying. "Pat was told," says Stevenson, "that entrepreneurship was not a good place for him to be, if he wanted a successful academic career. It was not yet mainstream enough."

Liles taught Starting New Ventures twice a year for three years (1970–1973) and met with significant success. Students loved him. Nevertheless, heeding the counsel of senior faculty advisors, he left the field of entrepreneurship to pursue other, more "mainstream" academic interests. His withdrawal from the teaching of entrepreneurship only underscored the unspoken rap on the subject: that it was a dead end, likely to be fatal to the tenure hopes of anyone who took it up. Both Windsor Hosmer and Frank Tucker had championed the cause at the ends of their careers. In fact, no one since Myles Mace had gambled on entrepreneurship as a young faculty member. With the unhappy example of Pat Liles fresh in people's minds, who would now risk stepping up to the plate?

RISK TAKERS IN QUIET NEIGHBORHOODS

The truth is, several individuals already had stepped up, in two separate fields. But the terminology they used, as they studied and taught issues related to entrepreneurship, was deceptively off-center.

One of these individuals was Professor James Reiser Bright, who was fascinated by a subject of great interest to entrepreneurs, investors, and general managers alike: technology and innovation. Bright's Technological Innovation course was first offered at HBS in the fall of 1964, and continued as a fall-term offering for several years. In the 1967–1968 school year, Bright taught the course in both the fall and the spring.

His classes explored the ways in which inventions and discoveries come to light and how they can be turned into marketable new products. The course, renamed Management of Technical Innovation in the fall of 1971, passed into the hands of Richard Rosenbloom and Modesto Maidique. The course remained in the second-year curriculum until 1984. For nineteen of the twenty-two semesters the course was available, however, the number of students enrolled was fewer than a hundred (and sometimes was as low as a few dozen). Perhaps because things "technical" did not yet appeal to a broad enough group of HBS students—the Web and Internet were still far in the future—the course did not gather momentum or generate offspring.

The other off-center field, which ultimately proved far more important to the long-term health of entrepreneurship at the Harvard Business School, was real estate.

This story begins with a low-profile course that appeared in the spring of 1967. Professor Phil David's Urban Land Development course originated as a seminar aimed primarily at doctoral candidates. In response to heavy pressure from M.B.A. students, however, David's low-profile course was pushed to center stage the following year. In the spring of 1968, 150 M.B.A. candidates (and a lone D.B.A. candidate) sat themselves down for instruction in the vagaries of urban land development. The number rose to 210 in the following fall.

What was going on here? Urban Land Development, while not designed explicitly for entrepreneurs, turned out to cover precisely the kind of ground that a budding real estate mogul would want covered. As the course catalog put it, "The problems of site acquisition, planning, zoning, financing, construction, rental and sale are considered, together with the relationship of the project to the social, political, and demographic forces influencing its market."

David was a skilled and popular teacher, and he taught about *deals*. M.B.A. students flooded the course, year after year. Almost 200 enrolled in the spring 1969 course, 209 signed up in the fall of that year, and 250 in the following spring.

After not offering the course in the fall of 1971, David passed the torch to a young assistant professor named Howard Stevenson. Then only three years out of the D.B.A. program and far from being an expert in the real estate field, Stevenson bravely faced a class of 187 second-year students in the spring of 1972.

"This course focuses on the general management problems of the real estate and shelter industry," Stevenson wrote in the course catalog. "Specific attention is given to financial analysis, market analysis, negotiations, financial sources, and the government's role. During the course, various viewpoints are assumed, including the developer; financial institutions as investors and managers of real estate holdings; [and] individuals considering real estate as an investment medium."

Years later, Stevenson admits to experiencing some trepidation as he ventured into real estate. "One of the scariest moments of my life," he says, "was when I walked into that classroom to teach real estate for the first time." Nevertheless, student response to Stevenson was enthusiastic, and in the early 1970s, real estate was a hot field. In the second run of the course, Stevenson and real estate together attracted 303 takers. Stevenson kept tinkering with his invention, looking for ways to make it more interesting, challenging, and systematic. Among other key steps, he recruited William Poorvu, a local real estate developer and investor, to help design and teach the course. (Poorvu had already done a stint at the School in the late 1960s, but had decamped to teach a real estate course at the Harvard Graduate School of Design.) Together, they retooled the offering and renamed it Real Property Asset Management for the fall 1973 semester.

Stevenson, like Poorvu, brought an intense personal interest in real estate to the course. But more important, he concentrated on the underlying patterns. What was different about real estate? What made it special? "I was thirty-one years old," he recalls. "I had done my doctorate. I had looked at service businesses like investment banking. I was struck by the fact that in those fields, you can make great money, but you have to do things *every day*. If you stop doing them today, there will be no income tomorrow. There must be businesses, I said to myself, where if you do something today, it pays off tomorrow and tomorrow and tomorrow. Right about that time, I decided assets were a pretty good thing."

In the spring of 1973, Stevenson taught a seminar called Real Property Asset Management (RPAM). When he taught it again in the spring of 1974, he gave it a new name (Real Property Asset Development) to avoid confusion with his retooled version of Phil David's course. Henceforth, students wanting to take Stevenson's Real Property Asset Development seminar (RPAD: "designed for students intending to specialize in the management of companies either owning or developing real property assets") first had to complete Real Property Asset Management.

Why are these acronyms of interest, a quarter-century later? Because according to Stevenson, RPAM and RPAD were direct precursors to many of today's courses in entrepreneurship. They were systematic, and they used *frameworks* to help explain the dynamics of an industry. Windsor Hosmer struggled in large part because he lacked such frameworks; Stevenson and Poorvu built on a strong conceptual foundation.

These frameworks have proven remarkably durable. "We used an intellectual scheme," he explains, "that is similar to the one that underlies today's courses in entrepreneurial finance, for example. We said that a successful real estate venture depends on the successful bringing together of people, property, deal, and context. In the Finance course, I think the words that are used are people, opportunity, deal, and context. So there's more than a little overlap."

Key to this framework was the real estate developer's time-honored tradition of using other people's money to make a deal work. In a sense, it was a distillation of the entrepreneurial challenge: perceiving and responding to opportunity despite resource constraints, and *minimizing one's own risks*. As Stevenson explains:

> *In real estate, you're like every other entrepreneur—you almost never start off with all the resources assembled. You say: I see a piece of property. I don't have the money. But I want it anyway. How can I get it? Let's see: I could get an option on the property. Then I could get a tenant on a prelease basis. Then I could get an architect to pull together some designs. And then I could ask the bank for a construction loan— and so on, and so on. In other words, you go through all the steps any entrepreneur goes through, as he or she puts together a deal.*

William Sahlman—now Stevenson's colleague, but in 1975 a somewhat bored second-year M.B.A. student—recalls RPAM as "simply the best integrated course I took at Harvard Business School." Students in the class had to examine every aspect of a real estate venture: the people involved, their incentives and past history, the environmental and regulatory context, the available (or accessible) resources, and the nature of the property involved. "You had to try to integrate all of those factors in the context of the present," Sahlman says, "and then look into the future to decide what made sense."

In Sahlman's opinion, few HBS courses offered this kind of integrated approach in the mid-1970s. Few offered the opportunity to work with "a project you could get your arms around." The companies studied in Business Policy—the course that for many years had been billed as the integrative device in the second year—were nearly all *Fortune* 500–class enterprises: complex, multilayered operations with problems that inevitably had to be greatly simplified in order to be presented in the confines of a twenty-page case. A real estate deal, by contrast, could fit comfortably within those same twenty pages and still retain much of its totality and complexity. "The way those deals and situations were described," recalls Sahlman, "you couldn't *help* but get the point. You understood that you couldn't do *anything* alone. You had to tap into these various resources: people, capital, property, regulatory, whatever."

Sahlman sees Stevenson's broad, integrated approach as "the fundamental core" of many courses that followed—and guesses that it must also have been at the core of successful entrepreneurship courses in the past. "It's probably what Myles Mace was teaching in 1947," he ventures. "And it certainly was a part of what Doriot was teaching in Manufacturing: an integrated, multiperspective approach to business. It carries forward in all of our courses today."

There was another factor, too. Bill Sahlman recalls being as impressed with Howard Stevenson the person as he was with the RPAM course. Stevenson was both demanding and flexible. In and out of class, moreover, Stevenson impressed Sahlman as someone who was remarkably unafraid to show vulnerability. "There was a very human side to him," Sahlman says. "He would share his mistakes with us. I remember that he had purchased a large piece of property in Lincoln for the purpose of subdividing it, only to discover that it didn't percolate. Here he was, teaching us real estate, and he was stuck with this piece of land that, shall we say, wasn't going to support other households. He shared this with us, and I've got to say, it absolutely differentiated him from lots of other people around the campus."

YET ANOTHER DEPARTURE

Howard Stevenson and William Poorvu together (and at times, Poorvu alone) continued to teach RPAM through the fall of 1977. In the spring of 1978, Stevenson guided fifty-eight students through his RPAD seminar—for the last time. On his own initiative, he was planning to leave the School.

It was, in a sense, a new version of an old story. Entrepreneurship courses commanded a huge following among students, but had almost no stature among academics. Against long odds, Stevenson was granted tenure as "a real estate guy"—the first one at HBS to be so honored. He had legions of admiring students and young alumni, but no colleagues (other than the part-time Poorvu). Suspicions about real estate as a legitimate field of inquiry lurked just below the surface. "In the process of the uncertainty of tenure," says Stevenson, "you want to understand what your options are. I spent a lot of time talking with senior faculty." And even though he ultimately was awarded tenure, he continued to hear discouraging commentaries. Immediately after his promotion to tenure, he recalls, a senior colleague took him aside and suggested that it was time for Stevenson to "start doing something important."

Frustrated by this attitude on the part of his colleagues and convinced that he would have few opportunities to make a real contribution in the real estate field at the Harvard Business School, Stevenson packed his bags. He took a seat on a board of a paper company in Springfield, Massachusetts, and this quickly turned into a full-time commitment.

Real estate soldiered on, now with William Poorvu alone at the helm. (In 1982, the School recognized Poorvu's contributions by awarding him the little-used title of adjunct professor; he later became the first part-time professor in the School's history to hold an endowed professorship.) But the larger field of entrepreneurship at Harvard Business School fell into a slump. For the next four years, starting in the fall of 1979, only two courses were available. Pat Liles's course, Starting New Ventures, remained on the books, but every year a different member of the faculty took it on. All too often in those years, the course catalog listed the instructor for Starting New Ventures as TBA: *to be announced.*

Nobody, it seemed, was eager to step into the shoes that Pat Liles and Howard Stevenson had vacated.

CHAPTER 7

A Constellation Appears

FOR MANY CHILDREN of the 1950s, outer space was the enduring fascination of childhood. Standing in the dark on suburban lawns across America in the first week of October 1957, they looked heavenward with their parents as the USSR's 184-pound Sputnik satellite silently sailed the night skies. Most never forgot the experience. Some never outgrew the fascination.

Three of those children, in later life, wrote the story that is told in this chapter.

One year after Sputnik, as one of many steps taken by the U.S. government to counter the perceived Soviet threat in the sky, the National Aeronautics and Space Administration (NASA) was created. But the Russians seemed always to be first, in those early years: the first dog in space, the first man to orbit the earth, the first multiperson spacecraft, the first woman in space. Americans waited for signs that their country could compete successfully in this strange new environment. One bitter disappointment followed another, including a string of aborted missions and a fatal fire on the launchpad that killed three of America's first-generation astronauts.

But those impressionable children of the '50s kept the faith. They drank up Stanley Kubrick's *2001: A Space Odyssey*, and waited. And waited some more. Eventually, their faith began to be rewarded. Overcoming long odds, the United States inched its way toward the moon. The Russians, meanwhile, fell behind, eventually abandoning the space race in favor of orbital endurance records and other more prosaic accomplishments. American technology, having fallen into disrepute in the dark days of Sputnik, was again triumphant. By the time Neil Armstrong took his famous step onto the moon's surface in 1969, Americans could afford to be generous in victory. This wasn't an act of colonization or conquest, they announced; this was a "giant leap for mankind."

And when the moon turned out to be an even more barren, forbidding, and uninteresting place than anticipated, some Americans (although now in much smaller numbers) looked beyond it. They dreamed of permanent space stations in orbit, beaming benign solar power down to an energy-hungry planet. They dreamed of space tourism and space-based telescopes. They looked toward Mars.

They looked up, and the stars and the darkness kept beckoning.

HIGH IDEALS

"Hey, we were all bitten by the space bug," admits Bruce Ferguson (M.B.A. '79). "It was a national obsession."[1]

But in truth, the young Bruce Ferguson spent very little time on suburban lawns in the heartland. He lived most of his childhood in places like Thailand and Nairobi. Ferguson's father was a regional director for the Peace Corps and later a U.S. ambassador to Kenya, which meant the family was mostly abroad, rarely staying in one place for more than a year or two.

But like most kids back home in Ohio, Utah, or wherever, Ferguson dreamed about outer space and about being an astronaut. With this end in mind, he started building rockets. "I experimented with homemade versions in grade school," he recalls. "They tended to burn up on the launchpad."

When he became old enough to purchase the necessary explosives, Ferguson graduated from homemade spacecraft and began ordering rocket kits through the mail. This was back in the days before product-safety issues had come to the fore, and some pretty powerful materials could be obtained by budding astronauts, with few questions asked. In the right combinations, those ingredients could push a toy rocket a long way into the heavens.

"The frustrating thing," Ferguson says, "was that no matter where I lived, I was never near any open spaces that were large enough. So whenever I launched a rocket, I lost it. Those things were capable of going pretty high, and they all just floated off somewhere. As it turned out, of course, this was good training for life."

Although he didn't know it at the time, Ferguson's frustration with rockets that just floated off somewhere foreshadowed a problem that would plague NASA for many years. During the '60s and '70s, every venture into space depended on an expendable launch vehicle, or ELV: a powerful, expensive rocket that was designed to be used only once. As the TV cameras focused on the orbiters, LEMs, and satellites that were being boosted into space, often with precious human cargo aboard, the mighty ELV—its task completed—dropped back to earth, forgotten even before its charred remains shattered on the ocean's surface and sank out of sight.

NASA's engineers knew that this was a wasteful and inelegant approach. (It was also a time-consuming and relatively inflexible way to launch—but it had the great advantage of being a known technology.) Over time, and under mounting budgetary pressures, NASA became increasingly eager to develop a reusable spacecraft. By the time Bruce Ferguson applied to colleges, in fact, NASA was almost fully preoccupied with planning for what the agency called a "space shuttle."

The name itself was a clue: NASA was downplaying the romantic, visionary, and patriotic themes of the past in favor of the practical. (A "shuttle," after all, was a humdrum vehicle—a bus, perhaps—that people took to the airport, or perhaps around a stalled commuter train.) And although Ferguson dreamed of being involved in space exploration, and told college admissions officers that he was aiming for a career in "science administration," in his heart he wondered if the reach for outer space would ever be exciting again.

Eventually, he concluded that it would not. Shortly after beginning his undergraduate work at Harvard, Ferguson struck out in a new direction. He decided to find a way to help the developing world, responding to the desperate needs that he had seen firsthand during his childhood years abroad. He began studying government, and completed the requisite courses and earned his bachelor's degree in three years. He married and stayed on at Harvard for a fourth year (picking up a master's degree along the way) while his bride finished her degree. She then accompanied him to India, where he did fellowship work for a year. "Our second honeymoon," he calls it. "No hot running water, no fridge. A great bonding experience."

Ferguson had then, and still has today, high expectations of himself. He is less a benchmarker and more a dreamer, in the idealistic sense of the word. "You always have great dreams about what you'd like to achieve," he explains, "and you measure your accomplishments against your dreams, as opposed to other metrics."

The pattern was set early in Ferguson's young adult life. After returning from India, for example, he entered the rigorous J.D./M.B.A. program at Harvard in 1977. "I walked back and forth across that bridge a lot," he recalls. (The Law School and Business School campuses lie on opposite sides of the Charles River.) "I couldn't resist the idea of getting five years of education in just four years," he says, only half joking. "It was just so *efficient.*"

As a joint degree candidate with a full complement of required courses at both schools, Ferguson had limited options in terms of elective courses. Before his fourth and final year, he scanned the course catalogs and reviewed those options. With a vague notion about following through on some business ideas that were knocking about in his head, he decided to hunt up a course on entrepreneurship at HBS. The only entrepreneurship-related course he saw offered in the 1980–1981 catalog was the Starting New Ventures course. It wasn't quite what he wanted. "I was looking for something that dealt more with *international* business," he explains, perhaps politely.

Ferguson's years at Harvard Business School came in an era when the entrepreneurship area had lost its champions, and indeed was in danger of disappearing altogether. Howard Stevenson, the entrepreneurial real estate professor, had left. In his wake, Bill Poorvu gamely kept the real estate course alive, but other faculty members turned their attention elsewhere. Starting New Ventures—briefly enlivened by the now departed Pat Liles—had lost momentum, and was sorely lacking in continuity.

So as Bruce Ferguson scanned the electives in the HBS catalog, looking for an appealing choice, he could find only one that seemed even vaguely aligned with his interests. That course was Creative Marketing Strategy (CMS), offered as a field study. The idea of getting out into the world and working on a concrete marketing project appealed to Ferguson. He signed up.

What was this "CMS"? Not counting Georges Doriot's unique Manufacturing course, the Creative Marketing Strategy course was the first field-study elective at HBS. It was the brainchild of Professor Harry Hansen, and—with its emphasis on creative, hands-on problem solving—took HBS students away from the classroom and out into the corporate world, where they researched and strategized about real dilemmas on behalf of real companies.

Enterprises ranging from start-ups to giants submitted problems based primarily on issues of marketing; when the student teams un-veiled their solutions in oral presentations a year later, senior managers (often the CEOs) of these companies attended. The corporations sponsored the projects, the results of which were generally kept confi-dential—and were sometimes acted upon. In 1976, for example, the U.S. Treasury Department decided—in response to conclusions drawn by its CMS team—to reissue the $2 bill.

Ted Levitt ran his own version of the CMS course during the 1960s and 1970s, a period considered by many to be its heyday. "I never thought of it as a 'field study' course," he later recalled. "I thought of it as a consulting project, where you helped the company deal with certain problems *as consultants*." Well over a year of work went into each project during Levitt's tenure. Every week, he held afternoon meetings with the student teams, and often the meetings ran late into the evenings.

"The projects we undertook were very serious," he recalls. "Every-one had to be committed. I hardly ever went home for dinner during the school year."

Over time, the course evolved to reflect the interests of its faculty sponsors. "Harry Hansen used to assign students to a team," says Levitt.

"He felt the students should learn to work with anyone and everyone in the group. I didn't do this. The students were stuck with the group for a year, and if the experience was unpleasant, this was quite a burden. So I let them decide for themselves whom they wanted to work with."

In many cases, strong relationships were forged during CMS projects. "These relationships led to people doing things together after they graduated," Levitt says, although graduates did not necessarily remain in the field they had studied for the CMS course.

So this was the context in which Bruce Ferguson, in the fall of 1980, was surveying postings of possible CMS projects. And unexpectedly, *there it was*: a project sponsored by NASA—NASA itself!—focused on the commercial possibilities of space. Deep in his gut, Ferguson remembers, he felt a rekindling of his boyhood enthusiasm. He eagerly asked if he could join the NASA-sponsored project. The six students already on board were hesitant to accept a seventh. Eventually, though, they acknowledged that Ferguson's legal training would be an asset, and welcomed him to the team.

Without knowing it, Ferguson was setting himself up for a major life detour. Now only a few courses and a few months away from his planned career in law and international development, he was soon to be armed with two more prestigious and hard-won degrees. He expected not much more from the NASA project than a gratifying visit to the haunts of his youth: outer space, rockets, astronauts.

SMALL TOWN, BIG VISIONS

One of the six original students on the CMS team that had laid claim to the NASA-sponsored project was a second-year M.B.A. student named Scott Webster. Webster spent his adolescence in the tiny mining town of Eveleth, Minnesota, in the northeastern corner of the state. Perched on the western slope of the iron-rich Mesabi Range, Eveleth offered only limited horizons. (One year, the town recorded the highest per-capita consumption of beer of any town in the entire country.) At some point during his high school years, Webster realized that he wanted more out of life than a job at the nearby U.S. Steel iron-mining operations.

"I needed to know how things *worked*," he says, "and mechanical engineering seemed the best route. I was also certain, early on, that I wanted to leave a mark of some kind, to do something very different."

Fortunately, the iron mines gave Eveleth a strong tax base, and its public schools prepared their students well. Webster attended the University of Minnesota, where he studied mechanical and electrical engineering. After graduation, he went to Minneapolis and began working at Litton Microwave Cooking Products. There, Litton's entrepreneurial young president—Bill George (M.B.A. '66)—impressed Webster immediately. "He was only twenty-nine then," Webster says, "and he was already a pioneer in this brand new phenomenon of microwave cooking."

But despite his respect for both the company and Bill George, Scott Webster resigned from Litton after only a few years, just three weeks shy of his twenty-fifth birthday.[2] "People down the hall from me were doing what I was doing," he explains. "They were managing microwave development projects, and they'd been there for years. Suddenly, I got worried that I'd be doing the *same thing* all my life."

In fact, the young engineer still dreamed of being a pioneer. Years earlier, in a moment of boyish egotism, he had pledged to himself that he would be the president of a company by the time he was twenty-five. It was getting a little late in the game, he knew. But he still wanted to give himself a shot at that dream.

"I resigned almost on a lark," he says. "Here I was, nearly twenty-five, and I still wanted to be an entrepreneur. Somehow, I was hoping to stay true to that pledge."

Webster first tried to develop some product ideas he had. "As a fairly conventional young man," he says, smiling, "I had come up with a new design for a loudspeaker." Over the next few months, though, he came to a sobering realization. While the University of Minnesota had indeed trained him well in the technical side of things—"how things worked"—he had absolutely no idea how to run a business. "I didn't have the first clue about finance or marketing," he admits.

He cast about for a solution. Eventually, he settled upon the path followed by Litton's microwave expert, Bill George, years earlier: business school. Webster secured a recommendation from George, applied to graduate programs, and then went back to work for Litton—this time as a consultant, with the express goal of saving money for graduate school.

So far in Webster's story, there are no rockets-by-mail or dreams of space travel. Did Scott Webster escape the space mania that affected so many others in his generation?

"Not at all," he laughs. "I watched all of the Mercury and Gemini expeditions, and, of course, Apollo. I always say that if I had been born twenty years earlier, *without any doubt* I'd have worked on Apollo. It was the signal event of our generation." But NASA wasn't making news in the '70s, and Webster—determined to be an entrepreneur and a very young company president—never thought seriously about opportunities in the space trade. As far as he knew, there *was* no space trade. Space was reserved for big companies (including Litton) that had contacts, government contracts, and years of experience in the defense business.

Webster found an unexpected calling during his first semester at Harvard Business School: marketing. He attributes this passion to the teaching skills and enthusiasm of Ray Corey, the HBS professor who was then teaching the required first-year Marketing course. "It was all new to me," Webster admits, "but I was hooked right away."

That marketing class in the fall of 1979 did more than introduce Webster to his destined field; it also introduced him to an intense young man named Dave Thompson. "We were sectionmates," says Webster. "Sitting next to him in some of our early classes with Ray Corey, I couldn't help noticing his *notes*. Very impressive—pages and pages of preparation, with graphs and matrices, and all in very fine, neat handwriting. That was the first thing I noticed. Then I noticed that he rarely spoke up in class, but whenever he *did* speak, he was spot on. It was interesting that he was so quiet, when he was such a clear thinker. The caliber of his mind impressed me, and I also liked the fact that he wasn't calling a lot of attention to himself."

HOTELS ON THE MOON

Some people know exactly what they want to do with their lives, and they seem to have known it forever. For Dave Thompson, that enviable certitude came (or *seemed* to come) from his thoroughgoing absorption with America's space program in the '50s and '60s.

Even as a little boy, Thompson had planned a career that would re-volve around rockets and spaceships. Growing up in small towns in rural Georgia and South Carolina, Thompson had sent literally hun-dreds of homemade and from-a-kit rockets up into the sky. Many of Thompson's rockets were "piloted," in a sense—first by grasshoppers, then by mice, and finally, due to the inspiration of a high school sci-ence fair, by monkeys.

"For the science fair," recalls Thompson, "I took the design of model rocket motors that you can buy in hobby stores and scaled it up. In the upper half of the rocket was a little seat where the monkey would sit. The thing could go over a mile high. It worked perfectly two out of three times—a good record back then, even for the U.S. government."

Today, in his office, Thompson displays a photo of the monkey-launching rocket: a six-foot-tall craft powered by five engines that put out fifty pounds of thrust apiece. He grins at his own enthusiasm, then and now. "Everyone knew me as the 'Rocket Kid,'" Thompson recalls a bit sheepishly. "They were all aware of my obsession."

Thompson went on to study aeronautics and astronautics at MIT; during the summers, he worked for NASA and Draper Labs, a defense "research tank" spun off by MIT in the wake of the student protests of the 1960s. He got his masters in aeronautics from CalTech in 1977 and took a full-time job with NASA. And although he subsequently held some high-flying positions—he was project manager for an advanced rocket engine—he never quite felt satisfied in his work.

"The space program was in its most depressing period," he ex-plains. "Nothing was flying. It wasn't what I had expected." In fact, be-tween 1975 and 1981, NASA sent nobody into orbit.

Depression, inactivity, boredom: All were the result of bad luck and bad planning, as Thompson saw it. "During the '60s," he explains, "the space program was way ahead of itself, although none of us realized it at the time. The country was caught up in a monumental rivalry with the USSR. We did a bunch of one-shot things, and *they* did a bunch of one-shot things. Tit for tat. But we failed to build the economic or social un-derpinnings that would enable those things to continue. As a result, the space program went through the doldrums. It ran out of steam. And it spent the '70s trying to figure out what it would do when it grew up."

Thompson is convinced that the promise of the 1960s—the promise of a future in which space played a central role—was not far-fetched. It simply wasn't delivered. "If you plot a graph," he says (reaching for a pencil and a pad of paper, and sketching out axes and ascending lines as he talks), "and you start with the '50s and '60s, and then track the trajectory of the space program through to the '90s, look what happens."

Thompson's trajectory line climbs steeply from left to right. But the reality of the space program in the 1990s is represented on his graph by a lonely dot far below that trajectory. "You end up in a very different place than where we are today. When we were kids, we were sure that by 1999, anybody who wanted to could fly into space just by buying a ticket, and it would cost about as much as it costs to take the Concorde to London. We thought there would be hotels on the moon."

As a young man eager for far more than NASA seemed to be offering, Thompson wondered what else he might do with himself. An odd idea was nagging at him. What about attempting some sort of commercial venture in space?

"It was crazy to think about it," he admits now. "The market was completely unknown and unproven. The technology, of course, would have to be state-of-the-art. The industry was more tightly regulated than most. Worse, it was an industry in which you'd almost certainly be in competition with the government." But his time at NASA convinced him not to dismiss the possibility out of hand. Many of the technologies developed for space exploration were underutilized by the government, or so it seemed to Thompson. Maybe one of these technologies could be adapted to support a private enterprise.

First things first, though. Private enterprise was a novelty for Thompson. If he wanted to start a company—*any* kind of company—he would need to broaden his range of abilities. Harvard Business School accepted him for the fall of 1979. There he met Scott Webster, whom he unwittingly impressed with his careful note taking and his highly selective class participation. For his part, Thompson admired Webster's solid experience in the corporate world. Clearly, Thompson decided, this was someone he could learn from.

So Thompson and Webster learned from each other in class, and socialized from time to time out of class. They signed up for the CMS field study together, and (with four other B-school colleagues) pounced upon the NASA-sponsored project. Then Bruce Ferguson walked in, and after some debate, the team decided that it might need a good lawyer—or at least, a would-be entrepreneur who would soon be a lawyer, and who by the way also loved rockets.

Even without considering the talents of the other four team members, these three—Webster, Ferguson, and Thompson—had a set of skills and interests that were complementary almost to an eerie degree. Webster, the lapsed small-town corporate engineer from the northern heartland, now couldn't get enough of marketing. Ferguson, raised around the world and trained in three graduate schools, already had a broad perspective and an intuitive understanding of complex legal and financial situations. Thompson, for his part, had a deep knowledge of a highly technical field and an insider's feel for the government, both as a boss and as a client.

"Of course, we didn't put all these pieces together on purpose," says Dave Thompson. "It was serendipity more than anything else. But even so, I soon had a *feeling* about this group. I started to think that if we worked together on this CMS study for NASA, just maybe it would lead to something more."

UNWELCOME FINDINGS

It is the fall of 1980. After many delays, NASA's gleaming white space shuttle is almost ready. After the long years of frustration, budget cuts, and relative inactivity, NASA is preparing to send the nation on its next great round of exploration.

NASA is also wondering how it can persuade the business community to help pay for the shuttle.

"The NASA-sponsored project we did for the CMS field study focused on microgravity," says Bruce Ferguson. "It's possible to use a low earth orbit to make new materials that can't be made on earth but would have value on earth. Take aluminum and zinc: They won't form alloys in earth's gravity, but put them in orbit, and they might.

NASA wanted us to research the possibilities—whether companies might undertake such ventures."

The CMS team had six months and a budget of about $40,000. Its seven members took field trips to enterprises within various industries and researched the opportunities that might reside in pharmaceuticals, semiconductors, optical glass, and other industries.

"In the end," says Webster, "we wrote a big report that said exactly what NASA didn't want to hear. The time was *not* right. American industries were not ready to step up and spend any kind of money to experiment on the idea that you could do something worthwhile in space."

One insurmountable problem was the expense. Even today, to buy an unsubsidized ride on a U.S. space shuttle, you would have to pay something like $50 million for your seat. (Tickets are not yet on sale, in any case.) Another problem was that very few companies had yet considered what the unique properties of space could do for them. It was a Catch-22: the prohibitive costs of space research discouraged such research, and the failure to conduct research meant that no one was discovering profitable uses for the shuttle.

NASA, hoping to achieve greater private-sector involvement in the space shuttle program, was disappointed with the results of the CMS team's report, which the agency received in the spring of 1981. ("They just barely thanked us," says Scott Webster.) To be fair, NASA had more important and gratifying things on its mind. *Columbia*—the first space shuttle—flew for the first time in April. Amidst all the hoopla, the wet-blanket report from the Harvard Business School team was easily forgotten.

For their part, the members of the CMS-NASA team were pleased to have played even a small role in the shuttle program. Now the course was over, graduation was upon them, and the team—along with the rest of their classmates—prepared to go their separate ways.

"Before we left, Bruce invited me to have breakfast with him at Quincy House, where he was a tutor," says Dave Thompson. The two of them sat at a long table among the undergraduates, eating waffles and sipping coffee. They compared notes on life at HBS, and, like near-graduates everywhere, wondered aloud what the future might hold for them.

At one point, Ferguson put his fork down on his plate and made an unexpected pronouncement. "You know," he said, "we really ought to start a space company."

Just like that, the idea was on the table.

"It was the first time anyone had articulated it," Thompson says. "It had been bouncing around in my head, but I wasn't going to say it out loud. It seemed too far out, too premature. And then Bruce simply said, hey, we ought to *do* this."

But the question remained: do *what*? Neither Ferguson nor Thompson had an answer, but they both felt the NASA-sponsored research they had done had helped clarify for them the opportunities in (and risks of) a private enterprise in space. They agreed to keep in touch and exchange any ideas they had. Maybe nothing would come of it—or maybe something would.

That summer, Scott Webster moved out to the Seattle metropolitan area, having landed a job marketing cutting-edge uses for ultrasound. Bruce Ferguson headed for Chicago to join the prestigious law firm of Kirkland & Ellis. Still searching for a way to follow his dream, Dave Thompson accepted a position with the Hughes Aircraft Company's Missile Systems Group in Los Angeles.

It could have all ended there. "In fact," says Webster, "it's very strange how the next step came about."

It came about when David Thompson, turning the pages of a trade publication, spotted an announcement of a space-related prize. The prize was offered by a new Houston-based organization, the Space Foundation, and it represented the foundation's first attempt at a national competition. (The organization, now defunct, had hoped to promote graduate work in the commercial development of space.) Dave Thompson decided he had nothing to lose. He put the CMS field study report in an envelope, mailed it off to Houston, and promptly forgot all about it. When word came back that the CMS team had won the award, Thompson was as surprised as anyone else.

Mildly elated, members of the team converged on Houston in October. The prize money was peanuts: Divided among them, it barely covered the round-trip airfares from points all over the country. But the recognition was fun, and the team enjoyed its unexpected reunion.

And more was still to come. "A lot of things came together there in Houston," says Webster, "and that awards ceremony was the catalyst."

HOW A "SPACE COMPANY" GETS CONCEIVED

So thanks to a fortuitous nod from the Space Foundation, Ferguson, Thompson, and Webster were together again only a few months after graduating from HBS. Along with the other members of the CMS team, they crowded into a low-budget hotel room on that October evening for an impromptu celebration. In the midst of these modest festivities, Dave Thompson said that he had an announcement to make.

"Bruce and I have decided to start a company," he said. "A space company." He looked at each person around the table. "So, who's game, and who's not?"

"I'm game," responded Scott Webster immediately.

At the Space Foundation awards ceremony earlier that day, Webster had heard featured speaker Ben Bova quote from James Michener's novel *Space*, and in that moment, he knew he had to work in the space industry. "The quote was about how each generation is presented with a frontier," he says now. "And if you didn't find a way to work on your generation's frontier, you would miss the meaning of your own epic, your own age. Our frontier was, and is, space, and I wanted to be there."

Webster's alacrity was the notable exception (and even Webster gave the project weeks of careful consideration before he officially signed on). The other M.B.A.'s in the room engaged in some serious hemming and hawing. Finally, one of them asked the question that seemed to be on several people's minds: "Dave, are you *crazy*?"

Thompson and Ferguson did not feel crazy. They had been bouncing ideas off each other all summer, and they were convinced that they had hit upon an idea that could work. Winning the Space Foundation prize, traveling to Houston—this simply fanned the fires that were already smoldering.

True, their first concepts for a space company were mostly duds. One idea—the "gas station in space" concept, whereby they would recapture the extra rocket fuel jettisoned from space shuttles, store it in a tank, and make it available to orbiting spacecraft in need of refueling—had potential in theory, but wouldn't become practical until far more rockets were coming and going in the vicinity of the gas station. "That summer," says Thompson, "NASA was predicting that in a couple of years they'd be launching a space shuttle every two weeks. So our idea was a bit ahead of its time."

But a more immediate opportunity had surfaced. Through his connections at NASA, Thompson had discovered that a potential project was coming together: the development of a Centaur upper-stage rocket, adapted for the space shuttle, that would help kick the heaviest-category satellites into orbit. Why not form a private enterprise, and offer to take a crack at the project? This was the idea that Thompson and Ferguson laid on the table that night in Houston.

Ultimately, of the seven CMS team members, only Thompson, Ferguson, and Webster decided to go ahead with the idea. As the trio well knew, there were very good reasons *not* to move forward. Most daunting, moving forward meant challenging the generally accepted idea that any private space-related venture was doomed to be unprofitable. Staggering amounts of money would be needed. To date, the money that had backed each and every successful venture had come from government sources. The drill was well known: Congress set NASA's budget; NASA then contracted with its "regulars" to take on aspects of the project that could not be accomplished by the agency in-house.

Given these circumstances, none of the trio of HBS grads was prepared to quit his day job. Instead, they worked long-distance to come up with a proposal. Their plan was innovative, phased, and contingent: They hoped to get a commitment from NASA to buy their finished upper-stage rocket (or at the very least, win the agency's seal of approval). They would use that commitment to raise the private capital needed to finance the engineering and testing. In effect, they would serve as project managers for the development of NASA's new rocket.

In April 1982, the three men incorporated their venture, calling it Orbital Sciences Corporation (OSC). By that time, their proposal to coordinate the Centaur upper-stage rocket project was nearly done. Here is where a measure of luck—after preparation, the entrepreneur's best friend—seemed to come into play. In June, just as OSC was putting the finishing touches on its plan, the Reagan administration unveiled its new National Space Policy. In keeping with

the administration's overall tilt toward the privatization of government functions, the government henceforth would continue to support the space shuttle program, but also would take steps to stimulate
private-sector involvement in that program.

In particular, said the Reaganauts, entrepreneurship in the space
field would be encouraged, and private investors in the space business
would receive special tax incentives. The timing couldn't have been
more perfect. During that same month, OSC made its pitch to NASA
for the Centaur project. But despite their lucky timing, OSC's
founders did not hear what they wanted to hear.

"The Centaur was a liquid-fueled, partially cryogenic upper-stage
rocket involving enormous safety issues," says Bruce Ferguson.
"Adapting it for the space shuttle probably would have been a $500
million program—in other words, huge. NASA listened to our proposal, and then they said, 'Thanks very much, boys, but why don't you
try something a little less ambitious?'"

Despite the privatization push of the National Space Policy, NASA
chose to develop the adapted Centaur itself. Perhaps to underscore its
willingness to work with private-sector entities, though, NASA
steered the founders of Orbital toward another potential project. This
one, which would require funding in the range of $50 million, seemed
to be of more manageable proportions.

The challenge, although smaller, was still formidable. With most of
its budget already allocated to other programs, NASA had been unable
to proceed with a new middle-range rocket—a "transfer orbit stage,"
or TOS—that would launch medium-capacity satellites from the
space shuttle. Orbital was encouraged to find a way to get the TOS
rocket designed and built in the private sector.

Thompson, Ferguson, and Webster considered the project. If they
wanted to take it on, they would have to put together a proposal similar to the one they had conceived for the Centaur. That plan had always been a long shot; the TOS, it seemed, was far better suited to
OSC's modest capabilities. And this, paradoxically, made the TOS a
more daunting prospect. Orbital's founders, now faced with a project
that might actually happen, knew they had to move very carefully. The
stakes were still high—$50 million—and the visibility of the project

potentially enormous. Orbital was not at risk of being the first company to fail at "privatizing space." But it was at risk of being the first to *succeed* at it.

In December 1982, Orbital Sciences Corporation made its second pitch to NASA. OSC would find private funds for the TOS project and would coordinate the project—providing, of course, that NASA would agree to buy the product, or at the very least, agree not to fund any competing projects.

"We told them we would start with their conception of the TOS, raise the capital, manage the project, and sell it on a commercial basis to all comers," recalls Scott Webster. "We told them we could get it done for less money than the government could, and we told them that our product would help them promote traffic on the shuttle."

NASA was impressed, but cautious. The agency first responded by seeking other proposals. "First they offered our idea to the big guys, like Boeing," says Webster. "Fortunately, nobody else was willing to come in. It seemed like a harebrained idea, and the big guys wouldn't touch it unless the government came up with the funding. To go ahead without the funding was inconceivable to them."

This attitude explains why Orbital ultimately got the chance to jump into the TOS game. It also defines the real contribution that OSC made to the larger field of space-related ventures.

"We reminded everyone of an old idea," Webster explains. "The idea is, you put up your money and you take your chances. Orbital applied this idea to an industry where nobody did that. We were ready to go about building this rocket as a private, commercial venture. Nobody else wanted to take the risk, and that gave us a straight, uncontested shot."

One week after OSC presented its proposal, NASA gave the company the green light. Suddenly, both the TOS project and Orbital Sciences Corporation were launched.

OFF THE GROUND—AND BACK TO EARTH

In December 1982, immediately after NASA's initial positive response to Orbital's TOS project proposal, Scott Webster said goodbye forever

to the marketing of ultrasound. He quit his job in Seattle, threw his belongings into a trailer, and drove south to Dave Thompson's house on
the outskirts of Los Angeles.

"I camped out there for six months," he recalls. "It was a frantic time."

By that time, Thompson was already devoting most of his waking
hours to Orbital. His wife, Catherine, was also in deep. She developed the vitally important ability to answer a 5 A.M. phone call with
a crisp, clear "Good morning, Orbital Sciences," and then put the
caller "on hold" under a pillow while Thompson struggled out of bed
to splash cold water on his face. Meanwhile, out in Chicago, Bruce
Ferguson had left his law firm and begun working for Orbital out of
his home office.

This full-court press was a simple survival tactic. OSC's "green
light" from NASA was not a true contract, or even an endorsement.
In fact, it was nothing more than a memorandum of understanding
that gave OSC six weeks to demonstrate the viability of the project.
If Orbital could come up with some substantial funding and enlist a
respectable aerospace contractor, NASA would give its approval to
the project.

Six weeks was an almost hopelessly narrow window of opportunity. Slim as the opportunity was, though, OSC most likely would
get only this one chance. Ferguson, Thompson, and Webster (and also
the occasional family member) plunged themselves into a frenzy of
activity.

They came to the scramble with one key resource. A successful
Houston oil and gas developer—Fred Alcorn, then a member of the
Space Foundation's board—had invested what he referred to as "walkin'
around money" in OSC. This $300,000 nest egg enabled Orbital's
founders to devote themselves full time to (1) finding a rocket builder
and (2) raising the much larger sums of money that would be needed.

Successes arrived faster than expected. The first piece of good news
came when Orbital persuaded aerospace contractor Martin Marietta
to agree to join the project—contingent on NASA's support—for a
fixed price of $35 million (this would cover engineering, develop-
ment, and testing). The only catch was that Martin Marietta insisted
on a no-risk deal: Tiny Orbital was on the hook to pay the huge defense contractor for its services, no matter what.

To their surprise, Thompson and his partners also met with some success on the money front. They had determined that they needed about $2 million to get the project off the ground. From the start, the venture capital firms they visited were very receptive. The combination of tax incentives, positive statements from NASA, and public encouragement from the Reagan administration seemed to be causing a ripple effect in the venture capital industry. Orbital's founders took advantage of these favorable winds, accumulating about $1.8 million in venture capital. They also collected some true believers—among them Fred Alcorn and a few former NASA officials—who agreed to join Orbital's board of directors.

At the end of an arduous six weeks, NASA and Orbital met again. This time, Thompson and his partners—arriving with a few prominent board members in tow—produced some hard evidence of their young company's abilities. They had Martin Marietta standing by, ready to sign on. They had money in the bank. Director Alcorn had secured a $2 million line of credit at his bank, and appeared fully ready to back the infant company to the hilt. Finally, NASA was persuaded: Orbital Sciences Corporation was for real.

The agreement between OSC and NASA provided that the latter would monitor the development of the TOS, supply the information necessary to make the TOS compatible with the space shuttle, and refrain from directly funding any competing projects. That was the good news. The bad news—which only confirmed aspects of the existing relationship—was that NASA put the burden of raising all necessary capital directly on the shoulders of Orbital, and wouldn't promise to buy even a single TOS rocket.

But the game was afoot. Orbital and Martin Marietta signed the fixed-price development contract (a highly unusual arrangement in this field), and almost overnight, a team from Martin Marietta began working on the rocket. Within a couple of months, however, it became abundantly clear that Orbital's initial funds would need replenishing. "We were spending almost $1 million a month," recalls Scott Webster. "So for about the next year and a half, the three of us became fund-raisers."

Ultimately, what kept Orbital alive was a research and development limited partnership conceived by Bruce Ferguson. The idea had first popped into his head in the course of the NASA-sponsored project at HBS. Later, while in Chicago, Ferguson had thought more systematically about R&D partnerships, and he recently had come to believe that such an arrangement might be the answer for Orbital. "Thanks to the tax laws back then," he says, "the partnership conferred tax benefits on the investors even if they weren't actively involved with the project." Investors were permitted to write off their losses immediately, even though returns might materialize somewhere down the road.

With these inducements in hand, Orbital's founders talked up the TOS project to individual investors, many of whom were affluent doctors and lawyers. It worked. All told, the trio of space salesmen raised $50 million in increments of $50,000. At that time, it was the largest pool of private capital ever assembled for a venture into space.

Perhaps surprisingly, Ferguson and his partners did not turn to their Harvard Business School classmates for help. "None of us was very alumni-group oriented," explains Webster. Ferguson agrees that the founders of OSC did not use their graduate school connections as much as they could have. "I have always been reluctant to try and raise money solely on that basis," he explains. "I would rather match the person to the project. If a Harvard connection is *in* there, so much the better, but I try not to get distracted looking for it."

On the other hand, Orbital's founders acknowledge the advantages that a shared experience may bring to the forging of an alliance between two people, or between an investor and a company. "It's as if you've already been introduced," Ferguson says. And it is possible that the HBS connection helped get Orbital through the door at Shearson Lehman, whose managing director—Paul Kinloch (M.B.A. '68)—ultimately provided invaluable assistance in shaping and promoting the R&D partnership. "We could not have raised the money without his support," Ferguson says, simply. Kinloch later joined the board of OSC.

It is also possible that having the Harvard Business School in their background helped the three entrepreneurs gain credibility with NASA. Jim Beggs, the administrator of NASA at the time, had an M.B.A. from Harvard (class of '55).[3] Again, Thompson and his partners did not trade explicitly on the fact that they had attended HBS, but conclude in retrospect that the association had an impact. In some cases, Ferguson says, "the credential may be absolutely essential. It means somebody reputable has looked at you and decided you are pretty smart, fairly trustworthy, and perhaps a reasonably safe bet."

Despite the success of his R&D partnership model, Ferguson continued to worry. "I often felt we were about to run into a brick wall," he says. "Sometimes it was the fact that we were almost out of money. Sometimes it was a performance milestone we had to struggle to meet. That first year, we were always getting way too close to that brick wall."

Dave Thompson acknowledges the psychological impact of the "wall" but suggests that the deep bonds the three men established as partners served to overcome the long shadows it cast. "Early on," he says, "we made a pact. We agreed that no matter how bad it got, we would hang on and keep the company going for six months *beyond* the day when we had pronounced it dead." That day loomed on several occasions, but the partners never made the pronouncement. "I think we just refused to say 'die,' in part because of the pact. Psychologically, in terms of our morale, this was essential to our success."

For Scott Webster—who remembers conducting business in his bathrobe as he made predawn calls to potential East Coast investors from Dave Thompson's kitchen in L.A.—the frenetic activity of those early months was tinged not only with desperation, but also exhilaration.

"On a good day," he recalls with a bit of relish, "we'd agree we had about a five percent chance of pulling this off. No, *three* percent. The deck was stacked against us. We were unknown and unproven. Most people thought we were coming out of left field. Nobody had done this before. And so on, and so on.

"Meanwhile, of course, we had to give away all the equity in order to build the company. But I can honestly say that in our case, the journey itself was the reward."

Webster, the company's marketer, had a particularly bumpy journey. His efforts to market the TOS rocket were discouraging, to say the least. He and Thompson left California in May of 1983 and set up shop in rented offices just west of Washington, D.C., in a Virginia Beltway suburb. In part, they made the move to get OSC closer to East Coast funding sources. "If we could get closer to New York City," says

Thompson, "our quest for capital wouldn't involve flying back and forth across the country continually." But the move was also intended to bring Orbital closer to its potential customers. Webster's marketing plans targeted not only NASA and the Air Force, but also commercial businesses that had (or might have) a need to launch satellites. Established satellite users like MCI, ComSat, and AT&T had strong presences in the nation's capital, so Orbital had to be there, too.

But Webster was getting precious little in the way of positive responses.

"One problem," he explains, "was that no satellite existed yet that could be plugged into the TOS. The right satellites were under development at that time, but they weren't ready yet."

When Bruce Ferguson relocated to Virginia from Chicago in August 1983, the company had eight employees on its payroll; the founders remained unsalaried. The company continued forward that year and the next, still in a kind of limbo. Despite its exotic aspects, Orbital at root was no different from any other company. Before OSC and its investors could see any returns, Orbital would have to find some customers and sell them some products. Work on the TOS project progressed; the limited partnership kept OSC in business, but futility was in the air. "We began to think nobody would *ever* step up," says Webster. NASA, for its part, followed the project closely, but still would not commit to a purchase.

Then, in early January 1986, after three years on the project, Orbital finally made a sale. NASA contacted the company and placed an order for two TOS rockets, one for the Mars *Observer* spacecraft, and another for the launching of the Advanced Communications Technology Satellite (ACTS), both planned for 1988 launches.

The Orbital team was ecstatic. The company, and especially its TOS project, crackled with newfound energy. Dave Thompson began wondering whether he might be able hire a few more people, and perhaps move to larger offices.

But within that same month—on January 28, 1986, to be precise—everything changed *again*. Early that morning, the space shuttle *Challenger* lifted off for what should have been its tenth flight into space. Then, less than two minutes after liftoff, *Challenger* exploded. All seven astronauts aboard the shuttle were killed—the first in-flight fatalities in the entire history of fifty-six manned U.S. space missions. It was the world's worst space disaster (until, unfortunately, it was matched by the February 2003 loss of the shuttle *Columbia*).

A massive investigation ensued. Ultimately, the cause of the explosion was traced to a faulty O-ring seal joining the steel segments of one of the shuttle's solid-fuel rocket boosters. But NASA also took note that *Challenger* was the first shuttle to launch carrying a Centaur upper-stage rocket in its payload bay. Both the *Challenger* and *Discovery* orbiters had been equipped with specialized plumbing and controls to minimize risks associated with the Centaur; the Centaur, moreover, was not implicated in the tragedy. But the Centaur got no second chance. After *Challenger* exploded, NASA decided that launching a shuttle with a fueled upper-stage rocket in the payload bay posed an unacceptable risk. Since that time, the Centaur has been used only on flights powered by unmanned expendable launch vehicles.

The loss of *Challenger* and its astronauts derailed NASA's space shuttle program, instantly and completely. For weeks, and then months, OSC waited to see what would happen next. The company could be sustained by progress payments from NASA, which by now had signed contracts with Orbital worth about $90 million. Even so, Orbital desperately hoped that NASA would soon resume its flights into space. But this was not to be the case. More than two and a half years would pass before another space shuttle was launched.

Six months after the *Challenger* disaster, moreover, NASA announced that all commercial payloads would be removed from the space shuttle and diverted to expendable launch vehicles. The agency also declared that henceforth it, too, would make greater use of ELVs, mainly to take pressure off its beleaguered shuttle program. At Orbital, hearts sank. The TOS rocket—designed to be compatible with the space shuttle, and rolled out for a public viewing just one week after NASA's announcement—suddenly had next to no market.

Orbital hung on desperately, subsisting on the contractually stipulated progress payments from NASA, but the future was uncertain at best. The company's already small staff began to contract further, as engineers and technicians sought jobs with brighter prospects.

In September 1988, a full thirty-two months after the *Challenger* explosion, NASA successfully launched the space shuttle *Discovery*. To the untrained eye, *Discovery* looked very much like *Challenger*. In fact, however, the new shuttle had the benefit of some $2 billion worth of safety enhancements and other improvements.

Orbital cheered the flight of *Discovery* and applauded the rebirth of the shuttle program. But this was not a moment of corporate salvation. In fact, by the time *Discovery* blasted successfully off its launchpad, Orbital Sciences Corporation—having struggled to survive for most of the previous three years against terribly long odds—had completely reinvented itself.

SURVIVAL—AND THEN SOME

Not long after the *Challenger* accident, the founders of Orbital began a search for a new chief engineer. Attrition had taken a heavy toll, and the company had lost nearly all of its key engineers and scientists. Now, they knew, they had to find someone who was not only exceptionally talented from a technical standpoint but also willing to take some risks. OSC's leaders knew this would be a critical hire. What they didn't know was *how* critical.

A member of Orbital's board who taught at MIT knew of a promising situation then developing back in Cambridge, Massachusetts. It seemed that a brilliant young assistant professor at MIT had recently learned he would not be receiving tenure. This young academic—Dr. Antonio Elias—was an acknowledged expert in astronautics and aeronautics. For understandable reasons, he was now very interested in entertaining offers from the nonacademic world.

So on a warm April day in 1986, Elias took the call when Dave Thompson called from Orbital's offices in Virginia. Thompson described his company—no longer an infant, and still struggling. He spoke candidly of the difficulties that were likely to lie ahead. And ignoring whatever protocols might exist, he offered Elias a job.

Elias, for his part, was flattered. He had only a vague memory of Thompson from MIT. (Thompson had been an undergraduate there while Elias was doing his graduate work). He found himself tempted by Thompson's offer, but he shied away from the prospect of uprooting his young family from their home outside Boston. Nevertheless, he agreed to meet with Thompson, who was coming into town for a conference.

"As soon as I spent time with him in person, I could tell we had the right chemistry," says Elias. "I agonized for months, but in the end, I joined Orbital."

Antonio Elias came on board as Orbital's chief engineer early in September 1986. At first, he spent most of his time overseeing the TOS rocket project—proceeding at Martin Marietta—on Orbital's behalf. "But by then we knew we had to get away from the space shuttle," says Scott Webster. "The problem was, we were still rocket guys at heart, so we still wanted to build rockets."

Elias, Thompson, and others at OSC elected to investigate the prospects of another upper-stage rocket project, this one proposed by the Air Force. "We flew out to a bidding conference in California," says Elias, "and on the red-eye flight back, we talked about who we could find to team with us on the project. We couldn't think of anybody. So I asked, 'Why don't we bid this project alone, without an industrial contractor or partner?'"

Without missing a beat, Dave Thompson turned to the flight attendant in the aisle. "Excuse me," he said, "but this man needs an oxygen mask, right away."

It was the first time anyone had suggested that OSC could (and maybe *should*) do more than coordinate and manage a project, and it was a turning point for Orbital. Today, a yellow oxygen mask mounted on a plaque hangs on the wall of Antonio Elias's office. "It's a memento of that moment on the plane," he says. "Right then, we began to change the way we thought about this company."

Orbital bid on the Air Force project as a solo vendor, and lost. In this case, according to Elias, losing was a very good thing indeed.

"First of all," he explains, "the Air Force canceled the whole project six months later, after several companies had spent millions on early designs. And secondly, once we didn't get *that* project, we began thinking more seriously about the business of launching small, low-orbit satellites."

As noted, the space shuttle was no longer available for commercial payloads, and expendable launch vehicles were once again the most popular option for satellite launches. This looked attractive—but Thompson and his team at OSC were completely new to the ELV business. They had no track record, no long-standing clients, and their investors were looking for a return. If Orbital wanted to compete and succeed, it would have to shake up the market.

Satellites at that time were typically very large, and orbited in a high-altitude location (more than 22,000 miles overhead) at a speed that kept them in the same position relative to the earth below. They offered a variety of useful services but always for a hefty price. Sending and receiving signals to and from a satellite so far away required a great deal of power, which meant both the satellite and its receiver had to be complex, which in turn entailed high costs. For most companies, the expense ruled out satellites for nonessential corporate use.

Herein lay Orbital's opportunity. Fred Alcorn, OSC's first investor and member of the board, presented the test case. Alcorn's company owned oil wells that were scattered across the vast reaches of Texas. In many cases, a well was out in the middle of nowhere, operating on an independent generator, and protected by little more than a chain link fence. An "oil rustler" (of which there could be quite a few, when oil prices were up) could easily plunder such a remote resource.

"All the thief had to do," Antonio Elias explains, "was cut the fence, walk in, and steal oil from the well. There was no alarm, no phone service, no effective and efficient way to watch over the wells."

Alcorn stated the problem in simple terms. His company needed to keep an eye on its remote and far-flung assets. In-person human security either cost too much, or was ineffective, or both. (Oil rustlers were a resourceful bunch.) A geosynchronous satellite could conceivably monitor the wells, but again, the cost would be prohibitive.

But what if Orbital could launch a system of smaller satellites—a network Elias calls a "constellation"—working together in low earth orbit? These satellites (circling between four hundred and five hundred miles above the earth) would be simpler in terms of design, less expensive to build and launch, and—by virtue of operating as a group—would supply more reliable service. The cost of the constellation could be shared among a group of subscribers; the coverage and advantages it offered would be unique, for no such system, private or government-sponsored, had yet been developed.

In the late winter months of 1987, Antonio Elias began investigating potential contractors, looking for someone who could build and launch the rockets he would need to put a constellation of small satellites into low earth orbit.

"But I returned from my road trip very depressed," he recalls. What he had learned was that the problem of expense still remained. No matter where he turned, the answer was the same: launch costs were prohibitively high. Yes, it appeared that inexpensive satellites could be constructed, but putting them in orbit still would require launching pads and powerful ELVs. The venture would be too costly for ordinary companies seeking new ways to monitor remote assets.

Back at Orbital's offices, Elias reported the bad news to Dave Thompson. "At the rate we're going," he joked sadly, "we'll have to build our own launcher."

"Antonio," Thompson replied, "the battlefield of small private launchers is littered with corpses—as you well know." The two men agreed that OSC should steer clear of the launching business.

But the pieces of the puzzle continued to rearrange themselves in the back of Elias's mind, and soon another idea began to emerge. The Air Force had recently launched an antisatellite rocket from an F-15 aircraft. As designed, the rocket did not have enough power even to get itself into a sustainable orbit—but what if the design could be changed? What if an air-launched rocket were built that *could* put a satellite into orbit, without the need for the whole elaborate launch-pad sequence?

The legend around Orbital is that Antonio Elias, trapped in a boring meeting on April 8, 1987, began to reconsider his conversation with Dave Thompson. If the launching business were *different*, perhaps Orbital would not need to steer clear. Elias—so the story goes—began doodling on a pad of paper, and set in motion a sequence of events that would change the company forever. What did he sketch? A picture of an F-15 carrying a satellite-equipped rocket—a new kind of launch vehicle that before long would be known to the world as Pegasus.

DEFINING THE NICHE: PEGASUS

In a little less than three years, the Pegasus rocket went from a doodle to a reality. It was put to the test on April 5, 1990.

Elias conceived the design himself. He worked out the basics of an aircraft-launched rocket that, if successful, would open up satellite options for the thousands of companies shut out by the costs of larger satellites, larger rockets, and launchpads.

Thompson listened to Elias's scheme, and quickly saw its merits. The ability to launch in the air would give Orbital a huge leg up against the competition. And in its fundamentals, the idea wasn't altogether untested. Years earlier, before the advent of Sputnik, the Air Force had had great success with its celebrated X-15 "rocketplane" by suspending it under the wing of a large B-52 airplane and then launching in midair. The B-52, in effect, was the X-15's launchpad. "In fact," says Scott Webster, "if Sputnik hadn't happened, the X-15 would have evolved into our primary space aircraft. Sputnik distracted us into thinking about how we could get a satellite into orbit as fast as possible. As a result, we lost sight of the X-15."

Elias, moving ahead with the plan, became discouraged early on by the problem of the rocket's initial descent. As a general rule, a rocket launched from an aircraft must be released without power and be allowed to fall a significant distance before its engines can be activated. (The risk otherwise is that the launched rocket will set fire to, crash into, or otherwise doom its launching vehicle.) But to turn this high-speed plummet into a powered climb, the rocket must consume huge amounts of fuel. "In fact, according to my design, our rocket would use up a large percentage of its total fuel right at the start of its flight," says Elias.

Dave Thompson watched over Elias's shoulder as he reworked the designs and went through a series of computer simulations. Finally, Thompson—the former Rocket Boy—asked an interesting question. "Have you tried putting a wing on it?"

Elias shook his head wearily. "No," he replied. "A wing wouldn't help. It would increase the drag, and make the rocket too heavy."

Thompson persisted. "I still think it needs a wing," he said. "It would *look better* with a wing."

To his credit, Elias considered the advice of his backseat driver—and suddenly it dawned on him that Thompson's stubbornness might reflect an age-old bit of wisdom about the relationship between aesthetics and aerodynamics. "It's been said," explains Elias, "that if something is aerodynamic, then it will be beautiful. Anybody looking at something aerodynamic will appreciate its beauty, and will be in awe of its shape, without even knowing why. I realized Dave was looking at the rocket and he wasn't in awe of its shape." If the rocket did not *look* beautiful, perhaps something was indeed missing.

Elias added a wing to the design, and ran the simulations. This time, the results were promising. "With a wing," he says, "the rocket was able to act like a small airplane. It didn't lose as much energy—in fact, it lost only a *fraction* of the energy—when it was dropped. The wing added weight, it added drag, but it was a net benefit."

These days, Dave Thompson looks back at the development of Pegasus with mock horror. "We bet the entire company on this one idea," he says. "We put *all* of our capital into it, and then some."

One of the many risks that the company took was to try a new sourcing approach for this project. As the design for the Pegasus rocket neared completion, Orbital contacted a Utah-based rocket motor builder (Hercules Aerospace Company, now Alliant Tech Systems) and proposed a venture partnership. Both companies would be well served: OSC wanted to stop depending on outside prime contractors, and Hercules—having been a subcontractor for years—was itching to play a more central role.

"They became stockholders and venture partners," says Scott Webster, "and we gave them a chance to share the front seat with us. They developed three brand-new optimized solid rocket motors specifically for Pegasus. We were going to have a very efficient, very economical rocket."

All of the other components were built at Orbital, which (as part of the larger Hercules joint venture) had acquired Space Data Corporations, a manufacturer of rockets, rocket electronics and data systems, launch facilities, and specialized space payload. When the deal was closed, OSC went from an organization with fewer than 40 people on the payroll to one with nearly 450 employees. "Suddenly, we could handle everything," says Bruce Ferguson. "We could design the products, we could build the components and assemble them, we could test them, and we could launch them."

After experimenting with various combinations—small and large airplanes paired with small and large rockets—Antonio Elias and his team at Orbital decided that the best launch value would come from a big plane carrying a big rocket.

"We borrowed our first plane from NASA," recalls Scott Webster. "It was the very same Boeing B-52 that had been used to launch X-15 rockets back in the 1950s. Our Pegasus rocket, not coincidentally, has virtually the same dimensions, weight, and center-of-gravity position as that old X-15."

The project was coming together, and soon a flightless prototype was completed and unveiled before the public at Edwards Air Force Base in California. Next, the real thing would be built: a three-stage solid rocket with a winged first stage. Pegasus would measure 49.2 feet long, weigh 40,000 pounds when loaded, and have a 22-foot wingspan. A Pegasus launch would cost about $6 million, or less than half the cost of the next cheapest option.

Orbital's first Pegasus customers began signing up. Fred Alcorn (with his unmonitored oil wells) was not among them; for the time being, the idea of putting a constellation of small satellites into orbit would have to wait until Pegasus proved its mettle. Instead, the first payload would consist of instruments for a NASA scientific experiment and a communications satellite for the U.S. military. Pegasus was scheduled for launch in the first week of April 1990. If successful, this rocket would be the nation's first privately developed space launch vehicle.

"We knew it would be a defining moment," Webster says. "It was sink or swim. There are a million ways to put a rocket together, but only one way to put it together and have it work. We would lose it all if Pegasus didn't work."

As the day of the launch drew near, Dave Thompson and his team at Orbital made preparations to take the company public. "This meant that everything was riding on Pegasus," Thompson says. "Our success, our reputation, any money we might have or might need in the future. Everything."

The price for the initial public offering (IPO) was set on the evening of March 22, 1990, with the IPO to take place the following day. But on the morning of March 23, the *Wall Street Journal* ran a front-page, column-one article about Orbital Sciences Corporation. The article reminded readers that the launch of Pegasus might fail—and that if that happened, the company itself was likely to fail as well. One subhead read: Start-Up Firm Faces Big Risks. Another labeled the founders of OSC as Three Harvard "Space Nuts."

Shaken, Orbital postponed its IPO.

"We decided to hold off," says Thompson, "until we could launch the rocket and prove them wrong."

The Pegasus team was exhausted, and morale—already low—had taken another beating. Nevertheless, team members regrouped for one final push. They began working around the clock to secure success for their rocket. Adversity became a friend. "You don't need eight and a half years and a thousand people and 1.2 billion dollars," Thompson told an interviewer, a bit defiantly. "We have a small team of very good, very dedicated people, and we can create magic."

Early on the morning of April 5, 1990, NASA's massive old B-52 rolled up to the runway at Edwards Air Force Base with the long white Pegasus rocket tucked snugly under its right wing. Every system on the rocket had been checked and rechecked. A control room full of technicians stood by expectantly, waiting for their moment. The morning wore on, consumed by a myriad of small details.

When the B-52 was finally ready to begin its lumbering takeoff, Antonio Elias was on board as the launch panel operator. "Whenever anyone questioned the safety of launching a rocket so close to an airplane," he says, "I reminded them that I would be up there with that plane. Obviously, I believed it would be safe."

Finally, the venerable plane rumbled down the runway and lifted off, trailing four streams of gray exhaust. Dave Thompson and his partners watched from the ground. Inside the control room, superstitious technicians crossed their fingers. All eyes focused on the video monitors, and on the picture of the big old plane rising into a cloudless blue sky.

On board, Antonio Elias had a terrible thought push its way into his head: "If I push the wrong button, it's all over."

The B-52 reached 40,000 feet, and Elias pushed the right button. Pegasus launched, cut free from its bonds to the B-52. For five long seconds, the rocket dropped silently down through the air. Then the rocket's graphite-composite motor ignited, hurling the white-winged projectile forward in a flare of fiery exhaust. Pegasus began to climb upward—a gentle angle at first, and then steeper and steeper, reaching for the heavens. The ground crew and technicians roared their approval—cheering, hugging, and high-fiving in delirious celebration.

When the B-52 taxied back in, Dave Thompson ran to welcome Elias back to earth. He embraced him, and offered his thanks. "That's the way to knock it out of the park!" he exclaimed.

Orbital's first air-launched rocket was a resounding success. Twenty days later, the company went public—its IPO price soundly defended (and even nudged a little higher) by its Pegasus triumph.

LIVING THE DREAM

Since that day in April of 1990, Orbital Sciences Corporation has used its Pegasus rockets to launch dozens and dozens of satellites. "Pegasus is still a mainstay of this company," Dave Thompson says. The memory of that April day is no less sweet for the passage of time.

But the air-launched rocket is now just one of many innovative products and services offered by Orbital. The company has followed through on its vision of a satellite-studded future. And while Orbital is today (in Thompson's estimation) as vertically integrated as such giants as Boeing or Lockheed, it also has branched out sideways into a variety of related businesses. Because there was no template available to guide the development of a "space business," OSC explored many directions. "We went horizontal," Thompson explains.

In fact, the company's ability to provide start-to-finish project coverage has emerged as one of its trademarks. "We can build a satellite for you; we can also launch it, and we can build the systems and ground stations you need to use it." As an Orbital customer, you can order your customized hardware—such as satellites, communications instruments, and handheld person-to-satellite devices. You can purchase software for processing the information that your satellites transmit to you, and you can buy into systems (linked to the Global Positioning System) that provide navigation and mapping information. If you're in the robotics or defense businesses, specialized electronics are available.

And, of course, you can sign up for a semicustomized launch. (To minimize expense, Orbital encourages its customers to share launches.) Launch vehicles now include Pegasus, Taurus (for larger payloads), and smaller suborbital rockets. As of the turn of the century, the vehicles had put a total of seventy-eight satellites into orbit. The company's "catalog" still includes its earliest product—the TOS rocket built for the space shuttle—which finally went into use in 1991, a year after Pegasus was launched. "It was good from a revenue standpoint up until 1994 or so," explains Thompson, "but the demand has almost vanished. This is mostly our own doing: The commercial launching of satellites has become so much easier that there's usually no need to go the shuttle route."

As it grew, Orbital relocated twice more. It has been in its current location—a clean, white building in Dulles, Virginia, distinguished by a large model of Pegasus outside the front door—since 1993. At times bursting at the seams, OSC has also rented office space elsewhere to accommodate expansion. The company now has two subsidiaries and two "affiliates": ORBCOMM (a communications system based on a constellation of small, low-earth-orbit satellites) and ORBIMAGE (an earth-imaging system with two satellites already launched and three more in the planning stages).

The constellation satellite system, ORBCOMM, merits special attention. Although other entities raced to do the same thing, Orbital's satellites were the first into orbit, and therefore represented the forerunners of major changes in the way we use satellites today. This achievement is the subject of *Silicon Sky*, by Gary Dorsey, who spent three years researching OSC from the inside with Dave Thompson's permission.

The seeds for ORBCOMM were sown before Pegasus was launched, back when the founders of Orbital first wondered whether commercial satellite services could be made easier, more affordable, and more reliable. A plan began to take shape—one that would depend on a system of twenty-eight low-earth-orbit satellites linked to a complement of stations on the ground. Largely through the efforts of Bruce Ferguson, ORBCOMM was established in 1989. By 1997, the company—having used the launching services of Orbital's Pegasus rocket—had ten satellites in orbit and could offer partial services. The constellation was completed in September 1998, and full service began. With additional launches, the network consisted of thirty-five satellites by the end of 1999.

In explaining ORBCOMM, Scott Webster brings us back to Fred Alcorn's oil wells: "If a remote well shuts down, it could take a week for the guy in his pickup truck to get there while he's making his rounds. Meanwhile, you've lost $50,000 worth of production. Or let's say you have a refrigerated rail unit traveling across the country, and it stops refrigerating. You have no way of knowing this, so about $300,000 worth of meat gets spoiled. This company can prevent these damages."

It's like "a magic carpet," Webster adds, for anyone running a company who is in search of extra asset-monitoring capabilities. "It enables you to travel anywhere at the speed of light."

Each of ORBCOMM's ninety-two-pound satellites circles the earth every ninety minutes, and the constellation's architecture is such that the orbits effectively "blanket" the globe. "Our satellites are identical in function and overlapping in coverage," says Webster, "which means redundancy is built into our system. This makes loss of service extremely unlikely."

Orbital, the parent company, changed as it expanded. Ferguson occupied a number of high-level positions there before leaving the company partway through 1997, aiming to start a (non-space-oriented) venture of his own.

"I'm amazed I stayed as long as I did," he says now. "It's a great company, but I've always liked to keep doing different things. From the time I was zero up until the age of twenty-six, I moved to a new place every eighteen months or so. I have a high threshold—maybe a need—for change."

Scott Webster left the Orbital family more recently (though he remains on the company's board of directors), departing in the end of 2001 to pursue a career as a sculptor. Webster had previously taken three years off from Orbital to recapture some degree of normalcy in his life. "I had become too one-dimensional," he explains. "I needed to decompress, I was hoping for more of a social life, and I wanted to travel a little."

During what he calls his "sabbatical," Webster met and married his wife. He also got his pilot's license and learned the art of bronze casting. "Bronze is an ancient medium," he explains, "and one that will last for many millenniums. My goal is to reflect our era. I also hope that each piece has enough beauty, durability, and intrinsic worth that it will someday be counted among a family's most valuable possessions. This is one way to become a part of history." Today, Webster is a full-time sculptor, with more than two dozen pieces completed, including a bronze Pegasus rocket poised outside a conference room at Orbital's headquarters.

DREAMS OF THE FUTURE

In 1999, the three cofounders of Orbital were honored with the Harvard Business School's Alumni Achievement Award. At a glance, it all seems like a fairy tale with a happy ending.

"Sure," says Thompson, "it probably sounds like fun. But to be honest, it's mostly fun in *retrospect*. You need to get five years past the bad stuff before you can look back and say, 'Gee, what a great time we had.'"

Bruce Ferguson agrees. "There were moments of happiness," he says, "but being an entrepreneur is a lot of hard work. It's a draining experience. What I liked best about Orbital was working with friends who are also very smart people. Everyone should try to do that in life: work with people who energize you and *make* it fun. I never could have done a project like this alone. It would have been too hard."

And there was more hard work to come. Like all companies, Orbital—and its descendants, ORBCOMM and ORBIMAGE, experienced growing pains and setbacks. In late 1999, for example, Orbital announced that it would restate its financial results from the beginning of 1997 through the second quarter of 1999, after investors raised questions about posted losses at ORBIMAGE; the parent company then faced a class-action lawsuit filed on behalf of shareholders.

Webster, who returned from his first sabbatical to resolve this crisis, worked out a settlement agreement that was entered into in 2000. Though this successfully dealt with the larger issue, Orbital was left with a depressed stock price, due in part to larger investor concerns industrywide about the near-term outlook for commercial satellite projects. In addition, Orbital found itself in what Thompson terms an "uncomfortably high debt position" due to its investments in both ORBCOMM and ORBIMAGE.

In response, the company, under Thompson's leadership, formulated a "back to basics" strategy consisting of three main elements. First, Orbital continued to focus on its core satellite and rocket manufacturing business. Second, as a byproduct of this decision, Orbital divested itself of a number of noncore units, with the proceeds used to rid the company of outstanding debts. And finally, Orbital reduced its investments in both ORBCOMM and ORBIMAGE. Both organizations have gone through Chapter 11 proceedings; ORBCOMM emerged in 2000, and is now operating with a more streamlined capital structure, no debt, and slower than anticipated but steady growth. ORBIMAGE is currently following a similar pattern, and expects to emerge from Chapter 11 before the end of 2003.

Orbital's own strategy, meanwhile, has been highly successful, thanks in part to significant increases in military spending on satellites and missile defense systems beginning in 2002. In August 2003, the company marked the successful delivery and launch of its 280th satellite. But the company's biggest recent breakthrough, reports Thompson, occurred in the first quarter of 2002, when it received a lucrative $950 million contract from the Pentagon—its single biggest contract ever—to design and build the interceptor rockets that are now being deployed in the national missile defense system. This seven-year contract promises to keep the company busy through the end of the current decade, and when viewed in conjunction with the increased government spending on satellites and various other international contracts, it seems to portend a rosy future for the company.

Orbital's accomplishments are enduring: the world's first privately developed space launch vehicle, the world's first operational low-earth-orbit commercial communications satellite, and the world's first handheld satellite communications device. Thompson feels that the near-term focus will be to capitalize on current areas of expertise, including practical-use satellites and rockets.

Meanwhile, though, the company continues to keep its eye on more distant exploration. One satellite currently being developed is destined to explore the asteroid belt, a previously unexplored region of space. And the company is also working on new technology that will enable new types of satellite systems in the not-too-distant future.

So the fascination with space endures at a company that—although its feet are set firmly on the ground—still looks to the heavens.

CHAPTER 8

A Nontrivial Pursuit

THE THREE FOUNDERS of Orbital Sciences Corporation, would-be entrepreneurs, completed their M.B.A. studies at a time when the field of entrepreneurship was losing ground at the Harvard Business School.

Entrepreneurship still had its proponents at HBS, of course. In 1978—the year before future Orbital leaders Dave Thompson and Scott Webster enrolled—Dean Lawrence Fouraker wrote approvingly of the number of HBS graduates engaged in small-business ventures and start-ups. M.B.A. students were still signing up in droves for Professor Howard Stevenson's real estate course. But by 1979, the number of courses related to entrepreneurship had dwindled to just two.

One reason for the implosion of entrepreneurial studies was the departure, in the summer of 1978, of Howard Stevenson (see chapter 6). At the end of a grueling process, Stevenson recently had been granted tenure by his senior colleagues, some of whom remained skeptical about his talents and interests. Stevenson, for his part, was just as skeptical about making his career at HBS. His primary fields of inquiry—real estate and small companies—didn't seem to be much valued at the School, and Stevenson thrived on a challenging peer group. If he stayed, and if that kind of peer exchange was not available to him, it would be hard to stay passionate about his work.

While he was wrestling with these career choices, he received a job offer from Preco Corporation, a Western Massachusetts–based paper company with whom he had had dealings during an earlier leave of absence. Preco's executives were looking for a vice president of finance and administration, and hoped to recruit Stevenson. They were pleased, and probably surprised, when their quarry left his hard-won tenured position and relocated to the often-forgotten city of Springfield, two hours west of Boston.

At least for a while, the job was a welcome change from academia. "It was a wonderful immersion in the realities of entrepreneurship," he recalls. "Right from the start, I had to play the entrepreneur's role. We wanted to put in a new recovery boiler for $14 million, we had $7 million of debt and $700,000 of equity, and I had to figure out how to do it."

But working at Preco turned out to be a short-term solution. Stevenson had lost none of his intellectual restlessness. After a few years as a paper-company executive, he found himself again considering his next career move.

"I had done what I could do there," he explains. "I'd had a lot of people working for me. I'd done a lot of systems work, I had dealt with a financial emergency during the oil crisis, and I had stared down Aetna in a potential restructuring situation." Half eagerly, half reluctantly, he embarked on a series of interviews with a venture capital firm in New York City. "I was bored," he admits. "I had started reading books on Russian history."

SETTING THE STAGE FOR A REVIVAL

During the late 1970s and early 1980s—in those years when Stevenson was on leave and the field of entrepreneurship at HBS was nearly dormant—several key players at the School were worrying about the problem of entrepreneurship. Some, working behind the scenes, were puzzling over how to revive the moribund field. The turning point came in 1980, when Harvard president Derek Bok asked John McArthur to become the School's seventh dean.

Bok's choice of McArthur had resulted in part from a letter McArthur had written to him in August 1979. Bok, who had publicly chastised the School for its alleged insular tendencies and (in Bok's view) a failure to move quickly enough into new areas of research, soon learned that he had roused McArthur (whom he already knew well from various administrative posts) to a spirited and thoughtful defense of the School. In his letter to Harvard's president, McArthur pointedly suggested that Bok would do well to celebrate the School's many accomplishments to date. But at the same time, McArthur—a savvy surveyor of the intellectual landscape at Harvard—readily acknowledged the need for improvements in the School's research and course development activities. One absolutely critical move, wrote McArthur, would be a far greater emphasis on the emerging field of entrepreneurship.

Soon after writing this letter, McArthur was tapped to lead the changes that he had been advocating. As dean, he began exploring (among other things) ways in which he could support the study and teaching of entrepreneurship. Realizing that student demand far outstripped the available seats in Starting New Ventures and Real Property Asset Management, he asked around the faculty for someone—a volunteer—who would take responsibility for developing new courses in the field.

Nobody volunteered. McArthur, frustrated but undeterred, continued his hunt, this time outside the institution. He already had a target in mind: his friend and former colleague, Howard Stevenson.

AN ESCAPE FROM UTAH

McArthur's quarry grew up in a small town in Utah. Throughout his teenage years, Howard Stevenson did everything he could to increase his chances of getting out and seeing a bigger world. The urge to seek broader horizons stemmed in part from his early childhood, when his family moved from place to place as a result of his father's military postings. But it also grew out of Stevenson's intellectual restlessness, which propelled him into motion from an early age.

"I entered every contest there ever was," he recalls. "I was in Junior Achievement and did all the things that one does there, largely to escape Utah. State math contest, state model United Nations, the American Field Service in France. In high school, I spent the summer between my sophomore and junior years in the first New Math program, at the University of Kansas. I would do *anything* that got me out of town."

But the urge to stretch and explore was counterbalanced by family circumstances, which imposed a certain degree of responsibility upon the restless young math whiz. "I was twelve when I started working in my uncle's lawnmower distribution company," says Stevenson, whose aunt and uncle lived next door to his parents in Utah. "My aunt taught me everything I ever needed to know about accounting. They had no children and became important role models for me. When I was sixteen, they went off to Europe for three months and told me to make sure the business kept running properly."

Stevenson's record of academic accomplishment (he was a National Merit Scholar), his unusual range of outside activities, and his obvious ambition helped him earn a scholarship at Stanford, where he completed a B.S. in mathematics. His professors and peers expected him to go on to advanced studies in math, but Stevenson went against those expectations. "I always thought of math as a language," he says, "and it was a disciplined way of thinking. Higher math is much like philosophy, which I always enjoyed. But"—and here he smiles broadly—"I decided that I didn't want to compete with *really* smart people, who tended to work *really* hard. That translated into no math and no physics." In 1963, therefore, he enrolled at Harvard as an M.B.A. candidate. At the Harvard Business School (he likes to claim he chose business over law because the business program was two years instead of three), he was awarded an M.B.A. with high distinction. His next choice: get a doctorate or go to Vietnam.

"When I graduated in 1965," he says, "the war was heating up. Like many people my age, I decided I'd rather be a doctor than a captain."

Soon after entering the D.B.A. program at Harvard, Stevenson began working with Professor Myles Mace, writing cases for a course on the management of international businesses. This was a decade after Mace's interlude as a senior executive with Litton, and long after his intellectual focus had shifted from small businesses to large. Stevenson, although not particularly interested in huge multinational corporations, was nevertheless struck by his supervisor's clear-eyed and practical approach to learning about business.

"I began to absorb some of the ways Mace thought about things," Stevenson says. "For example, he was very committed to getting the hard facts. That made good sense to me."

Even as Stevenson focused on business policy—a fairly typical concentration for doctoral students in that era who wanted to develop a generalist's perspective—he gradually became aware that he was not considered a rising star at HBS. None of the more high-profile faculty members had volunteered to serve on his thesis committee, for example, and that didn't bode well for the long term. But this tacit vote of "no confidence" didn't discourage him in the short term—in fact, Stevenson pursued his particular interests with gusto. In his casewriting, he increasingly concentrated on smaller companies. One was the Olivetti Company, which achieved extraordinary growth in the 1950s as a result of the powerful personal vision of Adriano Olivetti, but then suffered reversals after Adriano's death.

"What struck me about that situation," Stevenson says, "was that the Olivetti people were asking, 'What would Adriano do?' when they should have been asking, 'Where is the future?' Adriano would have asked where the future was, but this legacy didn't get passed on. The people he left behind didn't ask about the future; instead, they looked backwards for guidance."

Another case that impressed Stevenson was that of Howard Head, who created the first metal snow ski, built a ski company that dominated the market in the 1960s, and then moved on to revolutionize the tennis racket industry.

"One of the important teaching points in that case," says Stevenson, "is that there's a trade-off between personal importance and immortality. At Head Ski, Howard was in charge of everything, micromanaging every decision. At Prince Manufacturing, in contrast, he stepped back and let the organization build itself."

More or less accidentally, Stevenson had happened upon what turned out to be a lifelong interest. He wanted to continue investigating the ways in which small companies grew into successes—or went into tailspins. "The corporate bureaucracies didn't particularly appeal to me as subjects," he explains. "In 1970, after earning my D.B.A., I began to feel I was going in a direction that was different from the direction the School was taking, so I told them I wanted a leave of absence." The leave was granted, and Stevenson decamped.

His passion for small companies led him to accept a position as vice president of Simmons Associates—a small Boston-based investment firm headed by Matthew R. Simmons (M.B.A. '67)—where he helped raise venture capital for precisely the kinds of organization that had an appeal for him: small, scrappy, fast-moving companies that were intent on growth. Here, he was first introduced to Preco Corporation, the Western Massachusetts–based paper company where he later served as an executive. He also began working with real estate companies, and found that he was intrigued by the people and processes he encountered in that industry.

"Your typical real estate firm takes other people's resources and assembles them," he explains. "I was fascinated by this. I was also learning about how the good firms manage risk through multistage decision making."

The opportunities at Simmons were not compelling enough to keep Stevenson there beyond his two-year leave of absence. (One constraining factor was the 1968 market crash, which sent many small companies off the cliff edge and pushed Simmons itself to the brink.) In 1972, therefore, he began thinking about returning to the Harvard Business School. In this same time period, a real estate development company let it be known that it was interested in hiring Stevenson as its vice president of finance. When word of this low-key courtship got out, it not only provided Stevenson with another option, it also gave him an unexpected patina as an authority in real estate.

"At the School," he says, "they had heard about this, and they asked me to come back and teach a course on real estate. I had never read a book on the subject, but I said I'd be glad to do it. I had no idea what I would teach, but I figured I could find a book and read it faster than my students could."

In retrospect, the real estate courses Stevenson then developed (Real Property Asset Management and Real Property Asset Development, as described in chapter 6) laid the intellectual foundation for the development of entrepreneurship courses at HBS later on down the road. "I was teaching this concept of people, property, deal, and environment," he says. "In the entrepreneurship area, that became people, opportunity, deal, and context. But it's a framework that has its roots in the real estate industry."

Then came the tenure battle, and—in 1978—Stevenson's period of renewed soul-searching about whether he truly fit in at Harvard. "I asked for another leave of absence," he says, seeming to choose his words carefully, "but it was suggested that it was time for me to fish or cut bait. So I thought about it, and I decided to cut bait."

Stevenson went off to make paper in Western Massachusetts. Several years later—in the summer of 1981—he was still in Springfield, reading Russian history, and once again feeling the sense of mounting restlessness that so often seemed to overtake him. And that was when, out of the blue, HBS Dean John McArthur called and invited him to lunch.

ANOTHER SOBERING INTERLUDE

McArthur was not someone to go to such a lunch unprepared. He was well aware of his friend and former colleague's unusual career history. He also knew of the unhappiness that had surrounded Stevenson's most recent departure from the School. He had therefore taken a few calculated steps to sweeten his intended offer.

Most important, he had persuaded Arthur Rock and Fayez Sarofim, two successful graduates of the School, to endow the Sarofim-Rock Professorship. The chair carried with it terms that were new at Harvard: It was to be offered to a scholar and teacher who was willing to focus explicitly on entrepreneurship. At lunch, therefore, the dean was able to lay some inducements on the table. He wanted his former colleague to be the first incumbent of the Sarofim-Rock Chair. (This entailed mainly prestige, since the School's research was centrally funded.)

McArthur wanted Stevenson to come back to the School and "start something" in entrepreneurship. It was time, he said, for the School to *act*, and move forward on this critical issue.

Stevenson, as noted, was already thinking about his own next move, and had begun to explore opportunities in the New York venture community. His unhappy experiences at HBS, only a few years in the past, were still fresh in his mind.

But McArthur was well known for his ability to apply enormous pressure gently, and he now did so to Stevenson. "This time," he assured Stevenson, "it will be different." McArthur pledged his full support for whatever Stevenson decided to do at the School.

Stevenson agreed to consider this opportunity. Soon after this meeting, Stevenson received a visit from his former colleague in the real estate course, Bill Poorvu, who also encouraged him to re-enlist. The McArthur-Poorvu combination proved persuasive, and Stevenson returned to HBS in the fall of 1981.

Official tenure documents in hand ("I had never formally received them before," he explains, "and I did not commit to this until they arrived"), he made his way down the familiar shady sidewalks to his new office in Baker Library. "Arthur and Fayez had endowed the Chair," he says with a wry smile, "and there was a nice dinner. All in all, it was a very lovely welcome back." But after all the welcome-home fanfare died down, Stevenson took another hard look at his surroundings. Despite McArthur's clear commitment and Bill Poorvu's reassuring presence, the new incumbent of the Sarofim-Rock Professorship felt fundamentally isolated.

It appeared to be the same story all over again. Student surveys consistently revealed a high degree of interest in careers that involved small business and/or self-employment, and this interest was reflected in course-enrollment statistics. Time and time again, HBS had expressed its determination to embrace entrepreneurship as a subject worthy of serious academic attention. This embrace would attract high-powered scholars, who in turn would generate the conceptual frameworks necessary to develop good courses, which would help satisfy student demand. It would be a virtuous cycle. But more than thirty years after the introduction of Myles Mace's first New Enterprises course, the embrace had never happened. The prodigal son faced a steep uphill battle.

"Years had passed," he says, "but many of the same attitudes toward entrepreneurship prevailed. And the worst part was that in some ways, those colleagues were right. Entrepreneurship was like what Gertrude Stein said about Oakland: There's no there there."

In truth, the field of entrepreneurship had a notoriously shaky conceptual base. For example, one study demonstrated that 44 percent of entrepreneurs were firstborn children. This generated some interest among scholars of entrepreneurship—until a critic pointed out that 44 percent of humanity consists of firstborn children. The "personality" theory—that certain people are simply *born* to be entrepreneurs—seemed to Stevenson to be similarly bankrupt. No wonder self-respecting academics tended to run from the field of entrepreneurship.

Adding to the complexity of Stevenson's task was its lack of definition. Dean McArthur was celebrated for his purposeful indirection. He delighted in signing up high-powered talents and then turning them loose on a problem. If pressed, he was willing to state the problem, at least in oblique kinds of ways, but he was loathe to define the solution. "It was very typical of John," Stevenson recalls. "He said, 'Hmmm. This seems interesting and important. Why don't you do something?' And that was the last piece of guidance I got."

Some people find frustration in the lack of a well-conceived plan; others find opportunity. Stevenson was in the latter camp. He resolved to find a new framework for the study of entrepreneurship—one that was rigorous enough to achieve respectability within academia, but which would also make sense in the down-to-earth world of business. He also resolved to be opportunistic and open-minded as he cast about for this new framework. Because he didn't know what the answer might look like, he certainly couldn't guess where it might come from.

During his first six months back at HBS, therefore, Stevenson taught Business Policy while experimenting with different ways to structure a new entrepreneurship course. It turned out to be a sobering interlude. When confronted with a new idea or a new set of data about entrepreneurs, he found himself continually referring to experiences he had been through as an *executive*, rather than concepts he had developed as an educator. Again, the real world of entrepreneurship had very little to do with the then-current academic approaches to the field.

"What we were teaching then simply did not correspond to my experience in the trenches," he recalls. "And that troubled me a great deal." What were needed, clearly, were some fresh links.

GAMES PEOPLE PLAY

Business is not a game. On the other hand, games can definitely be a business—sometimes even a big business.

The popularity of games in our culture to some extent reflects the convergence of recent societal trends: more disposable income, more leisure time, higher levels of education, and so on. But in addition to these forces of contemporary life and culture, there is something deep, something *fundamental*, in human nature that drives us to play games.

A five-thousand-year-old backgammon board turned up in the ruins of a Mesopotamian town. Egyptians were playing a version of checkers as early as 1500 B.C. Chess, according to some authorities, originated in India more than a thousand years ago. Something in human nature drives us to *compete*, and a good game—one that balances skill and luck, and gives our imagination room to ramble—is a joy for the ages.

Of course, somebody, somewhere back in time invented these games. Those long-forgotten inventors have counterparts today—some of them driven only by the urge to come up with a great game, some by the desire to make money, and some by a dash of both. Whatever their motivations, these modern-day inventors are backed by companies eager to cash in on the latest game craze. And for good reason: Charles Darrow's Depression-era invention—a real-estate game called Monopoly—not only made his fortune, but also generated healthy profits for Parker Brothers for decades afterward.

Over time, a good game can become an industry, in and of itself. In 1978, luxury goods purveyor Neiman Marcus offered an all-chocolate

Monopoly set for $600. The Franklin Mint today offers nearly a roomful of Monopoly-related paraphernalia: the Collector's Edition ($595), the Collector's Edition table ($295), the official Monopoly Millionaire's Chair ($275, but of course one would need several to play the game right), a Harley-Davidson edition, the Collector's Edition game cover ($90), and an all-cotton Collector's Edition throw rug.

Only the hottest games sell themselves. The vast majority of games need help. Large game companies maintain their own sales forces, whose members call primarily on major buyers like Wal-Mart, Toys "R" Us, and other huge retail chains. Smaller companies (in the game industry and other businesses) often use manufacturers' representatives, or "reps," who call on potential buyers large and small.

In the late 1960s, Bob Reiss (M.B.A. '56), the cofounder of a national manufacturers' representatives company, specialized in "repping" games. One day, he was approached by a man who sought to persuade Reiss to rep a new chess game. By this point, Reiss and his partner had almost a decade of experience selling games (among other products), and having Bob Reiss agree to represent one's product was a step toward credibility in the relatively intimate world of games. Reiss was inclined to be discouraging, in this case.

"I turned this guy down several times," Reiss recalls. "He did a game with chess pieces shaped like figures from ancient Rome, using a very sophisticated mold. I didn't know much about chess, but I knew it wasn't a big item, so I kept turning the guy down. But he persisted and persisted."

Persistence was a quality that Bob Reiss admired—and which he himself possessed, in abundance.

GROWING UP IN BROOKLYN, New York, Reiss and his brother very early on absorbed the strong work ethic of their parents. What spending money the boys had, they earned themselves. Reiss returned milk bottles to the store for three cents apiece; he checked coats at the Broadway Theater; he made sandwiches and mixed milkshakes in his uncle's candy store.

"I had a thousand jobs," he remembers. "I think all of us did, growing up."

Reiss reached his full height—over six feet two—by age thirteen. He was lanky, but also quick and coordinated. Inevitably, the junior high school gym teacher in his New York City public school took him aside one day after class.

"Have you ever played basketball?" the teacher asked.

Reiss shook his head.

"Well," said the teacher, who also coached the basketball team, "you're going to start now."

Basketball opened new doors for Bob Reiss. He loved the game and soon became skilled at it. And establishing a pattern that recurred throughout his life, he found creative ways to capitalize on his skill. During high school, he spent summers at a Catskills resort where he worked as a waiter and resident ballplayer, playing in at least two games a week. A self-described "introverted extrovert," uncomfortable (even today) about socializing with strangers, Reiss learned to "work the tips" at the Catskills resort. "The salary was a dollar a day," he says, "but the tips were phenomenal." He forced himself to be gregarious with the guests on whose tables he waited, taking pains to memorize their names and learn something about their interests as soon as possible— preferably within hours of their arrival at the resort.

And he played an increasingly good game of basketball:

If you played ball, the guests wanted to impress you, so they tipped you even more. The rules were different then. A lot of the players were college players, and some were even pros—Bob Cousy was there the summer before I got there. The hotels were loaded with players, and those Catskills teams were unbelievable.

It was a fun way to spend the summer—and lucrative, too. My parents actually got concerned because I was sending so much money home. They wondered what I was doing up there in the mountains. But I had no expenses, and there was no way you could spend any money there.

Reiss was a committed athlete, and he was developing into a skilled one. His jump shot was good enough to overcome his unspectacular high school academic record, and in 1948, Columbia University found a place for him in its freshman class and on its basketball team. During his junior year, the team went undefeated and was ranked fourth in the country—a notable feat for an Ivy League school. In the off season, Reiss worked on boosting his grades, which tended to suffer during the season, and also sold football programs on commission for the student-run Program Agency. He eventually became the agency's manager, with a staff of thirty-five students working under him. "In my senior year," he says, "I made the rough equivalent of a year's tuition in just six or seven weeks. Aside from basketball, that was my most satisfying experience in college."

Both of these experiences left their mark on Reiss. Even as a college student, he could see parallels between basketball and business. He had an inkling that the game was teaching him lessons that he would draw upon for the rest of his life: *Work hard. Be prepared to make sacrifices. Never give up. Remember that you are playing for a team.* Basketball, like business, was fast and competitive, and he learned to throw himself wholeheartedly into the fray, while always knowing and respecting the rules. He found that *success*, especially hard-won success, gave him large doses of confidence and satisfaction. He became less shy and more assertive.

Following his graduation from Columbia in 1952, Reiss was drafted into the Army, where he coached and played on basketball and tennis teams, eventually becoming the cocaptain of a U.S. national basketball team that played in the 1953 Israel Olympics. But he had little interest in turning professional.

"If you liked insurance work or coaching, then pro ball was a great stepping stone," he says. "But I knew I wanted to go into business." So turning to his other passion, Reiss set his sights on the Harvard Business School. His roommate from Columbia, rejected by the Army because of a bad shoulder, had gone to HBS after college, and Reiss had visited him there several times.

"I sat in on classes, and I knew it was for me," he says. "The case method—none of this memorizing junk. *That* was definitely for me."

Only HBS would do, Reiss decided, and—having applied nowhere else—he pulled out all the stops to get admitted. He had heard that applicants sometimes went through a two-part interview process, first facing a pleasant interviewer and then one who was more challenging.

"So I made a point of standing up to the second guy," Reiss recalls, "and I think that's what he was looking for. And Columbia probably spoke up for me, too."

Once enrolled at Harvard, Reiss continued to develop the traits that his lifelong friends say came to define him: He was astute and observant, ambitious and opportunistic. He took every marketing course he could find. But during his two years at HBS (1954–1956), he found little else that dealt with issues of interest to entrepreneurs. The Management of New Enterprises course was still an elective option, but wasn't getting particularly good marks from second-year students. Windsor Hosmer and Frank Tucker had not yet stepped forward as advocates of small-business careers. Georges Doriot was in full flower, of course, teaching his Manufacturing course each year to a crowded Aldrich classroom full of transfixed faces. But when Reiss heard the word *manufacturing*, he pictured factories, employees, and overhead. Even at this stage of his life, factories held no appeal, so Reiss sidestepped the Doriot experience.

During June 1956, as graduation approached and representatives from major corporations swarmed the HBS campus in search of recruits, Reiss found himself studying the job postings that had been sent in by small companies. He spotted one from the Venus Pen and Pencil Company in New York City, which was looking for an assistant to the president. A meeting was arranged, and within the first three minutes of the interview, Reiss knew he didn't want the job. "It was a staff job," he explains. "Central office, politics, memo writing."

By coincidence, though, the company also had another opening: a position that entailed setting up a personalized pencil division. Whoever took this position would be almost entirely on his own. It would be a modest salary with bonuses based on sales. It would be sink or swim.

"I'm sure you wouldn't want it," said Venus's president apologetically.

"*Perfect*," Reiss thought to himself. Everything the company president saw as a negative translated into a positive for Reiss. "Basically," he says, "the guy was telling me to start a business, and he would pay for it."

Bob Reiss took the job. That first year at Venus was an intensive learning experience during which he got to know the business, the in-house resources, the buyers, and the channels of distribution. To Reiss, the incentives were clear and compelling: "The more pencils I sold, the more money I'd make." By the end of his third year, Reiss was earning more than Venus's national sales manager. The company's president, impressed by his young protégé's successes, urged him to take over product development for the entire country. This was a major corporate vote of confidence—but taking the job would require Reiss to relocate to Lewisburg, Tennessee, in order to be close to the Venus factories.

Reiss, who was then living in midtown Manhattan and relishing the single life, turned the job down flat. "Would *you* trade Manhattan for Lewisburg?" Reiss asked his boss.

"Well, I guess that's the end of that discussion," replied the president.

The two men then considered a different kind of solution. Reiss, eager to be in business for himself, wanted to launch his own manufacturer's representative company. While at Venus, he had learned a great deal about setting up and running a company, and he thought he might succeed if Venus hired him to rep the personalized pencils. "I was the only one that understood that business," he says, "so they needed me. I asked them to give me an exclusive contract and pay me a straight commission."

In 1960, Bob Reiss and a partner—Manny Lefkowitz, who had known Reiss since childhood and was then living in Washington—launched their repping company, Reiss Sales Associates, with the Venus Pen and Pencil Company as their first account. By any measure, Reiss Sales was a tiny operation, housed in a one-room office in New York City. "We had space for one desk and two chairs," says Reiss. But spacious offices would have been a waste of money, since Reiss and Lefkowitz spent most of their time on the road. Included in the rent was an answering service that handled their calls. A desk, two chairs, a phone, and a voice on the line when the entire staff of Reiss Sales Associates was out of the office: This, Reiss decided, was the perfect way to run a business.

Bob Reiss was not a typical manufacturer's rep. He brainstormed with clients and buyers about product development, and searched endlessly for new markets. He learned that competence and likability were critical, but not enough. In addition, you needed *persistence* to make a go of it.

And that was why he eventually he decided to strike a deal with the chess set maker who kept pounding on his door and pushing a chess set made with particularly fancy molds.

"Finally I said, OK, let's test it," he recalls. "Give it to me, no contract, no agreements, and I'll put it into Macy's, and you'll pay me for what I've sold. His set was beautiful. I put it into Macy's—and the thing starts flying out of the store. We did no advertising; it was all about the look of the set. So I said, *wait* a minute. We may have something here."

Reiss began convincing mail-order buyers and other department stores to carry the chess set. By the early 1970s, Reiss Games—a new company of convenience—had become the country's number-one seller of chess games. Meanwhile, a young genius named Bobby Fischer had done Reiss the favor of throwing the game into an international spotlight. The memorable 1972 match between Fischer and Boris Spassky sparked a Cold War–fueled craze for chess. Coffee shops and bars filled up with avid chess aficionados—some of whom couldn't tell a rook from a bishop, but who thrilled in placing bets on which chess piece Fischer or Spassky would move next.

"It was worldwide news," says Reiss. "Every move was on all the networks, and people who had never played chess before were running out to buy a set."

While the more serious chess players preferred to use a plain set, the decorative sets sold by Bob Reiss appealed to people who planned to display them in their living rooms. In many homes, the chess set was destined to function mainly as a piece of fine art. It would serve as a visual cue, tipping the visitor off to the household's high level of culture and intelligence.

The curious thing was that people in almost all income brackets were succumbing to the mystique of chess. "We ended up in Sears, JC Penney, all the catalogs," says Reiss. "Pretty soon, stores like Sears were revising their projections upwards from a thousand sets to thirty thousand! Our guy couldn't make the chess sets fast enough. At seven-thirty every morning, I'd find out how many sets had been made the day before, and I'd have to allocate them to the buyers. No buyer was going to get 100 percent of his order. In one way, it was horrible, and in another way, it was phenomenal."

MEANWHILE, MANY MILES TO THE NORTH, another game phenomenon was beginning to take shape. In 1979, a few days before Christmas, Canadian journalists Chris Haney and Scott Abbott were engaged in a mock-serious debate about their respective Scrabble-playing skills. The two men decided to resolve the dispute by playing a winner-take-all championship game. This prompted Haney to run out and buy a new game set, because neither of them possessed a complete set with all the game pieces intact. Offhandedly, as they were setting up the board for their grudge match, they calculated that this was the eighth time that one or the other of them had purchased a Scrabble game set.

The *eighth* time? Haney and Abbott suddenly found a subject they could agree upon: the potential profitability of a popular board game. (In fact, the iceberg was far larger than the two journalists ever suspected. Scrabble was then so popular that it could be found in *one out of every three* American households.) At that moment, they decided to invent a new board game based on current events. They quickly sketched out the basics of the game, and then—following the suggestion of Haney's wife—named it Trivial Pursuit.

At first, the going was tough. The rules and scoring of the game had to be developed, and the trivia questions had to be researched and written. Haney, a photo editor, and Abbott, a sportswriter, knew next to nothing about raising money and marketing a product. Haney's brother John and friend Ed Werner joined as partners and helped to persuade other friends and relatives to buy into the company. Finalizing the game and the financing took well over a year, but in the summer of 1981, with $40,000 in hand, the creators of Trivial Pursuit signed contracts with manufacturers. They would assemble the finished parts of the game themselves.

The first eleven hundred game sets—which cost $75 each to make—were sold to retailers for $15 apiece. (Haney and Abbott were not alone in choosing the initial-subsidy path: Thousands of early Scrabble games, made by hand at the rate of twelve an hour, were sold at a loss.) After the initial shipment in November 1981, the game attracted a following of serious enthusiasts, who spread the word. Additional orders began to pour in.

Despite their game's growing popularity, Haney and Abbott were having trouble getting credit. They were forced to halt production of the game sets until March 1982, when a venturesome bank finally came through and another twenty thousand games could be manufactured. By then, a bar in Ontario had set aside certain tables for playing Trivial Pursuit; another bar in Toronto began holding Trivial Pursuit nights on Fridays. By December 1982, one of Canada's largest games retailers had set up a Trivial Pursuit hot line. People waiting to buy the game would stand for hours in lines that routinely spilled out of the stores and into the streets.

South of the border, most game-playing devotees went about their daily lives without an inkling of what lay in store. But the first wave of Trivial Pursuit mania did not go entirely unnoticed in the United States. A few business-minded individuals had tuned in to watch and measure the fad, gauging its life and durability. And one of these sharp-eyed individuals was Bob Reiss.

CATCHING A WAVE

Those who know Bob Reiss say he's someone who will both take a chance and give a chance. His willingness to place a decorative chess set in Macy's—just to see what might happen—is one example of many. Often, he could persuade dubious buyers by encouraging them to "buy light" at first, and then buy more if the item proved itself a strong seller.

"He was always testing the waters," says Ron Goldstein, vice president of sales for the Valdawn Watch Company (created by Reiss in 1990 and named for his daughter, Valerie Dawn Reiss). "And he was always thinking of new ways to do the same old thing."

A new way to do a trivia game: This is what was on Reiss's mind during the summer of 1983, as he watched Trivial Pursuit fever sweep across Canada. More than a hundred thousand game sets had been sold there. Reiss knew that any game selling well in Canada would sell ten times that well in the United States. An opportunity was knocking— his business sense, plus twenty years of experience in the game industry, told him so.

"Do you remember when you could only get Coors beer out west?" asks Bob Reiss. "People would bring a six-pack back with them on the plane, saying, 'I got Coors beer!' like it was gold. Well, in the early 1980s, Trivial Pursuit was like Coors beer. It had the same *cachet*. It was expensive, and it had a lousy package with no graphics, but people were smuggling it across the border. So I knew something had to be there."

But as Reiss knew better than most, the toy and game industry could be a harsh and unforgiving environment. Most products had short life cycles—two years or less—and all were subject to the ups and downs of fads, fashion, and fickle young hearts. Every year, new toys pushed old ones off the shelves. The number of retailers was shrinking as a result of industry consolidation, and those that remained tried to stick with product lines that could support spin-offs and secondary lines. Reiss knew that a trivia game would represent a narrow category. Retailers would buy the game only if they were persuaded that the volume potential was enormous.

In Canada, this seemed to be the case with Trivial Pursuit. Sales of the game were soaring, and Chris Haney and Scott Abbott were looking for a U.S. distributor. Milton Bradley passed on the opportunity, as did Parker Brothers (which years before had also passed on an early version of Monopoly). Bob Reiss's latest company R&R—his one-man repping and consulting company for the toy industry—bid for the game, but was turned down. Haney and Abbott evidently assumed that a larger company, with more resources, was needed to ride the whirlwind that they had created.

Eventually, the Canadians licensed Selchow & Righter (coincidentally, the makers of Scrabble) to distribute Trivial Pursuit in the United States. Selchow introduced the game at the February 1983 Toy Fair.

At the Toy Fair—an annual trade show attended by thousands of manufacturers, distributors, and buyers—Trivial Pursuit turned very few heads. Selchow did little to promote it that spring. But despite its low profile and high price (between $30 and $40 retail, or two to three times the cost of other board games), the game began jumping off retailers' shelves.

Bob Reiss watched the numbers. By August, he was certain that trivia-game mania would soon explode all across the United States. Trivial Pursuit was still the only trivia game on the U.S. market in September, and it had sold 3.5 million copies. (Another 20 million would be sold in the next twelve months.) Two small U.S. games companies had already announced plans to produce trivia games in 1984, and Reiss figured the larger companies would soon be throwing their hats into the ring. It was time to make a move.

"I went to lunch with two friends of mine, Eddie Miller and Irwin Sperber, reps in the toy business. We talked about how to do a trivia game that would compete. Trivial Pursuit had just come out with an movie edition that was doing well, so when Irwin said, 'TV would be good,' I instantly knew he was right. Now the challenge was, how to pull that off?"

To give an R&R-produced TV trivia game credibility, Reiss decided, he would have to license the name and reputation of a universally respected television authority—and the best authority he could think of was *TV Guide* magazine. So, on October 17, 1983, he wrote a letter to the publisher of *TV Guide*. He had no contacts there and could pull no strings. All he could do was hope that his idea would get noticed, and perhaps generate some interest.

As Reiss himself is the first to admit, luck can be your best friend in such situations. When business school students today ask him what he would have done if *TV Guide* had ignored the letter, he replies, "Nothing. We had no Plan B." But as it turned out, *TV Guide* didn't ignore Reiss's letter. Bill Deitch, assistant to the publisher, read the proposal and then called Reiss, inviting him to come to the magazine's offices and discuss the idea in greater detail.

"We had been approached over the years by lots of people," Deitch says, "and we had turned them all down, except Bob. He's got some wonderful kind of innate charm about him. I trusted him and liked him, even though I knew nothing about him. We did the deal on a handshake."

In fact, the handshake was just the beginning, and many additional phone calls and letters were necessary before everyone reached agreement. But the details were nailed down quickly—and Bob Reiss swung into action. *TV Guide*, given a choice between manufacturing the game itself or collecting royalties on it instead, had opted for the royalties. It was up to Reiss to get the trivia game designed, manufactured, packaged, and shipped. He also had to find buyers, and all within a narrow time frame. The February 1984 Toy Fair was only two months away. No deadline could have been more real. "If we didn't make *that* fair, in *that* year," Reiss says, "we were dead."

A SCHEME AND A SURVEY

While two Canadian journalists were upending the American game industry and an American manufacturer's rep was plotting to ride the wave they had set in motion, Harvard's Howard Stevenson was himself hard at work, trying to come up with a systematic and compelling way to think about entrepreneurship.

Stevenson had spent the 1981–1982 school year at HBS quietly dismantling his own field and laying plans to rebuild it. He scheduled a colloquium on entrepreneurship for interested faculty members, at Harvard and elsewhere, and made sure to invite enough practitioners to provide a real-world perspective. He talked, he listened, and he kept his eye out for kindred spirits.

Fairly early in this process, Stevenson started playing around with an idea: that people who behaved in an entrepreneurial manner were responding principally to situational cues. In other words, entrepreneurship should be understood as a management *style*, rather than as a personal trait or innate instinct. "I felt we should look at opportunity-driven people," he recalls, "and figure out what they were doing and why they were doing it. And as it turned out, we were able to identify a very consistent pattern of behavior."

Eventually, Stevenson and a small group of colleagues settled upon a package of five behaviors that together helped define an entrepreneurial manager:

1. The tendency to seek out opportunities

2. A willingness to act quickly in light of an opportunity

3. Multistaged commitment of the resources at hand

4. Skillful use of leased and/or temporary resources

5. An interest in building a network rather than a hierarchy

Although Stevenson was quick to concede that a person's intrinsic attributes could play a role in his or her entrepreneurial inclinations and success, he argued that it was *external* forces and pressures—such as changing technology, economics, or consumer demand—that most often combined to encourage entrepreneurial behavior in managers. In other words, entrepreneurship was directly related to environment. Why was this important? Because it implied that entrepreneurship was a conscious response that could be learned. It was no longer a case of, "If you're not a born entrepreneur, you're out of luck." Instead, it was, "These are skills and attitudes that you can *learn*, and upon which you can draw when circumstances require you to do so."

In other words, schools of business had a legitimate role in educating would-be entrepreneurs. (This had been a matter of debate since graduate schools were first invented.) In a 1984 interview with the *HBS Bulletin*, Stevenson drew an analogy between this learning process and the experience of an athlete in training. "There are skills, attitudes, and a fundamental base of knowledge that education and experience can provide," he said. "You won't turn me into a world-class athlete by sending me out to practice with a coach, but I will certainly play a better game. Entrepreneurship is no different."

An important component of Stevenson's approach was the idea of a spectrum encompassing a range of management styles and methods. On this spectrum, no one style was edged out by another; the concept relied more on a *coexistence* of managerial methods.

"It isn't that one theory is right," says Stevenson, "and another theory is wrong. It's really about contingencies. If you're in a world where you think opportunities are springing up quickly, then don't try and plan, don't try and fully commit. Instead, be sure you involve other people. You're going to have to assemble resources faster than you can build them into a hierarchy, and you're going to have to manage through networks."

Working with the five components he had identified, Stevenson designed a new second-year course for the fall of 1983: Entrepreneurial Management. He developed and wrote cases focused on a wide range of industries and a variety of people. To the *Bulletin*, he explained, "We've tried to find situations where success or failure isn't based simply on an intuitive analysis, but rather where one's decisions *change* based on an understanding of the details."

Other members of the HBS faculty, including William Sahlman, became interested in developing additional aspects of Stevenson's theory. Meanwhile, two HBS entrepreneurs—Irving Grousbeck (M.B.A. '60, the cofounder of Continental Cablevision) and John Van Slyke (M.B.A. '70, founder and president of the American Management Company)—agreed to devote part of their time to teaching the Entrepreneurial Management course with Stevenson. During that first year, more than five hundred students elected to take the class.

The syllabus that greeted those students divided the course into five sections, reflecting the sequence of steps an entrepreneur typically takes in response to an opportunity:

1. Evaluate the opportunity (what created it, what time limits apply, where does the "window of opportunity" lie, what risks and rewards are at stake).

2. Assess required resources (determine what is needed and how best to control these critical resources).

3. Acquire necessary resources (obtain the crucial financial and nonfinancial resources through a variety of means)

4. Manage the venture (deal with operations, legal problems, growth, and bankruptcy).

5. Harvest the value (exit the deal via sale or public offering).

Stevenson wanted his course to connect to other interest groups at the School. Unlike other university-based centers of entrepreneurship, which often tried to disown the graduate program that had spawned them, this effort would reach out in every direction.

"I tried to establish relationships and build a network," Stevenson says. "I built as many ties as I could to the rest of the family. This differentiated us as a program. We would present an entrepreneurship problem to other areas, and ask them to bring their skills to bear on it. The point was that entrepreneurship is not *what* you study, it's *where* you study."

As he pushed ahead with his work, Stevenson took note of the changes he saw in the general business environment. The nation had experienced an abundance of opportunities after World War II, but the easiest ones to take advantage of—the low-hanging fruit—had all been exploited. New niches would have to be found, and they would be found only by skilled and aggressive individuals. This meant entrepreneurship was likely to become more visible, more respectable, and perhaps even fashionable.

And as Stevenson saw it, there were still more factors in play:

Another factor was that big firms were starting to downsize, conglomerates were breaking up, and capital was starting to flow more freely. Financial resources were becoming more mobile, human resources were becoming more mobile, and this caused intellectual resources to become more mobile.

And finally, we were seeing the rise of a phenomenon best embodied by Silicon Valley. Instead of handing over their money to trust companies, successful entrepreneurs were starting to reinvest in other businesses. They poured their resources back into new start-ups. People were beginning to invest in other people, so that in a very real sense, the next generation of entrepreneurs was being funded by entrepreneurs who were only slightly ahead of them on the development curve.

Like many other groups at HBS, the Alumni Office was keeping tabs on what Howard Stevenson was doing. The Administrative Director of External Relations, Paula Barker Duffy (M.B.A. '77), had reason to take a particular interest. One day, she stopped by Stevenson's office.

"Do you know anything about the alumni survey?" she asked.

He knew *of* it, he said, but didn't know much beyond that.

"Well," she continued, "you ought to take a look at it. I think we're about to learn something new about our graduates. A lot more of them are self-employed than you might expect."

Duffy had brought along a sampling of surveys for Stevenson to peruse. The lapsed mathematician was instantly intrigued by what he saw. "Until I saw those figures," he later told the *Bulletin*, "I had no idea of the extent of the phenomenon we were dealing with here at the School."

If Stevenson was correct in his thinking up to that point, then a changing business context was very likely to call forth more entrepreneurs. But even a cursory review of a sample of these alumni surveys seemed to show that entrepreneurship was *already* an organizing principle of huge numbers of HBS alumni. Further study bore out this initial interpretation. As Stevenson and Duffy began compiling statistics based on alumni responses to reunion-year questionnaires, they developed statistics that almost immediately began to change the way people thought about Harvard M.B.A.'s. Was HBS simply a finishing school for the *Fortune* 500? Evidently not: Nearly a *third* of the responding HBS alumni were self-employed. Nearly *half* described themselves as "entrepreneurs."

Subsequent in-depth analysis of the survey results revealed some additional telling facts. For example, the self-employed alumni felt their jobs provided more flexibility and more potential for fun. And they were not necessarily "rootless" or migratory. In fact, they changed jobs less often in a ten-year period than the non-self-employed alumni did.

This apparent job satisfaction seemed to bring about more overall satisfaction in life. According to the survey results, the self-employed alumni were more content than their counterparts. (So much for the image of the entrepreneur as chronic malcontent!) There was no evidence that self-employment led to a greater tendency toward divorce. In fact, the self-employed alumni believed their stress levels had gone down over time. Most of them felt they would make the same choices if they had to do it all over again. And about 43 percent of them (compared to 16 percent of the non-self-employed) replied "Never" when asked when they wanted to retire.

Stevenson puzzled over these figures. What lay behind them—especially the startling fact that half of the graduates of the School considered themselves to be entrepreneurs? What did this *mean*?

Ultimately, Stevenson decided that, wittingly or unwittingly, the Harvard Business School had been teaching the basics of entrepreneurship for many, many years. "The whole message of the case method," as he later explained to the *Bulletin*, "is that behind every situation lies an opportunity."

Students in a lecture class expect to be told the "right" answer to a problem. The tacit assumptions in this approach are (1) that there is a "right answer," and (2) that the person standing up at the front of the classroom possesses that answer. The case method, in Stevenson's opinion, created different expectations. "Our approach with the case method," he says, "has always been to say: Look, I know you don't have enough information—but given the information you *do* have, what are you going to do?"

The constant reiteration of that question—*what are you going to do?*—had an interesting consequence. In Stevenson's phrase, it "builds in a bias toward action." Don't just think about acting. *Act.*

GRADUALLY, word of the work that Stevenson and his colleagues were doing in entrepreneurship began to filter through the HBS alumni population. Some alumni attended Stevenson's initial colloquium. Others encountered Stevenson and his colleagues at reunions and other alumni functions. Still others read accounts in the *Bulletin*.

Many of these HBS graduates volunteered help of various kinds—financial support, leads on cases, or simply moral support. "We had a rather vocal constituency of entrepreneurs out there," says Stevenson with deliberate understatement, "and they were a large constituency that had been feeling somewhat ignored. Our work was helping them reappear."

In the later months of 1983, one of those HBS alumni called on Howard Stevenson in his office. "It's great, the work you're doing on entrepreneurship," Bob Reiss said. "I'm an entrepreneur myself. Next time you're in New York, come and see me."

SLAM DUNK

Bob Reiss stands before a classroom full of Columbia Business School students in Uris Hall. The day—February 22, 2000—is unseasonably warm. Outside, many of the young people now enrolled at Reiss's undergraduate alma mater are sprawled across the library steps, faces turned up to the sun. A few students in the classroom are wearing shorts. Reiss himself wears gray trousers and a sky-blue sweater that matches his eyes. He seems too tall for the low, white ceiling at the front of the room, and he paces around with an overabundance of energy.

"I want to see a show of hands," he says. "How many of you want to own your own business at some time during your life?"

Nearly every student in the room raises a hand high into the air.

"How about in the next four or five years?"

This time, at least two-thirds of the class raises a hand. The students look askance at each other, a little surprised to find such congruence in their ambitions. "This is new," Reiss says with obvious delight. "Take it from me: Ten years ago, you would have been aiming for big companies."

These students have prepared for class by reading the R&R case, written by Howard Stevenson and based on Bob Reiss and the *TV Guide* trivia game.[1] Like many case discussions, this one opens with a brief recitation of the bare essentials of the case: By October 1983, Selchow & Righter—the U.S. distributors of Trivial Pursuit—had fallen behind in filling orders for the game. Christmas sales went through the roof, creating a demand for similar games. Trivia games were expected to be the best-selling toys in the upcoming year, and at the February 1984 Toy Fair, it was clear that most major toy manufacturers were prepared to follow the trend. In fact, by the end of that year, the number of trivia games on the market would far exceed the number of interested customers.

TV Guide's TV Game made its debut at the 1984 Toy Fair. The pricing umbrella created by Trivial Pursuit enabled Bob Reiss's company to compete that year by offering a more affordable game while still making a tidy profit. Using a two-tiered distribution strategy, Reiss sold first to upscale retailers (who marked the game up 50 percent), and then to the mass merchandisers (who based their discounts on the marked-up price). Stores that wanted their names to appear in the *TV Guide* ads paid no fees, but were asked to place minimum purchase orders. The magazine's extensive circulation appealed to the retailers. Kmart bargained for exclusivity in the fifth and final ad.

The oversupply of different trivia games flooding the market by Christmas 1984 caused all such games to be heavily discounted. The wave had crested, hit the beach, and receded. But by then, 580,000 sets of Trivia Inc.'s *TV Guide* game had been sold.

After the basic facts of the case have been reviewed, Reiss asks them what they think of his foray into the trivia game arena. Do they see it as risky?

Clearly, the answer among the Columbia students is yes. They begin stating drawbacks, and Reiss scrawls them on the chalkboard as a list: "Challenges/Obstacles to Success." The list's first entry is "hostile environment," followed by details: The game was a copycat item, based on a fad, in a quickly changing industry dominated by only five major retailers. Also, the single-item company Reiss had created for this specific purpose—Trivia Inc.—would not be popular with buyers. It had no other products, no sales force, no infrastructure, and no production or shipping capabilities. And its window of opportunity was very, very narrow.

"Anything else?" asks Reiss.

"Well, yeah," one student replies, tentatively. "You were lacking capital."

"Yeah, let's get right to it!" Reiss says, writing "NO MONEY!" on the board in big letters. "We had *no money*! And don't forget, we needed six thousand trivia questions . . . with answers!"

He shrugs, grins an almost upside-down grin, and holds his hands up with an air of mock helplessness. The students laugh, and shake their heads. "So why in the world did we go *ahead* with this thing?" he asks, feigning incredulity.

As the hands go up, more slowly this time, Reiss prepares to make a new list on the board. He labels this one "Factors in Success."

At the top of *this* list, according to the first student who speaks, should be Bob Reiss himself—his experience and relationships. He had undeniable expertise, and even a measure of clout, in the toy and games industry. He knew games inventors and was able to persuade one of them, Alan Charles, to create the *TV Guide* game in less than a month. He also knew reps and buyers, and he was able to locate a part-ner for the project (Ira Weinstein, the "Sam Kaplan" of the R&R case) who provided some up-front financing and additional key contacts. Each person in the network trusted, and was trusted by, Bob Reiss. His personal appeal, knowledge, and good-guy reputation helped *TV Guide* decide to come on board.

TV Guide is next on the students' list of success factors. The maga-zine brought credibility to the product as a result of its highly recog-nizable brand name; it also brought the built-in ability to reach 17 million people through its normal circulation. In exchange for a pay-ment system of increasing royalties, the magazine agreed to throw in five full-page ads (valued at $85,000 apiece) at no cost, which meant Reiss could capitalize on the periodical's enormous penetration by advertising the game in the magazine itself. Last but not least, *TV Guide* insisted on controlling the creation of the trivia questions in-house. The magazine's staff would write and answer all six thousand of them, for $3 per question. "Not a bad deal," Reiss chuckles, continu-ing to scribble on the board as the students build their second list.

Third on the list is the fact that Trivia Inc. kept its up-front costs at a minimum, opting for variable costs over fixed at every opportunity. Very few expenditures were required before the games began selling. The game's inventor agreed to take royalties instead of a one-shot inventor's fee, while *TV Guide* agreed to an unusual arrangement whereby Reiss would pay the magazine *after* he was paid on sales.

"They asked me why I wanted this arrangement," Reiss tells the Columbia students. "I said, 'Because you're rich and I'm poor!' They seemed to like that answer, and they went along with it."

Other variable costs included assembly, storage, and shipping, all done under contract by Swiss Colony, a consulting client of Ira Wein-stein's (specializing in the speedy delivery of fresh cheeses) that had started to offer its mail-order expertise to other companies. Except for a small charge for reconfiguring their computers, Swiss Colony asked for no up-front fees, and instead collected on a per-unit-sold basis. Likewise, the factor—the agent who ran credit checks on Trivia Inc.'s customers and collected the money from them—worked on a per-centage basis, again requiring no up-front fees and no guarantees. All of this enabled Trivia Inc. to move forward quickly with its game.

"Convert fixed to variable," Reiss tells the class, hammering home one of his central points. "Think of it as almost a religion."

A student tentatively offers one last entry for this list: "Low break-even point?"

Reiss's face lights up. He is clearly delighted. "Great! Great! So what *is* the break-even? How many games did we have to sell before we made our first buck?"

This is a figure that can be deduced from the facts of the case, but only after careful calculation, based on subtle distinctions between fixed and variable costs. It is easy to get wrong. Several students volunteer guesses that range from 18,500 to almost 40,000 units. Reiss writes the various estimates on the board as each student explains his or her reasoning.

"OK," Reiss says, letting the class off the hook. "The right answer is, we only needed to sell 11,700 to break even." He then leads the class through the calculations that get to this answer. The students look chagrined. Reiss plows ahead:

> But why is that important, anyway? Well, at that time, we were able to design and launch our product for $50,000. Parker Brothers or Milton Bradley would have had about $250,000 in fixed costs if they had done the game, and they would have spent another $1 million promoting it. And they never *could* have moved on it as fast as we did. It would have been too late, and would have been too expensive, or not profitable enough, or both.

Reiss then holds up a well-worn game box, its colorful top awash in day-glo reproductions of *TV Guide* magazine covers. "This is the finished product. It's a collector's item now. As you can see, we were not real shy about using the *TV Guide* name."

A student raises her hand. "But why did you have to close out the game altogether? I mean, Trivial Pursuit has survived."

"You wanna know the truth?" asks Reiss, again grinning broadly. "Our questions were just a *little too hard*. The *TV Guide* people were such TV experts, they went overboard!"

A WIN–WIN SITUATION

The R&R case, authored by Howard Stevenson and featuring Bob Reiss, has been taught at Harvard for more than a decade. Often, it is the case used to begin a unit of study on entrepreneurship.

"It's not a normal case," Stevenson says now. "For one thing, it gives the answer. It took me five years to figure out how to really teach it. Now I have fun with it. I start by asking the class if the game business is risky. Their answer is always 'Yes!' And then you walk them through what Reiss did, and by the end of it, you ask them, 'So where's the risk?' And there *is* no risk. When you commit quickly, when you use available resources and spare capacity, you can manage the risk."

Students generally find the case appealing and easy to absorb. Like the real estate cases written by Howard Stevenson and Bill Poorvu many years earlier, it takes most of the business issues faced by a start-up company and places them into a context where the time frame is short, the personnel and other resources are limited, and there is a strong incentive to act.

The case is currently used at more than fifty other business schools across the United States, in programs ranging from undergraduate through graduate and executive education. And although Bob Reiss can't attend every class, he does accept invitations to show up in person as often as he can.

"Bob is one of those people," says Stevenson, "who are innately curious and yet tough minded. They believe opportunity comes through change, and yet they're very meticulous about the steps they take to bring about that opportunity. These are people who defy the stereotypes on both sides."

Reiss continues to be a businessman with fingers in many pies. Working with Ron Goldstein, he develops new products (among them are talking bears and musical umbrellas) and finds undiscovered markets. He published a book about entrepreneurship—appropriately titled *Low Risk, High Reward*—and sometimes accepts speaking engagements.[2]

"And just to close another loop," Reiss says, "I also got involved a couple of years back with the Program Agency at Columbia." This is the student-run organization that four decades ago helped Reiss supplement his college scholarship. "People have neglected it, but it's still going on."

And his involvement with young entrepreneurial hopefuls extends beyond the Program Agency. "I'm always talking to a couple of kids here, a couple there," he says. "I had breakfast with some of them yesterday—two kids at Columbia. When it's the right person, it's fun to watch somebody start out on the road to success."

Like Bob Reiss, Howard Stevenson has been an active mentor. When he first recast the entrepreneurship area at HBS, he also took responsibility for the basic readings course in the doctorate program. This positioned him to cross paths with every D.B.A. candidate who went through the School over the next eighteen years. Some he recruited for his area, others he didn't—but hardly any of the students left without some firsthand knowledge of Stevenson.

"My purpose," he says, "was twofold. First, of course, I wanted to infect everybody that came through, and then make off with the great ones. But more generally, getting to know all these high-potential people, and getting them to know us, fostered mutual respect among all our different areas of study."

In more direct ways, Stevenson has helped and advised many colleagues and former students as they navigated the waters he himself passed through decades earlier. "I never had a mentor myself," he says. "I've spent a lot of time meeting and talking to lots of people, which is more my style. And I think I saw some negative role models, which helped me be even *more* committed to mentoring."

In Stevenson's view, building an area of study at a business school is not far different from building a successful company. The lessons he learned while writing about Adriano Olivetti and Howard Head often pointed in one direction: *If you want to build something that will last, you can't make everything depend on you.*

"When you maintain yourself as the center of all networks," he explains, "the organization can't survive you. So you have to make a choice, a trade-off, if you want to build an organization. That's true whether you're growing a business or growing a faculty."

Stevenson's philosophy has always been to let the younger faculty members in his area choose when to teach and how to divide up the course assignments. "What you're trying to do," he says, "is give the young people their *best possible opportunity* to succeed. When you're building an area of study, you can't afford a lot of losses. You've got to hope that everyone becomes a star, and you've got to take steps to make it happen. You try to give them all an opportunity to shine."

CHAPTER **9**

The Magic of the Movies

THE MAGIC OF THE MOVIES—*la magia del cine*, as the trademarked
slogan of Mexican movie-exhibitor Cinemex puts it—is a global phenomenon. In most corners of the world, and in many places for the
better part of a century, more and more movie-goers have surrendered
to the power of flickering images on silver screens.

But sweeping statements about a global phenomenon almost always wash out interesting nuances, complexities, and shades of gray.
Country by country, and over the decades, the history of the movie
business has varied dramatically. And perhaps nowhere has that history
differed more dramatically across a shared border than in the United
States and Mexico.

And in those differences, as it turns out, lies entrepreneurial opportunity for those able to pursue it.

In the United States, Hollywood has steadily increased its power
and influence for almost a century. Yes, American kids growing up in
the 1960s and '70s watched a lot of TV—but they also went to the
movies, in such numbers and with such frequency that whole new
categories of films were invented for them. And yes, the malling of
America led to the decline of the gilded downtown movie palaces that
originally helped make Hollywood a cultural phenomenon. But it also
led to an explosion of suburban cineplexes and multiplexes, featuring

239

multiple screens, easy access, and ample parking. More and more, movie-going became a family affair. Box office receipts soared, decade by decade.

The story in Mexico was remarkably different. The so-called Golden Age of Mexican cinema—which began in the late 1930s—staggered to an end in the early 1950s. Throttled by price controls and local-content laws, which mandated that 50 percent of films shown be Mexican-made, the Mexican film production, distribution, and exhibition industries fell into steep decline. Ticket sales plunged. Splendid old theaters degenerated into decaying venues for X-rated films. By the late 1980s, movie-going was almost a furtive activity. Prosperous Mexican families vacationing in the United States went out of their way to take in a movie, and for many, it was a truly exotic experience.

This chapter brings together strands from two countries. It is a story of three HBS students—one American who loved films and the film industry, and two Mexicans who did not—who came up with a plan to conquer the film-exhibition business in Mexico City, and who then *implemented* that plan almost flawlessly. It is a story of what was, up to that point, the biggest venture-backed start-up in Mexican history. And to some extent, it is a story of visionaries losing control of their vision, and ultimately regaining control.

LONG CONVERSATIONS

In the spring of 1992, Matt Heyman and Adolfo Fastlicht began a conversation that, in one form or another, continued for a decade.

Heyman and Fastlicht were then finishing up their first year in Harvard's M.B.A. program. One day, Fastlicht—scion of a well-to-do Mexican family with substantial real estate interests—asked his American classmate why Mexico didn't have clean, well-equipped, and family-oriented movie theaters like those in the U.S.

Fastlicht expected his classmate to know the answer to his question. After all, as most future members of the class of '93 knew, Heyman had worked the exhibition end of the film industry. He talked incessantly about the movie business, both in and out of class. He sported a pony tail and an *earring*, for god's sake. If anyone at HBS could answer Fastlicht's question, it would be Heyman.

But in fact, Heyman couldn't answer the question. Intrigued, he consulted the industry bible—*Variety*, to which he subscribed—and was surprised at what he read there in an article on the movie business in Latin America. By almost every measure—screens per customer, attendance per screen, screens per theater—the Mexican theater industry lagged. Mexico was "underscreened," in the lingo of the trade. Heyman reported back to Fastlicht that there appeared to be some kind of opportunity there.

Almost from that moment, the two classmates committed themselves to building a business around that opportunity. But exploring their prospects proved to be a lot of work for two M.B.A. students who didn't have much spare time. Heyman and Fastlicht started thinking about a second-year field study, whereby they could get academic credit for making their investigations. Fastlicht suggested that he recruit a third classmate, Miguel Davila, whom he knew from a Thursday night poker game in which the dozen or so HBS Mexican students participated. Davila was smart, detail-oriented, and—although he didn't travel in the kinds of circles that Fastlicht frequented—well connected in his home country.

Heyman also knew Davila, even a little better than Fastlicht did. Like Heyman, Davila lived in the Soldiers Field Park housing complex adjacent to the Business School campus. They had met in the laundry room a little more than a year earlier, the night before first-year classes were to begin, and got to talking. The next morning, they both rose at dawn to participate in the time-honored HBS custom of arriving early in the Aldrich classroom building to claim the seats in which they would sit for the next academic year.

"I got the last sky deck seat," Davila recalls. "He got the seat in front of me, on the next deck down."

This, too, was the beginning of a conversation that continued for just over a decade.

NONCONFORMIST MAKES GOOD

Shortly before he arrived in this world, Matthew Heyman's family relocated from New York City to Los Angeles. Forever afterward, Heyman felt an affinity for the Right Coast as well as the Left Coast.

Heyman's father sold TVs and other appliances across the San Fernando Valley. The youngest of three children, Matt Heyman was smart, brash, and often in trouble with local authority figures. "I went along," he says in his fast, clipped, fractional manner of speaking. "Did whatever, bounced around."

His bouncing-around days came to an abrupt end during his senior year of high school, toward the end of a lackluster high school career, when his mother came down with a terminal illness. Heyman decided to help care for her. He enrolled at California State University at Northridge in 1981, to which he commuted while helping out at home. The experience of attending to, and ultimately losing, his mother forced Heyman to grow up quickly. "Once she died," he recalls, "everything in my life changed." He transferred to New York University in the fall of 1981, where for the first time he showed signs of both ambition and leadership. After little more than a semester at NYU, he ran for president of the undergraduate business school and lost by only a few votes.

By now, the once-wayward kid knew exactly what he wanted to do: become a world-class economics professor, teach at a leading research university, write brilliant tracts, and pick up the inevitable Nobel Prize along the way. After graduation from NYU in February 1984, he went to work in the economics group at Chase Manhattan Bank. While he was there, he saw his undergraduate thesis published in *The American Economist*. So far, so good; the plan was panning out. That fall, he relocated to the University of Wisconsin to begin working on his economics Ph.D. The Nobel was almost in sight.

There, though, Heyman's grand plan went off the rails. As he recalls:

> I realized I wasn't smart enough to win the Nobel Prize. I was smarter than most of the people I knew, but I wasn't smarter than these guys who were going to get their Ph.D.'s. But at the same time, I also learned that I could make things happen, and most of these guys around me could barely walk. So it was a question of realizing where my competitive advantage was.
>
> That's part of my personality, for better or worse. I like doing things I'm very good at. I hate doing things I'm not good at.

Heyman dropped out, returned to California early in 1985, and moved back in with his father. Needing a way to support himself, he scoured the help-wanted ads, which steered him toward some off-beat part-time employment opportunities. He reviewed loan applications for the Small Business Administration. He picked up billable hours building real estate–related financial models for Los Angeles County. This latter work led him to answer a newspaper ad placed by a California-based exhibitor that was looking for a real estate analyst. Heyman didn't get that job, but in the application process, he made some valuable contacts, which eventually led him to a colorful and influential character named Garth Drabinsky.

Drabinsky was a fast-moving, high-candlepower lawyer who was fascinated by the film-exhibition business and was taking steps to become a major player within it. With a partner, he was then assembling Cineplex Odeon, a Toronto-based exhibitor which by its heyday in the late 1980s controlled some 1,800 screens across North America. Drabinsky was impressed by Heyman's brains and persistence, and in 1986—after more than a year of intermittent contact—he hired the twenty-four-year-old to help Cineplex Odeon find and lease appropriate theater sites in the Los Angeles area. Four months later, Drabinsky sent Heyman to New York to run Cineplex's East Coast real estate operations.

Heyman spent much of the next two years in New York: first finding locations and leasing spaces for fast-growing Cineplex, and eventually shifting into corporate strategic planning. Although he enjoyed the theater business immensely and did well for himself and the company, he became embroiled in a power struggle between Drabinsky and a second Cineplex executive. (One wanted to platoon the up-and-coming Heyman to London; the other wanted to send him to Toronto.) Caught in the middle, Heyman bailed, leaving the company in 1988 in order to promote a high-stakes real estate venture. He returned in early 1990 to serve as Cineplex's vice president of business affairs, but by this time, the company was going through a wrenching restructuring, and Heyman decided it was time to begin the next phase of his life. In the spring of 1990, he applied to Harvard Business School, and was accepted.

He had some misgivings. He was then twenty-nine years old—at least a few years older than most of his prospective classmates, and with more than a few battle scars on his back. "I'd been kicked around pretty hard," he recalls, "taken my lumps, lost jobs. I was pretty insubordinate in my way of operating—it was my way or the highway." Would he fit in at Harvard? And would Harvard help him make his way in the film industry, to which he was now firmly committed, but in which he had already burned a bridge or two?

PRIVILEGE AND HUSTLE

Asked to recount the highlights of his own life, Adolfo Fastlicht first goes back many decades before his own birth, to tell the story of his grandfathers. Both fled the persecution of Jews in Eastern Europe following World War I. Originally hoping to emigate to the United States, they were thwarted by strict U.S. immigration quotas, and instead wound up in Mexico. His father's father was an orthodontist and a committed Zionist, who ultimately became the first consul of Israel in Mexico. His mother's father, Sam Kurian, set up shop as a haberdasher in Puebla, a small city about a hundred miles east of Mexico City. Over the years, Kurian transformed the modest shop into the leading department store in Puebla, and eventually expanded the operation into Mexico City. In addition to building department stores, Kurian founded a small chain of supermarkets, which gradually led the business into a deeper involvement in real estate and related investments.

Fastlicht's own father spent many years finding his own path. He never finished college, started and dropped out of both law school and medical school, parked cars briefly at the Los Angeles airport, became an art dealer, and worked with another family member in an auto body shop. Finally, he decided to get into the real estate field. With a partner, he created a development firm called Grupo K, which began in low-income housing and over the years branched out into several other specialties, including industrial parks, office buildings, and high-end residential developments. The business prospered, and as a result, young Adolfo enjoyed a privileged childhood. Although the family wasn't super-rich—only "garden-variety rich," Fastlicht says—they lived in an elegant home, vacationed in Acapulco and the United States, and sent their children to private schools.

But not just any private school: Adolfo and his four younger siblings attended the American School in Mexico City, an English-language school populated mainly by the children of embassy personnel and American executives stationed in Mexico. A small number of affluent Mexicans, including the Fastlicht children, also enrolled at the school. Instruction was in English, which Fastlicht's family considered important to their children's future success. (Both of his grandmothers were highly educated Americans, and his mother had studied psychology at the University of Wisconsin.) Fastlicht admits to being an undistinguished student through much of his school career in Mexico. Beginning in his junior year, however, he realized that if he hoped to continue the family tradition and attend college in the States, he would have to get serious about his studies.

And he felt another incentive to excel: Mexican college students almost universally lived at home during their college years. Fastlicht knew that to have a typical U.S. "college experience," he would have to attend school outside of Mexico. He began earning high marks.

Accepted by several U.S. colleges, Fastlicht chose Boston University, mainly because he had visited Boston, had friends there, and loved the city. He enrolled in BU's business program and eventually specialized in hotel management, in part because Grupo K was then considering investments in Mexican hotels. He earned good grades, was active in various school organizations, and generally reveled in the life of a college student.

In his spare time, he also launched a few businesses. One was an importing company, which brought cheap Mexican silver jewelry into the United States. Fastlicht put together a sample case, attended trade shows, and tried to sell the big New York jewelry establishments. "Tiffany's didn't treat me very well," he laughs. "*Nobody* treated me very well."

With some friends, he also started a company that packaged mints —two to the package—for restaurants and other commercial clients interested in pushing their logos out into the world. This business fared somewhat better than the jewelry trade, and in fact is still operating today. But Fastlicht knew he wasn't going to make his fortune in the mint business. As his college graduation neared in the spring of 1989, he became increasingly convinced that he knew where his future lay:

> *I always had the notion to come back and work with my family. I never really interviewed seriously with the American hotel chains, although I did talk with Marriott, Sheraton, and a few other big ones. I said to myself, "Well, that's a possibility," but I always knew deep down that I would come back and work with my family.*

Meanwhile, his life took an unexpected turn. A close friend from home was applying to the Harvard Business School, so Fastlicht ventured up the Charles River to take a look. He was fascinated by what he saw there—"it blew my mind," he says—and immediately submitted his own application. (His packet included a reference from renowned author and philosopher Elie Wiesel, one of his professors at BU.) Harvard said yes, but deferred Fastlicht, telling him to go get two years of real-world experience.

So Fastlicht went home to Mexico—specifically, to Acapulco, where Grupo K had just purchased a 130-room hotel that had seen better days. Fastlicht took over the management of the troubled property, and also developed a 41-unit residential condominium complex. "Very complicated, very interesting," he recalls.

And somewhat hard to leave. Many of his Mexican friends were already "ahead" of him on the career track, having worked part-time in college. Now, after two years of working in the fast lane, Fastlicht was about to take himself off the track again to attend graduate business school in the States. "I was out of synch," he says, "but in the end, that was my decision: to go."

WORKING FOR IT

Miguel Davila is proud to say that, like his father, he is a public accountant. His pride comes not only from having followed in his father's footsteps, but also from the high status enjoyed by CPAs in Mexico.

In no sense did the senior Davila belong to Mexico's privileged elite. One of nine children, he grew up in one of the roughest sections of Mexico City, near a state penitentiary. Against long odds, he secured a college education, began working as a private-sector accountant, and in the 1970s went into government work, where he eventually rose to the position of undersecretary of budget for the Finance Ministry.

At home, the senior Davila was a stern taskmaster, determined to instill his own brand of independence in his children. As Miguel recalls:

> *He was a very strong character, very strong personality. He was the type of father that your friends were scared of—when he got home, everybody ran away. He's chilled out a lot recently, but when we were young, that was his style. So in that sense, and others, he was a very strong influence on me.*

Miguel Davila grew up on the western side of Mexico City, where he attended the local Catholic schools. The one exception came in ninth grade. His family sent their children to boarding schools in the United States for a year to foster both their independence and their fluency in English. Davila was sent to a Salesian Brothers school in Tampa, Florida, which he recalls as a "weird" place—"mostly for troubled kids, something like an orphanage." Students were expected to earn their keep by making a contribution to their school or the local community, so Davila wound up working in the school's auto shop, repairing school vehicles and the cars of local people. "An interesting episode," he concludes.

After graduating from a Catholic high school in Mexico City, he enrolled at the Autonomous Technological Institute of Mexico, a private college and the most highly regarded economics think tank in Mexico. He soon gravitated toward public accounting:

> *This was about the time when the public accountants in Mexico were stepping into a lot of very high positions in the Mexican government. That's how I saw my own father—as a very successful government official. There was a group called the Mexican Institute of Public Accountants for the Service of the State, of which my father was president*

at one point in time. So I saw it as a way of going into government, and doing well, like my father.

In 1987, while still in college, Davila talked his way into a job with the economics investigation department of the Banco de México, Mexico's central bank. The department normally hired only economists; Davila—then an accountant-in-training—offered to take any sort of economics exam that the bank might throw at him. The bank accepted his challenge and put together an informal "entrance exam," which Davila aced, earning himself a position conducting macroeconomic research for the central bank. In the back of Davila's mind, from the outset, was the knowledge that the Banco de México was one of the only public-sector institutions that sponsored graduate studies abroad.

Meanwhile, Davila was actively involved in running a small business, which he had started a year earlier. (It was his second venture, actually: His first was a small-scale stationery business that he ran with a friend for a year during high school.) This enterprise, purchased from a retiring businessman, comprised a chain of specialized spare-parts stores for Volkswagen bugs, which were and are ubiquitous in Mexico, constituting most of Mexico City's taxi fleet. "I could see a big business," he recalls. But it was essentially an inventory-based business, and Davila—not finding it a particularly gratifying pastime—turned it over to his brother and another employee to run on a day-to-day basis.

Gradually, Davila realized that he wanted to earn a graduate business degree abroad—not only to broaden his private-sector options, but to get a taste of the kind of collegiate life that he hadn't yet experienced. (Like most Mexico City college students, he had lived at home throughout his college days.) But the Banco de México offered scholarships only in *public* administration, which wasn't what Davila wanted. So in 1989, he began a series of discussions with the director of McKinsey & Company in Mexico, Bernard Minkow. Davila told Minkow that he wanted to go to the Harvard Business School, and that local scuttlebutt said Minkow could help make that happen. Minkow suggested that Davila come work for McKinsey for a year or so as a business analyst to strengthen his private-sector resume and make himself more attractive to Harvard. So in 1989, Davila left the Banco de México and moved over to McKinsey, planning to enroll at HBS in the fall of 1990.

First, though, he had to get in. He fought a losing battle with the graduate business school admissions test—"bad," he says, with obvious distaste, "bad, bad, bad. A humbling experience. You can't believe how much I hated that exam." Worried that his relatively low scores would wreck his chances at Harvard—even though HBS had recently dropped the GMAT requirement—he applied to a dozen schools in the U.S. and Britain. Finally, in June 1990, Harvard accepted him, but on condition that Davila work another year. He stayed at McKinsey, and this extra year—although not in Davila's plans—proved a godsend. He got married that summer, found a place to live with his bride, finished his undergraduate thesis, helped his brother shut down the auto-parts store, and secured much-needed scholarship money from McKinsey, the Fulbright program, and the Mexico Harvard Foundation.

In the fall of 1991, Davila and his wife moved into Soldiers Field Park, where—in the basement laundry room on the night before the first day of classes at the Harvard Business School—Davila ran into a pony-tailed movie buff named Matt Heyman. A little more than a year later, he found himself huddling with Heyman and Adolfo Fastlicht on a subject of almost no interest to him: the Mexican film-exhibition business.

GETTING REAL

At that point, Davila—who had spent the summer between first and second years exploring the worlds of money management and banking—had unusually good options. Well before the beginning of the formal recruiting season at HBS, he had a job offer in hand from the private-banking arm of Goldman Sachs, which would have placed him back in Mexico City. He also had a standing offer from McKinsey, which included the opportunity to pick any McKinsey office in the world for his first posting. But Fastlicht won him over by laying out what he and Heyman had learned so far about the sorry state of Mexican cinema—and what kind of opportunity that might represent. Recalls Davila:

Adolfo asked me to meet him for coffee in Kresge. I knew him fairly well from the poker game, but he lived off campus in Back Bay somewhere, and traveled constantly. Me, I was counting the cents. You know: a different thing. But he tells me about this scheme to do movie theaters in Mexico. It sounded reasonable to me, and worth looking into. After all, I'm at Harvard—the capital of capitalism, right? A couple of friends want to look into a business, I'd have to be stupid to say no.

I said, "Yeah, but what do you need me for?" Adolfo said, "Well, Matt knows the industry. My family knows real estate. And your family's in government, and you're a consultant with all these business-plan and implementation skills." But really, I think they just needed a third guy, and somebody thought of me.

Using the same arguments, they recruited a fourth second-year student, Eric Jarnryd. Jarnryd was a Mexican-Swede who had been living in Boston for several years, and—although he never shared Heyman's and Fastlicht's passion for pursuing an opportunity in the movie business—he agreed to round out their proposed field-study team.

Meanwhile, outside events helped propel the project forward. A new law passed in December 1992 reversed forty years of government controls on the Mexican film-exhibition industry. The new legislation mandated sweeping changes. The government decided to sell off the theaters that it had come to own, over the years. It would back off on film production, exhibition, and distribution. The local-content requirement that was generally ignored but constituted an ever-present background threat to the industry would be reduced to 10 percent. And most significant of all, price controls on tickets (which had limited the price of admission to about eighty cents) would be lifted. For the first time in decades, the roadblocks to investment in Mexican cinemas would be removed.

With this final inducement, the team approached HBS professor Howard Stevenson and asked if he would sponsor their proposed Entrepreneurial Management field study. Already further along than most such teams—and clearly committed to the outcome of their study—they had little trouble persuading Stevenson to serve as faculty sponsor.

"The first thing you ask yourself about any proposed field study," says Howard Stevenson with a grin, "is, *Is this an absolutely stupid idea?*" Neither the faculty nor the students should be involved in an effort that's doomed to fail, he explains, mainly because the learning experiences are limited. A good field-study topic has enough dimensions to engage all the team's members for a full semester, and is also "researchable."

Stevenson pushed the team hard. Creating a new Mexican theater chain, he warned, would be an enormous challenge. Nothing about the movie-exhibition industry—securing real estate, working out relationships with film distributors, accounting for profits—was straightforward. Existing chains most likely would take steps to defend their established turf, perhaps by applying muscle to the distributors. And Stevenson told the team that they were probably underestimating the capital requirements involved in leasing mall sites and building high-end theaters with food courts and other amenities.

"The thing was very capital-intensive," Stevenson recalls, "and we talked about that a lot. If someone was going to put a lot of money into Mexico, they would insist upon making a lot of money for assuming that risk. So how much control could the 'idea guys' maintain, in that kind of environment?"

The group overcame Stevenson's initial objections, but that was only the beginning of the hard work. The bar was raised high—in large part because the four team members were committed to building a *real start-up*. As Fastlicht recalls:

> *Really, school became secondary, at that point. It was a very intense process. We dedicated our lives to it. Matt's apartment on campus became the headquarters of the company. We started acting as a company.*

One thing that real start-ups do is raise money. "We thought that we'd get the thing funded before leaving school," Davila remembers, "and we'd be like champions, right?" They looked first to the U.S. exhibition industry, hoping to set up a joint venture, but found no serious takers. Several companies offered to buy the idea for a flat fee, usually in the low to middle five figures. The Cinemex team, determined to exploit their own idea, resolutely declined all such offers.

So Fastlicht and Davila made several trips to Mexico, both to conduct market research and to hunt for funding. (Davila wound up using some of his tuition money to meet his expenses, and Harvard therefore withheld his diploma until he paid off his tuition bill months later.) Fastlicht called on longtime family friends in Mexico, explaining what this new company was doing and offering potential investors a piece of the still-imaginary action. But he met with skepticism, even within his own family. His father cautioned that Organizacion Ramirez, the dominant player in Mexican film exhibition, would never permit an upstart to intrude on its well-established turf. Others warned Fastlicht that organized crime played a decisive role in this largely cash business, and that no respectable investors would go near the industry.

On April 12, 1993, the team completed their field-study report, a ninety-three-page document describing in convincing detail a Mexican film-exhibition company called Cinemex, following the tradition of ending the names of Mexican companies with the suffix "-mex." More convinced than ever that they were onto something, they entered their product in the relatively low profile business plan contest that was then being sponsored by the student entrepreneurship club. The Cinemex plan took first prize in the competition. They did less well at the University of Texas's international business plan competition, which they entered in hopes of winning some prize money to cover their mounting expenses. Publicly, the panel of Texas judges told the Cinemex trio that their plan was too expensive. Through back channels, the Harvard team learned that the judges found them a little too "arrogant."

THE PLAN

The Cinemex business plan that was submitted to Howard Stevenson, and entered in two business-plan contests, called for a sixteen-theater company with 158 screens. The exact location of those theaters was not specified, but since Mexico City was by far the largest Mexican movie market, and since good data were available only from that city, the plan focused largely on Mexico's capital. If and when the team secured funding, they would conduct an investigation to determine exactly how to deploy those resources.

Cinemex, according to the plan, would focus on upscale mall locations with plenty of parking. All theaters would have multiple screens, permitting an efficient use of employees (through staggered start times), economies of scale, greater selection at each site, and less exposure if and when a particular film bombed. Customers could use their credit cards to reserve seats in advance over the telephone, a new concept in Mexico.

Films would be booked according to a strategy developed by Matt Heyman and designed both to meet Cinemex's needs and to appeal to film distributors. Instead of booking one megahit into multiple screens in the same theater, Cinemex would book fewer prints of that film, and thereby give that product a longer run in that neighborhood. Distributors would appreciate the fact that their films had "legs" in Cinemex theaters, and—not incidentally—the film would make more money for Cinemex over the long run, since film-rental fees generally drop week by week over the course of a run.

Perhaps most important, Cinemex would provide an end-to-end, and *high-end*, entertainment experience. Entrances would be of polished marble, and the floors would be covered by high-quality carpets. Neon would abound. Employees would wear company-supplied uniforms. Concession stands would have selling stations, numbering roughly one per screen; they would be large, and stocked with high-quality treats. (All popcorn would be popped on-site, and Cinemex would introduce "candy by the pound" concession stands as well.) The theaters themselves would be state-of-the-art, featuring the highest quality sound and projection technologies, as well as stadium seating with extra legroom.

In short, Cinemex would provide Mexican movie-goers with an unprecedented entertainment experience: *la magia del cine*. Customers would pay more, and they would get more. And from an owner's point of view, investing more—in upscale locations, technologies, and décor—would generate greater operating profits and ultimately create a more valuable company.

STILL NO MONEY

The money hunt continued. Through classmate Larry Friedberg, Heyman made contact with Friedberg's father, A. Alan Friedberg, the legendary former chairman of the Loews theater chain, who ultimately came on board as the team's "mentor partner." Friedberg read the Cinemex business plan, liked what he saw, and jumped into the search for funding. As a first step, he introduced the Cinemex team to Claneil Enterprises, a privately owned holding company that had previously invested with Friedberg when he purchased USA Cinemas. Although things heated up briefly, Claneil ultimately declined to invest.

This pattern recurred several times. Prospective investors would get interested, the romancing would intensify, but then the courtship would end, often without explanation. A major buyout firm, for example, called the team down to New York for a series of increasingly friendly meetings—and then simply stopped taking calls from the Cinemex group. Harvard's endowment managers, approached in this same time period, liked the idea, but eventually explained that their guidelines prohibited them from investing Harvard's endowment into Harvard student ventures.

"We got shot down by everybody," recalls Heyman. "Occasionally, you'd see them get a spark in their eye, and then they'd blow us out. It was very hard."

Time was running out. June arrived, and when the class of '93 graduated, there was still no money in sight. Davila and Fastlicht returned to Mexico, still trying to secure local funding. They scored a public-relations coup when they extracted a verbal commitment from the owners of the prestigious Santa Fe mall, in an upscale Mexico City neighborhood, for a theater lease. This up-and-coming retail location was hotly contested by the existing players—Ramirez, U.S.-based AMC, and Mexican media giant Televisa—and Cinemex got the commitment partly because it had made a compelling presentation to the mall's owners, and partly because it was willing to pay top dollar. Subsequently, the Santa Fe owners backed off their commitment—requiring Cinemex to go through a "beauty contest" bidding war—but the initial round of publicity was key. "We needed that like air," explains Fastlicht, "because it provided us with huge word of mouth. It was very, very important for the company."

Heyman, meanwhile, struggled to push things forward in the States. He had exhausted his savings at business school and now had little financial running room. He moved to New York City, staying in close touch with both Friedberg and the Mexican contingent. (He hedged his bets, to some extent, by extracting a respectable job offer from Blockbuster Video.) Heyman had no phone in the summer of 1993; instead, he took messages on a Skytel pager and returned his calls on borrowed phones. But despite everyone's best efforts, Cinemex *wasn't happening*, so Heyman made plans to relocate to the West Coast. He packed up his modest possessions and pointed the car toward New Jersey to begin a cross-country trek.

As he approached the outskirts of Atlantic City, his pager started beeping. "Go back to New York," the urgent message from Fastlicht in Mexico read. "You've got a meeting with J.P. Morgan."

Heyman turned the car around, dug a suit out of his luggage, and went off to a meeting with yet another potential investor in Cinemex. He wasn't optimistic.

FROM NO TO YES

The Morgan connection grew out of a cocktail-party conversation that had taken place several months earlier. A former high school friend of Fastlicht's—Ricardo "Rich" Joyel, who had graduated from HBS the previous year—had heard about the Cinemex plan when Fastlicht and Heyman first started batting the idea around. "It was immediately evident to me that this was a good business plan," Joyel recalls, adding that it would have been equally obvious to any Mexican who had visited the States:

> *Like teenagers anywhere else, I went to a lot of movies in high school. We took the conditions as a given—long lines, crumbling buildings, inedible concessions. But once I had spent time in the States, it was perfectly obvious that there was a lot of room for improvement in the entertainment industry. So when I saw Adolfo's business plan, I had no doubt that it would succeed.*

At that point, Joyel was working for his father in the family business, Corporacion Frigus Therme. The company, and Joyel personally, considered investing in Cinemex. But the timing wasn't right, and both Joyel and his company passed on the opportunity. A few months later, though, he discussed the Cinemex concept at a cocktail party with a fellow Mexican, Christian Valdelièvre, a member of the HBS class of '83. Now, several months after that informal discussion, Valdelièvre wanted a copy of the Cinemex business plan.

To an unlikely degree, Valdelièvre was already an expert in the world that Cinemex hoped to conquer. In the late 1980s, as a vice president of investment banking at J.P. Morgan in Mexico City, Valdelièvre had spent about a year investigating an opportunity to purchase the basketful of decrepit theaters that the Mexican government had taken over years before, and now was talking about privatizing. At that time, Valdelièvre concluded it made no sense to try to build a new theater chain out of existing assets. For the most part, the government-owned buildings were too far gone as well as being technologically outmoded. In addition, movie-goers now wanted to see movies in smaller theaters in more suburban settings.

At the same time, Valdelièvre had come to the conclusion that there *was* an opportunity here—for a new chain of multiplexes in Mexico. His Morgan client was not interested in doing this alone, but indicated that he might think about it with an experienced partner, so Valdelièvre went to the States and met with several of the large movie theater chains. Just as negotiations were heating up with Dallas-based Cinemark, the Mexican client backed out. Valdelièvre closed the file and assumed he was finished with the exhibition side of the Mexican film industry—until, that is, his conversation with Rich Joyel in which he first heard about Cinemex. Eventually, Valdelièvre called Fastlicht and asked for a copy of the business plan.

Valdelièvre recalls being somewhat miffed when Fastlicht asked Morgan to sign a confidentiality agreement:

> *Honestly, I thought to myself, who the hell does this kid think he is? I'm from* Morgan—*what is he talking about, confidentiality agreement? But of course we signed it, and then he sent the business plan.*

> *At that point, I was really impressed. All of the details that we had re-searched were in there. It was pretty clear this could work.*

Valdelièvre was so convinced, in fact, that he himself wanted to invest in the plan. He brought it to the attention of J.P. Morgan Capital, the venture investment side of the firm, with an aside that he was planning to invest, and that Morgan might want to look into it as well. Morgan Capital did look—and looked hard. Though they had some initial objections, Valdelièvre worked closely with them over the next several months to convince them of what he himself already believed: *This plan could work.*

In the end, Valdelièvre proved something of a guardian angel to the fledgling company. Not only did he play a large and critical role in convincing Morgan to invest in Cinemex, but he also made a personal sacrifice at the eleventh hour to make the deal go through. Though Morgan Capital initially had told Valdelièvre that there was nothing preventing him from investing, the firm decided at the last minute that Valdelièvre's participation could be construed as a conflict of interest. Realizing that they had placed him in a difficult position, Morgan offered Valdelièvre a choice: He could invest and they would walk away, or vice versa. Clearly, Morgan's involvement was more important to the venture than his own, so Valdelièvre walked away.

Once again, time passed—so much so, in fact, that Fastlicht assumed that yet another money trail had gone cold. But it hadn't. In late summer, Fastlicht got a call that Morgan's New York office was very much interested in the plan. Could the potential investors come down to Mexico and discuss it with the principals?

Davila and Fastlicht pounced on this opportunity. They rented a meeting room in a local hotel, arranged to buy popcorn from a nearby theater, persuaded their wives (Marian and Sharon, respectively) to serve as hostesses, and scheduled a meeting—not only with J.P. Morgan, but also with Andy Bloom of Chicago-based JMB Realty and other potential investors.

The date was September 2, 1993. The Cinemex team, now including movie mogul Alan Friedberg, had put together a tightly scripted dog-and-pony show. Friedberg played the industry sage, speaking persuasively about the merits of the project. Heyman, Davila, and Fastlicht all did a turn at the mike. Their pitch was straightforward: *We need $6 million to get this thing off the ground, and we want 60 percent of the business to make it worth our while.*

The crucial moment arrived. Fastlicht recalls what happened next:

> *Toward the end of the meeting, my maternal grandfather, Sam Kurian, may he rest in peace, stood up. Didn't even let us finish. He said, "I've heard enough. I'm in. I'm committing a half a million bucks." And people started whispering, and talking. And finally Morgan said, "OK, we're interested." It was fantastic.*

But it was fantastic only up to a point. Over the following few days, the real bargaining began. Heyman, Davila, Fastlicht, and Friedberg quickly reduced their ownership demands to 40 percent, but they still had a lot to learn about the power of money. On October 8—coincidentally, Davila's birthday—Morgan made its formal offer. Morgan would put in $8 million. The partners would have to kick in a total of $100,000. They could earn a 2 percent equity share each time they achieved one of five annual targets, and could also qualify for two more 5 percent blocks of stock depending on the value of the company when it was sold.

It was a bitter blow to the entrepreneurial quartet—so much so that Friedberg quit the venture in disgust. For their part, Heyman, Fastlicht, and Davila—although now eligible for a scant 20 percent of the company, collectively—felt that they had little choice but to plunge ahead, and hope for a more favorable arrangement somewhere down the road. As Heyman recalls:

> *I wasn't happy with the deal. I wasn't happy with the salary. I wasn't happy about moving to Mexico. And yes, the deal took the wind out of my sails entirely. But I was trapped. I wasn't in a position to tell these guys to go fuck themselves.*

The deal formally closed in January 17, 1994, for a total of $21.5 million: the biggest venture capital start-up in Mexican history, up to that point. The three partners immediately set to work making their dream into a reality.

From the beginning, they imposed a distinctive discipline on their business, running it as what Adolfo Fastlicht describes as a "quasi-public" company. They retained high-profile lawyers, auditors, and accountants, thereby incurring greater expenses than might have been expected. They saw two compelling reasons to do so. First, building robust systems would permit the kind of rapid growth that the founders anticipated. And second, keeping bulletproof records would someday facilitate a harvest—the sale of the company either to the public or to an acquiring company. "We always said," recalls Fastlicht, "that this was a vehicle that had to give our investors their money back, and hopefully with a good return."

By midyear, they could point to signs of momentum. For example, Cinemex had signed its first lease, in the Altavista neighborhood, scoring a coup against their better-known competitors. (The founding partners celebrated by taking all four of their employees out to dinner.) This was no slam dunk, despite their celebrated financing successes. Because of the unsavory reputations that Mexican theaters had earned over the years, mall developers in Mexico were still extremely reluctant to put theaters in their properties. And although money talked, Cinemex didn't have much to recommend it *except* money: no existing theaters, no track record. Once again, Fastlicht called in some local chips, and again the hungry young company paid top dollar for its second premium site, including more than $1 million up front in "key money" to close the deal.

With the Santa Fe and Altavista sites under contract, and with money in the bank, Cinemex began catching people's attention. It appeared that if the company could wave enough dollars, it could conquer Mexico—and perhaps even territories well beyond Mexico.

A CRISIS CREATES OPPORTUNITY

But once again, lightning struck, this time in the form of a governmental action. In December 1994, as Cinemex was pushing ahead with both its Santa Fe and Altavista sites, Mexico announced a devaluation of the peso. This precipitated the worst economic crisis in the modern history of the country, and it abruptly ended an era of relative stability and growth. Aiming for a 20 percent devaluation, the government overshot the mark badly. The peso sagged by a full 50 percent, and the Mexican economy staggered. "Nobody knew what hit 'em," Fastlicht recalls grimly.

For Cinemex, there were both dark clouds and silver linings. Almost overnight, the value of the dollar-denominated investments in Cinemex was cut from $21.5 million to just over $13.8 million. This forced a time-consuming renegotiation of those commitments, which ultimately were restored to their original levels.

But meanwhile, a second and happier phenomenon occurred: The competition left town. All but one of the international movie chains that were then making plans to invade Mexico dropped those plans hurriedly. (The lone exception was Dallas-based Cinemark USA, which was well along in its development of a "12-plex"—a twelve-screen cinema complex—in Mexico City.) Domestic powerhouse Ramirez, which had theaters under construction all across Mexico, put many of its projects on hold. The industry hunkered down and held its breath.

Cinemex's three founders called a strategic huddle. Perhaps it didn't make sense to keep thinking about conquering all of Mexico. Maybe it made more sense to focus exclusively on the Mexico City market, where approximately half of the tickets sold nationwide were purchased. The metropolitan area was one of the most densely populated in the world. ("Think seven Manhattans put together," says Heyman.) It was also one of the most congested. At most times of day, and well into the night, no sane person ventured across town for a movie, since a trip of only a few miles might require an hour or more in the car. Wouldn't lots of screens in the right neighborhoods of Mexico City—far more than had been contemplated in the original business plan—make sense?

The competition had decamped. Fastlicht was now getting the first shot at prime locations, and future lease terms promised to be far more favorable to Cinemex than past ones. Maybe by the time those anxious competitors returned, Cinemex could seize the strategic heights in the capital city.

With this narrowed focus, the trio set out to lay the foundations for a revised company. They finished plans for their $3.5 million Altavista theater, consciously aiming to build the best theater in Mexico.

(Whereas competitor Ramirez then spent about $75,000 per screen on projection and sound equipment, for example, Cinemex budgeted around $120,000 per screen.) They started hiring college students for entry-level positions, dressed them up, and paid them about three times what organizations like McDonald's were paying comparable new hires. They created the first Mexican implementations of conveniences that were already well established in the United States—for example, Linea Cinemex, the phone- and credit card–based system that theater patrons could use for advance ticket sales.

In short, they carried out almost to the letter the business plan that they had developed at Harvard a little more than two years earlier. Much had happened in those two intervening years, but to a remarkable extent, the plan hung together.

THE BATTLE OF ALTAVISTA

As Opening Day at Altavista approached, however, Cinemex's personnel head, Miguel Davila, faced one of his biggest challenges: asserting control over the workforce that he was in the process of hiring.

For more than seventy years, almost every aspect of the Mexican film industry—from production through distribution and exhibition—had been controlled by a single union, the STIC. The union wielded its power aggressively, and on the exhibition end of the business, this created huge inefficiencies. By contract, the person behind the counter who sold the popcorn couldn't dispense soda, and vice versa. (If you wanted both, you had to go through two lines.) Personnel could not be fired or even reprimanded. Particularly offensive to exhibitors was the *similares* system, which required theaters to hire two people to fill each job opening: one union worker and one nonunion *similar* (or roughly, "equivalent"). As Davila explains:

> *You had two payrolls. You had the nonunion guy, the* similar, *who got no benefits, or pension, or perks, but did all the work. And then you had the union guy who got all the benefits and perks, but did no work. And these union people got to inherit their jobs, and also sell their jobs. No wonder the industry in Mexico had gotten into disarray! If you weren't able to fix that, you simply couldn't make it.*

According to Mexican law, every company with more than twenty employees is subject to unionization. Unions find it relatively easy to gain control of workplaces—even where the workforce may not want representation—and companies find it difficult to dislodge entrenched unions. Many new companies, therefore, seek out a so-called progressive union with which to do business. Progressive unions differ from company unions in that they are truly independent organizations, representing employees from multiple companies; on the other hand, they are generally more willing than conventional unions to work with management. Taking a cue from a labor attorney, Miguel Davila got in touch with Justo Sierra, a union that concentrated mainly on foreign companies in Mexico, and asked whether that union wanted to organize Cinemex. As Davila explains:

> *I got myself a great labor lawyer—a young guy, very bold, with new ideas, and who was willing to take risks. We planned out our legal strategy to get what we needed within constitutional and legal bounds. Then we sat down with the union and worked it out. We agreed on the way we wanted to handle the company, and the way we wanted to look at the workforce. We agreed to support each other.*

Cinemex and the union struck a deal—but this was not the end of the story, of course. Rival Cinemark, which had pointed the way toward a new labor-management relationship, soon found itself in deep trouble as a result of that strategy. Picket lines and threats of violence prevented the opening of new Cinemark theaters in Monterrey and Aguascalientes. How would Cinemex avoid a similarly chaotic situation at Altavista, which was then nearing completion?

Davila first made sure that he had the Labor Ministry solidly behind him. Drawing on his connections with government officials, he arranged a series of meetings to make his pitch for support. "I did a lot of campaigning with them," he says, "pointing out that we had put a lot of money into the company, and wanted to do good things for the city and its people."

One day in the summer of 1995, a month before Altavista was scheduled to open, Davila was sitting in his office talking with a group of reporters from *Reforma*, the city's most popular newspaper, about the imminent opening of Cinemex's first facility. Just then, an aide came into the room and told him that the manager at the nearly completed Altavista theater was on the telephone with an urgent message. Something like 150 people—members of the displaced union, as well as what appeared to be their family members ranging from grandmothers to infants—had seized control of the theater.

Davila decided to go to the scene at once. Thinking fast, he invited the reporters to come along with him and see firsthand what Cinemex was up against. As the caravan sped toward Altavista, Davila also tipped off local television and radio outlets about the breaking story. By the time Davila arrived at the theater, he remembers, a full-fledged press corps was on the scene, awaiting the next development:

> *So I go inside the theater, and there's a big fat guy with his big body-guards standing around him. And I start going crazy:* Why is he in my theater? He's a robber! He's invading my property! *So he gets upset, and throws himself against me like he's going to punch me. His guys realize just in time that this is all with the cameras rolling, and they pull him back before he actually punches me. But what the press reports is that gangsters are attacking the executive management of the company. Gives them a very bad rap, to say the least.*

Eventually, the intruders—facing a barrage of charges ranging from invasion of property to kidnapping—left the theater, only to set up picket lines inside the mall blocking every entry to the theater. But Davila already had mapped out a strategy for this phase of the fight. On the theater's marquee, he announced an 8:00 P.M. showing of a film. When eight o'clock came and went with no patrons entering the theater, the picketers celebrated their victory and went home for the night. At that point, by prearrangement, some five dozen policemen converged on the shopping center and took control of all of its entrances, effectively establishing a new perimeter in the mall's parking lot. When the picketers returned the next afternoon, they found themselves restricted to demonstrations outside the building.

The final phase of the conflict came a few weeks into this standoff. By tradition, new theaters generally open on Friday nights, but Davila knew that Cinemex would be asking for trouble if it followed that industry tradition. So instead, he simply opened the theater mid-week with no advance notice:

One Wednesday afternoon—August 2nd, 1995—there were very few protesters outside. So we told our police to open up for people to come in. We lit up the box office, pulled open the curtain, opened up the refreshment stand, and invited people in. I think we got two customers. But the minute we turned that first projector on, even with only a few people in the theater, we had basically won the battle. After two or three days of watching us draw bigger and bigger crowds, the guys outside gave up and went home.

The Battle of Altavista tested Cinemex's young managers, several of whom received death threats. Davila, in particular, drew fire from angry unionists. (Between the founding of the company and the opening of Altavista, his weight dropped from sixty-five to fifty-eight kilos.) But Altavista set a successful pattern for Santa Fe—the second Cinemex theater, which opened in October 1995—and subsequent theaters. Whenever Fastlicht and Heyman identified a promising theater location, Davila drew up a collective bargaining agreement covering that site—in most cases, even before a lease had been signed. And although the displaced union made another run at Cinemex in the spring of 1997, the company now controlled its own destiny.

A HIT AND TWO FLOPS

The Altavista and Santa Fe theaters demonstrated that Cinemex and its concept could succeed in Mexico City's affluent neighborhoods. But no one knew whether that same concept could succeed in poorer neighborhoods. In terms of the raw numbers—screens per capita—Mexico City was underscreened. But did that deficit really reflect an unexploited opportunity? Or were people simply too poor to go to the movies? After all, Cinemex's average ticket price (then around $3.35) was about equal to Mexico's daily minimum wage. Suppose people in poor neighborhoods were offered the full Cinemex experience at a discounted rate. Would they put up their hard-earned pesos? No one knew the answer.

Cinemex decided to find out. The company leased space for a ten-screen complex in Los Reyes, a poor neighborhood near the women's jail in Mexico City. Even as they closed the deal, Cinemex's founders understood that they were running a critically important experiment, the results of which would define the potential of Cinemex. How big *was* this business, actually? If Los Reyes bombed, the repercussions for Cinemex would extend far beyond one disadvantaged neighborhood. From that point on, Cinemex would be limited to being a niche player in Mexico City's relatively few upscale neighborhoods—in other words, not much of a company. "If Los Reyes doesn't work," says Heyman, "it's over. There's no business here."

But Heyman, for one, was optimistic:

Admittedly, I was a foreigner, and didn't understand this market that well. But I knew that in the U.S., some of the best-performing theaters are in poor neighborhoods. They do huge attendance. They run the highest concession sales, because when people go to the movies there, they go to dinner at the movies. Plus, real estate costs less. So they can be harder to run, but they can be very profitable.

Heyman also had some specifics on theater-going in Los Reyes. Very close to the proposed Cinemex sites sat two old "twins" (two-screen theaters). "Hey, we're not *crazy*," he says. "We knew those twins were kicking ass, doing huge numbers, like three thousand people per screen per week. That certainly affected the way we thought about Los Reyes."

Construction began in 1995, and in May of the following year, the theater opened for business. But very little business got conducted, despite the fact that tickets cost about half of what they did in other Cinemex theaters. In fact, for several days, very few patrons ventured into the gleaming new facility. Local people stood outside the lobby—peering in through the glass doors, but refusing to come in.

Davila puzzled over this, and soon grasped the problem: These people simply didn't believe that this dazzling place had been built for *them*. He instructed his employees to go outside, mingle with the crowd, and encourage them to come in and look around. Gradually, tentatively, they did. Some had never walked on wall-to-wall carpeting before; they knelt down and rubbed their hands in wonderment across the high-end Durkan carpeting in the lobby.

Los Reyes proved that poor people *could* be wooed and won—thereby vastly enlarging Cinemex's potential market. But the experience of Cinemex Masaryk, on the other end of the economic spectrum, proved that Cinemex could guess wrong, too. Heyman yearned to add an "art house" to the growing Cinemex chain, and thereby plant the seeds for an art circuit in Mexico City. The first step would be to create a theater in which movies with a small but well-defined "highbrow" audience could be screened more or less profitably. Most major American and Canadian cities have one or two such theaters, in which foreign films, cult favorites, and other non-blockbuster films find their audiences. Significantly, only a small number of prints of each film circulate, almost guaranteeing that the audience will be concentrated enough to sustain the film—and also the theater. It's not unusual for an art film to run for weeks, or even months, at a New York or Boston art house.

For its art house, Cinemex settled on the upscale Polanco neighborhood, in part because Polanco had a high concentration of Mexico City's Jews. "In the U.S.," says Heyman, "if you want to have a successful art theater, you put it where the Jews are." So Cinemex constructed a beautiful state-of-the-art facility—a four-screen, seven-hundred-seat multiplex serving not only popcorn but also draft beer, hard liquor, cappuccino, and pastries—in heavily Jewish Polanco, and began booking art films.

But the Casa de Arte, which opened in September 1996, bombed. "A disaster," says Heyman. "The disaster of the company."

Two things went wrong. First, Heyman's reading on where Mexico City's cultured elite resided was simply wrong. (They tend not to be Jewish, and they tend to live not in Polanco, but in the southern part of the city.) But more important, Cinemex simply didn't have the muscle needed to restrict the number of prints entering the city. Under strong pressure from other exhibitors, distributors continued to supply limited-market films to all exhibitors, and as a result, the art films that were supposed to carry the Casa de Arte failed miserably. "The distributors ruined the business," Heyman says with disgust.

"Those particular films need to be treated differently, or they just become crappy commercial films." Although the Casa de Arte still limps along at a break-even pace, it hasn't lived up to the company's expectations, and seems to have no prospects of doing so.

At about this same time, Cinemex also ventured into the live entertainment business, an ill-fated move that no one at Cinemex much likes to talk about. "We lost four million dollars on it," Fastlicht recalls ruefully. "Everything that we could have done wrong in that business, we did. It was a textbook case of how not to do a business."

Curtly, Davila agrees. "It wasn't one of the most luminous stories in the history of this corporation."

But the good news far outweighed the bad in Cinemex's first few years. By the end of 1996, the company had built and opened six cinema complexes with sixty-one screens—and had captured 25 percent of Mexico City's box office. In this same period, moreover, the company's founders not only laid plans for even more growth, but also defined their respective roles in ways that would make that growth possible.

DIVISION OF LABOR

"If you wanted to bet against Cinemex from the beginning," says Miguel Davila with a slight smile, "you would have bet against the three of us getting through the process safely, in one piece—no?"

The "three-headed monster"—as insiders sometimes referred to the company's leadership triumvirate, all of whom held the title of "director"—ranks as one of the more interesting and unlikely aspects of the Cinemex story. Few companies prosper with three equally powerful leaders at the helm, but Cinemex managed to do so. The secret may lie in the fact that although the cast of three main characters stayed the same for more than a decade, the company in the same period grew rapidly. As a result, the three directors' roles, and the ways in which they interacted with each other, evolved significantly.

Fastlicht, given his family ties, began in the real estate side of the business, scouting suitable locations for new theaters and negotiating leases. (His father, an established player in the local and national real

estate games, was the company's first board chairman.) His partners referred to him as the company's "ambassador." And although Heyman
and Davila—who for the first three years of the company's existence
came early, stayed late, and worked weekends—sometimes begrudged
Fastlicht his time on the golf course with local movers and shakers,
they instantly forgave Fastlicht his golf outings when he closed a deal
on yet another highly sought-after location.

Not long after the company opened its first theater, Fastlicht added
a critical new role to his portfolio: the sale of on-screen ads. He had no
prior experience in ad sales and got the job mainly because he was the
one who advocated for it. "Very many things you wound up in charge
of," he explains, "because you identified an opportunity, and then you
went for it."

The idea of selling on-screen ads wasn't new—the Ramirez theaters had a long tradition of "sponsors," whose commercial messages
would precede films in Mexican theaters—but theater ads remained
an underexploited concept. Fastlicht first retained Televisa, a diver-
sified entertainment company and the world's largest producer of
Spanish-language TV programming, to serve as Cinemex's sales agent,
on the theory that Televisa already knew the business and had multiple outlets. After three years, Cinemex "repatriated" the effort, working directly with advertisers to develop ads specifically for exhibition
in theaters. Most often, this involved creating advertising materials
that could be repurposed for both theaters and television—but making sure that the theater versions were both high-quality and distinctive. By the turn of the century, Cinemex was garnering the single
biggest piece of what appeared to be a $40 million screen advertising
business nationwide, although the aggregate numbers were notoriously unreliable.

Davila, who says he enjoyed his Service Management course at
Harvard more than any other single offering, emerged early on as the
operations guy, trying to set and hold the company to the highest possible standards of service. Recruiting, hiring, training, accounting,
defining and documenting policies—all fell into Davila's domain. He
worked mainly behind the scenes, only occasionally stepping forward
to tackle a pressing challenge.[1]

The year 1999 presented one such challenge. The Mexican government then began making noises about reregulating the cinema industry—in other words, retrenching from the 1992 liberalizations that had made Cinemex possible. Specifically, the legislators proposed a 5 percent tax on box-office receipts, which threatened to shrink exhibitors' margins dramatically. They also contemplated a law that would once again raise the local-content requirement—this time from 10 percent to 30 percent. These local-content rules were generally ignored by exhibitors, in part because there weren't enough Mexican films to go around, but there was always the threat that they might be enforced one day.

Davila personally led the charge to head off the proposed reregulation. He had the benefit of good timing, in the sense that Mexican democracy was evolving rapidly toward a legitimate multiparty system. Along with viable political parties came lobbying and lobbyists and the opportunity to apply industry pressure to wavering legislators. Davila—in collaboration with other theater-industry executives—moved swiftly and effectively, getting the 30 percent local-content requirement reduced back to a manageable 10 percent, getting the proposed 5 percent box-office tax eliminated, and moving box-office receipts into the national VAT (value-added tax) structure.

This last change had a significant positive impact on Cinemex's bottom line. Cinemex, along with all other exhibitors, had been paying a VAT on every expense it incurred, but had been prohibited by law from collecting a VAT on box-office receipts. Henceforth, they could collect from theater-goers the taxes that were paid on those visits.

"It was a very positive move, worth something like six points of EBITDA," says Fastlicht. "Miguel spearheaded the whole thing, and did a fantastic job of it."

Davila made a point of going to every corporate recruiting session to talk with prospective employees. During orientation, he met with each new hire and gave the rookie the Davila perspective on the company's history and traditions. He visited at least a few theaters every week, trying to keep in touch with Cinemex's growing workforce, and stressing an "open-door" policy. "I told them all that we had just one rule," he says. "And the rule was, *have fun.* We're in the business of entertaining, and if you can't get entertained, you can't do your job."

Matt Heyman, the third head on the three-headed monster, was the "movie guy." While working in Cineplex Odeon's real estate department in his pre-HBS days, Heyman had taken every opportunity to hang out with that company's film department, learning how to book and exhibit films. ("I always wanted to be head film buyer," he explains. "That was the only part of the business that I wanted to do long-term.") But an odd pattern prevailed at Cineplex: It was the real estate group that projected attendance and revenues for proposed new sites. "That struck me as strange," Heyman recalls. "I mean, shouldn't the *film* department also be putting their asses on the line, in terms of projected revenues? And conversely, why should real estate have the right to force particular locations down the throat of film?" Determined not to recreate these mistakes, Heyman (with the encouragement of Davila and Fastlicht) made sure that the film-buying function at Cinemex was tightly linked to the strategic planning and real estate functions.

As Cinemex prepared to open its first Mexico City theaters, Heyman's most important job was to devise a booking and exhibition strategy that would give Cinemex the greatest possible leverage with the distributors. The postdevaluation decision to concentrate Cinemex's efforts in Mexico City, Heyman explains, made this strategy much easier to pursue:

> *It's the way it was in the U.S. when I was young: You had one dominant chain in each market, and each chain more or less controlled its own market.*
>
> *But then all the chains went national, and "national" had no value, because the distributors could play one chain off against another. The whole trick is to be able to control film, and to have at least a little push on these characters, because they're not easy guys to push around. The way I always put it is, "I know I can't knock you out if I take a swing at you, and I probably can't even give you much of a black eye. But I'd like to be able to wake you up a little bit." And that's what concentrating in Mexico City did for us.*
>
> *I learned a lot of this while I was working with Cineplex in Toronto and New York. They made just about every mistake you can make.*

Instead of focusing on New York City, for example, they started build-
ing in Atlanta and North Carolina. I think understanding those mis-
takes had a very positive impact on Cinemex.

As noted, the three-headed monster evolved over time. In Cinemex's early days—that is, before there were very many theaters into
which Heyman could book films—Fastlicht and Davila made some
effort to keep their voluble partner somewhat under wraps. This was
in part because they wanted Cinemex to be perceived as a Mexican
company, and it made no sense to put the American partner out front
(especially an American partner who didn't particularly crave the
Mexican limelight). But it was also because they suspected that Mexico City's business community wasn't ready to handle Heyman's
"American" approach to business. Heyman wanted lawyers and tight
legal agreements, they recall, whereas the Mexican culture called for
doing business on a handshake—even when large sums of money
were at stake. Over time, they say, Heyman knocked off some of his
own rough edges, and eventually, Mexican businesspeople came to
enjoy dealing with him. "Eventually," recalls Davila, "it got so he could
throw a fit and nobody would go crazy about it. Six years ago, they
might have."

The three-headed monster also worked, in large part, because the
three partners trusted each other's instincts implicitly. "I could trust in
them with my eyes closed," says Davila, "to do the thing the way I
would do it, or better." And in his own way, Heyman returns the
compliment:

> *Miguel is a very ethical guy. He's the most ethical guy I know. Some-*
> *times I wanted to kill him for it, because sometimes I didn't think the*
> *question at hand was one of ethics. Yeah, we had to be squeaky clean,*
> *but we didn't have to give all the money away!*

The three-headed monster worked because the company's rapid
growth created ever-broader spheres of influence for each of them—
and kept them out of each other's hair. In the early days, all three partners worried about almost every decision—down to the uniforms that
in-theater employees would wear—and squabbles inevitably cropped

up. Eventually, though, Heyman ran the film department and concession stands unilaterally. Fastlicht ran real estate development and screen
advertising single-handedly, and Davila ran operations without input
from his colleagues.

As the demands of the business gradually pulled the partners apart,
however, they realized that they had to take steps to formalize their
communications. They began meeting for breakfast at a local restaurant every Tuesday morning, comparing notes and making plans in a
reasonably nonharried context.

At these meetings, an interesting decision rule prevailed. The partners sought unanimity. If they didn't reach consensus, they settled for
a two-to-one vote, with the assumption being that the odd man out
would go along with the majority's decision. But they added a distinctive Cinemex twist: When a particular decision lay at the heart of
one partner's sphere of influence, that partner got what Davila calls a
"quality vote," which could outweigh the other two partners' votes.
When it came to booking films, for example, Heyman had the quality
vote. In matters relating to on-screen advertising, explains Davila,
Fastlicht ultimately made the call:

> *Say Adolfo was pushing, once again, for more of those minutes of on-*
> *screen advertising. Matt and I don't like those minutes, no? So we would*
> *try to say where we thought the line should be drawn. But in the end,*
> *we had to let Adolfo go a little bit beyond that, because he said he has*
> *to. Well, he was the one who knew what was happening in that market.*
> *He knew what he needed to give to a client so we wouldn't lose him.*

Similarly, when it came to scope and quality of service, Davila
tended to get the quality vote. Heyman confesses that he would have
gladly lowered the company's service levels to enhance the company's
profitability. "But hey," he says, shrugging his shoulders, "Miguel ran
that area, right? I'm wasn't going to get into a fight over that. Except,
of course, that we had to have the best theaters in the *world*, period."

Quality votes weren't cast lightly. When Fastlicht insisted that the
Cinemex concession stands carry red licorice—a taste he acquired in
the States—concession-king Heyman gave ground. "Even though it
didn't sell for shit," Heyman says flatly, "and importing and relabeling an
American product is basically a nightmare. Plus, *I* like red licorice, too."

And finally, the three-headed monster worked because the three partners didn't worry much about interpersonal politics or pecking orders. They led substantially separate lives, and rarely crossed paths outside the office. Personal relationships waxed and waned within comfortable zones. In the early days, says Davila, he and Fastlicht probably enjoyed the closest bond of friendship; later, he says, Heyman and Fastlicht came to have the most in common.

TAKING FIRST PRIZE

In its first half-decade of operations, Cinemex had an amazing run—both in relative and absolute terms. A few numbers help make the point. At the turn of the century, Mexico had only the thirteenth-largest economy in the world, but ranked fifth in terms of theatrical market. And Mexico City accounted for something like 38 percent of all box-office receipts in the country. (The second largest Mexican market is the city of Monterey, which accounted for 11 percent.) This is a greater percentage than would result in the United States if you combined the grosses in New York, Chicago, and L.A. So conquering Mexico City *counted*.

In 1996—Cinemex's first full year of operations—the company had 65 screens in 5 buildings, and captured around 16 percent of the Mexico City market. By the year 2000, Cinemex had 317 screens in 27 buildings, and owned just over 50 percent of the market. And that market had grown enormously—from a low of 28 million tickets sold in Mexico City in 1995 to 42 million in 2000. So Cinemex grabbed an ever-increasing share of a rapidly growing industry.

But the Cinemex story is more than just a tale of conquered territory. It is as much a tale of *transforming* a market and an industry. Professor Jim Heskett, a service-management expert who wrote an HBS case on Cinemex, recently was reminded of this fact in an informal discussion at Harvard. "We had some Mexican participants in our Latin American teaching program here," he explains. "We got to talking about Cinemex, and they said, 'You know, you don't really realize how completely they changed the industry.'"

Indeed, to some extent, "Cinemex" and "the movies" became interchangeable. "Which cuts both ways," recalls Heyman. "We were at risk of becoming a generic, like Kleenex."

Strategies for building the Cinemex brand got on the table almost at the inception of the company. Early on, Davila and Fastlicht made the case that a rapid expansion of Cinemex would lead naturally to the creation of a strong brand, which in turn could be leveraged to the company's advantage. In other words, a generic experience—going to the movies—could be branded, if the company played its branding cards right. Davila, in particular, believed that a strong brand would help the theater business, and might eventually extend beyond that business.

Heyman didn't believe it. After all, entrepreneur Richard Branson had tried something similar in the U.K.—buying up a group of theaters and applying his Virgin brand to them—and stumbled badly. But the occasional mistake aside, such as the live-entertainment distraction, Cinemex succeeded where Branson failed. By the year 2000, Cinemex had emerged as a powerful brand, with the opportunity to branch out in the future.

"Hey," says Heyman, "they were right, and I was wrong. The conditions were right. The moon and stars aligned. We worked hard, and we were lucky."

Meanwhile, the bread-and-butter numbers remained amazingly strong. In recent years, Cinemex has averaged about 90,000 customers per screen annually, one of the highest such totals in the Western Hemisphere. Although Cinemex's financial data are private, Heyman told the *New York Times* in 2001 that the company would probably earn operating income of about $44 million on revenues of $140 million.

In 2001, Cinemex's accomplishments were formally acknowledged by the industry, when the company was named International Exhibitor of the Year at the ShoWest convention in Las Vegas. "That felt good," says Heyman.

MUNDO E

About eight miles from Cinemex's headquarters in the upscale Lomas de Chapultepec district, alongside a busy four-lane divided highway that bisects a lower-middle-class neighborhood on the north side of the capital, squats "Mundo E," an enormous entertainment center put together in the late 1990s by a local developer. Next to a huge Coke sign is the trademark Cinemex red ball and logotype. And from an ad-jacent signpost hangs a tattered-looking sign for the All-Star Café.

"Out of business," says Matt Heyman, shaking his head as his chauffeured car pulls into Mundo E's parking lot on a hot October day in 2001. "Stupid concept."

Since Opening Day in December 1998, Cinemex has been the anchor tenant at Mundo E. The complex's developer came up with a futuristic/fantasy theme for his property, and Cinemex agreed to carry that theme into its cavernous lobby space. (When it opened, the Mundo E Cinemex—with nineteen screens and forty-five hundred seats—was the largest multiplex in Latin America.) Neon is every-where, most notably as a frame for oversized posters promoting current and coming attractions. Huge multiscreen video walls show previews, and speakers pump out movie soundtracks at high volumes. A thirty-foot-high obelisk, resembling a scaled-down Washington Monument, points toward a vaulted ceiling adorned with a faux blue sky. "Our obelisk," confirms Heyman. "Don't know what it means. If anything."

On this day, five of the theater's nineteen screens are showing Mexican products. The largest theater has 936 seats, and the smallest has 91. "I'll now show you the best screen in the world," he says proudly, opening a door and steering his guest into a darkened the-ater, where a subtitled Hollywood film is in progress. The screen is indeed impressive, mainly because of the high-end Sonido Cinemex projection and sound system. But Heyman returns to the lobby with a scowl on his face.

"*Muy tranquillo, no?*" he asks a nearby employee in a snappy uni-form. The employee shrugs and puts his palms up. He clearly recog-nizes Heyman. "This sucks," Heyman continues under his breath. "Rush hour, and no one in there. This is a bad thing."

The centrally located concession stand offers Mexican-produced candies, most of which closely resemble American candy brands. The popcorn is popped on site. "People here put chile and lime on their popcorn," Heyman says with a grimace. "To me, that's the most dis-gusting thing in the world. I mean, it's *watery*. The popcorn just *loses* it." The overhead menus stress combinations—for example, a large soda and a large bag of popcorn. "We're totally combo driven," Heyman confirms. "We want to drive our transaction size higher and keep our cycle time as low as possible. It's not rocket science."

Off to one side of the lobby sits "La Locura"—another Cinemex trademark, translating to "The Craziness"—a smaller stand that sells self-service, one-price candy by the pound. But unlike the treats at the main concession stand, these candies are aimed at local tastes. The *tamarindo* fruit—dried, and eaten with chile and salt—is a perennial favorite. "They're all acquired tastes," says Heyman to his American guest. "That one that looks like Good 'n' Plenty? Forget it. Definitely something that you wouldn't like."

Back in the parking lot after this whirlwind tour, Heyman turns and looks again at Mundo E. "If this theater were in Boston," he says flatly, "it would be the best theater in Boston. In fact, it's one of the best *in the world*. Hey, you can tell me you don't like our style, but you can't tell me any other theaters are *better* than ours."

THE GOLDEN CAGE

Early in 1999, Cinemex's three principals concluded that it was time to deliver on their promises to their investors. They decided to put the company up for sale. Not surprisingly, they turned to their longtime partner, J.P. Morgan, to handle the deal.

Morgan may not have been the best choice. Although accounts of what followed vary, some within Cinemex grew frustrated by what they saw as Morgan's lack of understanding of their industry, and the investment banking house's seeming lack of interest in the property that they were trying to sell (and in which they owned a sizable stake). Morgan set up an auction, in part to generate excitement and lure more bidders into the process, but as it turned out, no more than two bidders ever expressed real interest in Cinemex. The auction fizzled.

But even Cinemex's disappointed founders acknowledge that larger problems well beyond Morgan's control helped kill the sale. In the summer of 1999—just when the Cinemex auction was supposed to be heating up—the U.S. theater-chain industry melted down. Years of overconstruction had led to an industrywide overcapacity, and the result was predictable. Eleven U.S. chains went into bankruptcy in 1999 alone. Investors ran as fast as they could from the movie-exhibition business, and one company they ran from was the upstart chain in Mexico City.

Ironically, there was no compelling reason—other than a stampede mentality—to run away from Cinemex. As Fastlicht recalls:

If I remember correctly, we had projected that we would have cash flow of around $22 million that year, and we actually exceeded those numbers. The asset here was essentially untouched by the carnage then going on in the U.S. Our financial structure was, and is, a thousand times healthier than most of the U.S. equivalents. But the industry all but died, and most of our potential buyers were in that industry, and were in a sorry state. They weren't going to buy us; they were simply trying to survive.

Fortunately, the failed auction remained more or less invisible to the Cinemex workforce, so morale didn't suffer. But the inability to harvest Cinemex forced another round of introspection on the part of the company's three founders.

Heyman, more than his colleagues, was bitterly disappointed. The best time for a respectable harvest had come and gone, he believed—an opinion shared by his partners—and the chances of a healthy industry, a healthy Mexico, and a healthy Cinemex converging in the near future seemed to be practically zero. "I've never had an interest in being an international executive," he said shortly after the auction failed, "and now it looks like I may be trapped in that role for the rest of my life." And Mexico, he stressed at that time, was not where he wanted to spend the rest of his life:

I'm really a New York guy, an L.A. guy. I mean, that's where I come from. That's where I'm most comfortable. I'm not comfortable here. This is a society of "who's your mother, who's your father." It's a society where having a name and using it is real important, and I don't have a name to use.

I grew up in L.A. To me, the ultimate sign of making it is dressing like I dress right now, jeans and a T-shirt, and driving a 911 convertible. Well, I've got a bulletproof truck here, and the damned thing cost me more than a 911 costs in the States, and I get zero pleasure out of driving that thing.

Look: The business is a pleasure. Being in this office is a pleasure. Sitting here talking about Cinemex is a pleasure. Fighting over film terms—how much I'm going to pay—is a pleasure. In fact, dealing with everything in this business is a pleasure. But put me on the street in Mexico, and tell me, "You don't have Cinemex anymore, but you have money," and I'm out of here, man. Goodbye. I'm gone.

Heyman's unhappiness about his self-imposed exile sometimes irritated his Mexican partners. Both Fastlicht and Davila recommended early on that Heyman make a serious effort to put down roots in his country of residence—learn Spanish, make new friends, get involved in a community—but this was advice that Heyman never took to heart. (To be fair, Heyman did marry a Mexican woman in 1998, and learned to speak passable Spanish.) Davila recalls that he regularly pointed out to his partner that there would have been no comparable opportunity for him in the United States:

I said to him a thousand times that if this had been L.A., he could never have done what he did. He wouldn't have had the underdeveloped market or the financing opportunities. And meanwhile, he would have been up against ten thousand people just like him with venture capital up the wazoo. The point is, you only get to do things like this in markets like this.

But Adolfo Fastlicht, too, recalls that he was disappointed when, in the wake of the failed auction, his universe of options contracted sharply. He worried about a declining quality of life in Mexico City, and about security issues in a city where—despite improvements in the standard of living on the national level—the bulk of the population remains desperately poor. "Living here versus not living here," says Fastlicht soberly, "was not something that only Matt worried about."

And unlike his colleagues, he felt no special passion for the film-exhibition business:

I always saw this adventure—the Cinemex adventure—as a vehicle in a race. You pick a car, and you try to get to the finish line. I liked this business very much. It is fairly easy to manage, and it is not one of those obscure, complicated manufacturing processes that are subject to cyclical conditions around the world. But I never came into the business saying,

"I love the movie world" or "I want to be associated with this for the rest of my life."

Nor did I come into this business thinking I would be here for twenty or thirty years. If that happened, well, great. Things happen for reasons. I didn't have a time clock that said, "Hey, if I'm not out in five years, I'm going to be really angry!"

In the wake of the failed auction, Davila remained firmly committed to a career and a life in Mexico's capital city. He began wondering aloud about the possibility of buying out his partners and Cinemex's other owners, and taking sole charge of the company. Davila was not alone in this dream—Fastlicht, too, had considered the possibility of a leveraged buyout—but Davila began to contemplate this scenario with particular interest. He had always had dreams of going into politics, and he had hoped that Cinemex would create the wealth that would someday enable him to run for public office. ("Poor politician equals poor politician," he says, quoting his father on the necessity for personal wealth in the game of politics.) But as long as Cinemex remained unsold and unsellable, Davila's career in politics would have to wait.

So, as Cinemex regrouped for the next phase of its existence in the new century, it presented a mixed face to the world. With around two thousand employees and annual sales of nearly $150 million, the equivalent of a medium-sized company in the United States, Cinemex enjoyed the status of big fish in its Mexico City pond. Because it dominated its local market, knew its core business better than anyone else, carried very little debt, and had money in the bank, Cinemex was reasonably well inoculated against small mistakes.

But the founders who had made the company what it was were restless. None felt particularly indispensable. In fact, they shared the conviction that the "three-headed-monster" structure eventually would have to be dismantled. Talented younger people wanted to move up the ladder, and the company could not flourish—Davila, Fastlicht, and Heyman all agreed—if it couldn't offer credible advancement prospects to those young managers.

As they put their own dreams on hold, in other words, Cinemex's founders knew they were putting other people's dreams on hold as well.

EPILOGUE: THE CAGE OPENS

Sometime in 2001, Cinemex's founders began seeing daylight again. A number of U.S. exhibitors were then coming out of bankruptcy. Canadian-based Onex Corp. and several other large concerns were acquiring these companies, and trying to effect a roll-up of the exhibition industry. Although much of this consolidation was focused on the United States, it seemed likely that the same kind of thing soon would start to happen offshore as well.

With these trends in mind, Cinemex approached archrivals Ramirez and Cinemark in December 2001 to see if either or both of those companies was interested in acquiring Cinemex. The deal they proposed was straightforward: *Meet the return-on-exit threshold specified in the original Cinemex lending agreements, and you can own the company.* But—cautioned Davila, who handled most of these negotiations—you have to move before the end of May, when the return threshold goes up again. Faced with this opportunity to rid themselves of the upstart Cinemex, and to divide up Cinemex's screens to their mutual advantage, Ramirez and Cinemark indicated that they were very interested.

Then, reminiscent of the early hunt for backers, nothing happened. After several months of total silence, Fastlicht, Heyman, and Davila huddled again, and decided on a new course of action: They would find an investor who would put some equity in, and they themselves would do a leveraged buyout. At Heyman's suggestion, Davila contacted Onex—the acquisitive Toronto-based conglomerate with annual consolidated revenues of some $16 billion, which already owned the third-largest exhibitor in North America, Loews Cineplex Entertainment—and proposed an equity investment. Onex, too, expressed interest. And then Onex didn't call back.

Then, in May 2002, Cinemark called back. The U.S. firm agreed to the original deal proposed by Cinemex, but with a significant condition: The company, which was then trying to go public, wanted 180 days to pay. (They hoped to use the proceeds of the IPO to pay for the Cinemex deal, among other things.) A letter of intent arrived in Mexico City. All that remained was for Cinemex to sign the letter and send it back before the following Wednesday.

In the modest executive offices at Cinemex, there were mixed emotions. Aside from the delayed payoff—not conditional on the IPO, but still worrisome—the deal essentially called for the obliteration of Cinemex, and the division of its assets between Cinemark and Ramirez. The Cinemex brand (and presumably, much of the Cinemex team) would disappear. And although emotion was never going to determine the outcome, neither was anyone in a hurry to sign and return Cinemark's letter of intent. Davila, in particular, had misgivings:

> *I must say that of the three of us, I was probably the one who was most upset about the prospect of selling to the competition, and seeing the company broken apart. I really wanted the company to live on. I wanted to see the company, the name, and the people who we had put together continue on—and that was a strong motivation for me.*

Then, unexpectedly, *Onex* called back. With some urgency, the Canadians invited Cinemex to New York for further talks—an invitation that made Fastlicht, in particular, uncomfortable. Was this a real overture, he wondered aloud to his two partners, or simply a feint designed to throw the Cinemark deal off track? Fastlicht made an interesting suggestion to Davila: Tell them that if they're serious, they can come to *us*.

Onex's first representative arrived in Mexico City on Sunday night, and a team of negotiators arrived the following morning. It soon became clear that all the prolonged silences of the previous few months were the result of a proposed merger between Onex and Cinemark. When that deal fell apart, Onex felt free to go after Cinemex.

The deal took shape. At the appropriate juncture, Fastlicht called Cinemark, told them another suitor had entered the game, and offered them the chance to up their offer. Cinemark declined, reminding Fastlicht that the deadline on their offer was fast approaching. With some anxiety, Cinemex let the Cinemark deal go, betting instead on the ongoing negotiations with Onex.

It turned out to be a good bet. By June, a scant forty-eight days after the real negotiations started, the deal was done. (The Cinemark IPO, meanwhile, fizzled.) The sale price was $300 million, with Onex taking 58 percent ownership and Los Angeles–based Oaktree Capital

Management taking the remainder. Miguel Davila would remain on as (sole) CEO of the company, and Adolfo Fastlicht would stay on as a consultant. Matt Heyman, at long last, would go home.

J.P. Morgan—the original investor that had ridden out a bumpy decade with Cinemex—expressed its satisfaction with the deal. "This investment," said a Morgan spokesman, "is a prime example of successful investing in Latin American companies with proven business models, strong management teams, and experienced investors."

Matt Heyman, for one, got a chuckle out of being cast as a poster boy by J.P. Morgan:

> *If you look in the J.P. Morgan annual report from 2002, there we are on page 8—shitty little Cinemex. Now, by the way, the reason why we ended up there was that Morgan had such a bad year. So that was kind of fun.*

As of this writing, Miguel Davila soldiers on at Cinemex, and Adolfo Fastlicht consults to his former company and looks for opportunities in real estate. After living on the beach in Key Biscayne for a year, Matt Heyman moved his family to Los Angeles. There, he indulged himself with his long-deferred Porsche 911: metallic black with beige, full leather, and loaded-to-the-gills interior. "Awesome," says Heyman, flatly.

Looking back, he has mixed feelings about the Cinemex experience, and also about the *end* of that experience. "I made twice as much money in twice as much time as I expected," he says. He misses the other two heads of the three-headed monster, with whom he was in an intense relationship for a decade. He misses the business. He misses the satisfaction of betting heavily on *Spiderman* over *Titanic*, and being proven right. "Mexico was the only territory in the world," he boasts, "where *Spiderman* beat the biggest movie of all time."

On the other hand, he's rich enough to stay home and play with his four-year-old.

And on the *other* hand, he's a little surprised to find himself looking for the next thing, the next opportunity. "I need to *do* something," he says, restlessness in his voice. "I'm going fuckin' *crazy*, you know?"

CHAPTER **10**

Not Your Average
Study Group

STUDENTS JOIN STUDY GROUPS at the Harvard Business School in part to enrich their educational experience—and in part to survive the first-year curriculum.

Early in the first semester of the M.B.A. program, it becomes clear to even the most self-assured young M.B.A. candidates that they may not flourish in the classroom based solely on their own best ideas. The fact is, almost everyone has strengths and weaknesses, which are likely to be floated to the surface in the case-based classroom discussion. So, better to team up with a small number of congenial-but-complementary sectionmates and go over your cases as a group—*after* you've thought about them on your own, and *before* the classroom discussion.

This is the story of a study group that came together in the fall of 1995. More specifically, it's the story of three members of that study group who became good friends through that experience. With the help of other HBS classmates, faculty, and alumni, these three section-mates—Dave Perry, Stig Leschly, and Paul Conforti—went on to do extraordinary things.[1]

GETTING ACQUAINTED

It's September 1995. Five recently admitted M.B.A. candidates—Chris Kermoian, Beth Minehart, Paul Conforti, Dave Perry, and A. J. Sen—are meeting every weekday morning at 7:00 A.M. at Kresge dining hall. As a rule, they are bleary-eyed from staying up late reading cases the night before. They grab coffee and as much breakfast as they can stomach, and sit down to compare their individual notes.

They have come together mostly by accident. Kermoian and Conforti are suitemates. Minehart lives directly below them. Somehow, they have bumped into Perry—who lives in another wing of the residence hall—and Sen.

And although the grouping doesn't reflect systematic planning on anyone's part, these five young people turn out to complement each other fairly well. Kermoian is a scientist by training; Perry is a chemical engineer out of the Oil Patch. Sen is an electrical engineer. Minehart has a background in marketing and sales, and Conforti's background is in operations and finance.

Study groups are voluntary associations, of course, and their memberships can change. In this particular case, A. J. Sen eventually withdraws, and he is replaced in the study group by a somewhat reserved music lover named Stig Leschly, who is enrolled in Harvard's demanding J.D./M.B.A. program.

For the balance of the school year, the members of this group learn things about business, about each other, and—just as often—about themselves. Paul Conforti, for example, has always thought of himself as ambitious. Now, in the company of Dave Perry, who strikes him as *hyper*-driven, he relocates himself on the spectrum of ambition. For his part, Perry has always had great confidence in his own intellectual horsepower; nevertheless, he has recruited Leschly into the group in part because he has decided that Leschly is the smartest person he has ever met.

If you run into somebody who's even smarter than *you*, probably the best thing to do—after getting over the shock—is to pick that person's brains every morning over coffee.

ESCAPE FROM THE REFINERY

David Perry grew up in what he cheerfully calls the "middle of nowhere": Boone County, Arkansas.

He also grew up in the middle of a business. His parents ran an agricultural lime and fertilizer business in Magnolia, a hamlet in the southern part of the state. The business was right next to the house—in fact, the company's office was *in* the house—so Perry's childhood featured warehouses, trucks, and the comings and goings of huge volumes of chemical fertilizers. His father ran the outside operations, while his mother kept the books.

Perry started working for his father at the age of six. His pay was a quarter an hour. Almost immediately, he began driving a tractor, and became something of a local attraction. Farmers liked to watch as the pint-sized employee drove heavy equipment to and fro, loading up their waiting trucks with fertilizer. Every year, his father gave him a quarter-an-hour raise. By age twelve, Perry was making deliveries to farms (and getting paid $1.75 an hour). A year later, he ran the business for several weeks while his father recuperated from a heart attack.

When Perry was fourteen, the family moved to Harrison, the county seat, located in the northwestern corner of Arkansas. But some things didn't change. Throughout his teenage years, Perry made money and saved money:

I didn't have any way of spending it. There was nothing to spend it on. I didn't go to a movie until I was around fourteen. My dad wouldn't let me buy a car. So by the time I finished high school in 1986, I had saved thousands of dollars.

Not enough, unfortunately, to buy him a way out of Harrison. Although Perry's parents believed strongly in the value of a good education, they didn't have the money to send him to college. But, his strong high school academic record won him an appointment to the Air Force Academy, which offered him a free education in return for military service. He leapt at the chance. "When you're an eighteen-year-old male," he recalls, "the idea of being a fighter pilot, flying a jet, sounds like the most exciting thing in the world."

But Perry soon discovered that he hated the regimented life of the Academy: the 5:00 A.M. wake-up call, inspections at 6:00 A.M., uniforms, mandatory meals, rules about whom plebes could speak to, places where plebes were not allowed to walk, and so on, and so on. "In fact, *nobody* likes it," he declares, "but some people tolerate it well, and others tolerate it poorly. I was one of those people who tolerated it poorly."

Then came the football injury. Before getting hurt, Perry could picture himself as Tom Cruise in *Top Gun*; now, if he remained on his track into the Air Force, he might serve out his multiyear military hitch watching TV monitors in a missile silo in North Dakota. By the end of his second year at the Academy, in the spring of 1988, Perry knew he wanted out. Ignoring his parents' strong advice to the contrary, he transferred to the University of Tulsa.

Perry graduated from the University of Tulsa in the spring of 1990 with a degree in chemical engineering. This qualified him for a job at Exxon's Benicia oil refinery, a relatively small operation (as oil refineries go) not far from San Francisco. Within five years, he was managing several hundred people and a large piece of the refinery.

But Perry found himself getting restless. The oil industry had a growth rate of 1 percent a year. This meant that Perry would move up the ladder only when people ahead of him got *off* the ladder. "You hire in as an engineer when you're twenty-two," he says, "and you get promoted forever. And that's it." Interviews with local high-tech firms proved fruitless; he couldn't find a position with enough responsibility. Perry's piece of a small oil refinery was bigger than an entire Intel chip plant—and no one was about to turn over an Intel plant to a boyish-looking twenty-six-year-old.

So Perry decided it was time for more education. Once again, his parents back in Arkansas winced when they heard David's new plans: an advanced degree. In business. At *Harvard*.

Perry arrived at Harvard in the fall of 1995 fully intending to start his own business. He had notions of getting involved in an early-stage technology-based company, although he had no idea what form such a company might take. The first-year curriculum at HBS, focused in large part on various functional skills, didn't relate much to his prior experiences. "I knew things like how to hire people and how to fire people," he recalls. "I knew how to inspect welds in the middle of the night on a two-hundred-foot tower. I knew *nothing* about corporate finance."

On the other hand, unlike some of his classmates, Perry wasn't the slightest bit in awe of the academic world. Five years at an oil refinery—culminating in a serious explosion and fire just weeks before his scheduled departure—had focused Perry on getting out of Harvard exactly what he needed to get.

A DANISH IMPORT

Stig (pronounced "Steeg") Leschly was ten years old when his parents decided to leave Denmark and settle in the United States. They had grown up in near-poverty during World War II and had worked their way up into the Danish middle class. In 1979, however—frustrated by what they saw as the constraints of the northern European welfare states—they became part of a larger wave of migration from Scandinavia to America in the 1970s.

Speaking no English, Stig and his three brothers enrolled in the public schools in Princeton, New Jersey. Sometime around the eighth grade, Leschly realized that he *liked* school. School was a meritocracy, he decided: The more talented you were and the harder you worked, the better you did. So he applied himself, and the boy with the softly accented English became the valedictorian of Princeton High School's class of 1988.

This was good enough to get Leschly admitted to the college down the road—Princeton University—where he studied literature and contemplated going for a Ph.D. Meanwhile, he also worked summers to help pay his tuition. One summer, for example, he ran a business storing Princeton students' furniture over the summer. As he recalls:

I was the founder and manager of Princeton University Furniture Storage and Rug Cleaning. This basically involved renting twenty tractor-

trailers and stuffing them full of furniture. In one of those trailers, I put
all the rugs. I'd roll them all out on the pavement in August, down by
the gym, and ten of my buddies and I would wash them. Want to get a
good workout? Try washing 150 rugs in a parking lot in August in cen-
tral New Jersey. That's a good workout.

Graduating *summa cum laude* and Phi Beta Kappa from Princeton
helped Leschly land a job at McKinsey. Curiously, so did the rug-clean-
ing gig. "McKinsey seemed willing to overlook the literature part," he
recalls, "because they liked the part about cleaning rugs in the August
heat. In fact, that's all they wanted to talk about." What McKinsey didn't
know was that Leschly had hedged his bets, somewhat: He had also applied to Harvard Law School in his senior year at Princeton, and been
accepted. He deferred enrolling at Harvard to try consulting on for size.

He soon found that there were parts of the consulting life that he
liked. (He worked on interesting engagements at AT&T and Lorillard;
he learned to think more systematically about problems; he enjoyed his
interactions with his McKinsey colleagues.) But there were other things
that he didn't like. "Client service was not my cup of tea," he admits.

And more fundamentally, Leschly was growing increasingly troubled by issues of race, class, and poverty. As a young child in Denmark,
Leschly had encountered few minorities and few people who were
less affluent than his own family. In the United States, it seemed, you
couldn't get away from the poor and disadvantaged—even if you were
fortunate enough to work in the fast lane at McKinsey. This gnawing
sense of social injustice, combined with Leschly's intense feelings of
patriotism toward his adopted homeland, led him to look for another
path. "I wanted to try to make things better," he explains, "so I decided
to take a job in a public school." Harvard again obliged by deferring
him, and he began contacting public school systems.

His lack of a teaching certificate derailed this plan slightly. Instead
of teaching at an inner-city public school, Leschly wound up as the
assistant principal at St. Mark the Evangelist School in central Harlem,
just north of Harlem Hospital. Founded in 1912, St. Mark's taught kinder-
gartners through eighth-graders—mostly black, and mostly poor. Like
many inner-city Catholic schools, St. Mark's was in desperate financial

straits because the parish that supported it was nearly bankrupt. This fact of life, Leschly recalls, largely determined his own day-to-day reality at St. Mark's:

> *The nun who ran the place, Sister Catherine, said to me, "You can teach—sure. But I don't need help teaching. What I really need help with is figuring out how to patch the roof."*
>
> *So it was an amazing year of my life, just trying to help keep that school together. It wasn't a particularly Catholic institution, by that point. I'd say 80 percent of the kids there were Baptist, along with a few Muslims. The kids called me "Brother Steve," because the only white men in that part of Harlem were the friars—the brothers—who came to the school, and "Steve" was about as close to "Stig" as they got.*

"Brother Steve" was willing to work at street level, but—thanks in part to his McKinsey training—he also tried to look systemically at problems. He decided that there really was a legitimate role for the private sector in helping schools like St. Mark's. As a result, he helped the Archdiocese of New York set up a program whereby young professionals would sign on with struggling schools as assistant principals in charge of operations. Today, ten parishes in New York City have young investment bankers and consultants trying to "patch the roof."

Meanwhile, Leschly had decided to pursue his twice-deferred Harvard education, but now with a new twist: as a joint J.D./M.B.A. candidate. ("Sister Catherine wrote a recommendation for me for the M.B.A. program," he recalls with a smile. "Probably the only such letter they got that ended with the phrase, 'I will hold you in my prayers.'") He started at Harvard Law in the fall of 1994, with a hazy notion of becoming a world-class law professor.

But a job at a New York law firm in the summer of 1995—between his first year at the Law School and his first year at the Business School—got him thinking about his career path once again. The year at St. Mark's had taught Leschly that he wouldn't be happy if he didn't ground his career in something that he cared about deeply. Consulting alone didn't cut it, and now it was becoming clear that life as a high-powered New York lawyer, or a law professor, wasn't going to cut it, either. There had to be something more. But what would *that* be?

In the fall of 1995, during his first weeks at the Business School, a lapsed chemical engineer named Dave Perry invited Leschly to join his newly formed study group. Leschly liked and respected this Perry character, and he could already see that the Business School's case method was different from what he had encountered on the other side of the Charles River. So he was happy to sit at the breakfast table in Kresge with Perry and his friends—Kermoian, Minehart, and Conforti—and attempt to crack cases.

OCEAN STATE ROOTS

Like Dave Perry and Stig Leschly, Paul Conforti came from a family of strivers: people who worked hard and wanted better for their children.

He was born and raised in Cranston, Rhode Island. As far back as he can remember, both of his parents worked—his mother working a night job to bring in extra money, while his father was a sales engineer for several different equipment-supply companies. The senior Conforti was laid off when his company moved out of state. He then took a job managing a warehouse for a small but ambitious company called Ocean State Job Lot, a deep-discount retailer that bought and sold odd lots of discontinued products, overruns, and cancelled orders. He went to night school, got a certificate in human resource management, and wound up running HR for Ocean State. Paul speaks with obvious pride of his father's accomplishments and the attitude that lay behind them:

> He had two mottoes: "Do your best" and "Who gives a shit?" In other words, you work hard, you do your best—and then, who gives a shit what happens afterward, because you already know that you've given it your all?

But upon getting out of the Cranston public schools, where he had performed well academically, Paul Conforti didn't know exactly what he wanted to work hard at. He had applied to a handful of liberal arts schools and also to Rensselaer Polytechnic Institute. By the time his acceptances started coming in, Conforti was leaning toward majoring in business, and RPI was the only school he'd applied to that offered an undergraduate business major. So somewhat by accident, he wound up in Troy, New York.

At RPI, Conforti continued to make good grades (ultimately graduating *summa cum laude*) as he majored in management. In his senior year, he became president of the Student Union—a branch of the student government that ran a portfolio of student-related businesses, with an annual gross of around $6.5 million. The experience confirmed his growing interest in business, and before leaving college, Conforti decided that he one day would attend the Harvard Business School.

First, though, he wanted some real-world experience. He signed up with the Travelers Insurance Company's operations management program, and spent a year and a half based at the company's home office in Hartford, Connecticut, working on total quality management (TQM) projects. One involved the consolidation of twenty-five health-claims offices and a dozen dental-claims offices into a handful of "super-centers." At the end of that process, Conforti asked for the opportunity to run one of the new centers he had created, and (at the age of twenty-two) wound up heading a staff of forty in Albany, New York, which he recalls as an intense but fun experience:

> *You don't usually get phone calls at a claims service center telling you what a wonderful job you've done. So turning these people's experiences around, and putting a smile on their face at the end of their interaction with us, really fired me up.*

When Metropolitan Life subsequently purchased this piece of Travelers' business, Conforti was asked to consolidate his super-center with one of Met Life's similar facilities. He moved from Albany to Utica, New York, and took charge of a $14 million business with a staff of 250. "An absolute mess," he recalls. Over the next seven months, he stabilized the Utica facility—and also pursued his deferred dream. He applied to, and was accepted by, the Harvard Business School.

DESIGNING A CONTEST

While Leschly, Perry, and Conforti were meeting over coffee with their study-group colleagues, trying to stay on top of the cases and courses of the first-year program, two second-year students were wrestling with a different kind of challenge. Bill Nussey and Alison Berkley (both M.B.A. '96) had to come up with a topic for a paper for Professor Josh Lerner's Venture Capital and Private Equity elective.

Berkley was a congenital entrepreneur. Throughout her childhood, she had launched a string of enterprises, pushing products ranging from barrettes to stationery. Upon enrolling at the School, she had gotten involved with the Small Business and New Enterprise Club and was elected its president in the fall of 1995. This was one of the largest clubs on campus, with some 350 members.

In their scouting for a paper topic, Nussey and Berkley had scrutinized a business plan contest that MIT had been running for several years. The MIT contest, which was open to all MIT students, had been gaining in visibility. In 1996—the year Nussey and Berkley looked the competition over—the first-place prize was increased from $10,000 to $50,000, generating a lot of buzz and media attention.

"It seemed to us," Berkley recalls, "that HBS was going to fall behind the times." Why shouldn't the Harvard Business School have a contest of its own? And why couldn't that contest be funded by venture capitalists, who in return would get a sneak preview of bright ideas being put forward by second-year HBS students?

Lerner approved the field-study topic, and Berkley and Nussey set to work. They researched how other schools ran business plan contests, or otherwise channeled their students' entrepreneurial instincts for the benefit of both the students and the institution. They looked for ways whereby professional investors (in addition to students, faculty, and alumni) could be involved in the program as judges. They explored various mechanisms for funding the plan at levels that would guarantee student interest and participation.

This was more than an academic exercise for Nussey and Berkley. They very much wanted the School to accept and *act* on their final recommendation. But their topic was larger than the confines of a second-year field study. If their emerging proposal was to have any chance of actually being implemented by the School, at least two additional people—Professor William A. Sahlman and Dean Kim B. Clark—would have to become its champions.

CHAMPIONS, WITH CAVEATS

Bill Sahlman was then an informal leader of the entrepreneurship faculty group. The product of an entrepreneurial family—two generations before him had operated a Tampa-based shrimp company—Sahlman majored in economics at Princeton. Already interested in the stock market and investing, Sahlman applied for admission to the Harvard Business School after graduating from Princeton; the School admitted him, but deferred him for two years so that he could get some work experience.

Sahlman spent a year in the securities analysis business in New York. Enough was enough, he decided. He wrote a letter to HBS arguing that he'd learned everything he needed to learn in that particular job, and that he'd appreciate being admitted a year ahead of schedule. The School agreed, and Sahlman arrived at Soldiers Field in the fall of 1973.

This was a difficult time in academia. The Vietnam War raged, generating passions and divisions in all walks of life. The M.B.A. class that matriculated in the fall of 1973 included young people like Sahlman— and at age twenty-two, he was one of the youngest—but it also included a large contingent of students who had completed tours of duty in Southeast Asia. "They were *men*," says Sahlman, "and we were boys." Sahlman didn't feel out of place, exactly. After all, he had analyzed more than a hundred businesses during his stint on Wall Street, and understood much more than many of his classmates about how businesses actually worked. And yet many of those same classmates knew a lot more than Sahlman about how the *world* worked. "This led to some interesting section dynamics," he recalls.

Sahlman was a skydecker—HBS slang for those students who purposefully grab seats in the back rows of the Aldrich amphitheater classrooms, as far as possible from the professor down in the "pit." One of Sahlman's sectionmates, who sat much closer to the professors—remembers Sahlman's distinctive presence in the classroom:

> *He was insightful, very bright. He sat way up there in the back and made these incredibly sarcastic comments. He would spar with the professors, and because he was so bright, he'd get away with it.*

He was one of two really young members of the class. But even so, he came across as this forty-year-old dude. He was like this old man in the back, telling us all, "No, you guys are wrong about that." So we were always getting into arguments with him.

For the most part, Sahlman enjoyed his first-year courses. But it wasn't until early in his second year at the School, when he enrolled in Starting New Ventures, that he became passionately involved with the curriculum. Unfortunately, the passion took a negative turn. Phil Thurston, a veteran of the School's Production area, was then teaching the entrepreneurship course. One of the first cases Thurston presented infuriated Sahlman:

It was a case on an import/export business, run by a former marine, who was this very, very, tough guy, as in, "The goal of business is to win. You should do anything you can do to win!" Well, I hated this guy. To me, he was the epitome of all that was bad about business. He got way under my skin. So I went home that afternoon to my wife Carol, and said, "Hey, I'm not enjoying this. I think I'll quit, and go get a job."

Carol Sahlman suggested to her husband that he give the Business School another chance. ("She talked me down off the ceiling, somehow.") And as it turned out, Sahlman was then on the verge of a remarkable transformation: from disaffected second-year student to a candidate for the faculty. The transformation began when Sahlman started working directly with senior Finance professors—including Jay Light, Robert Glauber, and Gordon Donaldson—and continued as a result of his exposure to Howard Stevenson's Real Property Asset Management course. With their encouragement, Sahlman applied to, and was accepted into, the Ph.D. in Business Economics and the Doctorate in Business Administration (D.B.A.) programs.

Then came another unexpected turn. Bob Glauber invited Sahlman to spend a year in Switzerland, working on cases with him. The School had an unusually strong faculty contingent at its outpost in Vevey that year, and Sahlman remembers his European tour of duty as an incredibly valuable experience. "I wrote some twenty cases all over Europe," he says, "from Oslo to Milan. I was with a group of very interesting people doing interesting things, and learning all about European business, which was very different from business in the States."

Upon his return to the United States, Sahlman entered the Ph.D. in Business Economics program and spent a year in Cambridge working with Harvard luminaries like Michael Spence, Martin Feldstein, Jerome Green, and Richard Caves. His dissertation—"a long time in the writing"—dealt with interactions among investment and financing decisions. "An econometric study with lots of data, lots of equations," he recalls laconically. "All worthless, I might point out."

He joined the HBS faculty in 1980 and plunged into teaching first-year Finance. It was not a successful experience:

If we were to talk about course evaluations, for instance, I was surely one or two standard deviations below the average. At that time, I was of the opinion that I knew a lot more about everything than anybody, and so I tended to fight with my students. If somebody said something that I disagreed with, well, I'd take 'em on. A small portion of the students enjoyed that. The vast majority hated it.

In 1982, while Sahlman was still doing battle with first-year M.B.A. students, Howard Stevenson asked him if he would be willing to write a note for Stevenson's upcoming colloquium on entrepreneurship. Stevenson wanted a paper on how entrepreneurs should think about finance. Sahlman, sensing an opening that might allow him to bring together several of his long-standing interests, took the assignment.

Several senior Finance professors counseled Sahlman against drifting into the Entrepreneurship camp—a camp that consisted mainly of Stevenson, at that point. "They gave me some clear feedback that this was a truly life-threatening, or at least career-threatening, move," Sahlman recalls. Undeterred, Sahlman used the opportunity presented by Stevenson to organize his thinking about the financing of new and growing ventures. This turned into not only a paper, but also a new second-year elective, Entrepreneurial Finance, which he introduced in 1984. Shortly thereafter, he formally left the Finance group and joined forces with Howard Stevenson.

Entrepreneurial Finance, it turned out, was the right course at the right time. Enrollments were high, and—for the first time—students gave Sahlman consistently high marks. ("A nice change," he admits.) And the strong conceptual work that underpinned the elective positioned Sahlman for promotion from assistant professor to associate professor, and later from associate to full professor. These promotions came at a time when the School not only was debating, once again, whether entrepreneurship was a legitimate field of study, but also whether outstanding course development could lead to tenure. Sahlman's success seemed to answer both questions in the affirmative.

Through the early 1990s, Stevenson and Sahlman built the Entrepreneurship area into a freestanding and vigorous faculty group. With help from a growing cadre of junior colleagues, they continued to refine and broaden the conceptual underpinnings of entrepreneurship sketched out by Stevenson a decade earlier. To Stevenson's list of five entrepreneurial behaviors, for example, Sahlman added a sixth: a focus on team-based, rather than hierarchical, compensation systems. Enrollments in entrepreneurship courses continued to climb steadily. Entrepreneurial Finance, Sahlman's brainchild, was regularly oversubscribed. Meanwhile, other faculty groups—sensing that there was a new dynamic at work, in the economy of the mid-1990s—began incorporating entrepreneurial concepts into their own courses.

Then came a change that might have derailed the entrepreneurial enterprise: a change at the top. Over the previous decade and a half, both Stevenson and Sahlman had benefited substantially from Dean John McArthur's steadfast support. In the fall of 1995, however, McArthur stepped down and was succeeded by Kim B. Clark.

Sahlman watched this transition warily. Before Clark's elevation to the deanship, he had been the head of the TOM (Technology and Operations Management) faculty group. This was a group with which Sahlman hadn't had much contact over the years. The TOM-ers—a tight-knit group clustered in the basement of Morgan Hall—focused on practical, nitty-gritty, operational issues; the Finance and Competitive Strategy types in the upper reaches of Morgan didn't have a lot of contact with them. Sahlman knew Kim Clark mainly as a genial, soft-spoken colleague who maintained strong ties across the river to Harvard's economics faculty and was well thought of by his TOM peers.

Sahlman also knew that Clark had earned a reputation as a solid researcher through his inquiries into productivity in the automobile industry. So when Clark called Sahlman in for a meeting early in his tenure, Sahlman had some apprehensions. In fact, he steeled himself to hear that this new dean (like most deans before him) was skeptical about entrepreneurship as a field of study. After all, hadn't it been almost a century since the auto industry was a hotbed of entrepreneurship? Would the new dean pull the plug on the risky field that Sahlman had ventured into?

To Sahlman's relief, the answer was no. Yes, Clark had an enduring interest in productivity, and yes, the auto industry had indeed been one of his principal laboratories for exploring this interest. But productivity issues led naturally to a consideration of the management of technological change, innovation, and product development, and these issues in turn led Clark into industries beyond autos: pharmaceuticals, medical devices, software, disk drives, and consumer packaged goods.

In fact, the TOM group that Clark had led, prior to becoming dean, had become increasingly focused on the *dynamics* of business. As Clark explains:

> *We argued that it was increasingly important in business to become good at dynamics—at changing your product, at bringing new things in, at introducing new technologies, at entering new markets, and so on. In fact, we did some work that showed very, very clearly that even in a relatively stable business, the firms that were capable of managing dynamics effectively achieved a huge advantage over their competitors.*

So dealing with change was critical for fast-moving Silicon Valley ventures, as Clark saw it, but it was equally critical for Ford and General Motors. The implications for the School's curriculum were enormous. Far from pulling the plug on entrepreneurship, Clark wanted a radical intensification of the efforts then being led by Howard Stevenson and Bill Sahlman.

"You're doing great things," he told a surprised Sahlman. "The problem is, you're not doing *half* enough." If entrepreneurship was indeed what Howard Stevenson had been arguing it was—a *way of managing* that would be of increasing relevance in the late twentieth and early twenty-first centuries—then the work of the Entrepreneurship group obviously had to suffuse the entire HBS curriculum.

SO IN THE SPRING OF 1996, Alison Berkley and Bill Nussey, champions of a business plan contest for the Harvard Business School, took their case to the two individuals most likely to make the final call: first Bill Sahlman, and later Kim Clark.

Sahlman had already done some systematic thinking and writing about business plans in the real world, and saw clear limits to their value. The *people* behind the plan were the critical variable, he believed; the plan itself was of secondary importance:

> When I read a business plan, I read it from the resumes first, and I ask, "What have these people done in the past that would lead me to believe they can do something interesting in the future?" If I can find a good answer to that question, then I look at the rest of the plan.

Sahlman was even more skeptical about the value of a business plan contest in the context of a second-year business school curriculum. A business plan, he believed, is only as good as the experience and expertise of its proponents. In other words, people who don't understand an industry intimately shouldn't be writing business plans about it. Most business school students are young and inexperienced. Lacking the necessary domain expertise, business school students who write business plans tend to focus on *communicating* effectively, rather than designing viable companies.

Another potential objection to a business plan contest, Sahlman told Nussey and Berkley, was the distraction it might pose to second-year students. People could write business plans for the rest of their lives; they would get only one chance to take elective courses at the Harvard Business School. And at least *some* students might make choices that would prove unwise in the long run.

"The School's biggest concern," confirms Berkley, "was the potential distraction from the curriculum. They were worried that people would use their whole second year as a launching pad for a business, and that the learning that was supposed to be going on wouldn't happen. And that was a valid objection."

Dean Clark, too, expressed reservations about a School-sanctioned business plan contest. He told Berkley that he was determined to defend the primacy of the educational mission of the School. He could not allow a tail to wag the dog—even if the proposed tail was a contest that students were clamoring for. He also pointed out that there were perils to the School in seeming to endorse a particular business plan. What if the resulting business failed spectacularly? Would that reflect badly on the School? Would the investors in that business feel that they had been led astray by the School? If Harvard allowed third parties to provide in-kind services to contestants, did that represent an implicit Harvard endorsement of those third parties? And on a more philosophical plane, should Harvard be in the business of awarding prize money to students, or helping outsiders to do so?

Over the course of several months, the team of Nussey and Berkley worked with Sahlman to revise their proposal in ways that would make it more acceptable to the School. The judging process was simplified. The prize money was to be distributed more broadly. Instead of a single large prize going to one winner, a $20,000 prize would go to the first-place winner, and three runners-up would receive $10,000 each. Most important, though, was the decision to require that the business plans be written for academic credit. This would require faculty sponsorship of each competing team, which in turn would ensure that the contest would be tied into the academic mainstream of the School.

"We also saw it as a way to educate the faculty as well as the students," Sahlman adds. "If they actually got involved in critiquing these plans, they couldn't help but get pulled into new ways of looking at things."

Nussey and Berkley graduated in June 1996, but institutional planning for the business plan contest continued into the fall. (Students continued to have input through the participation of Jennifer Scott and David Rosenblatt, two members of the M.B.A. class of 1997.) Increasingly, the emphasis was on helping students learn how to work in small, high-performance teams that were focused on ideas that were *scalable* and *commercializable*. Teams would be told that a specific domain expertise was absolutely essential. If they didn't have that expertise, they would have to figure out a way to get it.

The Harvard Business School Business Plan Contest was formally announced in the fall of 1996. Second-year students interested in participating were encouraged to organize themselves into teams and formally commit to the process in December.

Two of our three study-group protagonists—Paul Conforti and Dave Perry—already had definite ideas about businesses that they'd like to found. The challenge of the contest appealed to them, and the prize—$20,000 to the first-place winner—would be good seed money for their venture. (Neither Conforti nor Perry planned to come in second.) So why not take a shot at winning this new contest?

ROOM FOR DESSERT

Paul Conforti remembers the exact moment he first realized that he would someday be in the restaurant business.

He was working at the Travelers home office in Hartford. He used to pass the same restaurant every day, going to and from his car. One day, he stopped on the sidewalk and found himself staring into the mirrored-glass windows of the restaurant, and suddenly got the strong conviction that someday, somehow, he would be a restaurateur. He wrote about this epiphany in one of the essays on his application to Harvard, and concluded his essay by writing that he wanted to open a restaurant when he graduated.

So he arrived at Harvard with restaurants on the brain, and he spent many hours in his first year of the M.B.A. program brainstorming with classmates about how he might realize his dream. One night— at an evening meeting of the study group at the California Pizza Kitchen in Harvard Square—this brainstorming headed in the direction of desserts. As Conforti recalls:

Everybody started talking about the scientific *nature of the dessert process, versus the very unscientific nature of what's called the "savory" side of cooking—chicken, steak, and so on. Desserts are very scientific, very recipe-based.*

And we went on from there. You can freeze desserts and ship them. Desserts are a product that people are very passionate about. Along with drinks, desserts have very high margins. So I said to myself, "This is worth looking into," and I continued to noodle with the idea throughout the first year and into the second year.

In the opening days of that second year, Conforti sent out an e-mail to his classmates. He told them that he had a concept for an upscale, dessert-focused restaurant, and that he wanted to write a business plan for the restaurant. He hoped to put together a year-long field study to that end. Was anyone else interested?

Two classmates—Kristen Krzyzewski and Kim Moore—said yes. Along with Conforti, they persuaded Ray Goldberg, a senior professor and a leading authority in the field of agribusiness, to sponsor the field study.

On the face of it, Kristen Krzyzewski was as unlikely a restaurateur as Conforti. A Phi Beta Kappa graduate of Cornell with a degree in economics, she had spent four years after college with Crown Sterling Suites, a hotel management company. She ultimately assumed responsibility for structuring and managing Crown Sterling's employee benefits and risk-management systems.

Kim Moore, too, seemed destined for something other than the restaurant trade. Born and raised in Houston, Texas, the daughter of a railroad switchman for the Union Pacific Railroad, Moore had first thought of going into medicine. ("Then organic chemistry steered me straight.") After earning a degree in journalism from the University of Texas in 1989, she moved to New York and spent five years working for ABC News as an associate producer. The job was glamorous, but the next step up the ladder was into the management of broadcasting, in which Moore had no particular interest. Moore decided to strike out in a new direction:

I decided that I should try to do something that I knew the least about. The thing I knew the very least about was the world of business. And I had met any number of interesting people who had graduated from the Harvard Business School. So I applied, and got in.

In the summer of 1996, between her first and second years at Harvard, Moore took a job at the Texas-based H.E. Butt Grocery Company. The $8 billion privately held firm—the subject of several MIS-focused HBS case studies—was renowned for its mastery of both technology and retailing. Moore got an immersion in retail real estate, sales per square foot, and other key concepts, especially as they related to tangible goods and food. "In short," she explains, "I got comfortable in the world of retail."

Together, Conforti, Moore, and Krzyzewski spent a good part of the 1996–1997 school year figuring out the economics of restaurants, through both library research and in-person interviews with restaurant owners. They sought out anyone and everyone on the HBS faculty with ties—even the most tenuous ties—to restaurants and food retailing. "We drew them down pretty good," Moore recalls. "As one professor later said, we completely drained the entire staff of any knowledge they might have had of the restaurant business."

In December, when the call for entries for the Harvard Business School Business Plan Contest went out, Conforti, Krzyzewski, and Moore decided to enter. Through the late winter and early spring, they wrote up a formal business plan for a company they called Room for Dessert, based largely on the field-study report that they were preparing for Ray Goldberg.

The final version of that plan, as submitted to the contest sponsors in the spring of 1997, opened with a flight of fancy: five paragraphs describing "a day in the life of Room for Dessert." But the fanciful language ended with the executive summary that followed:

> *Room for Dessert is a full service, fine dining restaurant serving desserts and beverages (coffee, tea, wine, and spirits). The concept also includes a retail store featuring take-out desserts, wine, spirits and signature ingredients. Units will be located in high foot-traffic areas in metropolitan markets and surrounding upscale communities. The management team has the following objectives:*
>
> • *Secure $600,000 funding to open a start-up unit in Boston during the third quarter of 1997*
>
> • *Prove the business model generates $1 million in unit sales and 35 percent cash-on-cash returns*

- *Establish 10 units in the Northeast by the end of 1999*
- *Grow into a national chain, with over 40 units and $50 million in sales by the end of 2002*

It was a cogent, forcefully stated plan. And it didn't lack for ambition: forty units within five years. But if Bill Sahlman had applied his critical first test of a business plan to this particular scheme—*who's behind it, and how credible are they?*—he would not have been impressed. As the resumes at the back of the plan made clear, none of its three authors had any relevant restaurant experience, or even any direct retail experience. Anticipating this objection, Conforti and his colleagues included an artful paragraph at the end of their executive summary:

> *The RFD founders are passionate about the food industry; experienced with service operations, public relations, and execution under pressure; and educated by Harvard Business School. They are also in the process of building a management team and board of directors with unparalleled restaurant industry experience. The resulting combination of professional management and restaurant savvy creates a team well-positioned to pursue this opportunity.*

In other words: *Trust us; we'll go find some people who know how to do this, and throw a net over them.* The trio of would-be restaurateurs submitted their plan to the contest organizers and waited for the verdict.

A B2B VISION

As he finished his first year at Harvard, Dave Perry landed a summer job in the San Francisco office of a major consulting firm. He completed this assignment in early August 1996 and returned to Cambridge to help found a biotech start-up, Virogen, with several molecular biologists.

This relationship continued, and even intensified, as Perry began his second year at HBS. His classmates worried that he was overextended—twenty hours a week at the biotech firm and a full course load—but Perry thrived on the pressure. He had loaded up his schedule with entrepreneurship courses, and suddenly, everything he was studying made sense. "I was starting a business," he explains, "and so I was dealing with all these problems in real time. How do I finance this? How do I hire the right people? And the result was that I turned in a pretty good academic performance."

It was in this context that Perry first heard about the inaugural run of the Harvard Business School Business Plan Contest. He invited three of his classmates—Jon Callaghan, Lisa Janssen, and former study-group colleague Stig Leschly—to form a team with him. "Jon had a venture capital background," Perry recalls, "Lisa knew about branding, and Stig, of course, was Stig." The four-person team, from the outset led by Perry, began looking for the right venture to write up.

Their first choice was a company that was to be called Innovation Partners, which would serve as a sort of patent clearinghouse for bringing good ideas to market. Perry had noticed in his refinery days that there were lots of engineers who would walk into his office with patentable ideas, but with no clue as to how to protect and commercialize those ideas. But this structure—essentially a service business, and therefore difficult to scale up without hiring large numbers of bodies—seemed unworkable.

Then the team turned to an idea that Perry had stumbled upon at Virogen. In the context of intensive life-sciences research, many of the highest-paid individuals were molecular biologists. Perry was astonished to discover that some of these researchers spent as much as five precious hours per week—or roughly 10 percent of their working hours—combing through the catalogs of companies that made specialty chemicals, looking for the materials they needed to conduct their experiments.

Not all companies offered all the necessary chemicals, so researchers maintained a large shelf of catalogs from a wide range of manufacturers. These catalogs were bulky, but despite their bulk, they weren't necessarily *useful*. The information they contained got stale quickly. Newly introduced products weren't included. *Comparing* product lines, apples to apples, was extremely difficult.

The Perry-led team entered the business plan contest in December 1996 fully intending to write up a plan for Innovation Partners. By February, though, the team had switched its focus to a concept that Perry was calling Chemdex. Chemdex would intermediate between the producers and users of life-science chemicals. It would do so entirely on the Web, as an "on-line distributor of specialty chemicals, biochemicals, and reagents."

Of course, there were existing distributors who were already well entrenched in this particular value chain. In fact, there were some two hundred of them who printed all those catalogs, took phone orders, and shipped out of their warehouse inventories. But by using Internet-based technology, Chemdex would do an end-run around these distributors. It would woo away their customers in part by offering improved information flow. Comparison shopping on the Web would be far easier than through catalogs.

Chemdex's second advantage would grow out of "disintermediation"—that is, taking middlemen out of the equation. Chemdex proposed to bypass existing distributors and reallocate their margins to others in the value chain. These margins were considerable, ranging from 40 percent to 200 percent. Substantial savings would be passed on to both manufacturers and end users, and the rest would go to Chemdex.

Perry envisioned a Chemdex that would operate on an enormous scale, and effectively be a single-source supplier in its field—comparable to the New York Stock Exchange or the SABRE airline reservations system. The best way to get there, Perry decided, was to avoid subscription or usage fees. Already in place were several players who charged fees, ranging from modest to hefty, for access to their proprietary databases. None of these competitors offered a state-of-the-art transaction capability, though. If Chemdex could build and deploy such a capability first, using the lure of a no-fee environment, it would have a significant competitive advantage.

It is difficult today to put this idea in context. Although Amazon, Yahoo! and Netscape recently had gone public in splashy ways—Amazon's April 1997 IPO netted $42 million, and the company ended its first day of trading with a market cap of $560 million—Perry and his teammates were looking at Web-based commerce a full year before the entrepreneurial Internet boom really exploded. True, some venture capitalists were homing in on the Internet as a field of vast opportunity. At Harvard, though, most graduating students were still focused on landing jobs at consulting firms and investment banks.

Perry admits that he was anything but a Web geek:

For all practical purposes, I hadn't been on the Internet prior to going to business school. But I'm an engineer, and I understand technology sort of intuitively. And Internet companies aren't really technology companies. The Internet technology only enables a business model. The hard part is understanding which business models work and which ones don't. Chemdex was simply the result of the biotech business I was involved in, and everything I was thinking about in business school: What is this phenomenon of the Internet, and which business models will it enable?

As a player in a vertical marketplace, Chemdex would be an old idea in a new channel. Keying off the new availability of Web search engines, companies like Yahoo! and Netscape had already made a splash in the B2C (business-to-consumer) arena. But very few entre-preneurs, in the spring of 1997, were yet thinking about what later came to be called B2B: business to business.

Dave Perry was one of them.

JUDGMENT DAY

"There's a legend out there," says Kim Moore, "that Room for Dessert won the business plan contest that year. Well, we didn't. Would have been nice, but it didn't happen."

In all, fifty-eight teams submitted plans in the first phase of the con-test. These were winnowed down to thirty-seven, all of which were read by faculty members Joe Lassiter, Mike Roberts, and Bill Sahlman. This trio of readers further narrowed the field to ten semifinalist teams, and those ten plans were forwarded to the contest judges.

Room for Dessert made it to the quarterfinals, but no further. Paul Conforti thinks, in retrospect, that his team's idea wasn't quite sexy enough from a financing standpoint, and that the sudden heating-up of the Internet killed any remaining chances they had of winning:

Our IT plan just wasn't interesting enough to a group of judges focused on high-tech opportunities. A restaurant concept wasn't going to be able to attract huge amounts of venture capital at such an early stage.

And remember, too, that the Internet stuff is really starting to take hold. Dave and Stig took the first class on business opportunities on the Internet. So it was starting to happen. And in the semifinal round, as I recall it, they took nine technology plans and one nontechnology plan—and we weren't it.

One of the ten plans that *was* taken into the semifinal round was Dave Perry's Chemdex. And when the four finalists were announced in late May, Chemdex was still in the running.

In the months leading up to Judgment Day—the ceremony was scheduled for Wednesday, June 4, 1997—Perry was a very busy second-year HBS student. He was still logging up to twenty hours a week at Virogen, his Cambridge-based bioengineering firm. He intermittently attended to his schoolwork. And he and his teammates—Jon Callaghan, Lisa Janssen, and Stig Leschly—were putting the finishing touches on the Chemdex business plan.

One other factor greatly complicated Perry's life, in this interlude: He was trying to make Chemdex *real*. Most participants in the business plan contest, including Perry's own teammates, thought of the contest as a sort of trial heat for the kinds of real-life contests in which they would soon be engaged. To Perry, Chemdex was on its way to being born, and the due date was coming closer all the time.

As with the Room for Dessert team, part of Perry's self-assigned homework was to talk to any HBS professor who had some relevant expertise and was willing to talk to him. Marco Iansiti, a specialist in new product development, was Chemdex's formal faculty sponsor, but Perry ranged much farther afield. "I probably talked to twenty or thirty faculty members," he recalls. "Marco was great. Joe Lassiter and Bill Sahlman were extremely helpful. Tom Kosnik, who was visiting from Stanford Engineering School that year, really pushed us along."

Meanwhile, Perry also ventured outside the School. He knew that if Chemdex was going to set a new standard in Web commerce, it would need deep technical expertise. Through a mutual friend, Perry got the California phone number of a technology wizard named Jeff Leane. Perry explained his plan and also told Leane that he had just received $25,000 in seed money from an investor in Nebraska. His near-term goal, Perry said, was to win the business plan contest and throw whatever prize money he took away from that contest into the seed-money pot. Chemdex was a *real* company, Perry stressed, and he needed Leane to help make it happen.

Leane was impressed—both with the plan and with Perry himself. Briefly, he hedged his bets, continuing to do some consulting work in California while he helped Perry work out the technical details of the Chemdex business plan. Pretty soon, though, he threw in his lot with Perry, and Chemdex had its chief technology officer.

All of this happened in the weeks preceding the formal announcement of the winners of the business plan contest. The seven judges who had reviewed the final ten plans included a number of prominent HBS alumni, as well as representatives from some of the firms that had sponsored the contest through in-kind contributions and other kinds of support.

The judges' responses had been compiled by Roberts, Lassiter, and Sahlman, and four finalists had been selected: American Veterinary Specialists, offering specialty pet care; David Perry's Chemdex, offering an online marketplace for buyers and sellers of specialty chemicals; MST, which proposed to "roll up" (or consolidate) the distribution of custodial services products; and Omnicom, which offered a new fax-switching technology.

Wednesday, June 4, was the day before Harvard's commencement. Second-year student David Rosenblatt, who had taken over from Bill Nussey and Alison Berkley as the student champion of the contest, spoke first, thanking the sponsors of the competition. He then introduced Bill Sahlman, who joked about being "why notted half to death"—first by Nussey and Berkley, and then by Rosenblatt. Sahlman recounted how the School had tried to come to grips with the field of entrepreneurship over the years, leading up to—among many other initiatives—this business plan contest.

Sahlman introduced Henry McCance (M.B.A. '66), the head judge and the managing partner of Greylock Management, the Boston-based venture firm. McCance stated that one of his jobs as managing partner was to recruit HBS grads to Greylock. He proudly pointed out that Bill Nussey—one of those who had pestered Bill Sahlman in the previous academic year—was one of two members of the M.B.A. class of '96 who had signed on with Greylock. He complimented the contestants, saying that their plans were generally of a high quality. Some plans, he added, were perhaps a *little* too cavalier about finding the necessary talent, and others were at least a *little* too optimistic about cash flow and how quickly revenues would ramp up.

He also offered an observation about the mechanics of the contest, and how they differed from reality:

> *When I spent a weekend, several weekends ago, reading these ten plans, I remarked to myself, "This is not what I do for a living." And by that I meant that at Greylock, we invest in, first, people; second, people; and third, people. It's the quality of the* team. *It's whether or not they are exquisitely suited for the venture at hand.*

McCance's closing advice, offered to all would-be entrepreneurs, was to "recruit the best human talent you can, at every level in your organization." Luck favors the talented team, McCance asserted; so move the odds in your favor with talented people.

Next, in alphabetical order, came ten-minute presentations by each of the four finalists: American Veterinary Specialists, Chemdex, MST, and Omnicom. Dave Perry, sitting near the stage as several of his classmates made their case for a roll-up in the veterinary field, was totally keyed up. For a while, it had looked as if his parents—who had accepted his offer to fly them to Boston for the event—might not make it. His mother had never flown before, and it had been an arduous trip: a two-and-a-half hour drive from Boone County to Springfield, Missouri; a flight to Denver; and then a flight to Boston. The connection in Denver was tight, and Perry used his frequent-flyer clout to get United Airlines to escort them from one gate to the next. They arrived at the School barely a half-hour before Perry's presentation. But Perry still couldn't relax: More than anyone else, he was aware of the holes, flaws, guesses, and long shots in his own team's plan.

When his turn came, Perry got up and presented his plan alone. It was *his* plan, in its fundamentals. He had spotted the market opportunity, and (with the help of his three teammates) had hammered out the plan and how it would be presented.

At first, Perry appeared ill at ease, clearing his throat nervously as he plunged into his PowerPoint presentation. Soon, though, he warmed to his task. He spoke with obvious commitment and excitement about *his company*, Chemdex. He emphasized that he was making a *progress report*. He had seed money in hand, he noted. (This was the $25,000 wired in by his Nebraska-based backer several weeks earlier.) He had made some important hires. (At that point, Jeff Leane was on board—or just about on board.) Chemdex was going to *happen*, and it would *revolutionize* the life-sciences marketplace. He sat down to a vigorous round of applause.

The third and fourth presentations were more like the first: team-focused, and arguably more oriented toward presenting an idea than a reality. Omnicom, the last team, comprised four young women in matching baseball caps sporting the Omnicom logo. Like Chemdex, Omnicom came across as a viable business proposition, and its fax-switching technology seemed to have the potential to grab a healthy share of a fast-growing telecommunications niche.

This was evidently what the judges—who had made their decision before these public presentations—felt, too. Following the final presentation, David Rosenblatt announced the first-place winner: Omnicom.

"I don't remember being disappointed that I didn't win," Perry says, choosing his words carefully. Several of his friends and section-mates think this is historical revisionism; they believe that Perry was deeply disappointed—disappointed that Chemdex (and all of his hard work to date) hadn't prevailed, and disappointed that his parents had come all the way from Harrison, Arkansas, only to see him come in second.

Immediately after the presentation of the awards, however, five venture capitalists handed Perry their business cards. "So I walked out of that room with a half-dozen potential venture contacts," he recalls, "and at the end of the day, that was what I was really there for."

GETTING THE MONEY

The summer of 1997 was, for David Perry, a frustrating and sometimes scary scramble for money. The business plan contest had given him access to a half-dozen venture capital firms, but none of these seemingly solid leads was panning out. He was $170,000 in debt, mostly as a result of education loans, and he had no savings to speak of. His prospecting resources were finite: the $25,000 from Nebraska, $5,000 in prize money from the contest (the other $5,000 came in the form of donated services from contest sponsors), and $25,000 in available credit on three personal credit cards. Drawing down these limited assets, Perry flew around the country looking for venture capital. But the money was running out, which meant that time was also running out on Chemdex.

A break came when a classmate called unexpectedly. Unbeknownst to Perry, this classmate had sent a copy of the Chemdex business plan to Robert Swanson. On the West Coast, Swanson (who has subsequently died) was considered a "godlike" figure (as Perry later put it, only half-jokingly). He was a partner at Kleiner Perkins, and went on to conceptualize and found Genentech—and by extension, in the eyes of many, the biotech industry. By the summer of 1997, Swanson was retired, managing his own money, and looking for opportunities. Swanson asked to talk with Perry, and Perry—who happened to be in the Bay Area that week hunting for capital—readily agreed. He brought along his newly hired CTO, Jeff Leane.

It turned out to be a memorable meeting. "We were scheduled to meet with him at either 8:00 or 9:00 in the morning," Perry recalls. "I had a 1:00 P.M. flight back to Boston, so I figured I was fine. At the outset of the meeting, he said, 'Tell me about yourself.' I said, 'Well, I have a chemical engineering degree.' And he interrupted and said, 'No, no, no. Where were you *born?*' So for two and a half hours, we talked about nothing but years zero to eighteen."

Perry pushed back his flight to 3:00 P.M. The interview continued, with Swanson continuing to probe into his guest's background, interests, skills, and ambitions. Perry pushed his flight back to 5:00 P.M. "One endless meeting," Perry recalls, "focused on Dave Perry and Chemdex."

At the end of the marathon session, Swanson said that he was interested in investing—provided, of course, that someone out in Chemdex's proposed marketplace would confirm that the scheme made sense. Would Perry and Leane mind, Swanson asked, if he sent the plan over to his friends at Genentech? Putting on their best poker faces, Perry and Leane told Swanson that would be OK.

Help was on the way from another quarter as well. Jon Callaghan, Perry's venture-capital-oriented teammate on the Chemdex business plan team, had landed a job with @Ventures, the venture arm of CMGI, the high-flying Andover, Massachusetts–based Internet firm. CMGI had made its reputation through a series of bold B2C Internet investments, some of which it had spun off for huge gains. Its @Ventures group stirred the pot at the very center of this vibrant action.

Callaghan—the newest partner in @Ventures' West Coast office— knew of Perry's money woes, believed in Chemdex, and thought that CMGI and @Ventures would be a good fit with the proposed business. But because he (along with his fellow teammates) owned a small piece of the still-imaginary business, he felt obligated to turn the opportunity over to his @Ventures colleagues.

A new round of discussions began. Although CMGI was as experienced as any other company in making B2C Internet investments, the B2B realm was mostly unknown territory. But the @Ventures team looked over the Chemdex plan and made a carefully considered proposal to Perry and Leane. CMGI would invest in Chemdex if the fledgling company would agree to a set of metrics that it would have to hit. These included, for example, getting a number of products online to demonstrate the company's ability to sign up vendors, processing a transaction successfully, and getting a buyer under contract.

Meanwhile, a positive signal came back from Genentech: Yes, the Chemdex plan made sense. As it turned out, Genentech's director of purchasing, Jim Latimer, was feeling some pressure of his own. He had recently learned that as a result of a new corporate policy, Genentech planned to be doing half of its purchasing over the Internet within three years. If this visionary Chemdex scheme actually *worked*, Latimer might have a useful way to start building toward that ambitious corporate goal.

As a result of these parallel sets of negotiations, Chemdex's first formal round of funding—Series A—came together in September

1997. The total amount of money raised to carry Chemdex to its next level, a working prototype along the lines defined by CMGI, was $750,000. The investors included Bob Swanson and CMGI, as well as Chemdex's original angel back in Omaha.

FUTURE CEO ON THE MOVE

By August 1997, the time had come for David Perry, newly minted graduate of the Harvard Business School, to relocate from his rented apartment at Soldiers Field Park to fabled Silicon Valley. There he would transform the dream of Chemdex into a reality.

But first he had to get there. He loaded all of his earthly possessions into, and onto, his 1987 Nissan Maxima. The car already had 198,000 miles on it and, according to its owner, "had its problems."

First Perry filled the trunk. Then he filled the back seat. Then he buried the front passenger's seat. Then he strapped some more stuff onto the luggage rack that sat above the trunk, and finally he tied his windsurfing gear and his bicycles onto the roof of the car. Then he pointed the car westward—initially toward the Brighton interchange of the Mass Pike, but ultimately toward the Land of Dreams.

He was a young man in a hurry. He wanted to reach the West Coast in three days. He planned to drive twenty hours, sleep four, and drive another twenty until he got there.

But the Maxima protested against this plan. Each time Perry hit a bump, the rear wheels—meeting little resistance from the car's aging shock absorbers—scraped against the wheel wells above them, fraying off a little more precious rubber with each bump. Whenever a cross-wind came up, the car shimmied alarmingly from side to side. The first time this happened, Perry pulled over in alarm. Eventually, he learned to countersteer against the shimmy and wrestle the car back onto an even keel.

The radio, which had not worked well for several years, quit in the Midwest. The air conditioner died as Perry was entering Wyoming, condemning Perry to a slog across the Utah and Nevada deserts with the car windows wide open. A layer of fine grit and powder settled over everything. The car began overheating. Each time he stopped for gas, Perry saw more deterioration in the rear tires. Eventually, the steel belting started to show through.

"So none of this is a comfortable feeling," Perry recalls. "But I'm thinking, 'If I can just get over the Sierras—up that eastern slope and over the top—it's basically all downhill into the Bay area, so I should be OK." He crossed the peaks of the Sierras late in the afternoon of his third day on the road.

What Perry hadn't counted on, as he began his downhill run on Highway 80, was simultaneous blowouts of both rear tires. He got towed into the nearest town, spent the night at a Motel 6, put two new tires on a credit card the next morning, and headed off again.

Using his cell phone on the cross-country trip, he had already rented an apartment in Palo Alto, sight unseen. He had directions to the apartment, and—only a day behind schedule—was bearing down on his destination.

"That's when the transmission quit," Perry continues. "After two hundred thousand miles lifetime, and after three thousand miles in the previous three days, the thing quits a half-mile from my apartment."

Strictly speaking, the Nissan hadn't *quit*; it simply refused to shift out of first gear. So Perry crept down legendary Sand Hill Road at ten miles per hour—passing fabled edifices that housed legends of West Coast venture capital and high technology, and creating a substantial traffic jam behind him. He limped into his apartment complex, unloaded his belongings, and had the car towed away.

"Thus I arrived," he laughs ruefully, "to start my multibillion-dollar company."

LAUNCHING FINALE

Back on the East Coast, meanwhile, newly minted M.B.A.'s Paul Conforti and Kim Moore were having a humbling summer of their own. Although field-study colleague Kristen Krzyzewski had decided to pursue her passion in health care with a start-up in Miami, Conforti and Moore were fully committed to making their restaurant—now called Finale—a reality. The decision to move ahead with Finale, Conforti recalls, came well before their elimination from the business plan contest:

> *Kim and I had both done some interviewing, and we'd both gotten some job offers. So we both had to decide whether or not we were going to do it. I had gotten some indication from the people at Ocean State Job Lot—where my father works, and my uncle is the CFO—that they were going to put some money into this. So I had that commitment, and my wife, Kristen, was supportive. So I said, "Kim, I'm going to do it." And she said, "OK, then, I'm going to do it, too."*

It was something of an anticlimax. (Moore thinks that just after making this commitment, she asked Conforti to pass the ketchup.) But one reason why they were both willing to commit to Finale was that they knew each other extremely well by this point—thanks to the year-long field study—and they knew that their skills were complementary. They knew that they would disagree in interesting ways, and that their joint product would benefit from that tension. As Moore explains:

> *I'll tell you, if he were left to his own devices, Finale would be a completely different concept. Same with me: a completely different concept. And in my opinion, neither of those solo concepts would be viable. When we put our two heads together, we come up with an answer that is much better than either one of us could come up with alone.*

Well before graduation, Conforti had already made the rounds of some potential backers, including Ocean State. One thing he heard consistently from these potential angels was that Finale would stand a far better chance of getting funding if its two would-be founders could show some relevant restaurant experience. (Conforti had tried the previous summer to get a restaurant job; no one was interested in taking on a Harvard M.B.A. candidate for ten weeks.) So he and Moore agreed that this was a priority. They both needed *some* kind of job during the funding search—to bring in at least a little money—and having night jobs would allow for fundraising during the day.

And finally, they agreed that it made sense for them to work at separate places to broaden their base of expertise. He would work the service side of a restaurant, and she would work the kitchen in some other establishment.

And so, three weeks before it opened in Brookline, Paul Conforti joined the waitstaff of the Kokopelli Chili Company and Southwestern Grill in Brookline. He told the owners that he had an M.B.A. and was interested in the restaurant business. More out of politeness than anything else, they asked, *an M.B.A. from where?* "I sort of looked at the floor and said 'Harvard,'" Conforti says. It didn't disqualify him: Soon he was serving burritos and refried beans.

Bringing in a little money ("a *very* little money") helped on the home front, Conforti recalls wryly—but more important, the experience immersed him in the restaurant trade:

> *It was important for me to be able to walk through the dining room with a trayful of dishes, to be comfortable standing at the table and opening a bottle of wine, and to run the cappuccino/espresso machine. And in such a people-intensive business, it's important to learn how to roll up your sleeves, and stand next to somebody and work with him, and listen to him, and help him, and earn his respect.*

Meanwhile, over on Route 9 in Chestnut Hill, Kim Moore was plating desserts four days a week at the Cheesecake Factory. Unlike Conforti, she didn't have a breadwinning spouse, so she needed the money. The choice of the Cheesecake Factory was quite deliberate: The chain was then (and still is) considered one of the best performers in the industry. Why not learn from the best, Moore figured?

She recalls her first day of work clearly. After going through a three-hour initiation program, Moore met with the general manager, who told her that she had been hired, and would be paid nine dollars an hour. Moore pointed out, politely, that she had an M.B.A. from Harvard. "Oh, OK," responded the manager affably. "*Ten* dollars an hour."

Moore soon learned that she was indeed passionate about the restaurant trade, at least in some of its aspects. For example, she loved her interactions with patrons. On the other hand, she *didn't* love standing on her feet ten hours a day. A disciplined person, she definitely didn't enjoy dealing with coworkers who didn't take pride in their work. "On balance, though," she concludes, "what Paul and I did showed our commitment to what we were doing. You don't leave HBS and plate desserts for ten dollars an hour if you don't *mean* it."

GETTING OPEN

Finale opened for business on July 1, 1998, in a less-than-optimal location: a ground-floor space on the easternmost tip of the enormous Statler Building and Boston Park Plaza Hotel, stuck between Boston's Bay Village and Back Bay neighborhoods. The restaurant's founders had hoped to set up shop on upscale Newbury Street, more than a few blocks away. But stratospheric rents in that prime retail district, as well as liquor licenses that ran upwards of $275,000, had pushed Finale to a less prestigious spot.

Still, Finale sat on the corner where busy Park Plaza and Columbus Avenue came together at an acute angle, creating lots of foot traffic. With windows along the lengths of its converging walls, the space looked as if it were perched on the prow of a ship—a ship pointed directly at Boston's theater district, several blocks to the east.

This reasonable proximity to the theaters, and the presence of lots of other restaurants in the neighborhood, seemed to promise good things. On the other hand, the last tenant in the space—a tapas bar named the Red Herring—had folded after only thirteen months. And the coffeehouse that had occupied the space *before* the Red Herring had also gone under. Making a go of Finale at 1 Columbus Avenue would be no slam dunk.

Nor had getting to Opening Day been easy. Between the summer of 1997 and the following March, the two entrepreneurs slowly pushed their dream uphill toward reality. They put $15,000 worth of travel, photocopying, and other expenses on their credit cards, and spent an equal amount on lawyers, accountants, and so on. Conforti (often alone, but sometimes accompanied by Moore) personally pitched the Finale concept to more than a hundred people. His goal was to raise $600,000, which was the sum needed to get a single restaurant off the ground to prove—or disprove—the concept. Inch by inch, mostly in increments of $50,000 or less, Conforti scraped together the necessary funds.

After signing their lease in March, the two restaurateurs plunged into the task of re-equipping and redecorating the former tapas bar. Counting the "key money" needed to buy out Red Herring's owners and the additional investments that the new concept required, Conforti and Moore shelled out $481,000 in a few short months. Gradually, the compact space was transformed into what one reviewer later called a "plush bandbox of a place," with red and brown velvet chairs, soft lighting, and a ceiling mirror over the pastry chef's work area (to give patrons a view of their food being prepared). But all this cost *money*—lots of money—and Moore and Conforti became acutely conscious that they had guessed wrong, on the low side, about just how much money this thing was going to require. As Conforti explains:

> *When we did the budget, we hadn't figured in the cost of buying somebody out of a lease. Once it became a buyout scenario, we knew that money was going to be tight. But that was the way it was. And then, of course, construction costs ran over, too. Just like that, our operating budget was blown.*

Meanwhile, they attended to the challenges of creating the new venture's menu. They scored a coup when they signed on Michael Hu, head pastry chef at the Waldorf-Astoria in New York, as an advisor. Hu was intrigued at the prospect of helping to build a restaurant from scratch with two ambitious Harvard M.B.A.'s, and accepted a modest ownership stake in the new venture in return for his consulting services. Hu's affiliation with Finale gave the restaurant much-needed credibility—and earned Finale discounts on equipment and services purchased from vendors familiar with Hu.

Kim Moore also found and hired Deborah Roth, a pastry chef whose fourteen years of experience included stays at some of the finest restaurants in the Boston area. Roth would serve as Finale's head chef on site, taking guidance from Hu in New York. Finally, acutely aware of their own inexperience in the restaurant trade, Conforti and Moore hired John Wahr, a twenty-year veteran in the business, to serve as general manager of Finale. Wahr most recently had managed the restaurant in the nearby Back Bay Hilton, with a staff of twenty-two, and seemed eminently qualified to oversee Finale's day-to-day operations.

While the staff was coming together, Kim Moore took responsibility for creating buzz about Finale. Working against her was the venture's minuscule marketing budget. Working in her favor, though, were her years of experience in the media world, her own style—an interesting mix of intensity and reserve—and an intriguing story to tell: *two Harvard M.B.A.'s do the unexpected.* Bringing these advantages to bear, she managed to get the restaurant written up in a number of local publications.

Meanwhile, she cut deals with both the nearby Wang Center for the Performing Arts and the Boston Ballet. Those two institutions offered their patrons 10 percent discounts on their purchases at Finale. In return, Finale got free publicity and access to several key mailing lists. Last but not least, people who happened by the restaurant in the weeks before its grand opening—tenants in the Statler Building, passing pedestrians, *whoever*—were given free samples of Finale desserts. *Anything (inexpensive) for buzz.*

STAYING OPEN

In the week following the July 1, 1998, grand opening, Finale gave mixed signals to its anxious owners. Tourist traffic was heavier than expected, in part because Boston's theaters stayed lit throughout the summer. (This was purely luck of the draw, and Finale got lucky.) Customers seemed universally satisfied with the Finale experience, and within a few weeks, Conforti and Moore were beginning to see repeat business.

But the restaurant did only about $5,000 of business in its first week—less than Moore and Conforti had hoped. Sales stayed at this discouraging level for several weeks. The bank account continued to evaporate, shrinking toward $10,000 toward the end of the summer: a razor-thin margin. And there weren't many more economies to be made, Conforti recalls:

Kim and I took $30,000 salaries for the first year of the restaurant. We took paychecks every other week, and accrued the other half as a liability to the company, because cash was so tight. So we were taking home the annual equivalent of $15,000 each.

Meanwhile, an extraordinary series of personnel misadventures began. A little more than a week after the ribbon-cutting, head chef Deborah Roth resigned for personal reasons. As her replacement, Moore hired a Rhode Island–based chef named Karen Kearny. In the third week of August, manager John Wahr quit, also discouraged by the long hours. And less than a week later, Kearny—only two weeks into her tenure as Finale's second head chef—resigned. Although Moore and Conforti picked up the slack created by Wahr's departure, they once again had to go looking for a new head chef. This time, however, they looked to their own kitchen. They persuaded their assistant chef, Nicole Coady, that she was up to the challenge, and Coady stepped into the head chef role.

The personnel merry-go-round both distracted and discouraged Conforti and Moore. Finding help in a tight labor market proved difficult, and neither owner had any more hours to give to Finale. Volume still hadn't picked up by the end of August. A dispassionate observer might have wondered if the handwriting was already on the wall for Finale.

Then, on September 2, came a timely break. The *Boston Globe* ran a long article on Finale on the front page of its Food section. *Globe* writer Alison Arnett had brought her daughter and two friends for an incognito dessert at Finale after a dinner in the North End—Boston's Italian district—and the foursome enjoyed themselves and their desserts immensely. Arnett then interviewed the restaurant's two owners, and produced a flattering story that was as much a personality profile as a restaurant review.

This was something like the cavalry coming over the hill in the third reel. In the wake of the *Globe* piece, business took off. Rather than sinking the Finale concept, it suddenly appeared as if 1 Columbus Avenue might actually validate it. Conforti and Moore exhaled—briefly—and then went back to their sixteen-hour days and their $15,000 take-home salaries.

Gradually, too, they rethought their business model. It was becoming clear that Finale's *real* clientele was not the after-theater crowd, but—as with the *Globe* critic—the after-*dinner* crowd. This came as something of a revelation to Moore, who had assumed that Finale would be in competition with neighboring restaurants to win the sweet-tooth trade. As she recalls:

> *We didn't anticipate that we would have so many people at nearby restaurants come to us for dessert. And thank God that happened, because we wouldn't be around if it hadn't. And as more restaurants opened around us, our business just kept growing.*

Conforti and Moore huddled and discussed this phenomenon. Could they actually work with other local restaurants, and come up with a proposition that was mutually advantageous? Could they help their competitors turn over tables—and sell more steaks and lobsters—by "partnering" on dessert at Finale?

But the testing of that scheme would have to wait. The two restaurateurs had their hands full, maybe even more than full, at 1 Columbus Avenue.

THE FINALE CASE

Joe Lassiter had been interested in Finale since well before its birth. As one of the three HBS faculty members who had winnowed down the entries in the 1997 business plan contest from thirty-seven to ten semifinalists, Lassiter had been struck by the simplicity and clarity of the Finale (back then, the Room for Dessert) business plan.

Not that Lassiter had any particular expertise in the restaurant trade. In fact, he was an oceanographer by training, and he wound up teaching at Harvard by a decidedly circuitous route.

Born and raised in South Arkansas, the nine-year-old Lassiter was captivated by a film version of *20,000 Leagues Under the Sea*. As soon as he was old enough—fourteen—he began spending summers on oceanographic research vessels run out of Panama City, Florida, by Texas A&M University. The fascination endured, and Lassiter wound up earning a master's and doctorate in ocean engineering from MIT.

Then came the first detour: The legendary founder of Teradyne, Alex D'Arbeloff, recruited Lassiter to work at his pioneering Boston-based high-tech company. Lassiter got to Teradyne when it had $50 million in annual sales; by the time he left twenty years later, it was an $800 million company. He recalls an amicable parting of the ways:

> *I left because I wasn't going to become CEO any time soon. A good friend of mine was going to get to be CEO. He was fifty-five and I was forty-five, and I wasn't about to wait another ten years. So I went off and did a start-up called Wildfire Communications, backed by Grey-lock and Matrix. And that was a ton of fun.*

The combination of the years at Teradyne and a good run at Wildfire gave Lassiter lots of economic choices, and he began looking around. He realized that he missed teaching—which he hadn't done since his days as a graduate student at MIT—and started trying to find a place that might hire someone with his odd credentials. One place, in particular, seemed to recommend itself: the Harvard Business School. As Lassiter explains:

> *At both Teradyne and Wildfire, I had met a tremendous number of people associated with the School. [West Coast venture capitalist] Pitch Johnson was one of our directors at Teradyne. So was [HBS dean] John McArthur. I knew Bill Sahlman because our kids had known each other for years. So when Bill called me up and said, "Would you like to come here and teach?" I said, "Sure."*

In August 1996, Lassiter arrived at HBS for a "teach the teacher" program designed to introduce him to case-method instruction. ("Hugely different from my MIT seminars," Lassiter says.) And a few short weeks later—on September 10, to be exact—he found himself in the pit, teaching his first case in his first HBS course. The case concerned a high-tech entrepreneur named Jeffrey Parker, and the course was Entrepreneurial Finance, the second-year elective introduced twelve years earlier by Bill Sahlman. Although Lassiter recalls having had a few butterflies in the opening moments of that first class, he also points out that he had some unusual advantages, going in to work that morning. Not only had he known the casewriter (Bill Sahlman) for many years; he also knew Jeffrey Parker himself, dating back to Lassiter's days at Teradyne.

The second-year students in the Entrepreneurial Finance class that morning included Paul Conforti, who later recalled Lassiter's class as the single most helpful course he took in sizing up and acting upon an entrepreneurial opportunity. In keeping with HBS tradition, Lassiter's students all signed a copy of the case he taught that first day; today, it sits framed on his office wall.

Gradually, Lassiter got accustomed to the rhythms of his new life. When the M.B.A. courses were in full swing, the hours were even longer than those Lassiter had kept in the business world. Then there were other periods when nothing much happened, and the professor was expected to create his agenda from scratch. In business, Lassiter says, someone is always *bringing you problems*; in academia, that's only true some of the time. The rest of the time, you're supposed to be proactive and creative. You're supposed to get involved in things.

In December, in the spirit of getting involved in things, Lassiter wandered into the lobby of Kresge, where the students in Marco Iansiti's New Product Development course were demonstrating their entrepreneurial ideas. One of the first students he ran into, he remembers, was a kid named Dave Perry:

> *He was there pitching this idea he had for managing inventors. He asked me what I thought, and I told him, more or less politely, that it was the dumbest thing I had ever heard of. Well, he kept right on selling me. He was a good salesman—very persistent. And I kept right on saying, "Hey, I think you're trying to solve* way too tough *a problem."*

Lassiter kept running into the persistent Perry, who turned out to be from Lassiter's home state of Arkansas. (*"No one's* from Arkansas," Lassiter jokes, "except me and this kid Perry.") In the spring of 1997, for example, Lassiter audited the Entrepreneurial Marketing course taught by Tom Kosnik, a visiting professor from Stanford. Sitting next to Lassiter in the class that day, in cutoff khaki pants, was Dave Perry. And when Lassiter signed on to help with the business plan contest, he found himself reading a plan for something called Chemdex, with Dave Perry's name on it.

He also read the plan for Room for Dessert (later Finale), and was struck by the clarity of the plan's executive summary. As he recalls:

Looking at the vast herd of plans that we saw in the contest—or for that matter, that I had seen while sitting in venture capital offices—you couldn't understand what the person was trying to do. You'd read the first page, and you'd have no idea what it was about. It would be littered with jargon, or hopelessly imprecise as to the scope or scale of the business they were developing. Not so with the thing that Conforti, Moore, and Krzyzewski wrote. It was crystal clear.

Lassiter wasn't particularly surprised when Room for Dessert got washed out in the quarterfinals of the business plan contest. But the plan stuck in his head. A few months later, he asked Conforti and Moore for permission to turn the plan into a teaching case. They agreed, and Lassiter and colleague Mike Roberts lightly edited the plan.[2] It went into the School's case inventory early in 1998, and Lassiter taught it in his first run in Entrepreneurial Marketing, which he had taken over from Tom Kosnik.

For all these reasons—and because Conforti and Moore continued to pick his brains in the months leading up to Finale's launch—Lassiter remained interested in the venture. He attended the restaurant's grand opening in July 1998, and watched as his former students suffered through those first several low-volume summer months. He shared their relief when the *Globe* write-up finally pushed Finale into viability.

And he decided that there might be another interesting teaching opportunity in Finale. Working with casewriter Matt Lieb, Lassiter crafted a case that carried the Finale story through September 1998—that is, just after the arrival of the *Globe* story.[3] Lassiter taught the new case, still in a draft form, for the first time in January 1999. It was "shopping week" for second-year M.B.A.'s, and no one took much notice of the tired-looking trio in student garb—a youngish man and two twenty-something women—in adjacent seats down toward the front of the classroom. Lassiter recalls the course of the ensuing discussion:

After we got the facts of the case out on the table, I asked the students what their launch criteria would have been. And one student said, "Oh, I wouldn't do this unless I had $50 million in the bank." And

another said, "Unless I got the corner of Newbury Street and Claren-
don, I wouldn't touch this."

A couple of the students—maybe 10 percent—liked what they saw.
A crisp economic model. The two highest-margin items off a standard
menu: alcohol and desserts. A straightforward manufacturing process,
which translates into a small kitchen, which in turn means more seats
out front. The possibility of multiple locations and multiple busi-
nesses—an OEM bakery operation, and then maybe a catering service.
And someday, maybe a branded product that's sold through grocery
stores. So a few students let themselves see and dream, but the bulk of
the class was really *down on it.*

Then Lassiter introduced the tired-looking trio to the class: Conforti, Moore, and Finale's third head pastry chef, Nicole Coady.
Conforti and Moore had persuaded Coady to come along and see
what this Harvard Business School thing was all about—and, as
Conforti remembers, smiling, she had just gotten an *earful*:

> *An hour and a half of being absolutely lambasted by a hundred really*
> *bright students, most of whom thought the idea was awful, that we were*
> *dumb to do it in the first place, that we didn't have any experience, that*
> *we should just lock the doors and leave, and that there was no way we*
> *were going to turn this thing around.*
>
> *It was fun.*

Lassiter had seen the "surprise guest" technique used to good effect
in other classes. But having Moore and Conforti up in front of the
class—looking not much different from all those critics up in the tiered
seats, speaking with conviction, and clearly enjoying their interactions
with each other—had a special impact in all those second-year students, who were not too far from having to make some difficult decisions of their own.

THE CHEMDEX CASE

Larry Katz, M.B.A. '97, had the benefit of a front-row seat during
the early months of 1997, when David Perry's plan for Chemdex was
taking shape. He had known Perry since the fall of 1995, when the

two of them wound up in the same section at the School. Katz and Perry had become close friends, and in the summer between their first and second years at the School had lived together in San Francisco, where Perry worked on his consulting assignment before moving back East. While on a hike that summer, Perry told Katz about his plan for creating a patent-service firm—a sort of venture capital firm for small but patentable ideas. This was the plan that Perry later shelved in favor of Chemdex.

Katz skipped the business plan contest ceremony in June 1997, but stayed in touch with Perry as his friend scrounged for venture capital, relocated to Palo Alto, and tried to make Chemdex a reality. As for his own near-term future, Katz decided to do a hitch as a research associate for Bill Sahlman, who was then trying to get the School's new California Research Center (CRC) off the ground. The initial focus of the CRC was to get good teaching cases written that were based on the business realities of Silicon Valley. In short order, Katz produced a number of cases on Amazon.com and several other "dot-com" phenomena.

One day, Katz decided that Chemdex would make a good teaching case. Katz was pretty sure that his friend David Perry would go along with the idea; this guess turned out to be correct. So one night in the late summer of 1997, David Perry took a few hours off from his increasingly desperate quest for capital and spent three hours with Larry Katz and Mike Roberts at the CRC, reliving the origins of Chemdex.

Roberts was a member of the M.B.A. class of 1983 who had served as Howard Stevenson's casewriter in 1984, during the first year that Stevenson taught his Entrepreneurial Management course. Many of the cases that Roberts wrote that year remained the backbone of Entrepreneurial Management for more than a decade.

Roberts joined the HBS faculty and taught Entrepreneurial Management (using many of his own cases) between 1986 and 1989. After a stint in business, he returned to HBS in 1991, and developed a new course—Managing the Growing Enterprise—that combined concepts from Roberts's experiences both in the academy and in business. Then, in 1993, he left Harvard again, frustrated (as he explains) by having to choose between two worlds:

The reason I bounced back and forth is that there were things in both universes that I really enjoyed. I loved the intellectual aspects of the work at Harvard. I loved the freedom and independence, the caliber of the people I got to work with, and the fact that so much of my job consisted of finding interesting stuff to learn about. The part I didn't like was that academic work was pretty solitary and ethereal. In the real world, I was accustomed to working with groups of people and getting tangible stuff done.

So when Howard Stevenson and Bill Sahlman made an overture to Roberts in the spring of 1997, Roberts listened carefully. The Entrepreneurship group, the two Harvard professors explained, needed an executive director who could coordinate casewriting, help with the business plan contest, and also help the California Research Center get off the ground. Roberts liked the proposed deal. "It gave me the opportunity to come back," he says, "do some casewriting and teaching, but swap the more traditional research for more administrative responsibilities. That looked like a good trade, and I took it."

A few months later, on one of his trips to the West Coast, Roberts sat in on Larry Katz's interview of Dave Perry. The two casewriters had the idea of taking the Chemdex story from its inception up to about the early summer—that is, when Perry left HBS and started talking with the Greylocks, CMGIs, and Bob Swansons of the world. This narrative slant required them to get a sense of the things in David Perry's background that might have helped lead to the birth of Chemdex.

In passing, Roberts asked Perry if he had taken any entrepreneurship courses while at HBS. The question was of interest to Roberts in part because he had recently completed a study of second-year enrollment data: How many HBS students took how many entrepreneurship-related courses? Because of confidentiality rules, the HBS registrar's office would only give Roberts the eight-digit ID numbers that corresponded to students, rather than the students' names themselves. This enabled Roberts to determine that, for example, Student #00000000 had taken one entrepreneurship course, whereas Student #99999999 had taken two.

The result, Roberts recalls, was a fairly predictable distribution:

Something like 90 percent of the students took one course, 50 percent took two, and 25 percent took three. Then it fell way off, and after five or six courses, there was a gap. And then way out on the end of the curve was this one person who had taken eight entrepreneurship courses. In other words, every course in this person's second year had been taught by someone in our group.

So one of the things I asked Dave Perry at that session at the CRC was which courses he had taken, and which were useful, and so on. So he rattled off this string of eight entrepreneurship courses he had taken in his second year. I was amazed. "Hey," I said, "you're the guy!" And he was.

Katz finished the case, David Perry released it, and "Chemdex. com" went into the HBS case inventory early in 1998.[4]

BUILDING A COMPANY

Chemdex actually came together in the living room of Perry's Palo Alto apartment and the kitchen of Jeff Leane's Menlo Park apartment. Perry's living room was large enough to hold interviews and conduct meetings; Leane's kitchen table was big enough to host Chemdex's servers, which were hooked up to Leane's cable modem.

Perry served as the company's "suit," spending much of his time on the road negotiating with the likes of Bob Swanson and beating the bushes for customers. Leane was the technical visionary who was winning belated recognition for his previous work with shopbots and other Internet-based intelligent agents. But their areas of expertise also overlapped in interesting ways. Perry was an engineer, and Leane had considerable business experience to draw upon. The result, says Leane, was a team with a strong sense of *all being in it together*.

This was a good thing, since the company was on the hook to produce a working prototype by January 1998 in order to meet the requirements laid out by @Ventures and CMGI in the September round of funding. Dave Perry, for his part, threw another log on the fire: He wanted to demo the prototype before his thirtieth birthday, coming up at the end of January 1998.

The Chemdex prototype was demonstrated successfully to CMGI and @Ventures in January 1998, the day before Perry's thirtieth birthday. Genentech officially came on board as a buyer under contract, thereby enabling Chemdex to meet another of CMGI's metrics.

The Chemdex team, which eventually moved out of kitchens and living rooms into a series of rented offices, continued to pour its skills and limited resources into creating a specialized platform for e-commerce. This, too, poured fuel on the Chemdex fire: Everyone involved in the effort, and savvy observers outside the business, realized that if the Chemdex model actually worked, it could be replicated across other "spaces." The same platform, in other words, could conceivably be used for dental supplies, airplane parts, or whatever. If the technology challenges could be solved, Chemdex's $1.3 billion potential market—itself growing at 15 percent per year—might some day be complemented by other even bigger markets.

ANOTHER RUNNER-UP

Stig Leschly kept in close touch with both Dave Perry and Paul Conforti, after their disappointments in the business plan contest and their graduation in June 1997. As a member of the joint J.D./M.B.A. program, Leschly's own graduation from HBS wouldn't come for another year.

Leschly was still absorbed by the challenge of combining passion and professionalism. He had tried consulting (McKinsey) and social work (the Catholic school in Harlem), and had walked away from both unconvinced. In the summer of 1994, after his first year of law school, he had taken a job at a New York law firm, and that hadn't grabbed him, either. What *really* interested him, he knew, was music. Not performing—he was not a musician himself—but tracking down and enjoying obscure tracks by favorite artists.

Leschly was something more than a fan; he was a fanatic. There was nothing he enjoyed more than touching down in a new town somewhere and haunting the local used-record store. He read *Gold Mine* magazine, the Holy Grail of vinyl record collectors, which featured display ads in which those out-of-the-way record stores listed their inventories. "If you were looking for the B side of some Armstrong album," he recalls, "that's where you'd go find it."

But *Gold Mine*, and publications like it, didn't really solve the problem. Early in 1997, therefore, even as Leschly was helping Dave Perry think through the Chemdex business plan, he also began working out an idea of his own. Couldn't somebody build a virtual marketplace to bring together all those out-of-the-way record stores with nuts like himself? Wasn't this a perfect application for the B2C (business-to-consumer) side of the Web?

While Chemdex and Room for Dessert went through their final redrafts and went off to meet their fate with the business plan contest judges, Leschly began looking for financial backers. He figured that he needed about $100,000 to build a working prototype of the Web site he was envisioning, which he planned to do in the summer of 1997. The money was soon forthcoming from family and friends, and—as Dave Perry headed west to make his fortune, and Paul Conforti signed on for a summer of waiting tables at the Kokopelli Chili Company—Leschly rented space in a warehouse behind a supermarket on Western Avenue in Brighton, about a mile from the HBS campus. He hired a Web expert and began working on a Web site that he called MusicFile.com.

The warehouse, coincidentally, was two blocks away from where Paul Conforti and his wife Kristen were living. As Conforti recalls, they welcomed their friend to the neighborhood:

> *At night, Kristen and I and our dog, Peanut, would walk over to Stig's office and chat with him, as Peanut ran around the office. We got takeout a couple of times, and just sat around chatting about the entrepreneurial crap we had going on, day to day.*

The project crept along throughout the following school year, as Leschly finished up his course requirements. But then came the second run of the HBS Business Plan Contest—in the spring of 1998—

and Leschly decided to throw his hat in the ring as a solo entrant. By now, Leschly recalls, his thinking had evolved considerably:

> *I had realized a couple of things. One was that the business of launching a Web site to organize trade for fanatical music collectors was a business, but not a big business. The big business was doing it for stamps, and coins, and model trains, and rare books, and music. So I lined up fifteen markets, which collectively represented an enormous business.*
>
> *There are twenty thousand stamp collectors in the world who each spend more than $30,000 a year on stamps. These people are oddballs. Also true for record collectors like me, and book collectors. You find them in conventions, regional meetings, swaps, and so on. You go up to one of them and ask, "Say—what's the coolest thing you own?" And they'll talk to you for half an hour. So I'm thinking that I have to build a product for all these pathologically insane, hard-core types, who were clearly mistreated as children.*

Leschly was not particularly interested in online auctions, à la eBay, which was just beginning to take off. He wanted to develop B2C software that would bring together hard-core buyers of all types with the goods that they were so desperate to find. Multiple markets would be aggregated under one technological umbrella. Gradually, MusicFile gave way to a new concept, which Leschly called e-Niche Incorporated.[5]

This was the concept that Leschly put on the business plan contest judges' desks in the spring of 1998. Leschly wasn't exactly sure what to expect—but he admits that he didn't expect to get washed out *immediately*.

Which is what happened. According to several surviving anonymous judges' sheets, the idea was too broad, too costly, and too vague. "Team lacks experienced people in relevant markets," wrote one judge. Another judge concluded that "there are a myriad of competitors—it is unlikely that aggregation in itself is of real value."

So now, exactly a year after Dave Perry and Paul Conforti failed to take first place, Stig Leschly had done even worse. But like Perry and Conforti before him, he still had confidence in his idea. Like Perry,

Leschly had signed up a world-class software engineer—Sridhar Rao, who had declined to make the trek to Redmond when his company was acquired by Microsoft—and Rao was far along in developing the working prototypes that would be needed for venture financing.

And like Perry and Conforti, Leschly was out of money. "Actually, $100,000 in debt," he corrects himself with a wan smile. So now, in the summer of '98—at the same time that Paul Conforti and Kim Moore were watching the bottom of the Finale bank account come into view—Leschly was wondering if his dream was about to fall to earth.

A HAPPY ENDING

Leschly began making the rounds of venture capitalists. To his surprise, he met with a very warm reception indeed. This was in part because by the summer of 1998, Leschly had been refining his idea for more than a year. He also had something to show for all that refining: the prototype of the MusicFile Web site, which was the leading edge of the company that Leschly was now calling Exchange.com. And perhaps most important, investors by now had fully bought into the Internet phenomenon. If it had "e" before it or ".com" after it, investors were interested. Over the course of nine months—between the summer of 1998 and early 1999—Leschly raised a total of $15 million in venture capital.

With money in the bank, Leschly and Rao plunged ahead. The staff of Exchange.com grew rapidly, reaching forty people before the end of 1998. One thing that these new legions did was contact several hundred of the biggest used-record dealers in the country and secure lists of their inventory. By Thanksgiving 1998, when Music-File.com launched, it was in a position to draw upon a database of *3 million* vinyl records. This was the audiophile's equivalent of heaven on earth, and it quickly became the leading Web site for rare and out-of-print music titles.

Leschly used the success of MusicFile to raise another $10 million in venture capital—this time from the Washington Post Company, which had passed on an opportunity to buy eBay and was trying to get back into the Internet game. Leschly used this latest cash infusion to buy existing companies that did things similar to MusicFile in other collecting realms. Out in Western Massachusetts, for example, he came across a husband-and-wife team who had launched a Web site called BiblioFind.com, which had compiled data from antiquarian book-sellers all over the country. Already one of the fifty largest commerce sites in the world, it generated almost $1 million per year in revenue and subscription fees. Leschly paid $6 million to bring BiblioFind into the Exchange.com fold.

The company continued to grow and evolve at a breakneck pace through the early months of 1999. Leschly remembers this period in something of a haze. He nearly lost his life in a skiing accident. He slept four hours per night. He gained twenty-five pounds. "We were working like dogs," he recalls. "And the world was changing around us. Things were going *nuts*."

Then—one day in March—Leschly received an overture from bookseller Barnes & Noble. The venerable chain was looking for a way to invade the out-of-print and used book market. As Leschly knew well, this latter market was actually more profitable than the traditional bookselling business, and Barnes & Noble had to get into this game.

Barnes & Noble's offer had the tone of an ultimatum: *Sell to us, or we'll buy your biggest competitor and pump money into them.* Leschly took the offer to his board and strongly advised against accepting it. The bookseller, he explained, could never pay enough for Exchange.com, because it wasn't *thinking big enough*. The company that invested in Exchange.com, he argued, should be the one that was thinking (for example) about taking on $30 billion online auction giant eBay. The board agreed.

Leschly knew of two such companies: Yahoo! and Amazon. And if you added eBay itself to the list—which might want to buy out a cred-ible threat to its own future—three. So on a Tuesday morning in March 1999, he flew out to the West Coast for meetings with all three of these companies. His first stop was in Amazon's home city of Seat-tle. Interestingly, Leschly learned that Amazon was only weeks away from launching an auction site to attack eBay head on. Meanwhile, though, Amazon also needed the kind of B2C, specialized retailing expertise that Exchange.com represented. The negotiations heated up quickly, Leschly recalls:

> *I met with Jeff Bezos and his team for six hours. And at the end of that they said, "We're not going to invest in you. We have to buy you, or compete with you. And we need to lock you up tomorrow morning." So I never got back on the plane to go talk to anyone else, and we negotiated the deal in a week.*

It took another two months to put the finishing touches on the deal, so the acquisition was not announced publicly until April 30, 1999. The sale price: $200 million.

In retrospect, it's easy to understand why Leschly sold and why Amazon bought. Although several of the venture capitalists on Leschly's board argued for staying the course and going public—an event already planned for the first quarter of 2000—Leschly subscribed to the bird-in-the-hand philosophy, and his position ultimately prevailed. For its part, Amazon saw Exchange.com as the best way to launch a flurry of vertical B2C solutions in the near term—and lay the foundation for an eventual launch of larger noninventory, fee-based B2C sites. And then there was the Leschly factor: One of Amazon's investors reportedly warned Jeff Bezos not to let Leschly and Exchange.com drift down the coast to eBay or Yahoo!

A few days later, HBS professor Joe Lassiter—who had been following Leschly's progress with great interest—found a message from Leschly in his voice mail. (Lassiter saved and later transcribed the message.) Leschly's voice sounded self-confident, as usual, but there was also a slightly guilty undertone:

> *Hi, Joe. Stig Lechsly calling. I don't know if you heard, Joe, but we sold our company to Amazon. It was announced last Monday. And today, on the cover page of the business section of the* Globe, *there's an article on Exchange.com and me. And I'm gonna read to you the first sentence in the article. Titled "Striking It Rich."*
>
> *The first sentence reads, "Stig Leschly still remembers the rejection his business plan got when he entered the Harvard Business School competition last year." So, Joe, I didn't know the guy was going to lead with this. And it is a true story, by the way—I got rejected in the first*

round. Um, so, I got you guys some press. I don't know if it's good press, or bad press. In any case, uh, no offense intended, Joe. Hope you're doing well. I'll talk to you soon. Bye.

Amazon quickly put Exchange.com's technology to work. In the fall of 1999, the company introduced its new "zShops" feature—an area on its Web site that brought together customers and third-party sellers using the Exchange.com platform. Today, this type of commerce represents a third of all of Amazon's volume. Visitors to Amazon's site experience several kinds of "platform commerce" that the Exchange.com technology helped make possible. When they click on a freestanding tab for "clothing," for example, or when they click sideways from a new book to a used or out-of-print book, they are drawing on the technology that Leschly and his Web expert put together in that Western Avenue warehouse.

WAY, WAY UP

Three months after the sale of Exchange.com was announced—in July 1999—Dave Perry's Chemdex made its initial public offering. Selling stock for $15 per share, the company raised $140 million. In a little more than two years, David Perry's business plan contest runner-up had gone from an unfundable pipe dream to one of the hottest of all B2B plays.

Before the year was out, there began to be disturbances in the field. Chemdex's business model encountered an unexpected snag. The neutral Internet exchange model—which seemed logical on paper—wasn't working. "It's the chicken-and-egg syndrome," explains Perry. Buyers were reluctant to make the transition to the exchange until their suppliers were on board, and vice versa. Nobody would make the first move, and Chemdex was caught in the middle.

Perry switched gears. He decided to try to leverage the Chemdex B2B transaction platform across other industrial marketplaces, while partnering with more established entities. Working with such bricks-and-mortar companies, Perry figured, would help transfer the financial risk for building the exchanges to the companies that would be using them.

Accordingly, Perry formed a partnership with IBM and DuPont in January 2000. Together, the three companies built an exchange called Industria, which dealt in factory equipment. In February, Perry and his colleagues created an umbrella structure to house the company's current and future exchanges. The new entity was called Ventro Corporation. Through this process, Chemdex became a subsidiary of Ventro. "It's a little bit like giving birth to your parents," a jovial Perry told his assembled employees as he unveiled the new corporate name.

This reshuffling of the corporate deck seemed promising, and the market responded positively. Ventro's stock appreciated at a dizzying pace, and the company's market cap reached $10 billion in March. Out in Omaha, Perry's initial investor marveled as his family's cash investments in Dave Perry's dream, totaling some $350,000, climbed toward a paper value of $50 million.

WAY, WAY DOWN

But the fix and the glory were short-lived. Part of the problem was Ventro's burn rate. "Their financing strategy, the Lear jets, the stories spun upon stories," says one observer close to the scene. "In part, it's a story of excess." By April, the company had run up another $250 million in debt.

And the business model, too, had flaws. Ultimately, only 144 corporate customers signed up with Chemdex—far fewer than the exchange needed if it was ever going to break even on the tiny transaction fees it charged.

The expectations game hurt Ventro, too. Perry was a *visionary*—invited to speak at Davos early in 2000, not three years out of business school—and Ventro was the *business model of the future*. As he explains:

Two and a half years after we were founded, we were a $10 billion company. There's a certain amount of pressure associated with that. You know you're ahead of yourself, right? I always thought that we might someday live up to expectations that people had of us, but it was very clear that the market expected more of us than we were going to be able to deliver in the short term.

The final and crushing blow, however, was the spectacular collapse in the year 2000 of technology stocks. The average B2B stock lost 35 percent of its value in March 2000 alone, and that was just the beginning. Ventro's stock plummeted from an all-time high of $243.50 per share to around $1 per share in January 2001.

This wasn't a setback; it was a rout. In December 2000, Perry took drastic measures. To preserve cash, he closed down Chemdex and Promedix—an exchange focused on medical equipment and supplies—and laid off about half of his 480 employees. The rout continued. By June 2001, most of the remaining employees were gone, and Ventro shares were selling for thirty-nine cents. Shareholders filed a lawsuit in federal court in San Francisco, alleging securities fraud by Ventro executives.

Perry launched a strategic review, looking for a way to get Ventro out of the woods. The answer that he and his colleagues eventually settled upon was to turn the company into a supply-chain software provider—a humble but reasonably practical vision. Perry brought in a new executive behind him and stepped down as CEO early in 2002.

Throughout this period, HBS professors continued to teach the original Chemdex case. Joe Lassiter, for example, opened his Entrepreneurial Marketing class with Room for Dessert, and in the second session taught Chemdex. And every year, whenever his schedule allowed, Dave Perry came back to Harvard to sit in on the Chemdex sessions. On September 11, 2001, despite troubles back on the West Coast, Perry turned up in Joe Lassiter's classroom. "I was there mostly because I told Joe I would be," he explains. "I felt like I owed him and the School, and that involves sharing both the things that go well and the things that *don't* go well."

Just as the case discussion was heating up, word filtered in that terrorists had attacked the World Trade Center. The M.B.A. students decided that canceling class wouldn't help the victims of the attack, and the class went forward. Lassiter handed out an article from the *Los Angeles Times* that described the ugly demise of Ventro. Against the chilling backdrop of events in New York City, Perry talked candidly about the pain of firing five hundred people, and of tearing down something that he had built, brick by brick.

Lassiter credits Perry for having the courage to come back and talk to the second-years about the unraveling of his dreams—and also for helping teach in the surreal and horrifying context of 9/11. "It was a remarkable series of classes," he recalls.

THREE STUDY-GROUP MATES

In the half-decade since they parted company at HBS, Perry, Leschly, and Conforti have stayed in close touch. Conforti had the interesting experience of riding in the jump seat of a Chemdex jet—with Perry in the back, doing deals—and having a front tire blow out, forcing an emergency stop on the last few inches of the runway. Conforti bought some shares in Chemdex and rode them all the way up—and most of the way back down. Leschly provided Conforti's Finale with a bridge loan that they needed between financing rounds. "He's good for it," Leschly says, simply. Perry eats at Finale whenever he's in Boston.

They also stayed in touch with Joe Lassiter, who at one point or another helped move each of their ideas along, and who today serves as an informal point of contact among the former study-group mates. Leschly got in the habit of sending barbed notes to Lassiter—for example, mock-complaining about the fact that no HBS case was ever written about *him*. In September 1999, when Perry, Leschly, and Conforti were all riding high, Leschly wrote to Lassiter:

> *joe—please say hi to paul and dave—and be sure to remind them that my brain is twice as large as theirs combined, that I carried them both through 1st year with my case analysis, and that dave should have given me shares, and that paul should have given me more free food.*[6]

And where are they now?

Dave Perry is running a biotech company called Anacor Pharmaceuticals. The company recently landed a $23 million contract to produce antibiotics for biowarfare defense. "I am conscious," he says wryly, "of the need to keep expectations somewhere behind my ability to deliver."

Briefly, Perry was worth several hundred million dollars on paper. He never sold a share of Chemdex/Ventro stock, so he's no longer a centimillionaire. He's philosophical on this point: "I've got more money than I ever thought I would have, during most of my life, and I've got a whole lot less than I did at one point." Now thirty-five years old, he is training for his first Iron Man event: a 2.4 mile swim, followed by a 112-mile bike ride, followed by a 26-mile run. "The winners will do it in about eight hours," he says. "You have to do it within seventeen. I'd like to do it in about eleven."

Stig Leschly is a lecturer at HBS. He spent two years at Amazon helping them build their first offerings in what is sometimes called "intermediated commerce." Briefly, he worked as Jeff Bezos's "shadow," to see if there might be a longer-term role for him at Amazon. After deciding that there wasn't, he took a half-year off and then relocated to Boston. As he explains:

> *I was thinking about what made Exchange.com a success, and I realized once again that it was all about getting my professional life rooted in something that I care about. So I decided that I wanted to spend the next ten years of my life working in public education. I began talking with two urban school districts—Seattle and Boston—about opening up and running new kinds of high schools.*

The Harvard Business School was then getting involved in public-education issues, and Bill Sahlman invited Leschly to set up his base of operations at the School. Since then, he has spent about 20 percent of his time teaching and the rest writing cases and (in collaboration with Harvard's Graduate School of Education) studying management practices in large urban school districts. He has launched a second-year elective on entrepreneurship and education reform, and has also taught the required first-year entrepreneurship course—the Entrepreneurial Manager—which opens with Howard Stevenson's case on Bob Reiss. "When I teach that case," he says, "I want the students to understand that you've got to know something about a space, a set of customers, a problem. You have to be an interesting person. You've got to go get *lost* someplace."

Paul Conforti and Kim Moore are still at 1 Columbus Avenue—and now, in a second Finale location at 30 Dunster Street in Harvard Square, not far from where Conforti first started focusing on the idea of a restaurant that specialized in desserts.

Harvard Square was a story in and of itself. When Conforti went looking for the money to open the second Finale, he happened to mention that fact to the manager of the parking garage across the street from 1 Columbus Avenue. *Why don't you call the guy who owns my garage*, the manager asked? *He's a fan of yours.* Discussions ensued, and soon Conforti had a deal for most of the money he needed to open Harvard Square.

Like Conforti, Kim Moore still believes in the Finale concept, and also believes that her experiences have been extremely valuable:

> *Some people can't deal with the fear of failure. If this thing blew up to-morrow, well, except for the good people around us, no big deal. It wouldn't be a reflection on me, or Paul. What it would mean was that I'd had five years of unbelievable learning—learning that you can't buy in any school. And I love it. And frankly, I'd rather hire a person like me than someone who's had an easy ride, somewhere.*

Finale's momentum continues to build. Whereas the Park Plaza location did $800,000 in sales in its first year and $1.2 million in its second, Harvard Square did $1.3 million in its first year. Conforti and Moore have opened a central production kitchen in Malden that will have the capacity to service not only Boston and Cambridge, but the next several Finales as well. They're currently eyeing locations in places like Portland, Maine, and Providence, Rhode Island.

But once again, Finale faces capital constraints. Neither Conforti nor Moore is much interested in shaking the bushes once again for enough $50,000 investors to fund the next round of growth—and yet that may be the only way to go, since Finale still flies below the radar of the venture capital community.

THE MORNING OF September 22, 2003—a sunny Monday morning—promised a beautiful and unseasonably warm day in Boston. Governor Mitt Romney's staff breathed sighs of relief; they had scheduled a ceremony for 11:00 on the South Lawn at the Massachusetts State House.

By 10:30, the forty or so plastic chairs on the lawn were full. Romney emerged from the State House, bounded down the well-worn granite steps, and took his place at a podium bearing the state seal. The governor made the first of two presentations, recognizing investments in Boston's inner city. Then Romney announced the winners of the Commonwealth's Entrepreneurial Spirit Award: Paul Conforti and Kim Moore.

Romney recounted the story of Room for Dessert/Finale, including the two founders' distinction of having taken the "lowest-paid jobs in the history of the Harvard Business School." As the crowd laughed, Romney continued:

> *Their perseverance has proved the pessimists wrong. Their dream—actually the fantasy of every child, which is to get into a restaurant where there is no broccoli, and no beets, and the only green is in the form of kiwis, or dollars—has come true . . . I just couldn't be more pleased to be able to present to Kim and Paul the Entrepreneurial Spirit Award from the Commonwealth of Massachusetts.*

Conforti accepted the plaque and thanked the governor on behalf of Moore and Finale's eighty-five employees. "We wouldn't be here today," he emphasized, "if it weren't for all of them." He thanked his parents—seated in the front row—and all the other people, present in person or spirit, who had helped make Finale happen.

Joe Lassiter was in the crowd that morning. He attended because he felt, and feels, that entrepreneurs don't get to celebrate their accomplishments often enough. "So you need to revel in those rare moments," he explains, "because it's a long journey with uncertain outcomes."

It's the journey itself, he suggests, that's the point:

> *There's been great passion in the life that these two have lived so far. They've been intensely alive. Will they create as much wealth as someone does by fluke, at the height of the Internet? Or as much tragedy as someone does at the depths of the Internet? I don't know. Will it be the life they want to lead? Will they be paid in the currency they want to be paid in? That's their judgment to make.*

And it's a journey of *discovery*, Lassiter concludes. "Remember," he says, "it took Moses forty years to take a three-week walk."

Shaping the Waves

ON JUNE 4, 2003, a small crowd gathered outside South Hall, a concrete, relatively modern looking building adjacent to the Harvard Business School's Baker Library.

The occasion was the renaming of South Hall in honor of Arthur Rock (M.B.A. '51), whose gift of $25 million to support the School's efforts in entrepreneurship had been announced in January. Rock was one of the most successful venture capitalists in history, and over the previous quarter-century, he had been consistently supportive of the School's entrepreneurship studies program. (In fact, his 1981 gift with classmate Fayez Sarofim of the School's first professorship in entrepreneurial studies helped reinvigorate those studies at a critical juncture.) The Arthur Rock Center for Entrepreneurship would serve as the nerve center for the School's entrepreneurship-related activities, which now comprise some thirty faculty members, approximately twenty first- and second-year courses, and a far-ranging course development and research program.

Rock himself was a somewhat reluctant guest of honor; he generally avoids fanfare related to his philanthropic activities. When the gift was first announced, Rock issued a brief statement:

The future of this nation lies with new ventures. They supply the new projects, the new technologies, and the new jobs. Harvard Business School has long been at the forefront in understanding the many facets of the entrepreneurial process—from the intricacies of finance to the art of leadership—and I am delighted to be able to do something that supports those efforts, both now and for the future.

On this June day, Rock—by nature a reserved, even taciturn individual—was more inclined to listen than to talk. After the dedication ceremony, he had lunch at the dean's house and then attended a series of presentations by young faculty members: Tom Eisenmann on the management challenges faced by companies building or deploying digital networks, Clark Gilbert on how large firms develop and nurture new ideas through "corporate innovation," and Stig Leschly on harnessing the tools of entrepreneurship for education reform.

Following the faculty presentations, Rock agreed to take questions from those in attendance. Not surprisingly, many of the questions focused on the highlights of his career as a venture capitalist and "angel" investor.

Did you know, going in, which of your investments were winners?

"No," Rock replied. "Except Intel. Then I was literally 100 percent sure."

Is it true that you still have the original Intel business plan?

"Yes. I wrote it."

How did you manage to be right so often?

"Well," Rock responded slowly, his long face betraying a touch of amusement, "the fact is, I was wrong more often than I was right."

PROBABLY MORE THAN WE KNOW, we live in an age of miracles and transformations.

So far, that age has straddled two centuries. We have left behind the century that brought us both the mass-produced automobile and the moonwalk. It was the century in which Alexander Graham Bell's invention—combined with a few others, of course—went from oddity to Internet. Ancient scourges were conquered by new therapies (and predictably, new scourges arose to take their place). The threat of global conflagration receded; terrorism took its place. People started talking less about "multinationals," and more about global competition and a global economy. Stocks and bonds were transformed from the exclusive province of the wealthy few to the daily preoccupation of the middle class. Charles Merrill's vision of bringing Wall Street to Main Street was realized to a far greater extent than he ever could have envisioned.

Throughout the twentieth century, in the business world, bigger was better. But the *definition* of bigness has changed, and that in turn has changed the rules. In 1940, New York's General Electric Company posted $450 million in sales; by the 1990s, the company's sales exceeded $60 billion. In the quarter century between 1950 and 1975, sales at St. Louis–based Emerson Electric jumped from roughly $37 million to more than $1.2 billion, while the payroll increased from 5,000 to 30,000 people. And at century's end, Microsoft Corporation, which was founded in 1975 and had sales of $39 million by 1980, had a market cap of around $500 billion.

Amid all this change, the future seemed like an uncertain, even a scary, prospect. Many companies concluded that consolidation on a global scale was the safest (and maybe even the only) path to survival. Bigness became the means to the end: *We'll do the same thing, but on a huge and global scale.* Megamergers prompted pundits to declare the Death of the Also-Ran. Brand equity became defined as an enormous competitive advantage. Soon, it seemed, the world would have one automaker, one bank, one insurance company, one appliance maker, one soft-drink company, one software company, and so on.

But there was another side to this picture.

In the United States, 1,745 technology companies went public between 1980 and 2000. The number of initial public offerings totaled fewer than a hundred in each of the years between 1975 and 1979; only thirty years later, that number had skyrocketed to an average of 652 per year between 1995 and 1999. And at the very end of the century, the total pool of venture capital *exploded*: A staggering 69 percent of the total venture capital funding of the last twenty-five years occurred in 1999 and 2000.[1] Venture firms raised $3.1 billion in 1990; they raised $104.8 billion in 2000.[2]

In other words, even as some of the world's largest corporations capitalized on their inflated stock prices to buy each other up—in some cases, a dance of the mastodons—there was at the other end of the spectrum an explosion of creative energy and investment. And although dot-coms soon fell into disrepute, they were only the most visible tips in a whole sea of entrepreneurial icebergs. Across a wide spectrum of industries and sectors, there continued to be an astounding wave of new-business formations.

Why? Certainly, a twenty-year national fascination with business and free enterprise, starting roughly with the inauguration of Ronald Reagan, was a contributing factor. Not since the 1950s, or perhaps even the 1920s, had capitalism been so thoroughly celebrated. But at least three other trends also contributed to the outsized wave of entrepreneurship at the end of the century. The first was the restructuring of corporate America in the 1970s and 1980s, which turned many talented and ambitious people away from traditional postwar career patterns in business. Traditionally, the *Fortune* 500 had offered good pay and benefits, a dose of prestige, and security. Now, all of that—and particularly the promise of security—was gone. (Many of the companies that had confidently promised lifetime employment were gone as well.) Middle managers, in particular, were suddenly redefined as dispensable. So when the severance package was offered, many of the most talented managers took it. They saw an alternative, and this was their passport.

The second trend was the great bull market of the 1980s and 1990s. The "wealth effect," first feared and then celebrated by Fed chairman Alan Greenspan, kicked in. People felt richer because of the huge appreciation in their stock portfolios. They spent more freely and thereby sustained the booming economy. (It became the longest boom in U.S. history.) And even though much of this new affluence was paper wealth, more and more people were emboldened to take career chances—to step out of the corporate ranks and act on long-suppressed entrepreneurial impulses.

And finally, a family of technologies reached maturity all in the same twenty-year time frame, just as their predecessor technologies were ending their useful lives. Personal computers became available in the early 1980s, at about the same time that advances in switching technologies and expanded bandwidth were beginning to make long-distance data transmission cheap and reliable. Modems tied the two technologies together, growing faster and cheaper every year. And decades of government investment in a nationwide network of linked computers—intended to keep communications alive in the wake of a nuclear holocaust or natural disaster—paid off in the form of the Internet, which became accessible to nontechnologists through the friendly interface of the World Wide Web.

Suddenly, there was something called e-commerce. Internet stocks became the darlings of the 1990s. Young people who found ways to exploit the Internet became overnight millionaires, or billionaires. The market capitalizations of tiny Web-based companies that had never made a profit exceeded those of sprawling, century-old retail empires. Young entrepreneurs leaving HBS—or in some cases, not quite out the door yet—could anticipate liquidity events in a matter of months, rather than the years (or even decades) that their predecessors had had to wait.

WHAT AND HOW TO TEACH

All of these changes prompted changes at the Harvard Business School. The protagonists in the cases became younger, and there were more zeros on the ends of the key numbers. The HBS Business Plan Contest came into its own. The faculty entrepreneurship cadre grew, and grew again.

The entrepreneurial precepts hammered out by that faculty became more focused and more systematic: *Distill the essence of the competition. Find underserved segments. Adjust the scope. Consider competitors' reactions. Think broadly about the value chain. Attend to your leading-edge customers.*

But the truth is that in the field of entrepreneurship, the Harvard Business School figured out *how* to teach much sooner than it figured out *what* to teach.

Since the 1920s, the School's dominant pedagogy had been the case method, designed to immerse students in a "slice of reality" and force them to grapple with that reality. This teaching technique proved enormously powerful, and more or less displaced the traditional lecture. (Georges Doriot, to whom we will return in a moment, provided a notable exception.) So when Myles Mace undertook to create a second-year elective in the management of new enterprises, he did what his colleagues had been doing for roughly a quarter-century: He called some contacts in the business community (in this case, the *small-business community*) and asked if he could come look over their companies, and maybe write a case or two based on that field research. Fortunately, classmate Louis Kovacs and others readily agreed.

What's the singular power of the case method, and why did it fit in so neatly with entrepreneurship teaching? Perhaps most important, it removes students from the realm of observers and makes *doers* of them. It makes them active participants in their own education. Before, during, and after class, they bounce ideas off each other, cooperatively evaluating business contexts and trying to anticipate and solve problems. In other words, there is a *bias toward action*. It's not enough to soak it up; you also have to *work with* what you've soaked up.

Case-method learning has a cumulative impact as well. As students wrestle with dozens, scores, even hundreds of cases, they begin to think differently. They begin to approach problem solving with new decision rules, which Howard Stevenson summarizes as follows:

1. *Everything can be improved.* Most cases state an emerging problem. (Many open with a cliff-hanger.) Most lay out a jumble of details—some relevant, some less relevant—and use a historical narrative to push the reader into the present-day problem. The unstated premise is that even if things don't look so bad on the surface, they can be made better. Put yourself in the shoes of our protagonist: How can you make his or her circumstance better? What specific operating changes would be likely to create positive results?

2. *Experts are often wrong.* In case-method teaching, this has two facets. First, that chief financial officer whose strong opinions you've been reading about in this case may be absolutely right about which direction this company should go in —or, he may be dead wrong. Which is it? And second, as

you prepare for and participate in the class discussion of this case, you encounter the strongly voiced opinions of your classmates, some of whom have already had experiences something like this. They weigh in forcefully. (They are experts.) And yet, in many cases, the consensus that emerges goes off in another direction entirely.

3. *The group's best effort is almost always better than the individual's best effort.* If individuals all around you—in your study group, in the classroom—use their deep experience and high candlepower to get to conclusions that they later recant, maybe there is power in the group. At the very least, having the solution "owned" by more than one person is a good thing. But beyond tactical considerations, the jointly derived solution usually beats any individual's best effort.

4. *So what are you going to do about this?* This is the bias toward action, mentioned earlier. It's not enough to recite the facts of the case, or to find fault with its principal actors. You have to be prepared to put yourself on the line and make a recommendation: *Here's what I think we should do, and why. Here are the trade-offs. This is why the benefits of my solution outweigh the risks.*

Most of the main characters described in the preceding chapters recall with great clarity their first exposure to the HBS classroom experience. "I sat in on classes," says Bob Reiss, "and I knew it was for me. The case method—none of this memorizing junk. *That* was definitely for me!" Forty years later, Adolfo Fastlicht sat in on an HBS class. "It blew my mind," he says simply. These were young people who were already biased toward action, and the case method fit their needs like a glove.

General Doriot, always the exception, remained disdainful of the case method throughout his long career at the School. He got away with flouting this central institutional norm in part by being a brilliant lecturer. But he also succeeded as a teacher because he put enormous weight on field studies. He believed that getting students out into the field was more effective than bringing the field into the classroom (in the form of cases). His students didn't have to make this choice, of course; they simply tacked on the Doriot/field-study experience to their education—and many found themselves transformed by that experience.

Over the years, many Harvard Business School faculty members have proven to be *opportunistic* teachers. When an effective teaching tool comes along, they find a way to appropriate it and bend it to their own purposes. Doriot had happened upon a powerful formula: Let teams of high-powered students put themselves together, define a problem, and battle their way toward a *joint solution* of that problem. The *process* is more important than the findings, whatever they turn out to be. (Doriot rarely even looked at the reports his students went to such pains to generate.) Professor Harry Hansen, trying to teach marketing in a new and compelling way, appropriated Doriot's field-study approach for his Creative Marketing Strategies course, which Ted Levitt in turn bent in new directions. Decades later, Howard Stevenson and his colleagues began sponsoring large numbers of student teams in self-directed field studies.

Not all such efforts resulted in Orbital Sciences Corporations or Cinemexes, of course. But even the investigations that came up empty proved to be important learning experiences for their participants. Those students learned about the real world, and they learned about themselves.

WAVE SHAPERS IN THE FIELD

All of which leads us to ask the obvious question: Who are these students of entrepreneurship? What are they looking for, and where do they find it?

Howard Stevenson and his colleagues have argued persuasively that entrepreneurs are made, not born. They point to entrepreneurship as a *style of management*—something that can be embraced and put to use in the right circumstances—rather than a set of innate characteristics. This is a prerequisite for teaching entrepreneurship in business schools. You wouldn't offer a course in how to have silver hair, or how to be more than six feet tall. You might *research* those qualities, and try to explain how they relate to certain kinds of behaviors—but you wouldn't attempt to *change* behaviors.

That being said, it's interesting to look across our cast of characters and tease out the qualities that many or most seem to have in common.

One is *high energy levels*. Our subjects tend to talk loud, or fast, or both. They are physically active. They get up early and stay up late. "We make our own energy," Bob Reiss notes in his book.[3] They work hard, parlaying pedestrian settings into grounds of opportunity.

By and large, they share a *love of the marketplace*. Many have a long history of entrepreneurship (usually on a small scale) before arriving at HBS. Down in Mexico, Miguel Davila sold office supplies to his high school, and while in college attempted to set up a car-parts empire. His compatriot, Adolfo Fastlicht, sold mints and jewelry in college. Alison Berkley, one of the moving forces behind the HBS Business Plan Contest, had previously launched a string of tiny enterprises, dating back to a childhood barrette business.

And on a related note, they are *skilled salespeople*. Bob Reiss—an indefatigable salesman—comes to mind first; Paul Conforti comes in a close second. But in fact, almost all of our protagonists have been willing to put themselves on the line. They sell their ideas to their classmates, their families, their friends, and ultimately their employees. They sell their business concepts to venture capitalists and other funders. (In the process, they also sell *themselves*, as leaders and spark plugs.) They sell their products and services, often into resistant channels. And in some cases, they sell their businesses. In all of this, they tend to be not reluctant, but eager. They understand that you don't have a business without sales, and that rainmaking is an indispensable quality.

Many are *repeat offenders*. "I'd do this again, and again, and again," says Dave Perry. Tom Stemberg backs his own business "offspring" financially and psychologically. Bob Reiss estimates that he's been personally responsible for fourteen start-ups and has helped many other young people take entrepreneurial plunges. Matt Heyman thought that, postharvest, he'd be satisfied driving around in a 911 Porsche wearing a T-shirt and blue jeans; but after a year of that, he started looking for the next thing to do. After Staples.com, Jeanne Lewis rehabbed a house, and then started looking for new opportunities.

All are *networkers*. One consistent subplot in this book is the many ways that HBS students and graduates build networks and then exploit those networks. Networks provide access to ideas, moral support, and money. Networks start in study groups, sections, and classrooms and extend out over the 68,000-member HBS alumni population. In the previous chapters, we've perhaps overemphasized the theme of companies (e.g., Orbital, Cinemex, Chemdex, Finale, and Exchange.com) that grew directly out of HBS classroom work and field studies. By the same token, we've certainly underemphasized the companies that HBS sectionmates and classmates started five, ten, and fifteen years after graduation. Building a network is one reason why ambitious young people decide to go to business school—and the HBS network is simply one of the most powerful and pervasive.

Most of our subjects possess a high degree of *intellectual curiosity*, although some might resist that particular phrase. They ask questions like, why does this work this way? Or, conversely, why hasn't anybody come up with a better way to do this? What's the *problem* here, and how can I get around it? John Diebold couldn't understand why wartime "automation" technologies couldn't be put to peacetime purposes. Dave Perry was stunned to discover that highly paid researchers were spending five hours a week—or roughly 10 percent of their work time— ordering laboratory supplies. *(Why can't this be done better?)* Adolfo Fastlicht couldn't figure out why Mexican movie theaters tended to be decrepit, outmoded, and off-putting, whereas U.S. theaters tended to be clean, technologically up-to-date, and inviting. And when classmate Matt Heyman couldn't answer that question, he didn't let it rest. He dug down until he found an answer.

Most have *an ability to see things as they are*, rather than as they have been described by others. Dave Perry once saw a TV newsmagazine report detailing the alleged dangers and abuses of Alaskan canneries. He called the local chamber of commerce, got himself a canning job, and salted away $7,000 for a summer's work. (Two summers later, he was netting $20,000.) Arthur Rock's New York colleagues were amazed when Rock announced that he was relocating to the West Coast. "People thought I was nuts," he recalled, "but I saw enormous opportunities." Harvard Business School professors had long described the dry cleaning business as a loser; Tom Stemberg and Todd Krasnow saw it differently.

Some possess a rare and enviable talent: the *ability to look into the future*. This is a particularly useful skill in the venture capital field. "I always had the ability to see where things were going, more or less," says Arthur Rock, not boastfully. "Not necessarily understanding them, but being able to figure out that some things were garbage, and other things had a future."

This may sound mysterious, but it isn't. It's a case of experience and intelligence coming to bear on a "boundable" business problem. When Bob Reiss assesses the U.S. market potential of an obscure Canadian trivia game, his "gut" tells him that the game will be huge. When Matt Heyman tours the down-and-out theaters of Mexico City, he can *see where things are going*—because, in large part, he's already been there (in another context). When Tom Stemberg surveys the balkanized office-supply industry—characterized by high margins, sweetheart deals, and middlemen—he sees a fast-growing, "consolidatable" industry. "A vision blindsided me," he recalls.

THESE ARE OUR "wave shapers," then—both inside and outside the academy. The challenges are very different, of course, but some of the same qualities can be found in both places: energy, curiosity, determination, and so on.

The membrane between the two realms of endeavor also turns out to be reasonably permeable. Teachers go out and *do*; doers come back and teach. Even when they don't go back, get their Ph.D., and earn a faculty position—as did Staples cofounder Myra Hart—most make the time to go back to argue and joust with students when their cases are discussed in amphitheater classrooms across the country.

What's the future? Inside the academy, at least at Harvard, entrepreneurship seems secure. All academic fields wax and wane over time, and entrepreneurship won't be immune to these cycles. But history suggests that once a set of powerful and *useful* ideas permeates Harvard's curriculum, those ideas tend to persist over the long run—influencing, and being influenced by, other good ideas. Entrepreneurship has achieved the status of *usefulness*, and therefore seems well positioned for continuing success.

Out there in the world, we can predict—quoting Dave Perry, who paraphrases George Bernard Shaw—that *all progress will continue to depend on the unreasonable person.* We can predict, too, that entrepreneurs will continue to be "unreasonable," which very often is the first step toward shaping the waves.

Notes and Sources

UNLESS OTHERWISE NOTED, direct quotes are from author's interviews. Company-specific statistics have been supplied by interviewees, or have been derived from public sources (e.g., corporate Web sites).

Many of the individuals and companies profiled in this book have been the subject of published HBS cases; these have been noted as relevant. Certain unpublished materials (including, for example, unreleased teaching cases) have also been consulted, with the authors' permission. Certain faculty papers also were made available for consultation. Notable among these were the papers of the late Patrick R. Liles, whose extensive collection of clippings (in the first four boxes of his papers, held by Baker Library Special Collections) were a primary source for the two chapters on the venture capital industry.

Also extremely helpful as background were Amar V. Bhidé's writings on entrepreneurship (for example, "The Road Well Traveled," HBS teaching note N9-393-277, and his 1998 HBS Division of Research working paper entitled "The Origin and Evolution of New Businesses); Nancy F. Koehn's "Entrepreneurial History: A Conceptual Overview" (HBS teaching note 9-801-368); and William A. Sahlman's many published works on entrepreneurial finance and business plans. Howard H. Stevenson's body of work on entrepreneurship—although it appears in this book mostly in the form of oral commentary—is also a foundation. And finally, Michael J. Roberts supplied background readings (including several of his own cases on entrepreneurship and entrepreneurs) and commentary on those readings.

Chapter 1

1. There is an extensive collection of HBS cases on Staples and its offshoots, several of which have been drawn upon in this chapter. These include "Staples.com" (9-800-305), and "Jeanne Lewis at Staples, Inc." (A and B, 9-499-041 and 9-499-042, respectively).

2. Staples 1995 annual report, 15.

3. Thomas G. Stemberg, *Staples for Success* (Santa Monica, CA: Knowledge Exchange, LLC, 1996), 40.

Chapter 2

1. Myles Mace, *The Board of Directors of Small Corporations* (Cambridge, MA: Harvard University Press, 1948).

Chapter 3

1. Citation from the "Hall of Fame" section of the Quartermasters Foundation Web site <www.qmfound.com/BG_Georges_Doriot.htm> (accessed 24 August 2004).

2. John Diebold, *Automation* (New York: D. Van Nostrand Co., Inc., 1952).

3. James A. Henderson and Edward R. Hintz, Jr., *Creative Collective Bargaining: Meeting Today's Challenges to Labor-Management Relations* (Upper Saddle River, NJ: Prentice-Hall, Inc., 1965).

4. From Flanders's 16 November 1945 speech to the convention of the National Association of Securities Commissioners, reported in the *Commercial and Financial Chronicle*, 29 November 1945.

5. "Research Venture Gets SEC Blessing," *New York Times*, 9 August 1946.

6. "Conservatives Join in Revitalizing Economy," *Finance*, 25 September 1946.

7. "Venture Enterprise of Unusual Management," *Boston Herald*, 14 August 1946.

8. "Conservatives Join in Revitalizing Economy."

9. Merrill Lynch, Pierce, Fenner & Beane, *Investor's Reader*, October 1947.

10. *Business Week*, 28 February 1953.

Chapter 4

1. "Businessmen's Risks," *Barron's*, 8 April 1966, 3.

2. Statement by Stanley M. Rubel before the Senate Small Business Committee, 16 February 1967.

Chapter 5

1. "The Prudent Boston Gamble," *Fortune*, November 1952.

2. *Barron's*, 10 June 1957.

3. Internal ARD documents in the Liles collection, especially the "March 1968 Summary."

4. DLJ, founded by three Harvard Business School graduates, has the distinction of being the only new investment banking company started in the post–World War II era.

Chapter 6

1. Patrick R. Liles, *New Business Ventures and the Entrepreneur* (Homewood, IL: Richard D. Irwin, 1974).

Chapter 7

1. Although Ferguson is officially a member of the M.B.A. class of 1979 based on his date of entry into the School (in the fall of 1977), his joint studies at both the Business School and Law School kept him at Harvard through the spring of 1981.

2. Litton Microwave recorded $35 million in sales when George became president; by the time he left in 1978, the division was doing more than $200 million. Moving to Honeywell, he soon found himself overseas as the president of Honeywell Europe; he later became president of Industrial Automation at Honeywell. In April 1989, he accepted an offer to join Medtronic, a leading medical technology company that specializes in implantable medical devices, and rose to the positions of CEO and chairman. For these accomplishments and others, George in 1997 received the Alumni Achievement Award: the Harvard Business School's highest distinction for its alumni.

3. Das Narayandas and John A. Quelch, "Orbital Sciences Corp.: ORB-COMM," Case 9-598-027 (Boston: Harvard Business School, 1997).

Chapter 8

1. Howard H. Stevenson and Jose-Carlos Jarillo, "R&R," Case 9-386-019 (Boston: Harvard Business School, 1985).

2. Bob Reiss, *Low Risk, High Reward* (New York: Free Press, 2000).

Chapter 9

1. James L. Heskett taught the Service Management course that Davila took, and subsequently (at Davila's invitation) wrote "Cinemex." (HBS teaching case N9-898-108), from which some material in this chapter is borrowed.

Chapter 10

1. Several of the principals (including Paul Conforti, Joe Lassiter, Stig Leschly, Kim Moore, and Dave Perry) shared documents used in the writing of this chapter.

2. "Business Plan for Room for Dessert," HBS teaching case 2-899-008.

3. Joseph B. Lassiter III, Michael J. Roberts, Matthew C. Lieb, "Finale," HBS teaching case 2-899-100.

4. William A. Sahlman, Michael J. Roberts, and Laurence E. Katz, "Chemdex.com," HBS teaching case 9-898-076.

5. This section is partly derived from the "e-niche incorporated business plan," provided to the author by Stig Leschly.

6. Transcription provided to the author by Joe Lassiter (with Leschly's permission).

Epilogue

1. Morgan Stanley Dean Witter, *Technology and IPO Yearbook*, 7th ed. (New York: Morgan Stanley Dean Witter & Co., 2000).

2. Peter Jacobs, "Venture Capital: Spurring Innovation and Growth," *New Business* (winter 2002), 21. Jacobs is citing Thomson Financial Venture Economics and the National Venture Capital Association.

3. Bob Reiss, *Low Risk, High Reward* (New York: Free Press, 2000), 17.

Index